Frazz 3.1415926535897932384626433832795028841971693993751058209749445923078164062862089...

Andrews McMeel
Publishing, LLC

Kansas City • Sydney • London

Other Books by Jef Mallett

Frazz: Live at Bryson Elementary

99% Perspiration

Frazz is distributed internationally by United Feature Syndicate, Inc.

Andrews McMeel Publishing, LLC
an Andrews McMeel Universal company
1130 Walnut Street, Kansas City, Missouri 64106

www.andrewsmcmeel.com

ISBN: 978-0-7407-7739-4

Library of Congress Control Number: 2008923476

Frazz can be viewed on the Internet at
comics.com/frazz

Introduction

When *Frazz* debuted, online rumors proliferated that "Mallett" was a pseudonym and that Bill Watterson had started a new strip about a grown-up Calvin from *Calvin and Hobbes*. As flattering as those rumors were, Watterson's influence on the artwork in *Frazz* is less important than the way the drawings communicate the cartoonist's ideas.

At a time when many comic strips look like memo-pad doodles, Mallett's strong, calligraphic lines make it easy for the reader to grasp an expression or a pose at a glance. The characters' expressions often reveal subtle emotions, in the tradition of *Peanuts*: worry, curiosity, incomprehension, suspicion, annoyance.

The poses reflect Mallett's ability to communicate a sense of gravity in his drawings. When Frazz tries to balance on a unicycle, the viewer can sense the uncertainty of his equilibrium, and that he's poised to throw his arms out to catch himself if he needs to. When Caulfield leaps through the air into a booby-trapped leaf pile, the back of his jacket lifts believably in the breeze. And when he lies amid the heaps of books he's knocked down, his T-shirt hangs off his torso with a convincing sense of weight.

The friendship between songwriter turned Bryson Elementary School janitor Edwin "Frazz" Frazier and the precocious Caulfield isn't just a plot contrivance: They both love to read and play tricks on Mrs. Olsen. Like the artists at the Jay Ward studio decades ago, Mallett uses words and makes references that readers may not get immediately or may have to look up. His strips include references to Kurt Vonnegut, Elmore Leonard, J.D. Salinger, and C.S. Lewis. And what other comic uses such recondite terms as callipygian, trebuchet, and palter?

When the characters comment on the world around them, it's a reflection of their personalities, not a political screed. Frazz is a dedicated triathlete, so it's not surprising that he urges Mr. Burke to abandon his TV at the curb, or complains about kids eating junk food. Mrs. Olsen may be a caricature of the dragon lady elementary school teacher every child had to endure for at least one year, but a rarely seen softer side gives her depth and believability. She loves to garden, and it's touching to discover this squat old woman once dreamed of becoming a ballerina.

In many comic strips, children serve as vehicles for what adults think is cute, adorably mispronouncing "pas-ghetti" or fretting about the Tooth Fairy's absence. Mallett remembers that elementary school is *not* fun for kids. It's an illogical, often scary place that forces children to confront bullies, spelling tests, arbitrary rules, spilled paint, icky lunches, humiliating P.E. classes, and stultifying lessons. Caulfield and his classmates have to go to school, but no one, not even Frazz, can make them like it—and they often don't.

Although pundits frequently announce the imminent demise of the comic strip, *Frazz* continues the tradition of blending words and drawings to tell humorous stories about recognizable characters—the combination of elements that made comic strips popular when they debuted more than century ago.

—Charles Solomon, animation critic for the *New York Times* and National Public Radio

Most of this book is for Jim Kravets, whose thirst for life matches mine, and whose faith in my talent has always exceeded mine.

Except for the callipygian strips. Those are obviously for Patty.

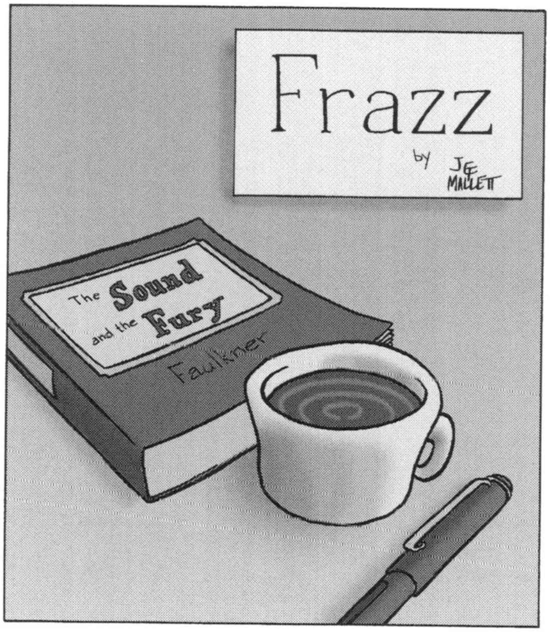
Frazz
by JEF MALLETT
The Sound and the Fury
Faulkner

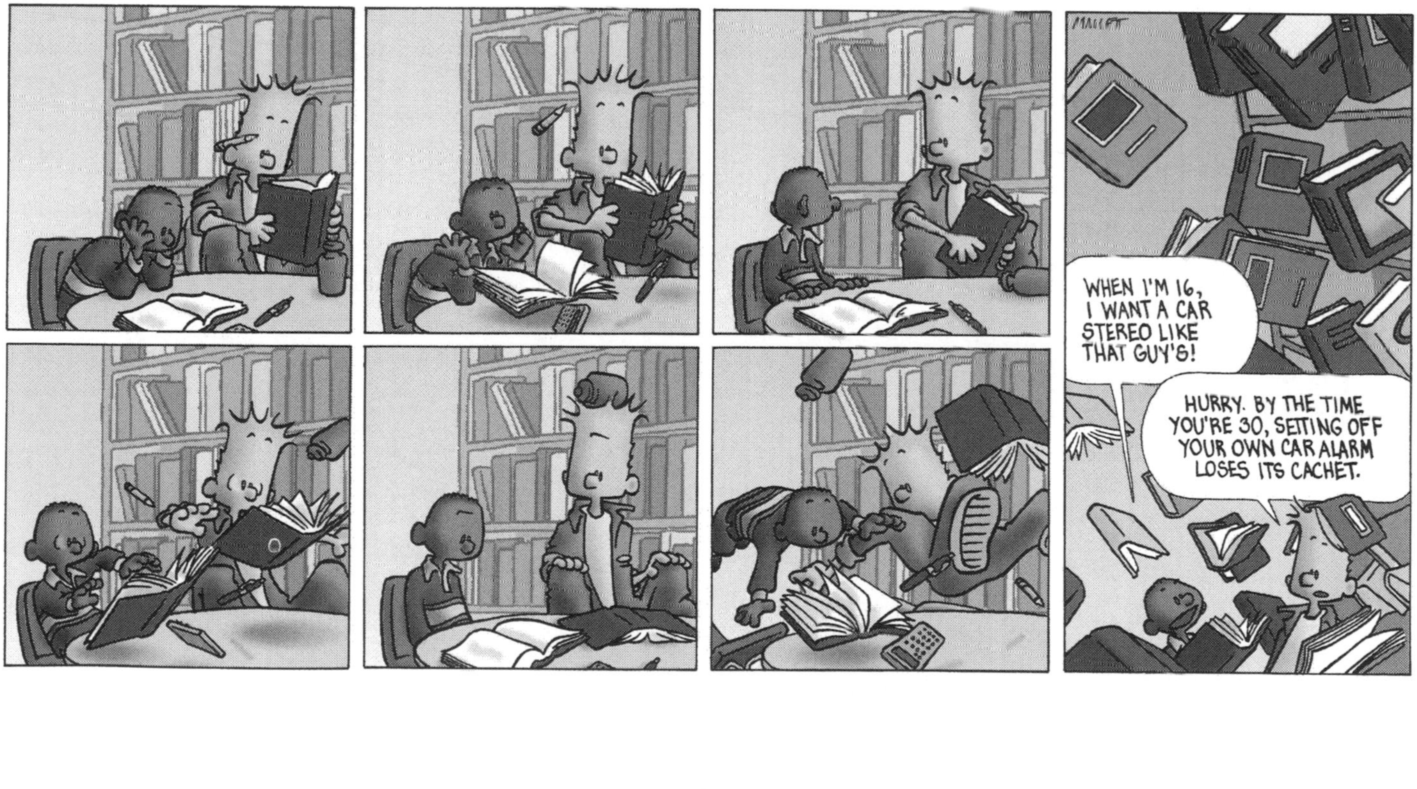
MALLETT
WHEN I'M 16, I WANT A CAR STEREO LIKE THAT GUY'S!
HURRY. BY THE TIME YOU'RE 30, SETTING OFF YOUR OWN CAR ALARM LOSES ITS CACHET.

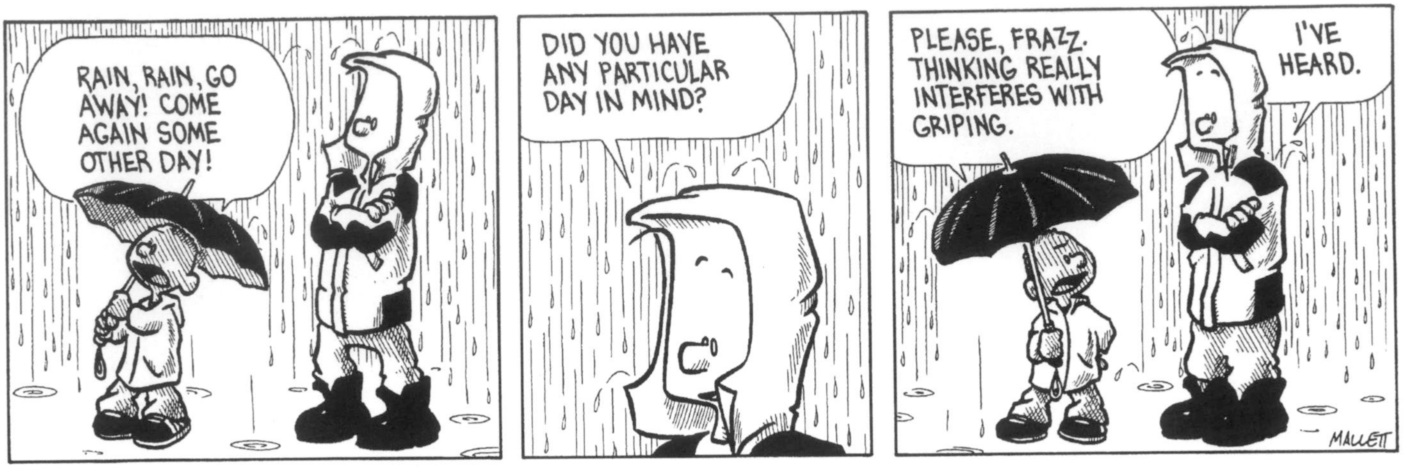
RAIN, RAIN, GO AWAY! COME AGAIN SOME OTHER DAY!
DID YOU HAVE ANY PARTICULAR DAY IN MIND?
PLEASE, FRAZZ. THINKING REALLY INTERFERES WITH GRIPING.
I'VE HEARD.
MALLETT

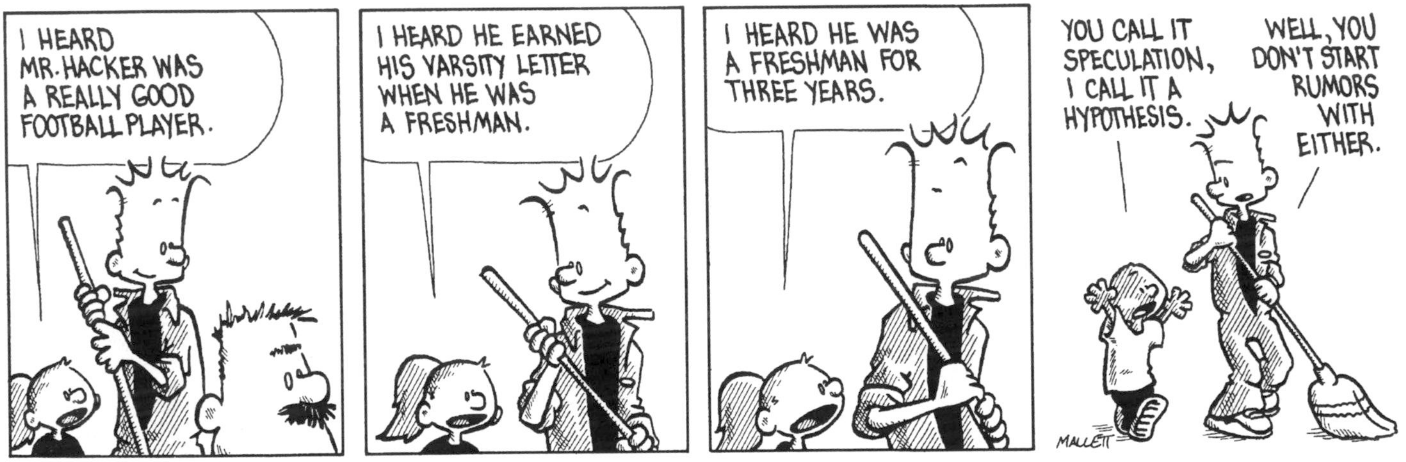
I HEARD MR. HACKER WAS A REALLY GOOD FOOTBALL PLAYER.
I HEARD HE EARNED HIS VARSITY LETTER WHEN HE WAS A FRESHMAN.
I HEARD HE WAS A FRESHMAN FOR THREE YEARS.
YOU CALL IT SPECULATION, I CALL IT A HYPOTHESIS.
WELL, YOU DON'T START RUMORS WITH EITHER.
MALLETT

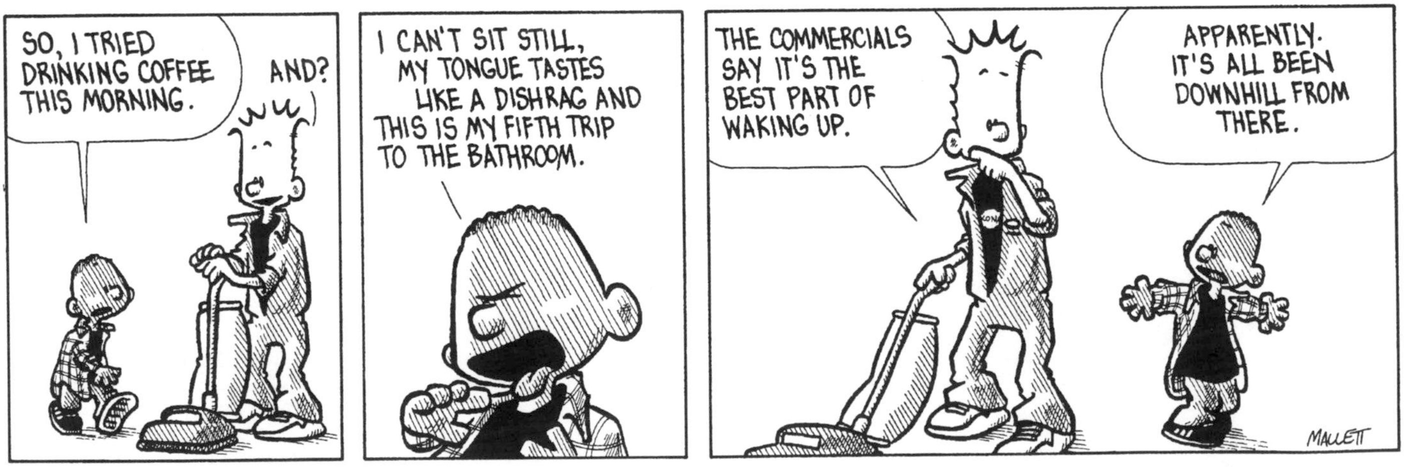
SO, I TRIED DRINKING COFFEE THIS MORNING.
AND?
I CAN'T SIT STILL, MY TONGUE TASTES LIKE A DISHRAG AND THIS IS MY FIFTH TRIP TO THE BATHROOM.
THE COMMERCIALS SAY IT'S THE BEST PART OF WAKING UP.
APPARENTLY. IT'S ALL BEEN DOWNHILL FROM THERE.
MALLETT

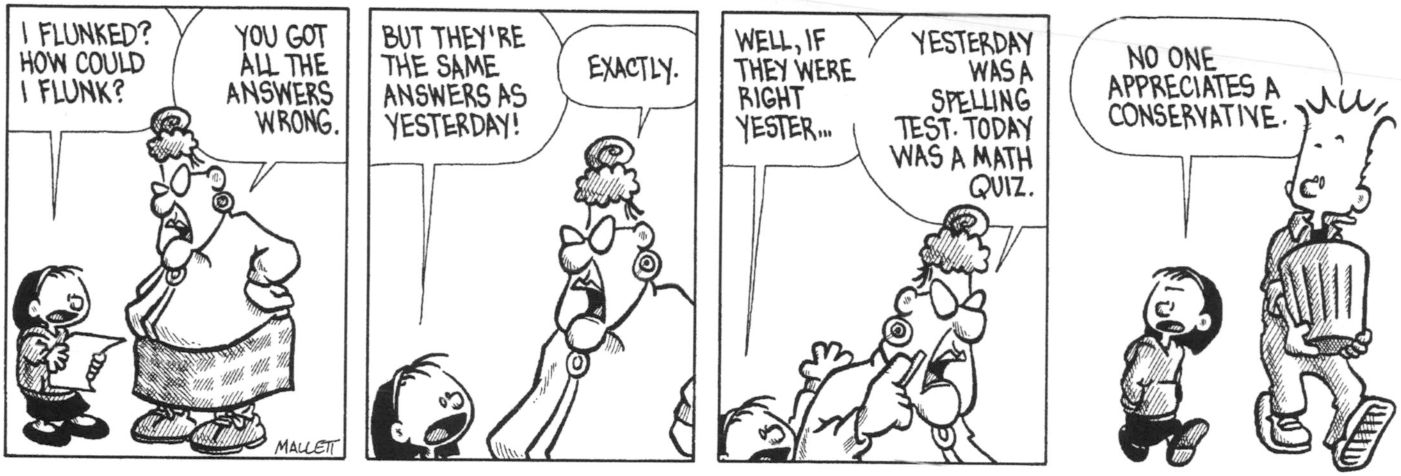
I FLUNKED? HOW COULD I FLUNK?
YOU GOT ALL THE ANSWERS WRONG.
BUT THEY'RE THE SAME ANSWERS AS YESTERDAY!
EXACTLY.
WELL, IF THEY WERE RIGHT YESTER...
YESTERDAY WAS A SPELLING TEST. TODAY WAS A MATH QUIZ.
NO ONE APPRECIATES A CONSERVATIVE.
MALLETT

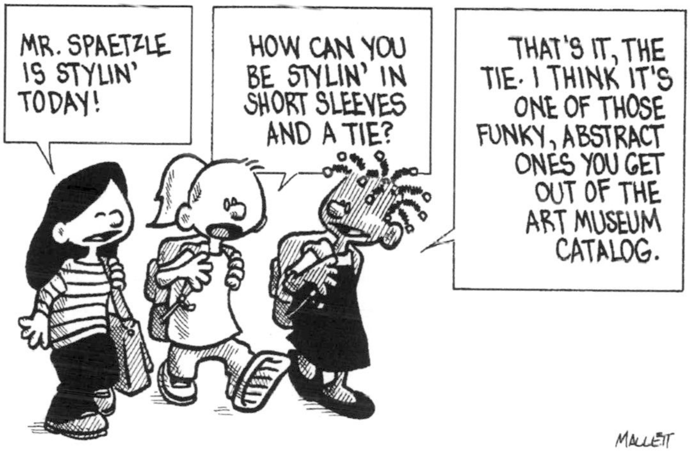
MR. SPAETZLE IS STYLIN' TODAY!
HOW CAN YOU BE STYLIN' IN SHORT SLEEVES AND A TIE?
THAT'S IT, THE TIE. I THINK IT'S ONE OF THOSE FUNKY, ABSTRACT ONES YOU GET OUT OF THE ART MUSEUM CATALOG.
MALLETT

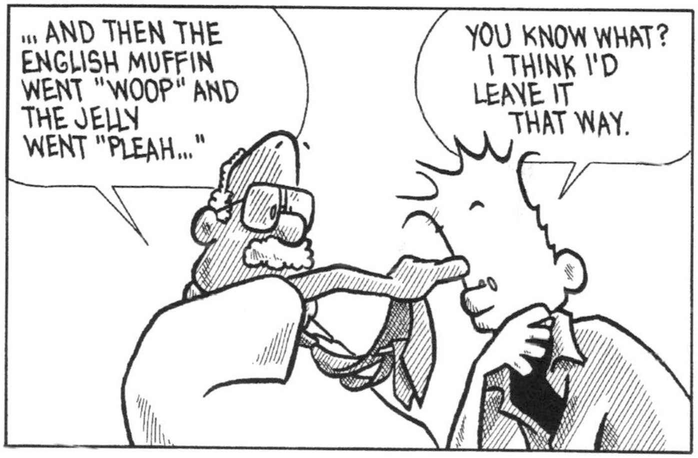
... AND THEN THE ENGLISH MUFFIN WENT "WOOP" AND THE JELLY WENT "PLEAH..."
YOU KNOW WHAT? I THINK I'D LEAVE IT THAT WAY.

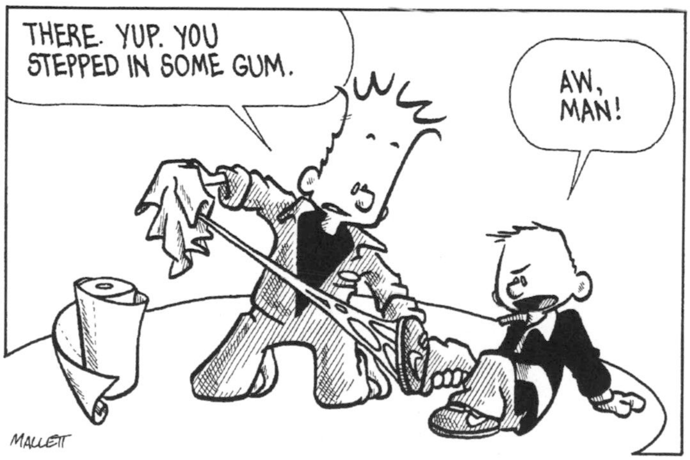
THERE. YUP. YOU STEPPED IN SOME GUM.
AW, MAN!
MALLETT

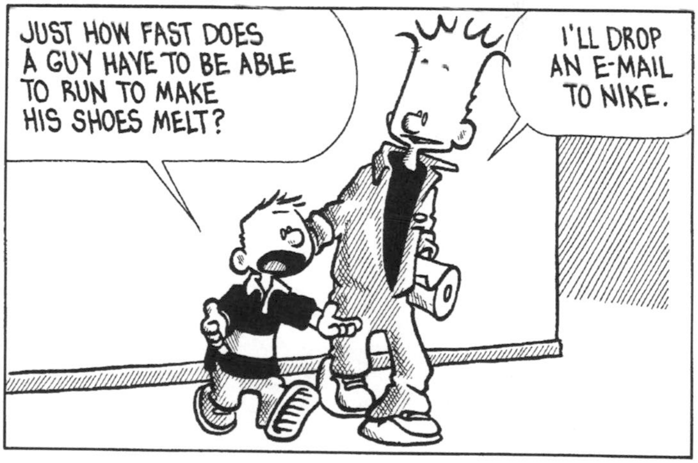
JUST HOW FAST DOES A GUY HAVE TO BE ABLE TO RUN TO MAKE HIS SHOES MELT?
I'LL DROP AN E-MAIL TO NIKE.

WHAT I WANT TO KNOW IS WHY WE CAN HAVE "JANITOR IN A DRUM" IN THE BROOM CLOSET BUT WE CAN'T HAVE "CATCHER IN THE RYE" IN THE LIBRARY.
DID MRS. OLSEN YANK IT AGAIN?
Frazz
LEMON FRESH
by JE MALLETT

HEY, FRAZZ! WHAT HAPPENS WHEN YOU MIX BLEACH WITH AMMONIA?
BAD THINGS. YOU GET A CHLORAMINE GAS.
WHAT'S THAT?
THAT IS A TOXIC CLOUD THAT WILL MAKE YOU AND ME AND ANYONE WHO'S NEARBY VIOLENTLY ILL.
INTERESTING.
HOW INTERESTING?
VERY INTERESTING.
NOW, WHAT IF SOMEONE WERE TO ACCIDENTALLY SPILL SUCH A MIXTURE DOWN A VENTILATION DUCT?
CAULFIELD, PLEASE TELL ME YOU DIDN'T...
OF COURSE I DIDN'T. BUT THERE'S A TUNA-FISH SANDWICH SITUATION OUT THERE JUST DYING TO BE PUT INTO PERSPECTIVE.
MALLETT

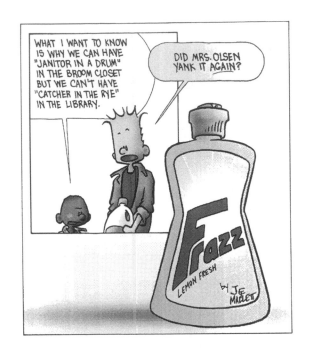

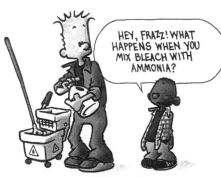

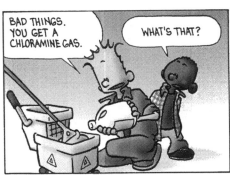

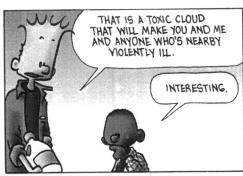

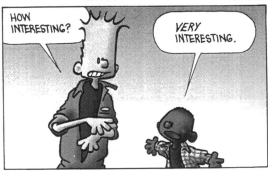

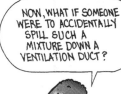

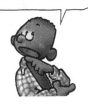

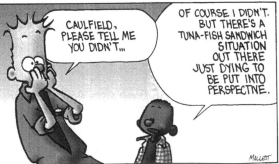

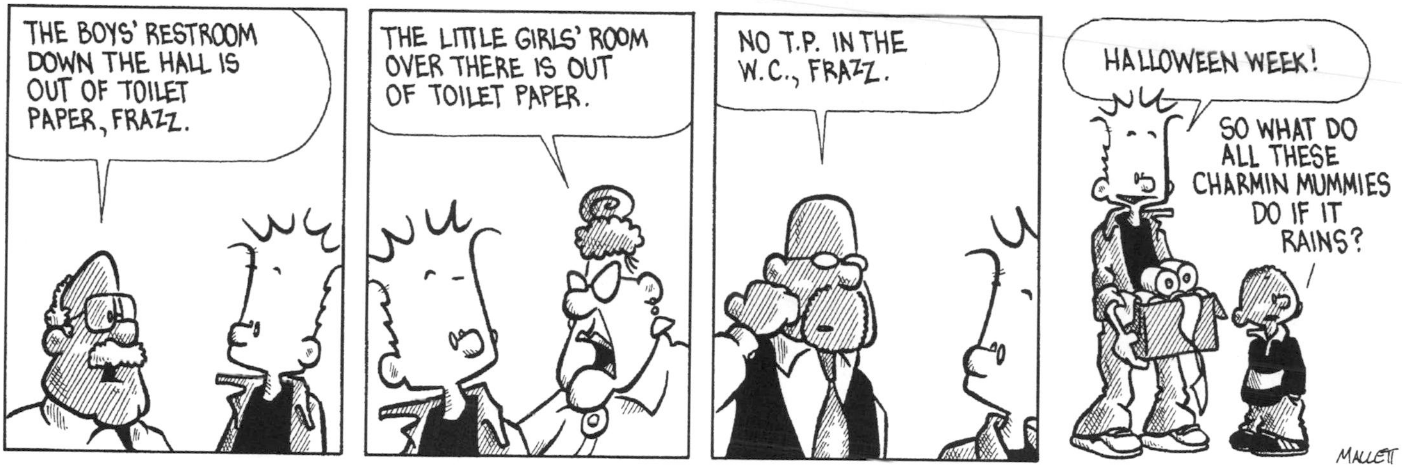
THE BOYS' RESTROOM DOWN THE HALL IS OUT OF TOILET PAPER, FRAZZ.
THE LITTLE GIRLS' ROOM OVER THERE IS OUT OF TOILET PAPER.
NO T.P. IN THE W.C., FRAZZ.
HALLOWEEN WEEK!
SO WHAT DO ALL THESE CHARMIN MUMMIES DO IF IT RAINS?
MALLETT

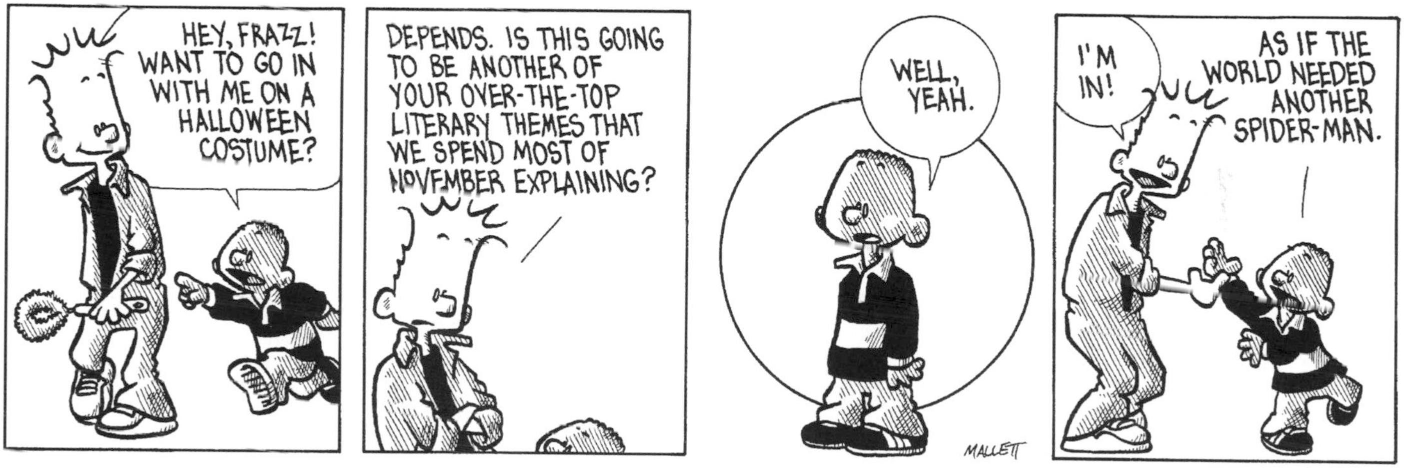
HEY, FRAZZ! WANT TO GO IN WITH ME ON A HALLOWEEN COSTUME?
DEPENDS. IS THIS GOING TO BE ANOTHER OF YOUR OVER-THE-TOP LITERARY THEMES THAT WE SPEND MOST OF NOVEMBER EXPLAINING?
WELL, YEAH.
MALLETT
I'M IN!
AS IF THE WORLD NEEDED ANOTHER SPIDER-MAN.

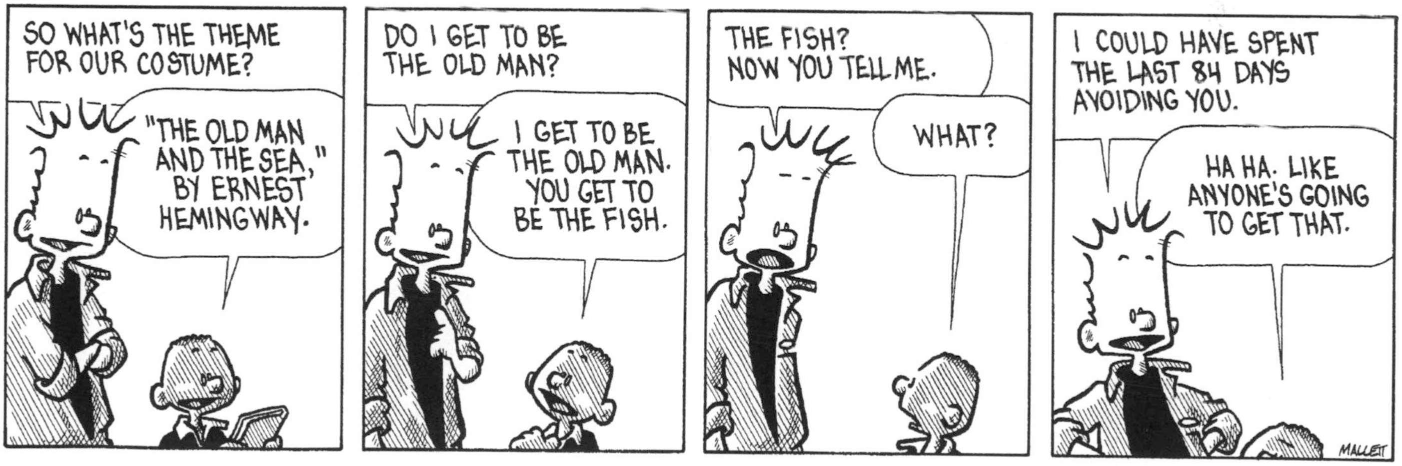
SO WHAT'S THE THEME FOR OUR COSTUME?
"THE OLD MAN AND THE SEA," BY ERNEST HEMINGWAY.
DO I GET TO BE THE OLD MAN?
I GET TO BE THE OLD MAN. YOU GET TO BE THE FISH.
THE FISH? NOW YOU TELL ME.
WHAT?
I COULD HAVE SPENT THE LAST 84 DAYS AVOIDING YOU.
HA HA. LIKE ANYONE'S GOING TO GET THAT.
MALLETT

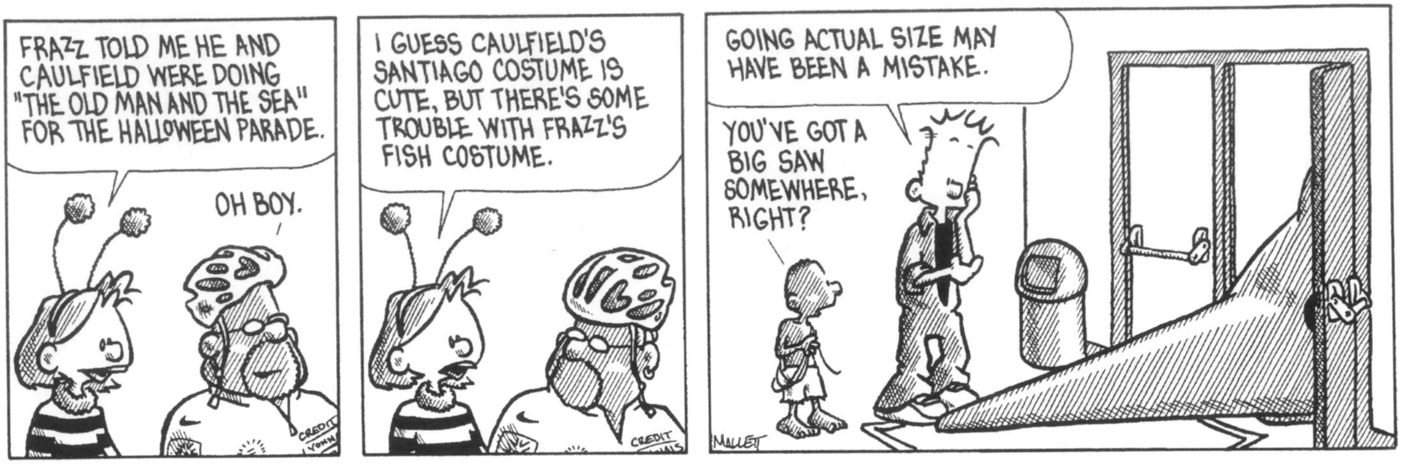
FRAZZ TOLD ME HE AND CAULFIELD WERE DOING "THE OLD MAN AND THE SEA" FOR THE HALLOWEEN PARADE.
OH BOY.
I GUESS CAULFIELD'S SANTIAGO COSTUME IS CUTE, BUT THERE'S SOME TROUBLE WITH FRAZZ'S FISH COSTUME.
GOING ACTUAL SIZE MAY HAVE BEEN A MISTAKE.
YOU'VE GOT A BIG SAW SOMEWHERE, RIGHT?
MALLETT

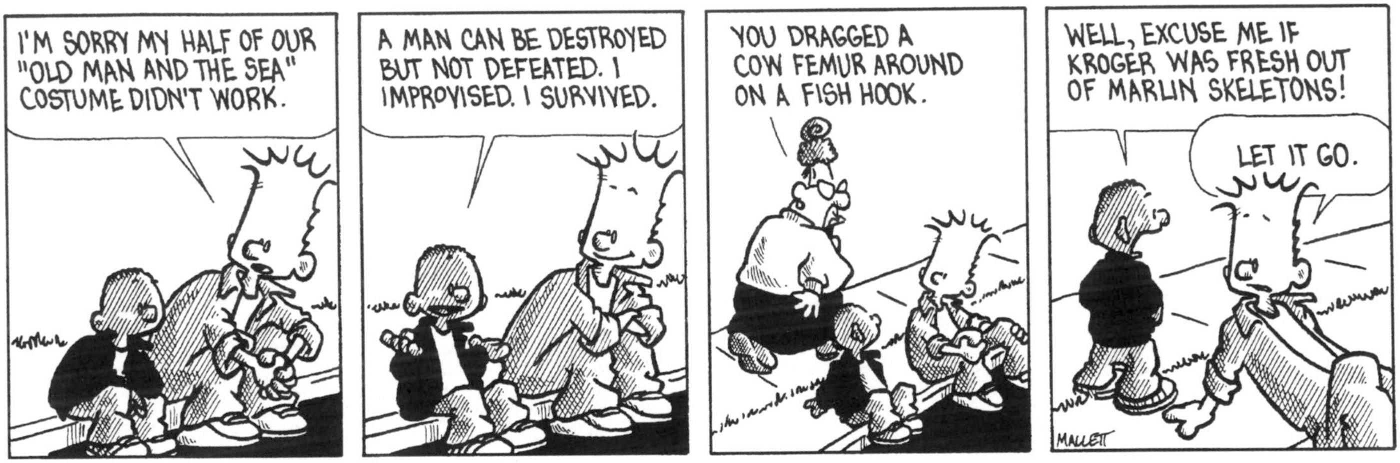
I'M SORRY MY HALF OF OUR "OLD MAN AND THE SEA" COSTUME DIDN'T WORK.
A MAN CAN BE DESTROYED BUT NOT DEFEATED. I IMPROVISED. I SURVIVED.
YOU DRAGGED A COW FEMUR AROUND ON A FISH HOOK.
WELL, EXCUSE ME IF KROGER WAS FRESH OUT OF MARLIN SKELETONS!
LET IT GO.
MALLETT

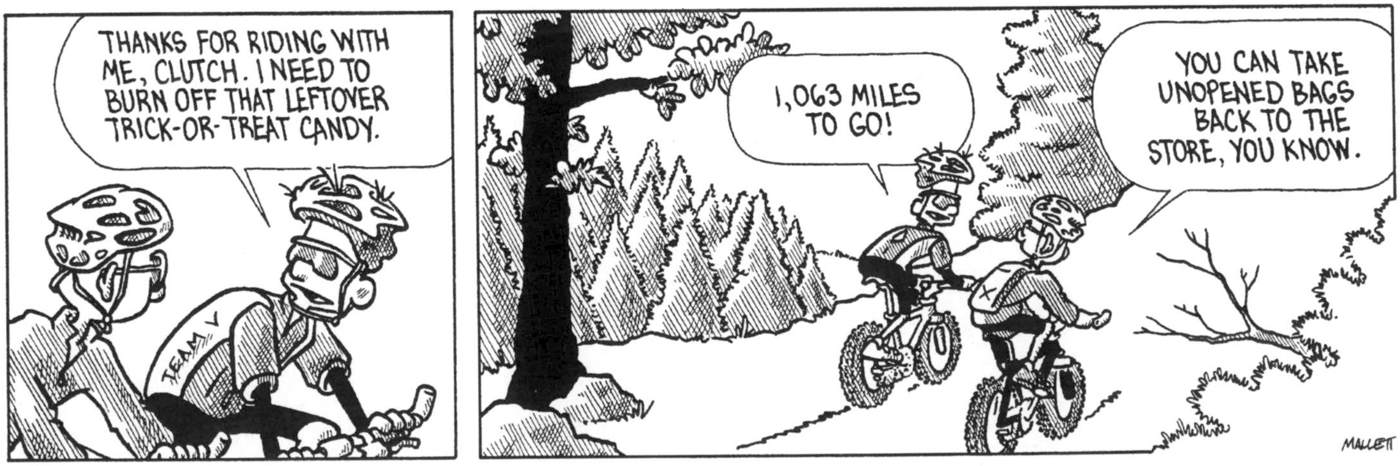
THANKS FOR RIDING WITH ME, CLUTCH. I NEED TO BURN OFF THAT LEFTOVER TRICK-OR-TREAT CANDY.
TEAM V
1,063 MILES TO GO!
YOU CAN TAKE UNOPENED BAGS BACK TO THE STORE, YOU KNOW.
MALLETT

FRAZZ

by Jef Mallett

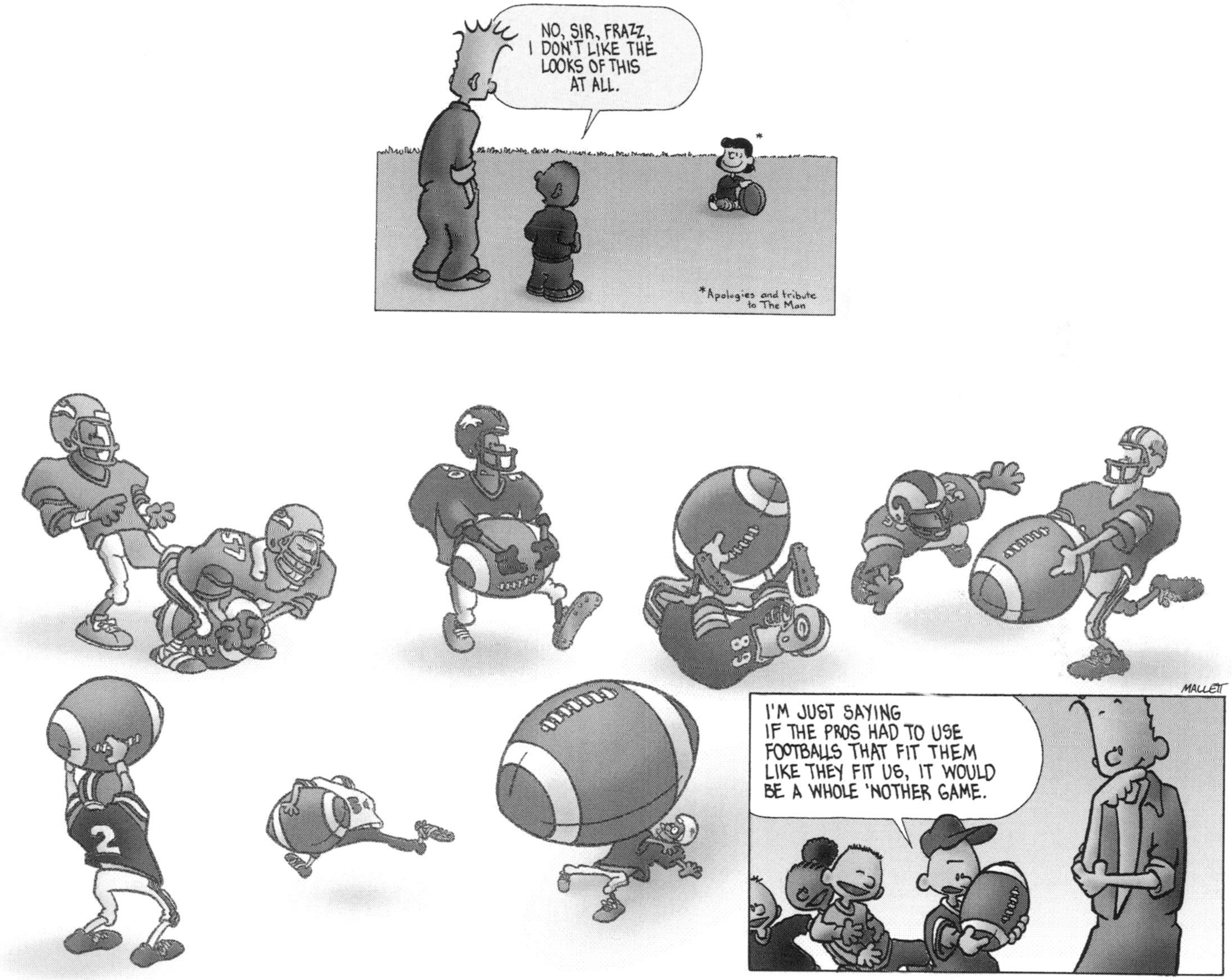

NO, SIR, FRAZZ, I DON'T LIKE THE LOOKS OF THIS AT ALL.
*
*Apologies and tribute to The Man
MALLETT
I'M JUST SAYING IF THE PROS HAD TO USE FOOTBALLS THAT FIT THEM LIKE THEY FIT US, IT WOULD BE A WHOLE 'NOTHER GAME.

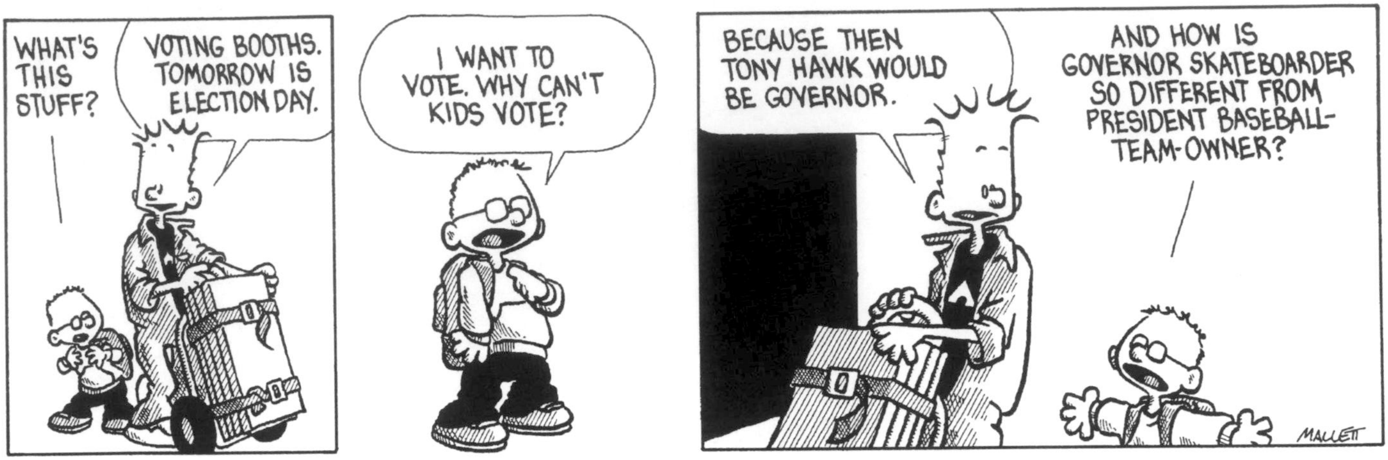
WHAT'S THIS STUFF?
VOTING BOOTHS. TOMORROW IS ELECTION DAY.
I WANT TO VOTE. WHY CAN'T KIDS VOTE?
BECAUSE THEN TONY HAWK WOULD BE GOVERNOR.
AND HOW IS GOVERNOR SKATEBOARDER SO DIFFERENT FROM PRESIDENT BASEBALL-TEAM-OWNER?
MALLETT

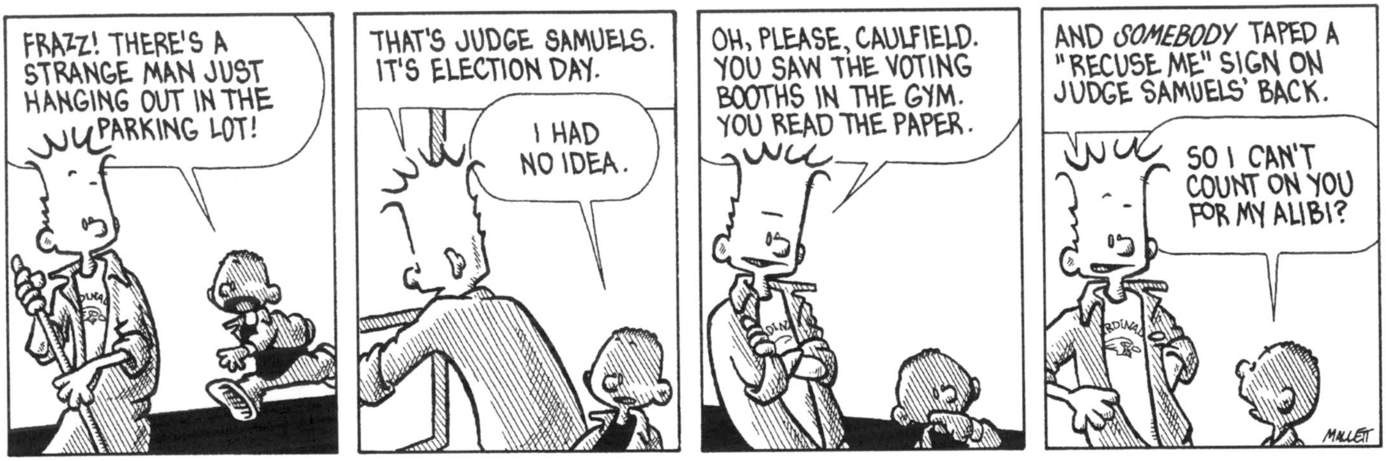
FRAZZ! THERE'S A STRANGE MAN JUST HANGING OUT IN THE PARKING LOT!
THAT'S JUDGE SAMUELS. IT'S ELECTION DAY.
I HAD NO IDEA.
OH, PLEASE, CAULFIELD. YOU SAW THE VOTING BOOTHS IN THE GYM. YOU READ THE PAPER.
AND *SOMEBODY* TAPED A "RECUSE ME" SIGN ON JUDGE SAMUELS' BACK.
SO I CAN'T COUNT ON YOU FOR MY ALIBI?
MALLETT

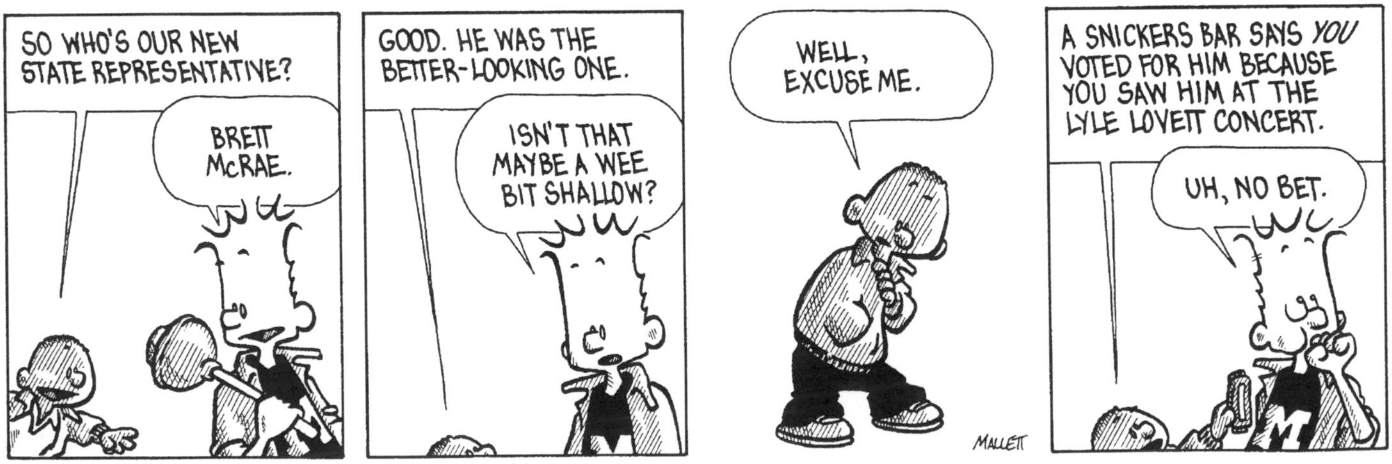
SO WHO'S OUR NEW STATE REPRESENTATIVE?
BRETT McRAE.
GOOD. HE WAS THE BETTER-LOOKING ONE.
ISN'T THAT MAYBE A WEE BIT SHALLOW?
WELL, EXCUSE ME.
A SNICKERS BAR SAYS *YOU* VOTED FOR HIM BECAUSE YOU SAW HIM AT THE LYLE LOVETT CONCERT.
UH, NO BET.
MALLETT

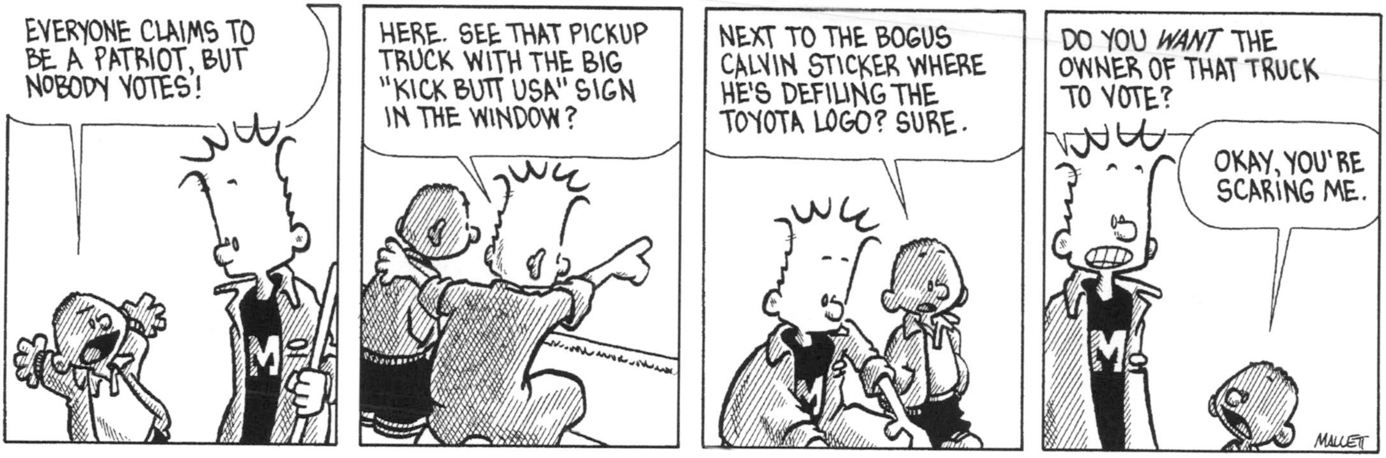
EVERYONE CLAIMS TO BE A PATRIOT, BUT NOBODY VOTES!
HERE. SEE THAT PICKUP TRUCK WITH THE BIG "KICK BUTT USA" SIGN IN THE WINDOW?
NEXT TO THE BOGUS CALVIN STICKER WHERE HE'S DEFILING THE TOYOTA LOGO? SURE.
DO YOU *WANT* THE OWNER OF THAT TRUCK TO VOTE?
OKAY, YOU'RE SCARING ME.
MALLETT

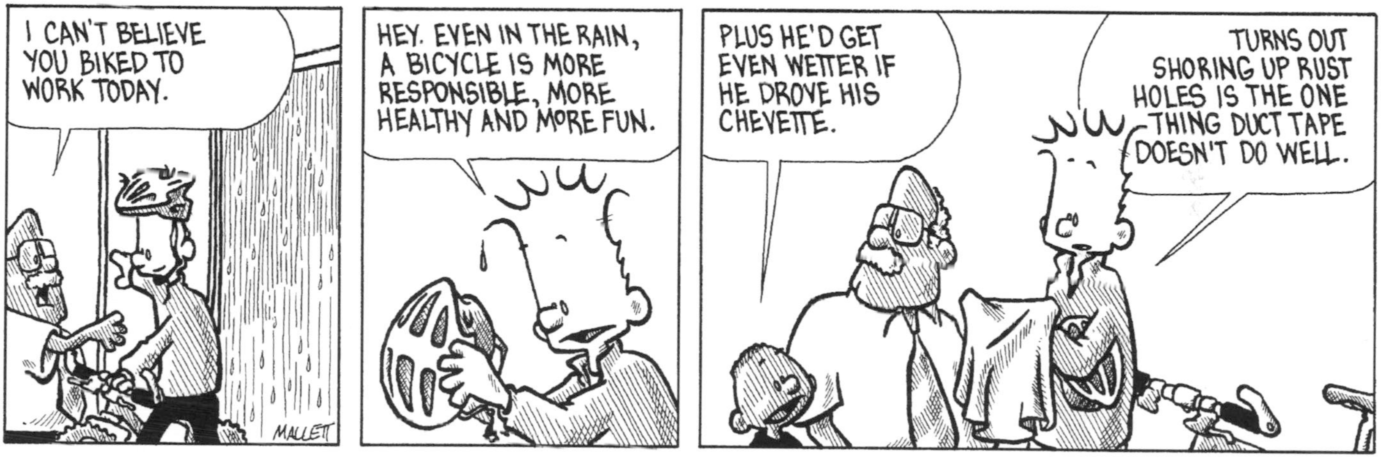
I CAN'T BELIEVE YOU BIKED TO WORK TODAY.
MALLETT
HEY. EVEN IN THE RAIN, A BICYCLE IS MORE RESPONSIBLE, MORE HEALTHY AND MORE FUN.
PLUS HE'D GET EVEN WETTER IF HE DROVE HIS CHEVETTE.
TURNS OUT SHORING UP RUST HOLES IS THE ONE THING DUCT TAPE DOESN'T DO WELL.

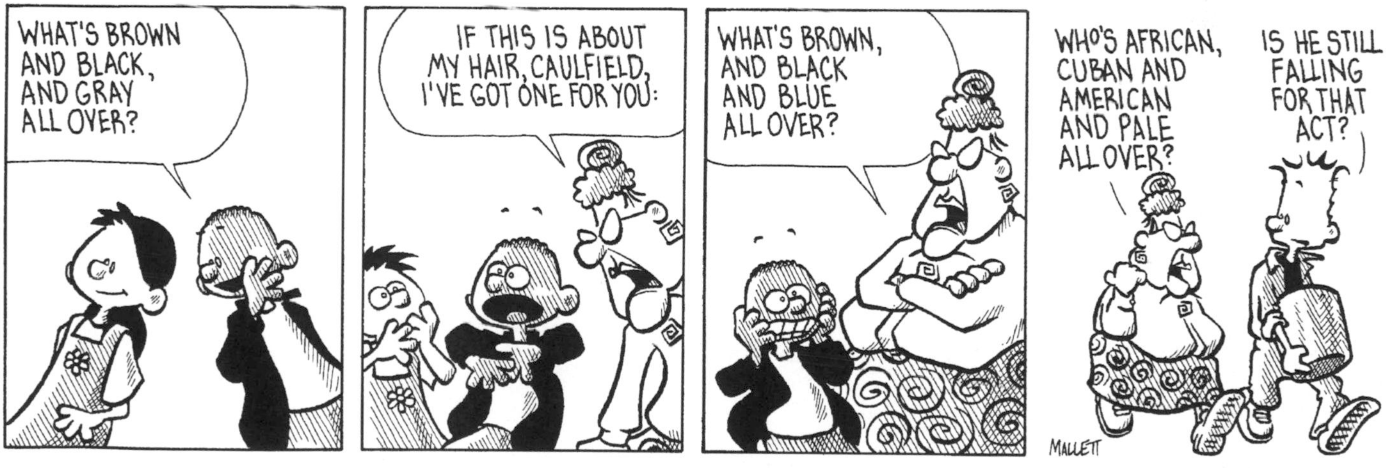
WHAT'S BROWN AND BLACK, AND GRAY ALL OVER?
IF THIS IS ABOUT MY HAIR, CAULFIELD, I'VE GOT ONE FOR YOU:
WHAT'S BROWN, AND BLACK AND BLUE ALL OVER?
WHO'S AFRICAN, CUBAN AND AMERICAN AND PALE ALL OVER?
IS HE STILL FALLING FOR THAT ACT?
MALLETT

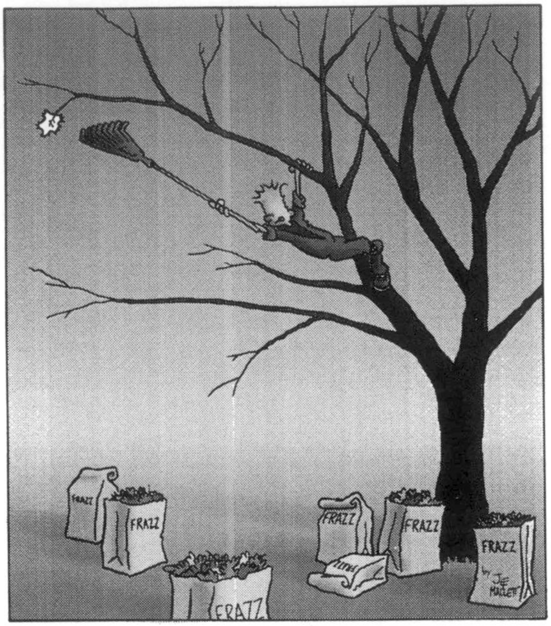
FRAZZ
FRAZZ
FRAZZ
FRAZZ
FRAZZ

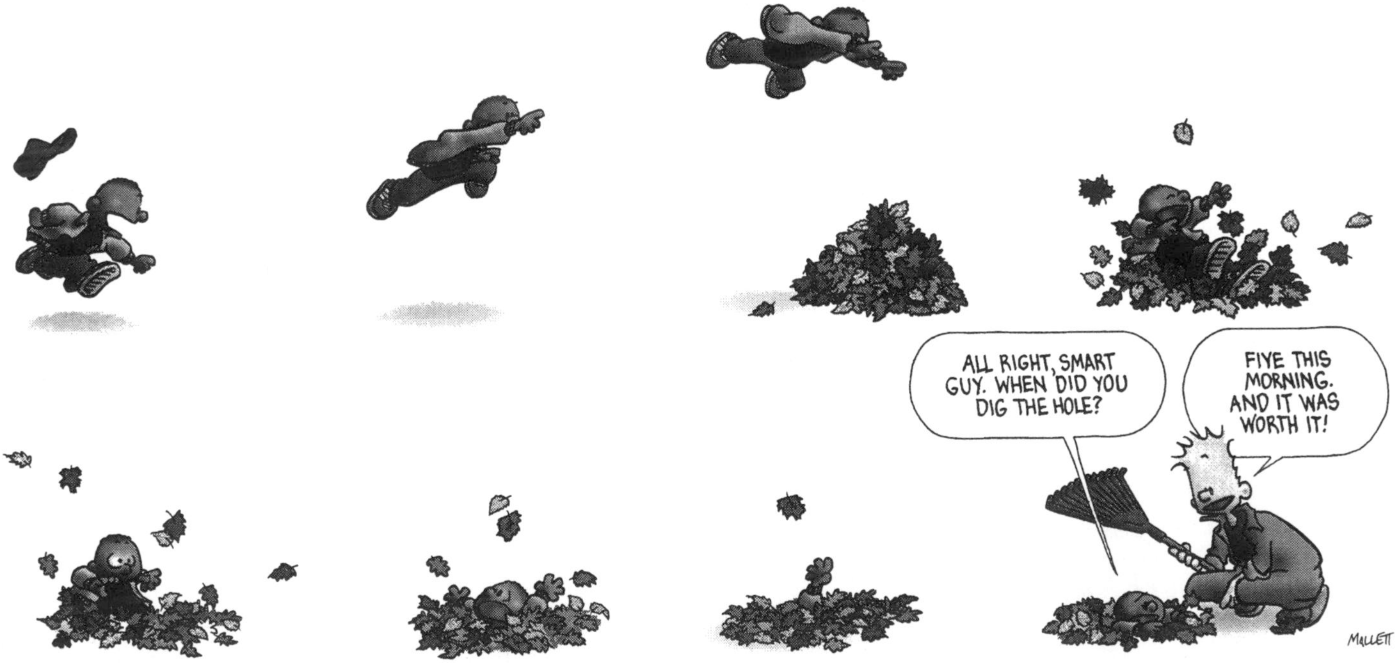
ALL RIGHT, SMART GUY. WHEN DID YOU DIG THE HOLE?
FIVE THIS MORNING. AND IT WAS WORTH IT!
MALLETT

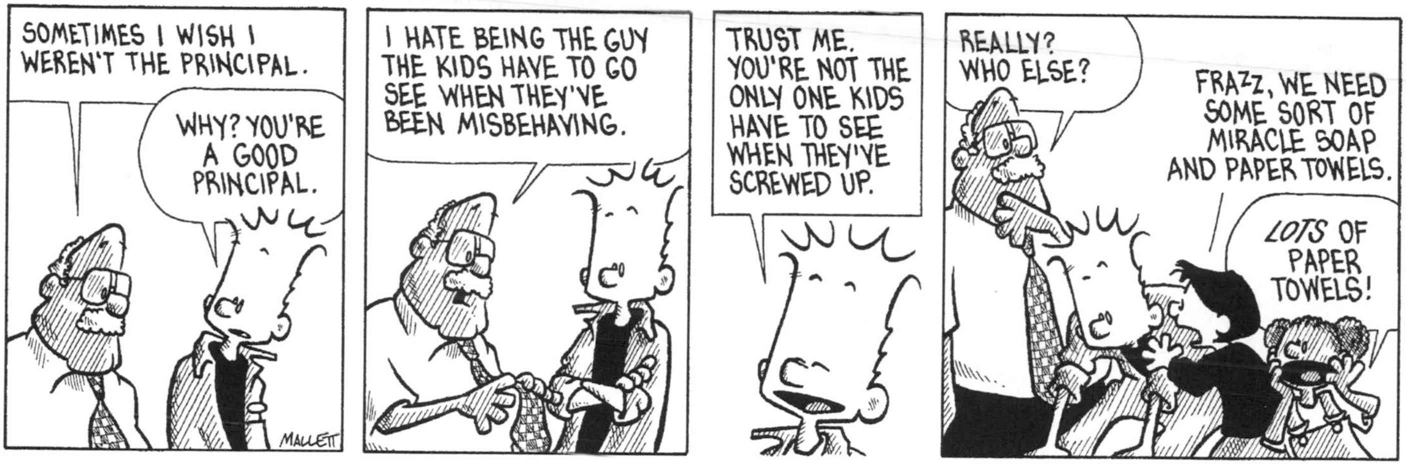
SOMETIMES I WISH I WEREN'T THE PRINCIPAL.
WHY? YOU'RE A GOOD PRINCIPAL.
MALLETT
I HATE BEING THE GUY THE KIDS HAVE TO GO SEE WHEN THEY'VE BEEN MISBEHAVING.
TRUST ME. YOU'RE NOT THE ONLY ONE KIDS HAVE TO SEE WHEN THEY'VE SCREWED UP.
REALLY? WHO ELSE?
FRAZZ, WE NEED SOME SORT OF MIRACLE SOAP AND PAPER TOWELS.
LOTS OF PAPER TOWELS!

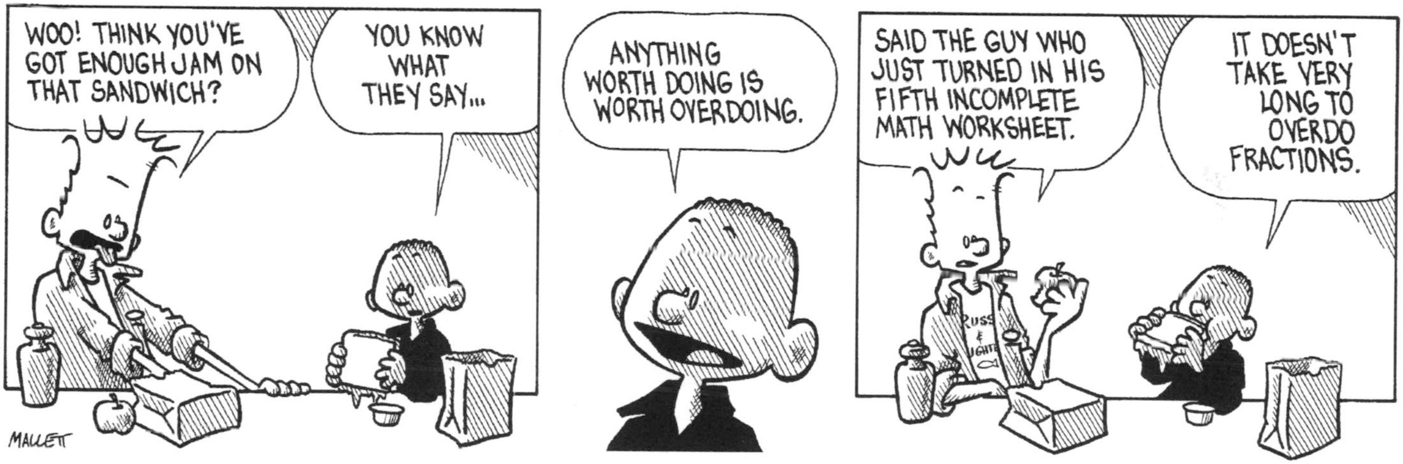
WOO! THINK YOU'VE GOT ENOUGH JAM ON THAT SANDWICH?
YOU KNOW WHAT THEY SAY...
MALLETT
ANYTHING WORTH DOING IS WORTH OVERDOING.
SAID THE GUY WHO JUST TURNED IN HIS FIFTH INCOMPLETE MATH WORKSHEET.
IT DOESN'T TAKE VERY LONG TO OVERDO FRACTIONS.

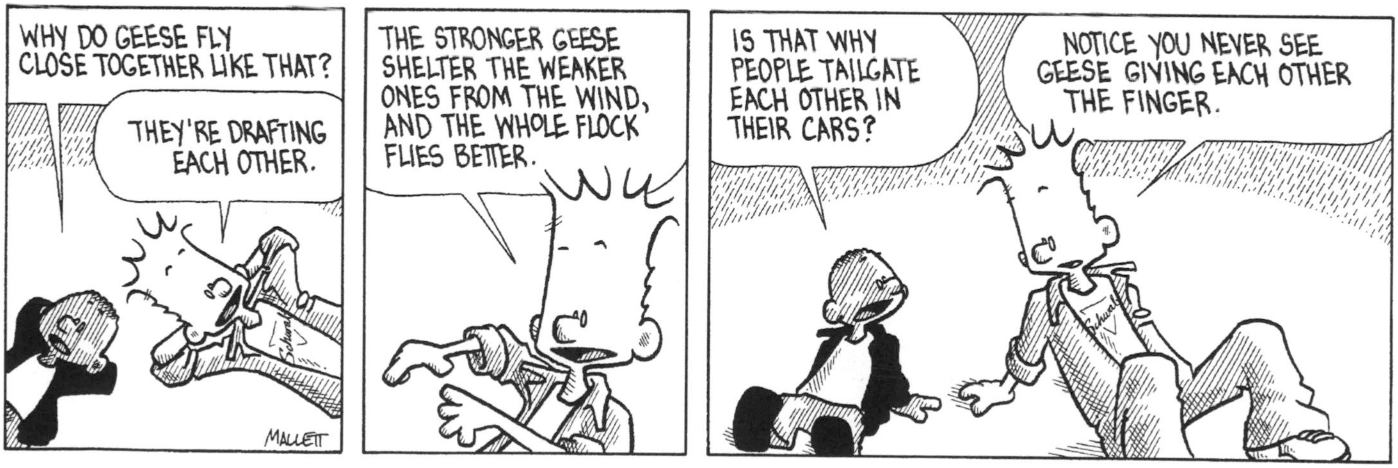
WHY DO GEESE FLY CLOSE TOGETHER LIKE THAT?
THEY'RE DRAFTING EACH OTHER.
MALLETT
THE STRONGER GEESE SHELTER THE WEAKER ONES FROM THE WIND, AND THE WHOLE FLOCK FLIES BETTER.
IS THAT WHY PEOPLE TAILGATE EACH OTHER IN THEIR CARS?
NOTICE YOU NEVER SEE GEESE GIVING EACH OTHER THE FINGER.

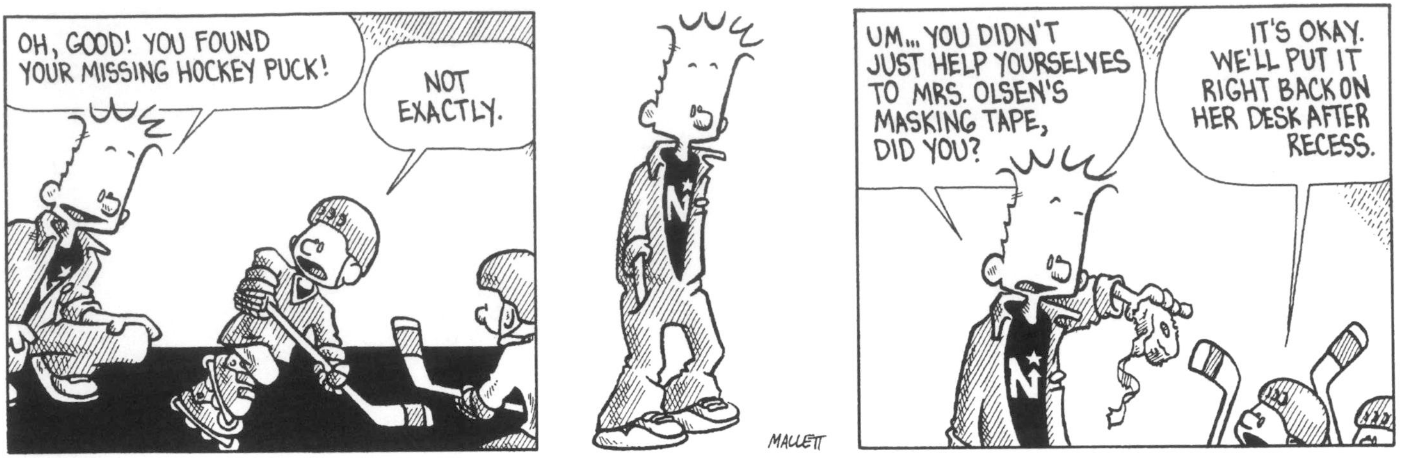
OH, GOOD! YOU FOUND YOUR MISSING HOCKEY PUCK!
NOT EXACTLY.
MALLETT
UM... YOU DIDN'T JUST HELP YOURSELVES TO MRS. OLSEN'S MASKING TAPE, DID YOU?
IT'S OKAY. WE'LL PUT IT RIGHT BACK ON HER DESK AFTER RECESS.

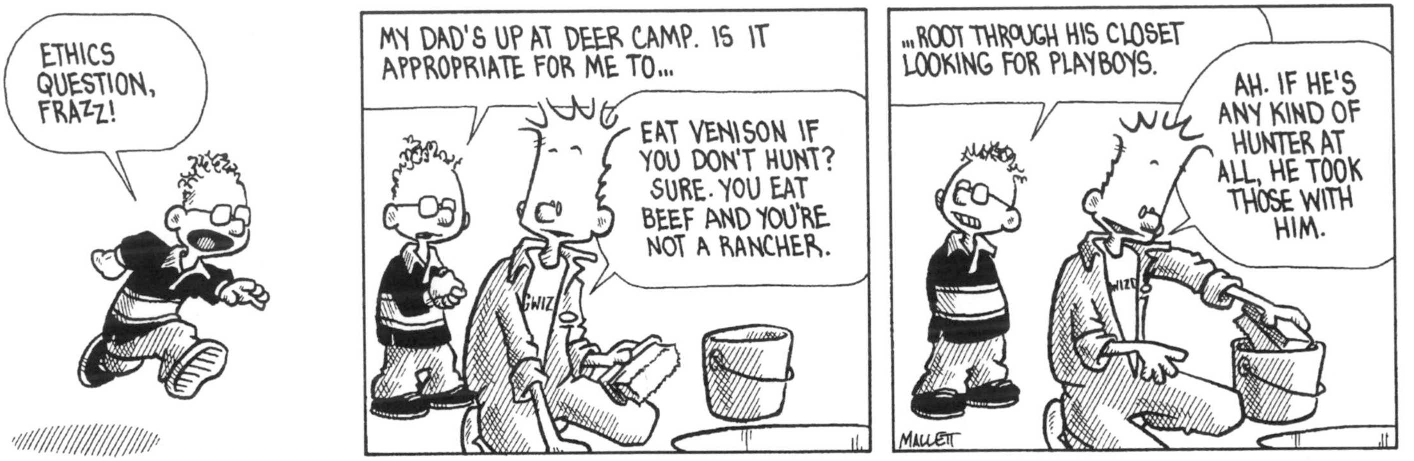
ETHICS QUESTION, FRAZZ!
MY DAD'S UP AT DEER CAMP. IS IT APPROPRIATE FOR ME TO...
EAT VENISON IF YOU DON'T HUNT? SURE. YOU EAT BEEF AND YOU'RE NOT A RANCHER.
...ROOT THROUGH HIS CLOSET LOOKING FOR PLAYBOYS.
AH. IF HE'S ANY KIND OF HUNTER AT ALL, HE TOOK THOSE WITH HIM.
MALLETT

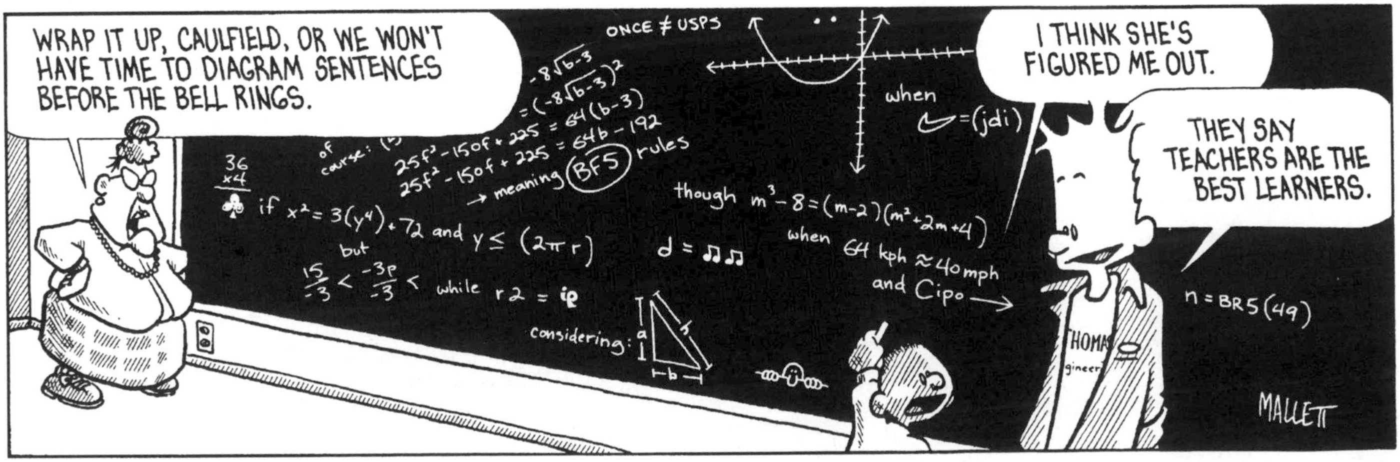
WRAP IT UP, CAULFIELD, OR WE WON'T HAVE TIME TO DIAGRAM SENTENCES BEFORE THE BELL RINGS.
I THINK SHE'S FIGURED ME OUT.
THEY SAY TEACHERS ARE THE BEST LEARNERS.
MALLETT

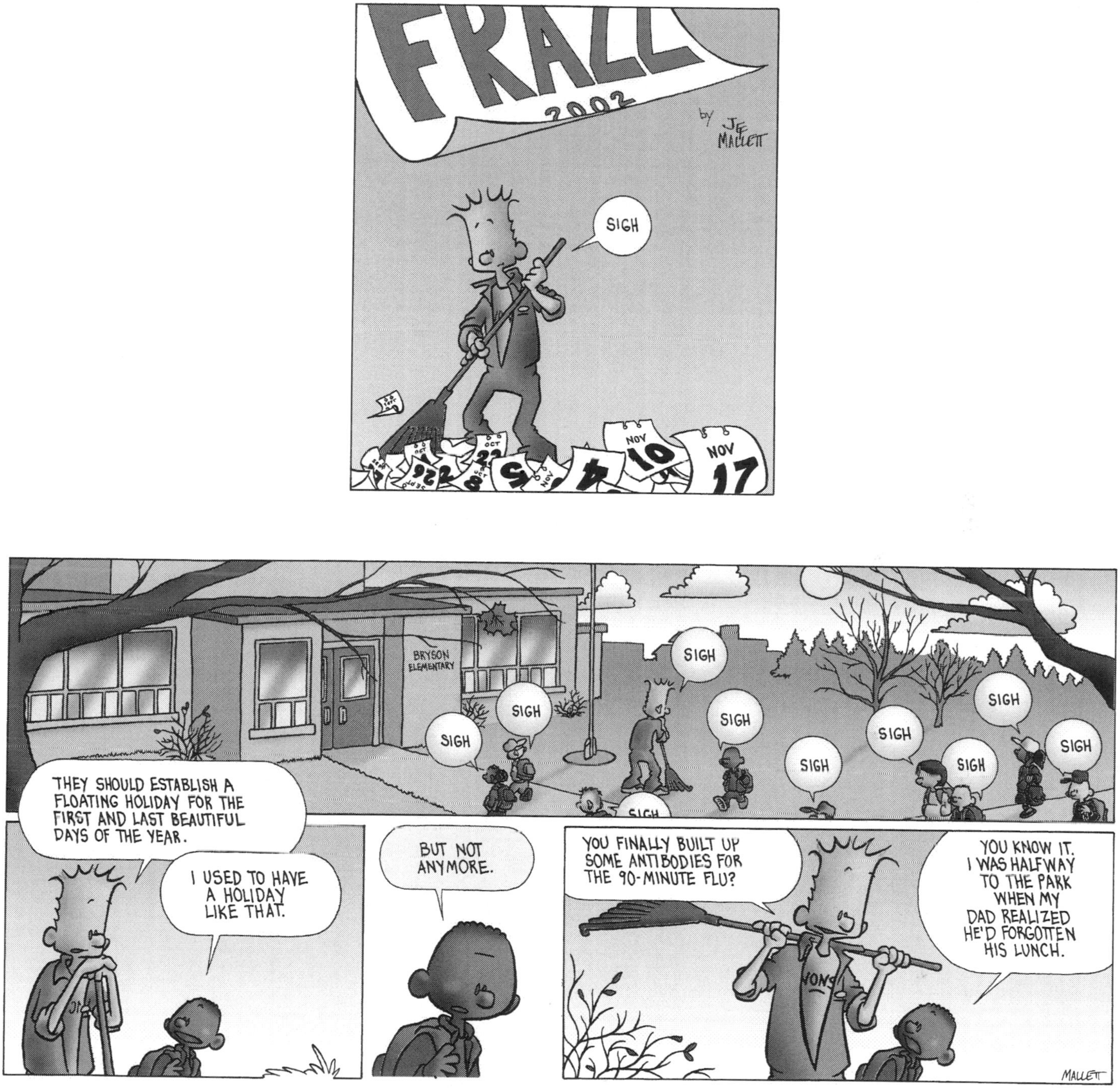
FRAZZ
2002
by JEF MALLETT
SIGH
NOV 10
NOV 17
BRYSON ELEMENTARY
SIGH
SIGH
SIGH
SIGH
SIGH
SIGH
SIGH
SIGH
SIGH
SIGH
THEY SHOULD ESTABLISH A FLOATING HOLIDAY FOR THE FIRST AND LAST BEAUTIFUL DAYS OF THE YEAR.
I USED TO HAVE A HOLIDAY LIKE THAT.
BUT NOT ANYMORE.
YOU FINALLY BUILT UP SOME ANTIBODIES FOR THE 90-MINUTE FLU?
YOU KNOW IT. I WAS HALFWAY TO THE PARK WHEN MY DAD REALIZED HE'D FORGOTTEN HIS LUNCH.
MALLETT

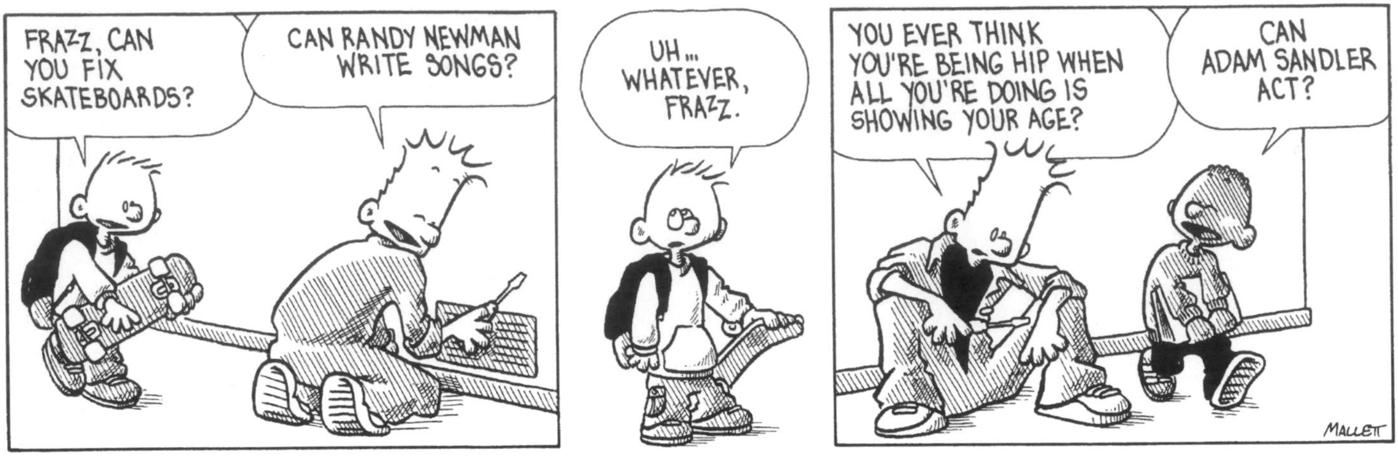
FRAZZ, CAN YOU FIX SKATEBOARDS?
CAN RANDY NEWMAN WRITE SONGS?
UH... WHATEVER, FRAZZ.
YOU EVER THINK YOU'RE BEING HIP WHEN ALL YOU'RE DOING IS SHOWING YOUR AGE?
CAN ADAM SANDLER ACT?
MALLETT

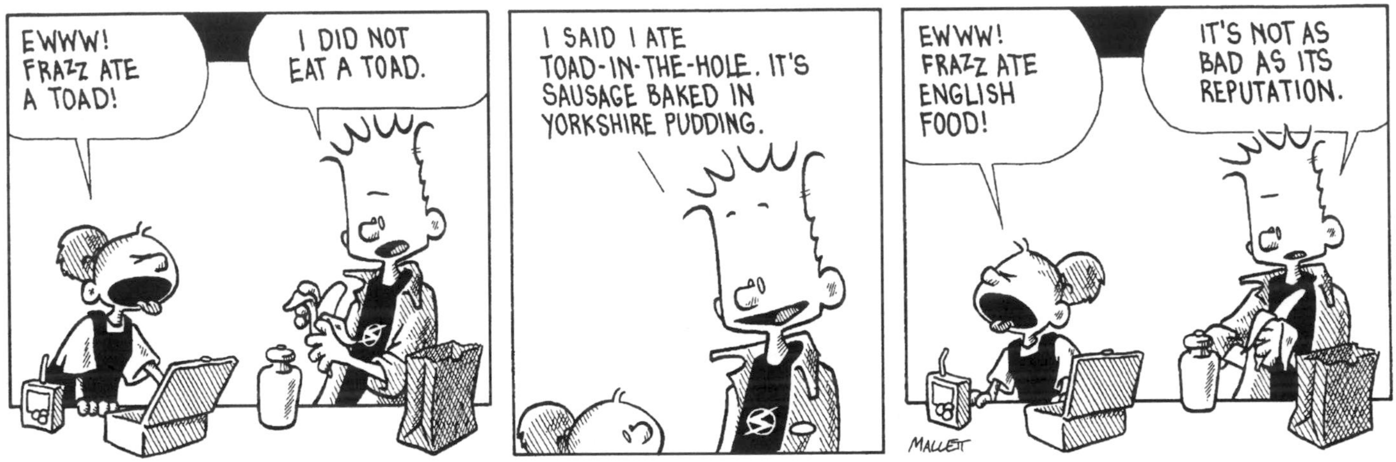
EWWW! FRAZZ ATE A TOAD!
I DID NOT EAT A TOAD.
I SAID I ATE TOAD-IN-THE-HOLE. IT'S SAUSAGE BAKED IN YORKSHIRE PUDDING.
EWWW! FRAZZ ATE ENGLISH FOOD!
IT'S NOT AS BAD AS ITS REPUTATION.
MALLETT

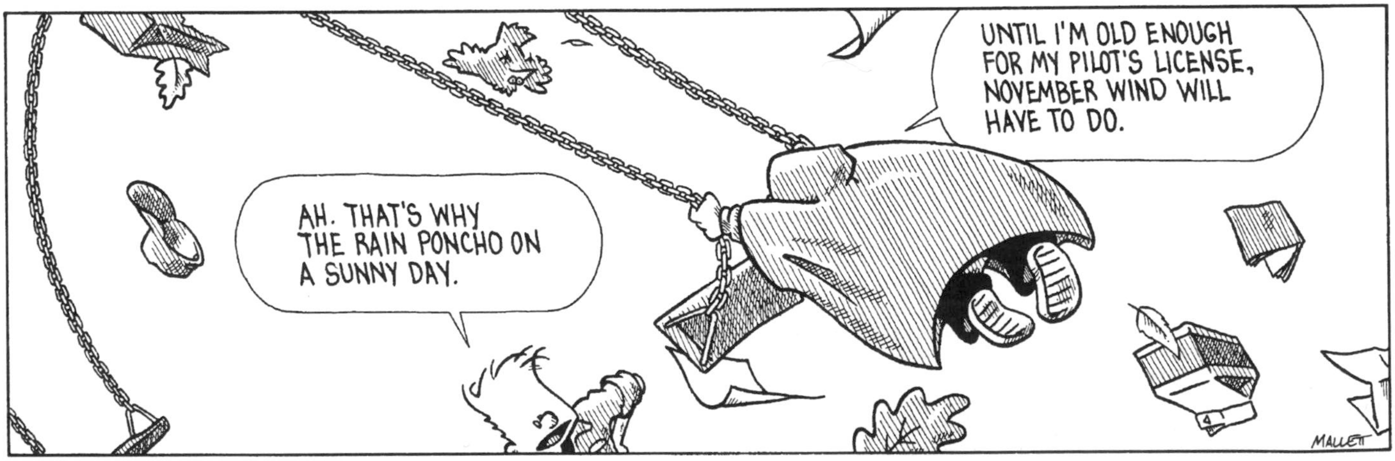
UNTIL I'M OLD ENOUGH FOR MY PILOT'S LICENSE, NOVEMBER WIND WILL HAVE TO DO.
AH. THAT'S WHY THE RAIN PONCHO ON A SUNNY DAY.
MALLETT

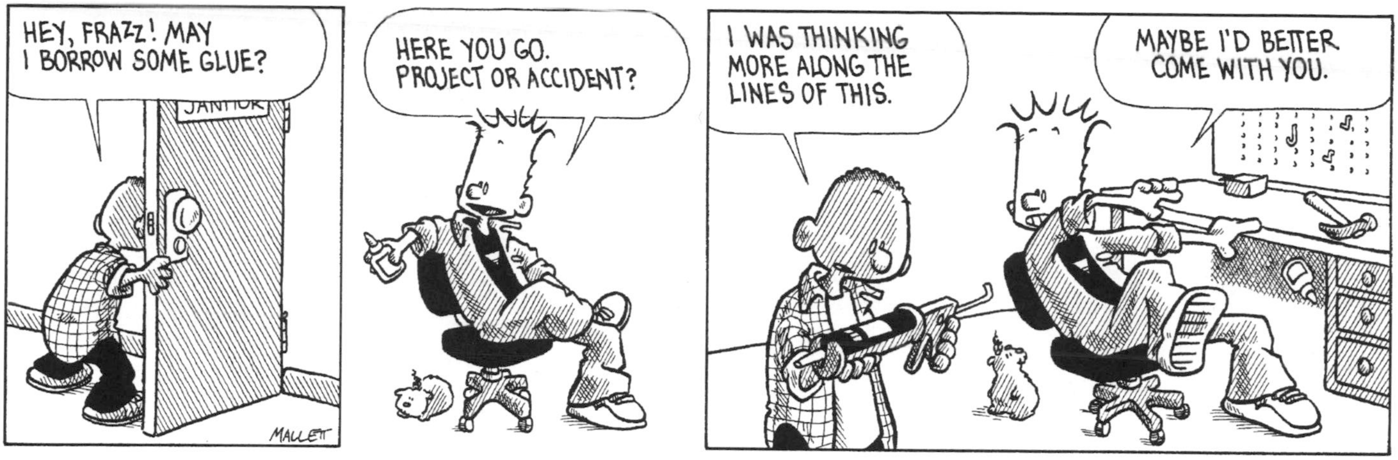
HEY, FRAZZ! MAY I BORROW SOME GLUE?
HERE YOU GO. PROJECT OR ACCIDENT?
I WAS THINKING MORE ALONG THE LINES OF THIS.
MAYBE I'D BETTER COME WITH YOU.
MALLETT

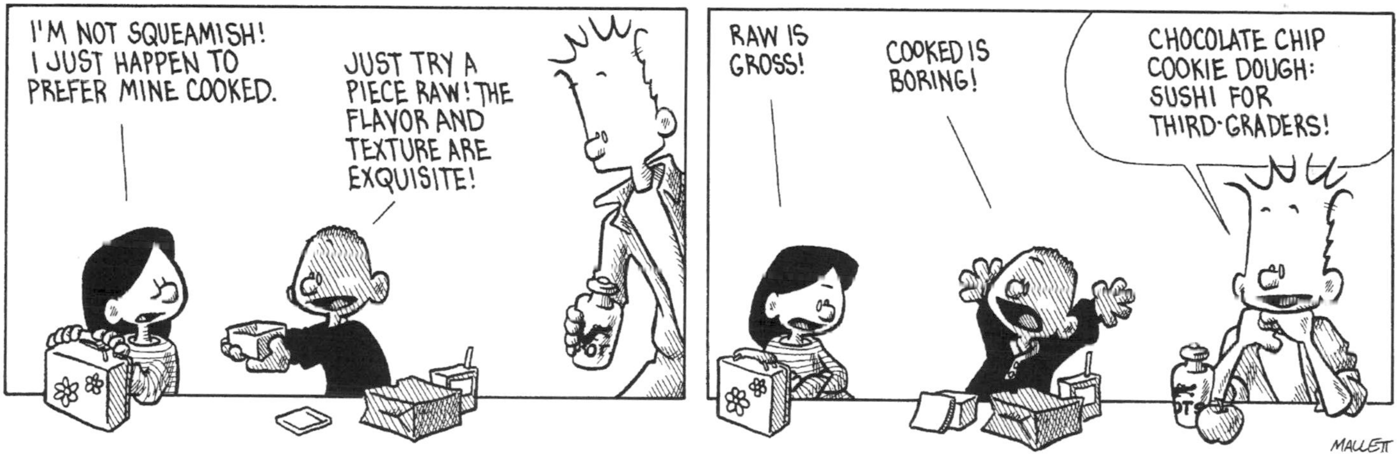
I'M NOT SQUEAMISH! I JUST HAPPEN TO PREFER MINE COOKED.
JUST TRY A PIECE RAW! THE FLAVOR AND TEXTURE ARE EXQUISITE!
RAW IS GROSS!
COOKED IS BORING!
CHOCOLATE CHIP COOKIE DOUGH: SUSHI FOR THIRD-GRADERS!
MALLETT

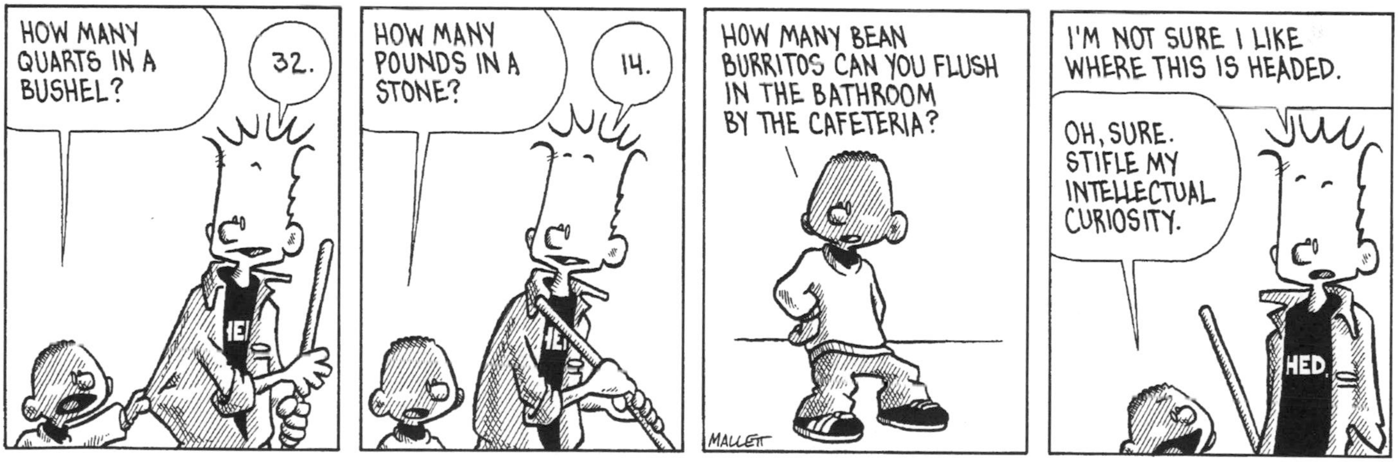
HOW MANY QUARTS IN A BUSHEL?
32.
HOW MANY POUNDS IN A STONE?
14.
HOW MANY BEAN BURRITOS CAN YOU FLUSH IN THE BATHROOM BY THE CAFETERIA?
MALLETT
I'M NOT SURE I LIKE WHERE THIS IS HEADED.
OH, SURE. STIFLE MY INTELLECTUAL CURIOSITY.
HED.

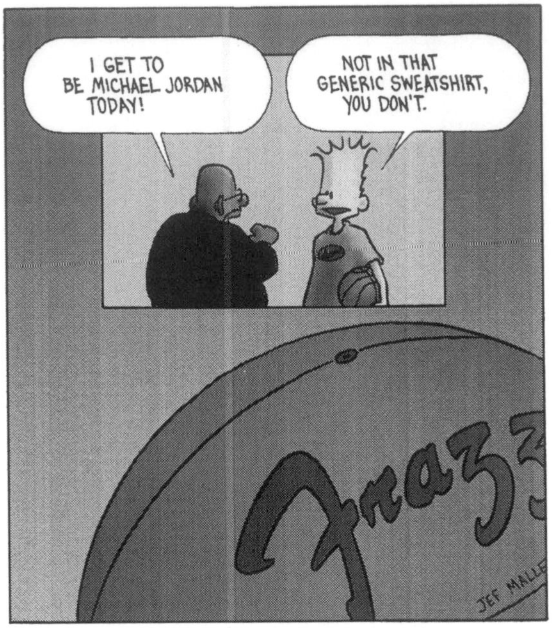
I GET TO BE MICHAEL JORDAN TODAY!
NOT IN THAT GENERIC SWEATSHIRT, YOU DON'T.

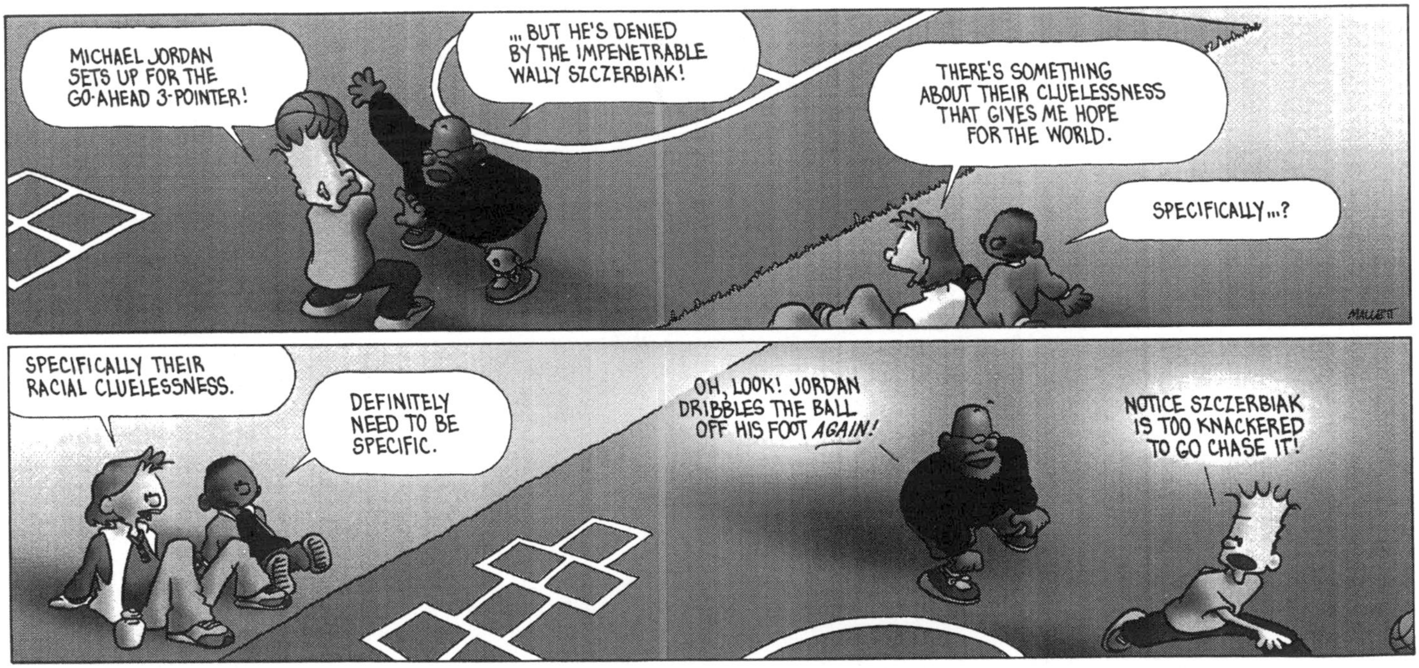
MICHAEL JORDAN SETS UP FOR THE GO-AHEAD 3-POINTER!
... BUT HE'S DENIED BY THE IMPENETRABLE WALLY SZCZERBIAK!
THERE'S SOMETHING ABOUT THEIR CLUELESSNESS THAT GIVES ME HOPE FOR THE WORLD.
SPECIFICALLY...?
MALLETT
SPECIFICALLY THEIR RACIAL CLUELESSNESS.
DEFINITELY NEED TO BE SPECIFIC.
OH, LOOK! JORDAN DRIBBLES THE BALL OFF HIS FOOT AGAIN!
NOTICE SZCZERBIAK IS TOO KNACKERED TO GO CHASE IT!

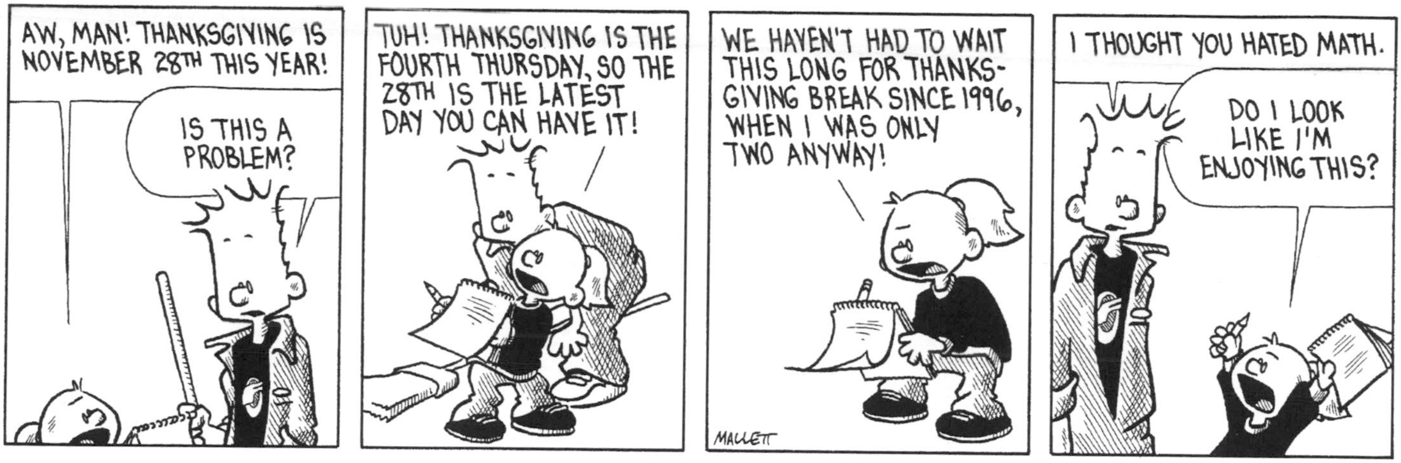
AW, MAN! THANKSGIVING IS NOVEMBER 28TH THIS YEAR!
IS THIS A PROBLEM?
TUH! THANKSGIVING IS THE FOURTH THURSDAY, SO THE 28TH IS THE LATEST DAY YOU CAN HAVE IT!
WE HAVEN'T HAD TO WAIT THIS LONG FOR THANKS-GIVING BREAK SINCE 1996, WHEN I WAS ONLY TWO ANYWAY!
MALLETT
I THOUGHT YOU HATED MATH.
DO I LOOK LIKE I'M ENJOYING THIS?

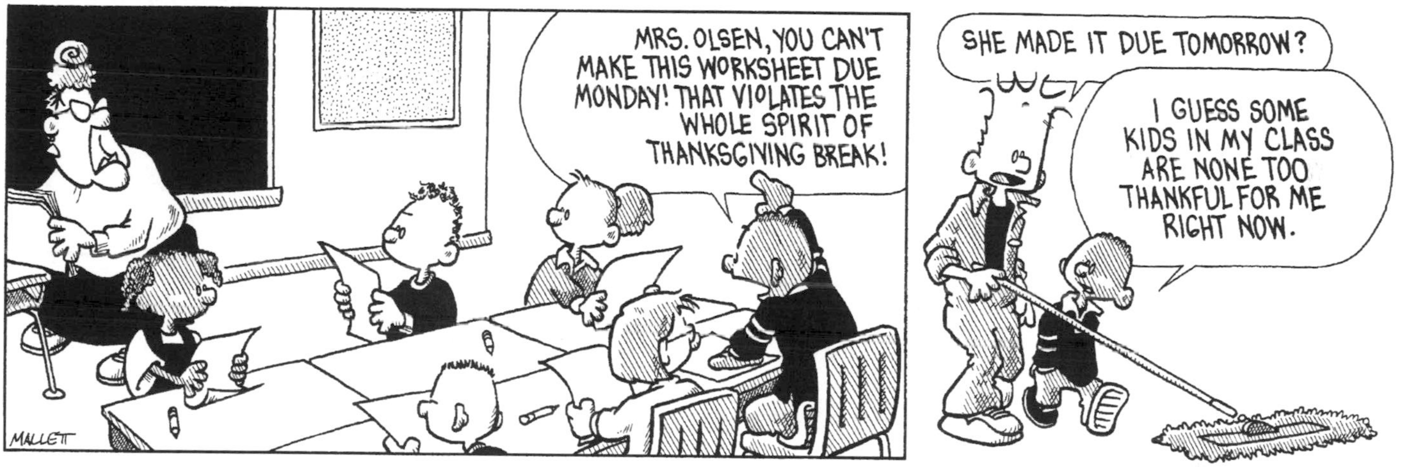
MRS. OLSEN, YOU CAN'T MAKE THIS WORKSHEET DUE MONDAY! THAT VIOLATES THE WHOLE SPIRIT OF THANKSGIVING BREAK!
MALLETT
SHE MADE IT DUE TOMORROW?
I GUESS SOME KIDS IN MY CLASS ARE NONE TOO THANKFUL FOR ME RIGHT NOW.

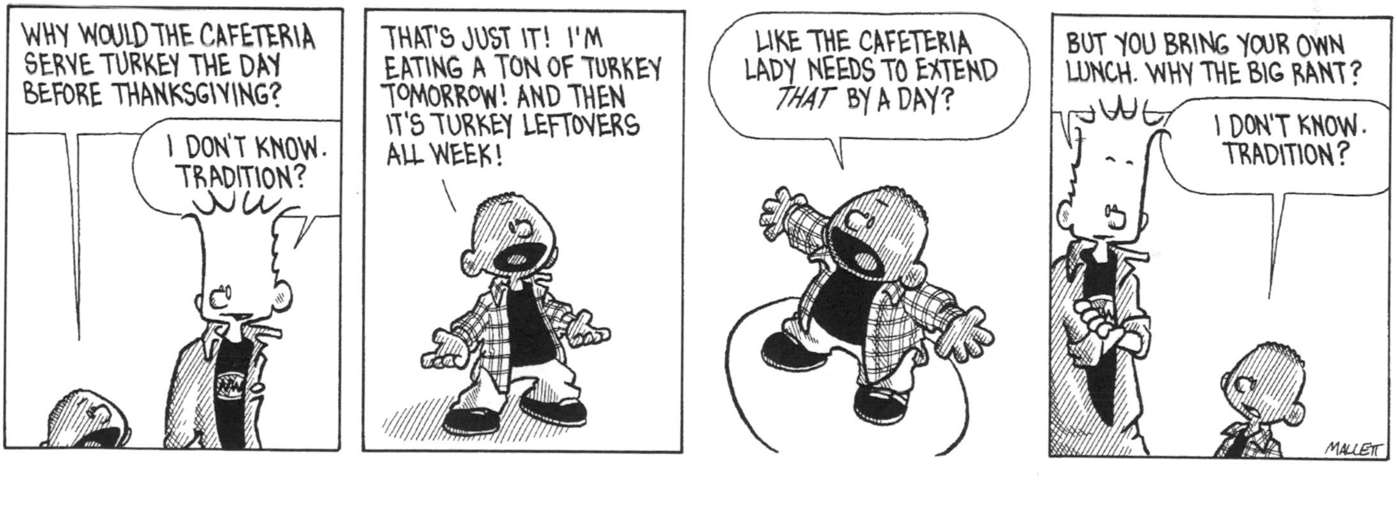
WHY WOULD THE CAFETERIA SERVE TURKEY THE DAY BEFORE THANKSGIVING?
I DON'T KNOW. TRADITION?
THAT'S JUST IT! I'M EATING A TON OF TURKEY TOMORROW! AND THEN IT'S TURKEY LEFTOVERS ALL WEEK!
LIKE THE CAFETERIA LADY NEEDS TO EXTEND *THAT* BY A DAY?
BUT YOU BRING YOUR OWN LUNCH. WHY THE BIG RANT?
I DON'T KNOW. TRADITION?
MALLETT

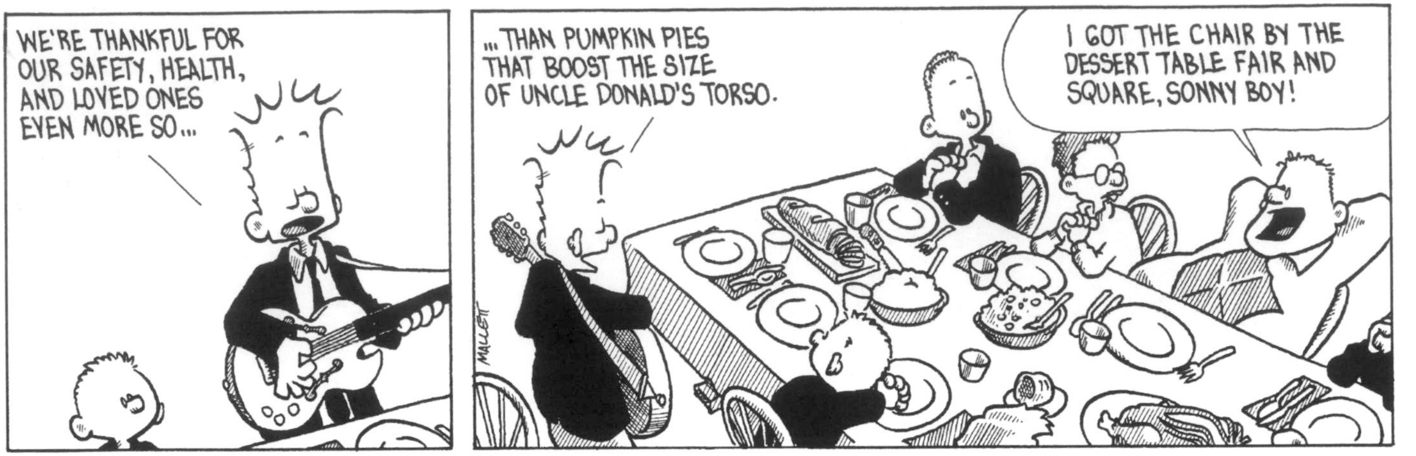
WE'RE THANKFUL FOR OUR SAFETY, HEALTH, AND LOVED ONES EVEN MORE SO...
...THAN PUMPKIN PIES THAT BOOST THE SIZE OF UNCLE DONALD'S TORSO.
I GOT THE CHAIR BY THE DESSERT TABLE FAIR AND SQUARE, SONNY BOY!
MALLETT

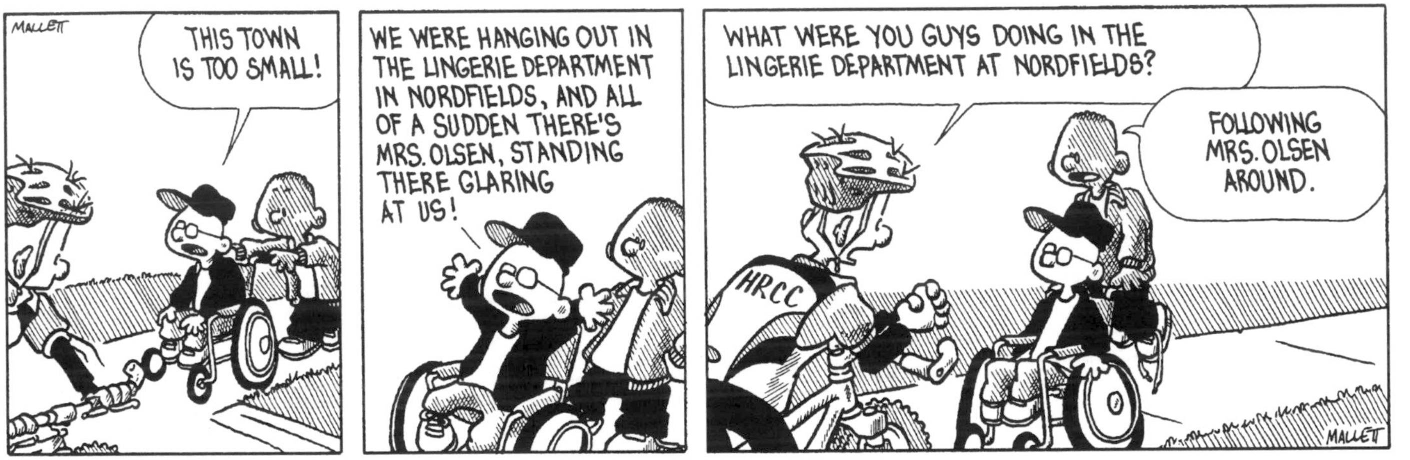
MALLETT
THIS TOWN IS TOO SMALL!
WE WERE HANGING OUT IN THE LINGERIE DEPARTMENT IN NORDFIELDS, AND ALL OF A SUDDEN THERE'S MRS. OLSEN, STANDING THERE GLARING AT US!
WHAT WERE YOU GUYS DOING IN THE LINGERIE DEPARTMENT AT NORDFIELDS?
HRCC
FOLLOWING MRS. OLSEN AROUND.
MALLETT

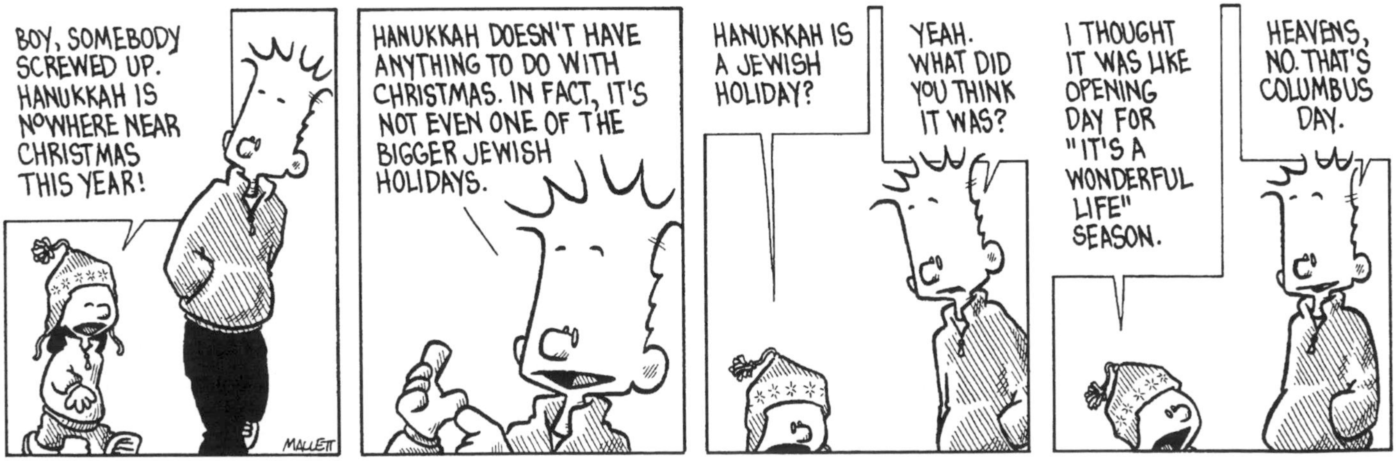
BOY, SOMEBODY SCREWED UP. HANUKKAH IS NOWHERE NEAR CHRISTMAS THIS YEAR!
MALLETT
HANUKKAH DOESN'T HAVE ANYTHING TO DO WITH CHRISTMAS. IN FACT, IT'S NOT EVEN ONE OF THE BIGGER JEWISH HOLIDAYS.
HANUKKAH IS A JEWISH HOLIDAY?
YEAH. WHAT DID YOU THINK IT WAS?
I THOUGHT IT WAS LIKE OPENING DAY FOR "IT'S A WONDERFUL LIFE" SEASON.
HEAVENS, NO. THAT'S COLUMBUS DAY.

Frazz
by JEF MALLETT
SO HOW OBNOXIOUS IS THE MOST OBNOXIOUS PERSON YOU KNOW?
RELATIVELY.

HEY, MISS PLAINWELL! DIDN'T FRAZZ INVITE YOU TO HAVE THANKSGIVING DINNER WITH HIS FAMILY?
NO. I FLEW HOME AND VISITED MY OWN FAMILY.
AREN'T YOU HIS GIRLFRIEND NOW?
I SUPPOSE I AM.
BUT I HAVEN'T BEEN FOR VERY LONG. AN INVITATION LIKE THAT MIGHT HAVE FELT A LITTLE PRESUMPTUOUS TO HIM.
MALLETT
BUT HE INVITED *ME*.
WELL, WITH YOUR DAD DEPLOYED OVERSEAS AND YOUR MOM HAVING TO WORK, FRAZZ THOUGHT YOU MIGHT ENJOY BORROWING HIS FAMILY.
I SURE DID! ESPECIALLY UNCLE GOOSE!
HE TAUGHT ME HOW TO PLAY BEATLES SONGS! LISTEN!
UNCLE GOOSE MAY BE THE OTHER REASON FRAZZ DIDN'T INVITE ME.

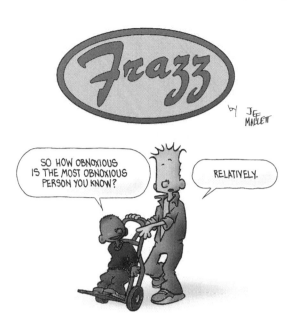

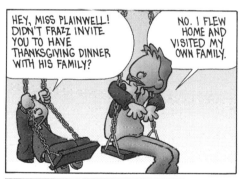

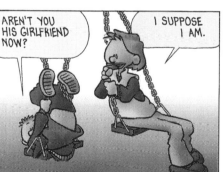

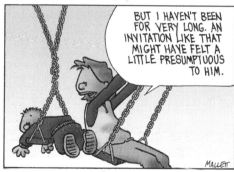

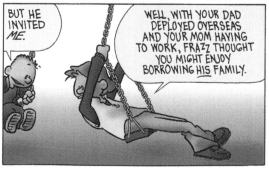

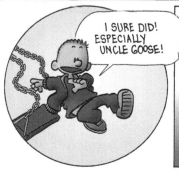

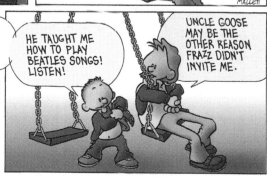

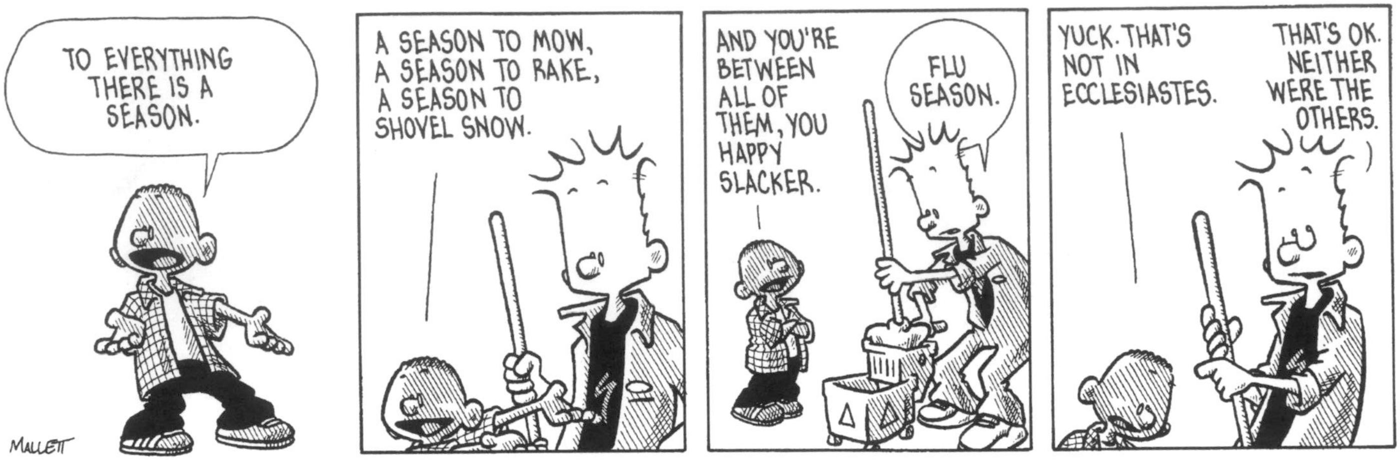
TO EVERYTHING THERE IS A SEASON.
MALLETT
A SEASON TO MOW, A SEASON TO RAKE, A SEASON TO SHOVEL SNOW.
AND YOU'RE BETWEEN ALL OF THEM, YOU HAPPY SLACKER.
FLU SEASON.
YUCK. THAT'S NOT IN ECCLESIASTES.
THAT'S OK. NEITHER WERE THE OTHERS.

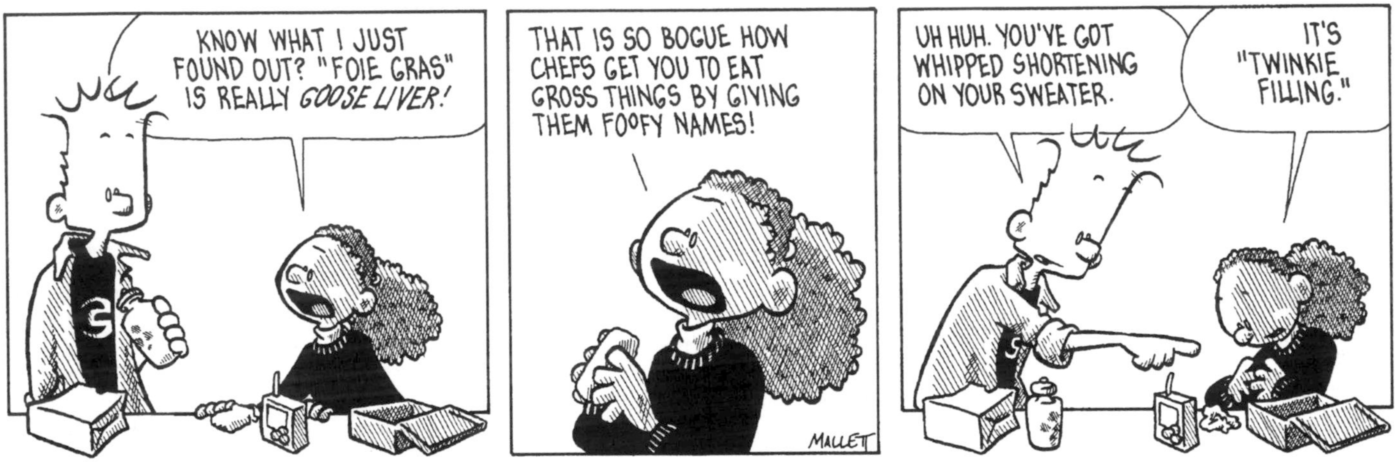
KNOW WHAT I JUST FOUND OUT? "FOIE GRAS" IS REALLY GOOSE LIVER!
THAT IS SO BOGUE HOW CHEFS GET YOU TO EAT GROSS THINGS BY GIVING THEM FOOFY NAMES!
MALLETT
UH HUH. YOU'VE GOT WHIPPED SHORTENING ON YOUR SWEATER.
IT'S "TWINKIE FILLING."

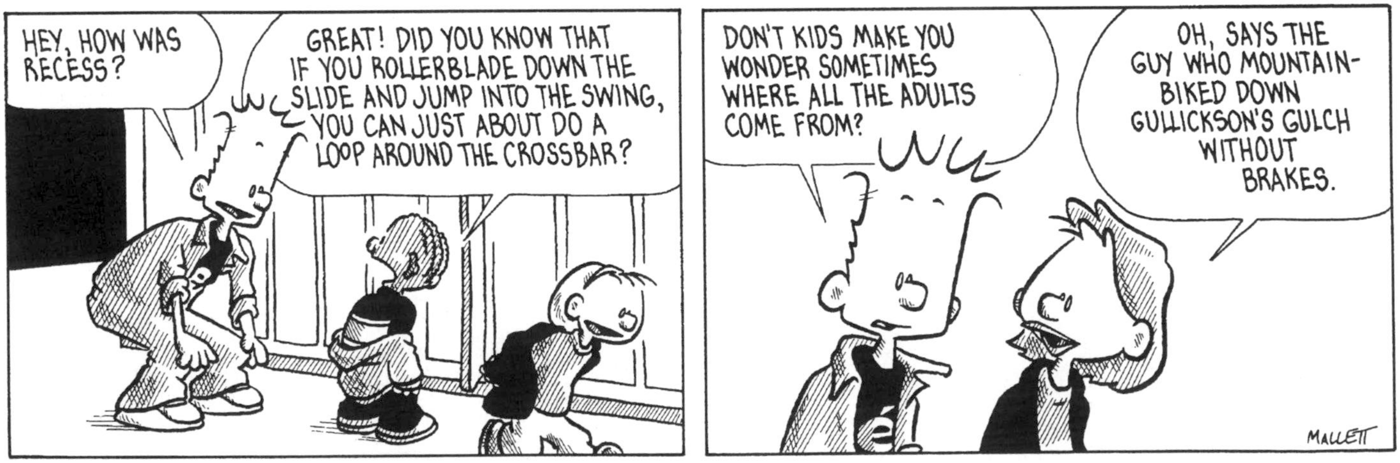
HEY, HOW WAS RECESS?
GREAT! DID YOU KNOW THAT IF YOU ROLLERBLADE DOWN THE SLIDE AND JUMP INTO THE SWING, YOU CAN JUST ABOUT DO A LOOP AROUND THE CROSSBAR?
DON'T KIDS MAKE YOU WONDER SOMETIMES WHERE ALL THE ADULTS COME FROM?
OH, SAYS THE GUY WHO MOUNTAIN-BIKED DOWN GULLICKSON'S GULCH WITHOUT BRAKES.
MALLETT

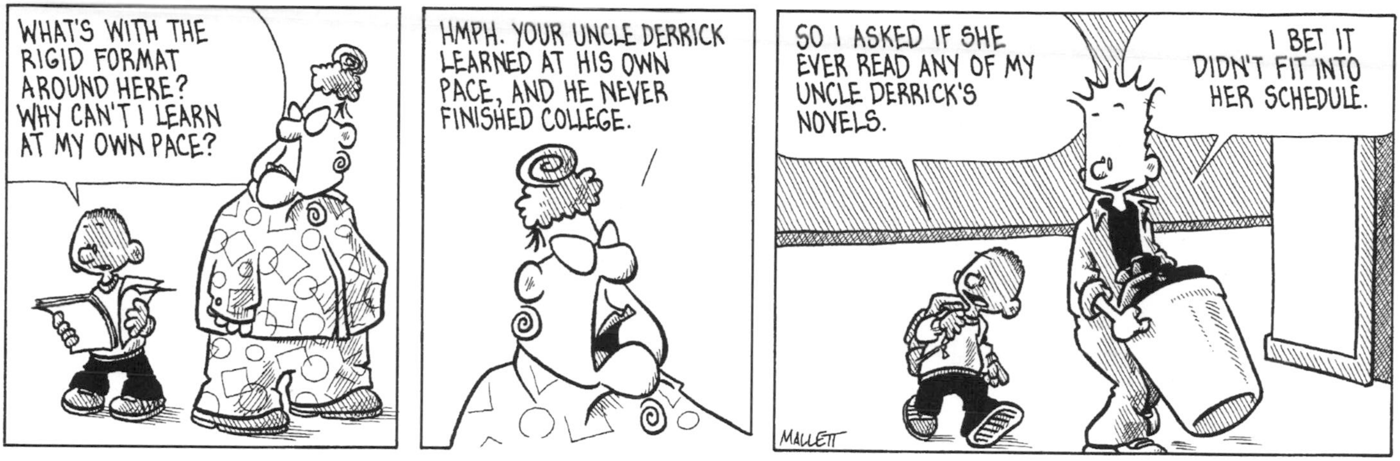
WHAT'S WITH THE RIGID FORMAT AROUND HERE? WHY CAN'T I LEARN AT MY OWN PACE?
HMPH. YOUR UNCLE DERRICK LEARNED AT HIS OWN PACE, AND HE NEVER FINISHED COLLEGE.
SO I ASKED IF SHE EVER READ ANY OF MY UNCLE DERRICK'S NOVELS.
I BET IT DIDN'T FIT INTO HER SCHEDULE.
MALLETT

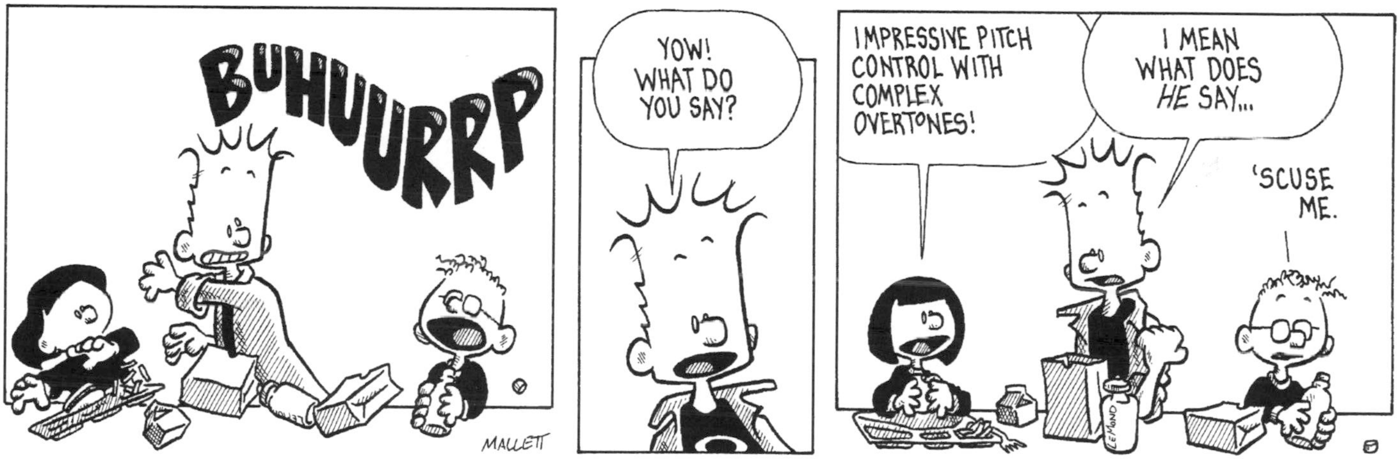
BUHUURRP
MALLETT
YOW! WHAT DO YOU SAY?
IMPRESSIVE PITCH CONTROL WITH COMPLEX OVERTONES!
I MEAN WHAT DOES *HE* SAY...
'SCUSE ME.
LEMONO

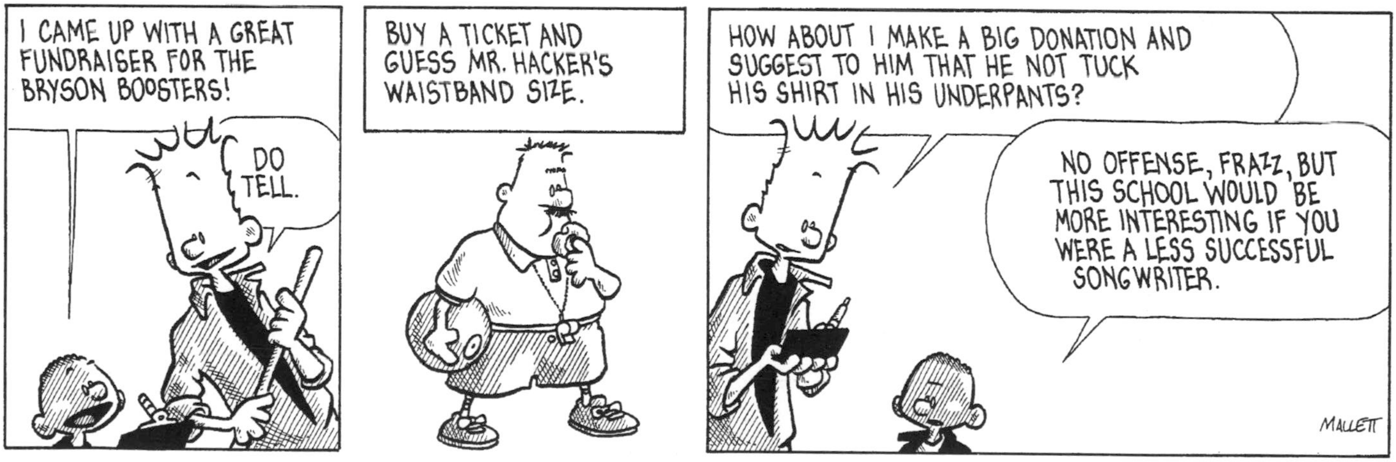
I CAME UP WITH A GREAT FUNDRAISER FOR THE BRYSON BOOSTERS!
DO TELL.
BUY A TICKET AND GUESS MR. HACKER'S WAISTBAND SIZE.
HOW ABOUT I MAKE A BIG DONATION AND SUGGEST TO HIM THAT HE NOT TUCK HIS SHIRT IN HIS UNDERPANTS?
NO OFFENSE, FRAZZ, BUT THIS SCHOOL WOULD BE MORE INTERESTING IF YOU WERE A LESS SUCCESSFUL SONGWRITER.
MALLETT

Frazz
by JEF MALLETT
ARE WE SCHEDULED TO APPEAR IN TODAY'S COMIC STRIP?
WE'VE BEEN PENCILED IN.

MR. SPAETZLE! DON'T FORGET, IT'S THE SECOND MONDAY OF AN EVEN-NUMBERED MONTH!
RIGHT! YES! THANKS!
LUNCH
THINK THINK THINK THINK THINK
SO WHAT'S THE SECOND MONDAY OF AN EVEN-NUMBERED MONTH?
THAT'S MESS WITH MR. SPAETZLE DAY!
MALLETT

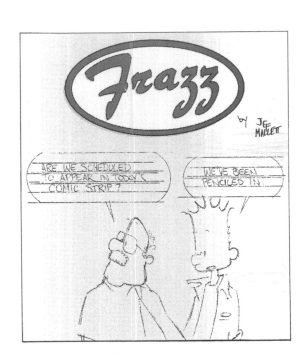

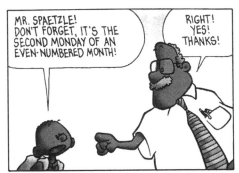

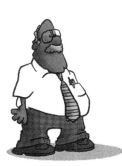

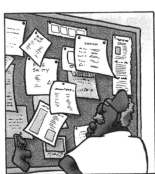

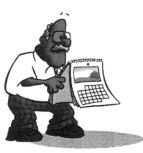

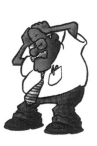

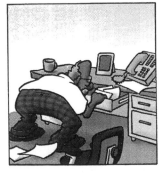

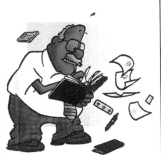

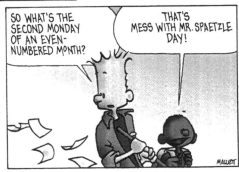

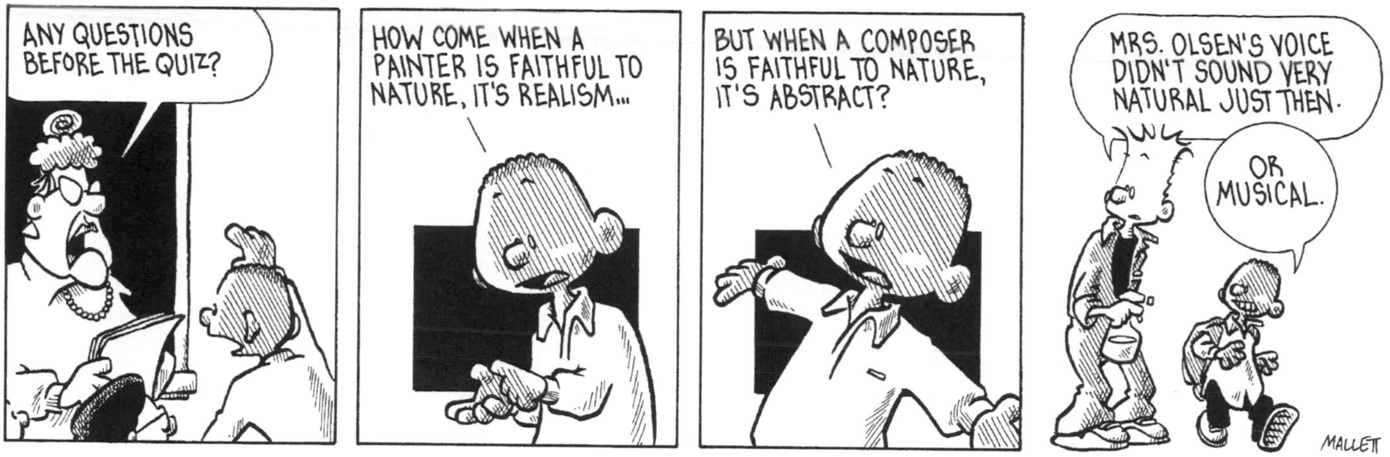
ANY QUESTIONS BEFORE THE QUIZ?
HOW COME WHEN A PAINTER IS FAITHFUL TO NATURE, IT'S REALISM...
BUT WHEN A COMPOSER IS FAITHFUL TO NATURE, IT'S ABSTRACT?
MRS. OLSEN'S VOICE DIDN'T SOUND VERY NATURAL JUST THEN.
OR MUSICAL.
MALLETT

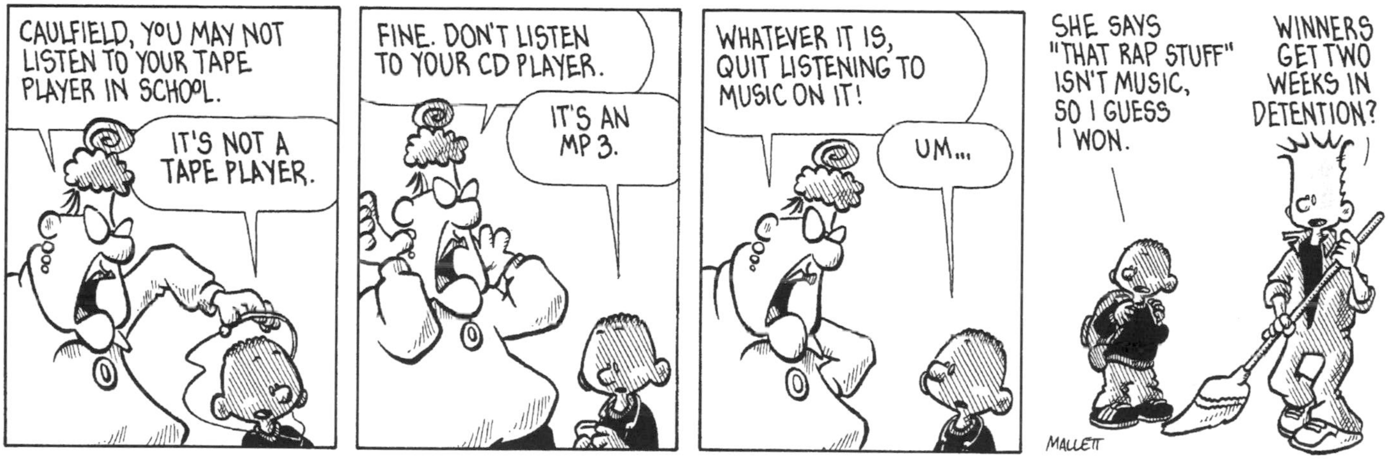
CAULFIELD, YOU MAY NOT LISTEN TO YOUR TAPE PLAYER IN SCHOOL.
IT'S NOT A TAPE PLAYER.
FINE. DON'T LISTEN TO YOUR CD PLAYER.
IT'S AN MP 3.
WHATEVER IT IS, QUIT LISTENING TO MUSIC ON IT!
UM...
SHE SAYS "THAT RAP STUFF" ISN'T MUSIC, SO I GUESS I WON.
WINNERS GET TWO WEEKS IN DETENTION?
MALLETT

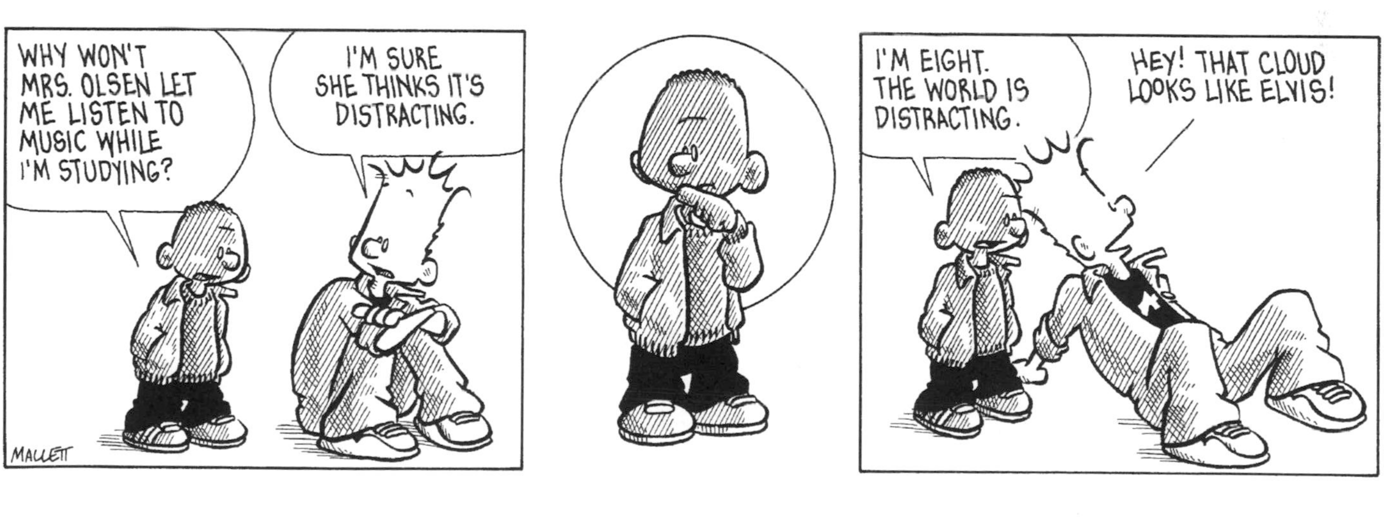
WHY WON'T MRS. OLSEN LET ME LISTEN TO MUSIC WHILE I'M STUDYING?
I'M SURE SHE THINKS IT'S DISTRACTING.
MALLETT
I'M EIGHT. THE WORLD IS DISTRACTING.
HEY! THAT CLOUD LOOKS LIKE ELVIS!

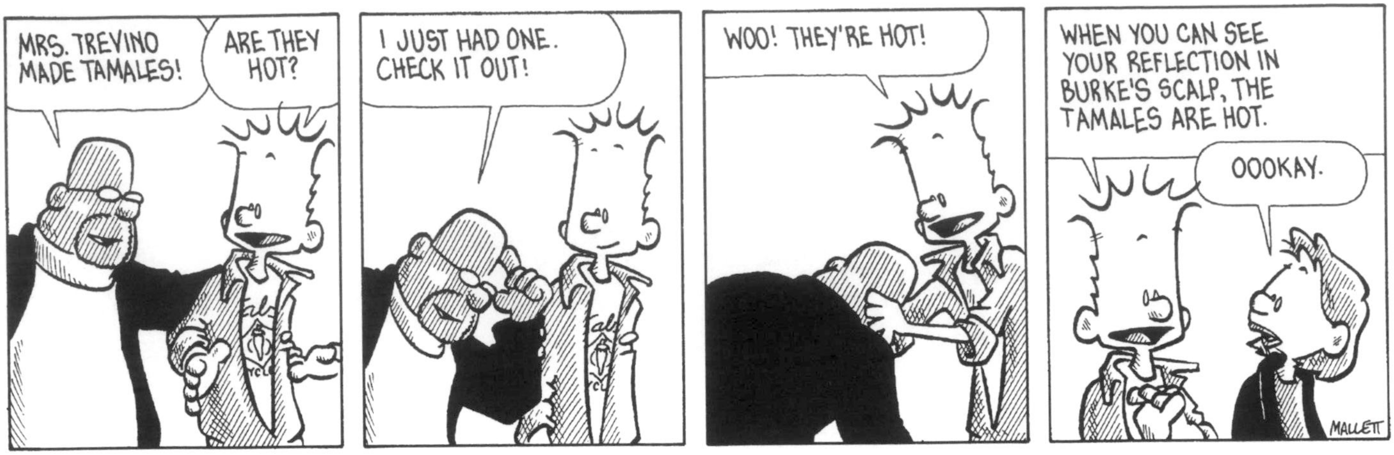
MRS. TREVINO MADE TAMALES!
ARE THEY HOT?
I JUST HAD ONE. CHECK IT OUT!
WOO! THEY'RE HOT!
WHEN YOU CAN SEE YOUR REFLECTION IN BURKE'S SCALP, THE TAMALES ARE HOT.
OOOKAY.
MALLETT

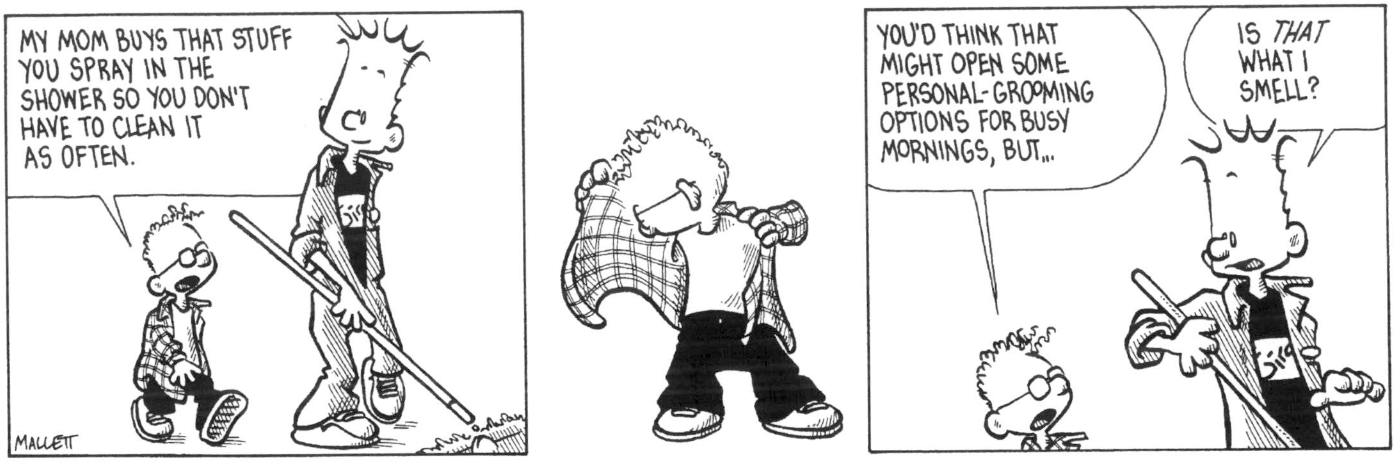
MY MOM BUYS THAT STUFF YOU SPRAY IN THE SHOWER SO YOU DON'T HAVE TO CLEAN IT AS OFTEN.
MALLETT
YOU'D THINK THAT MIGHT OPEN SOME PERSONAL-GROOMING OPTIONS FOR BUSY MORNINGS, BUT...
IS *THAT* WHAT I SMELL?

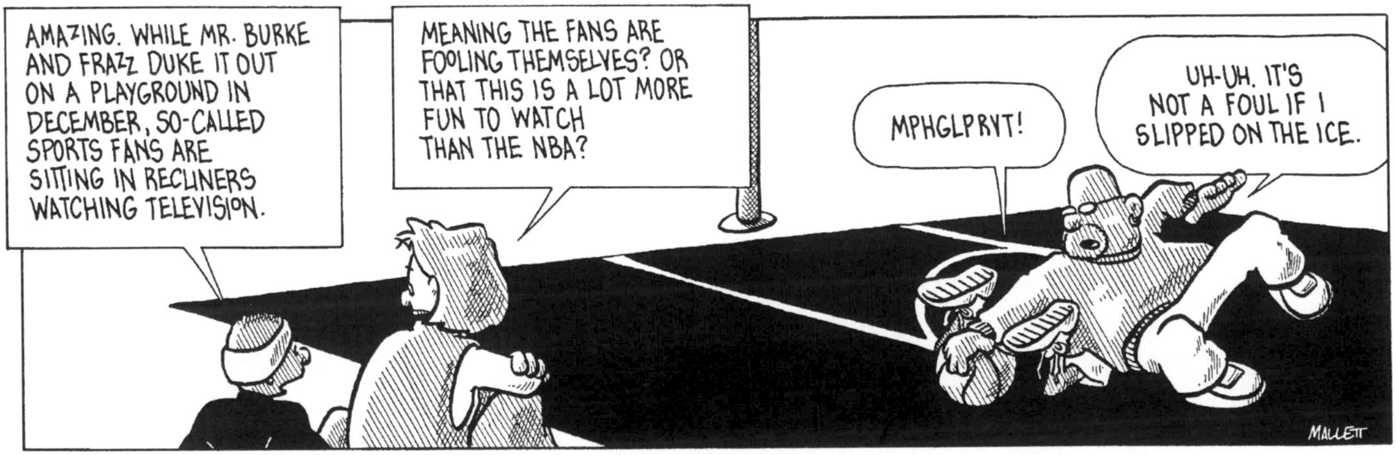
AMAZING. WHILE MR. BURKE AND FRAZZ DUKE IT OUT ON A PLAYGROUND IN DECEMBER, SO-CALLED SPORTS FANS ARE SITTING IN RECLINERS WATCHING TELEVISION.
MEANING THE FANS ARE FOOLING THEMSELVES? OR THAT THIS IS A LOT MORE FUN TO WATCH THAN THE NBA?
MPHGLPRYT!
UH-UH. IT'S NOT A FOUL IF I SLIPPED ON THE ICE.
MALLETT

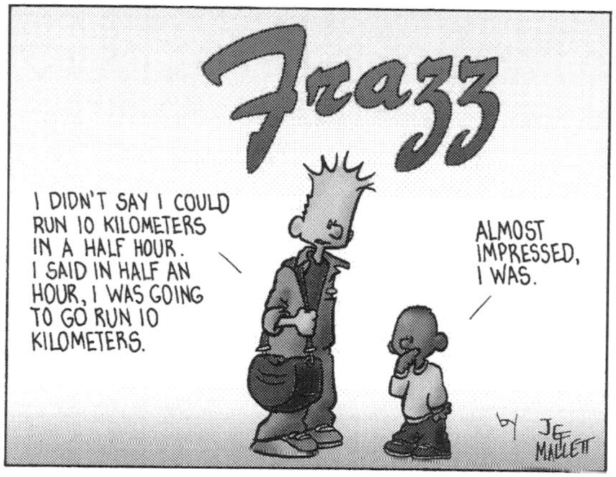
Frazz
I DIDN'T SAY I COULD RUN 10 KILOMETERS IN A HALF HOUR. I SAID IN HALF AN HOUR, I WAS GOING TO GO RUN 10 KILOMETERS.
ALMOST IMPRESSED, I WAS.
by JEF MALLETT

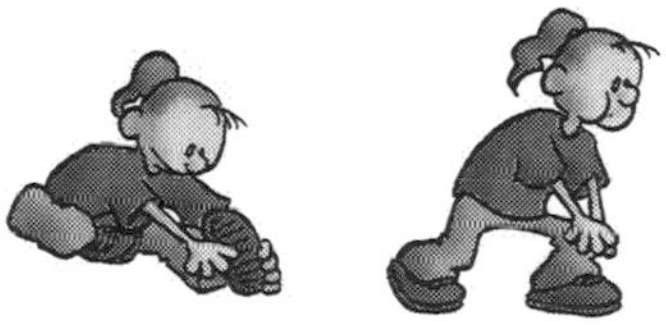

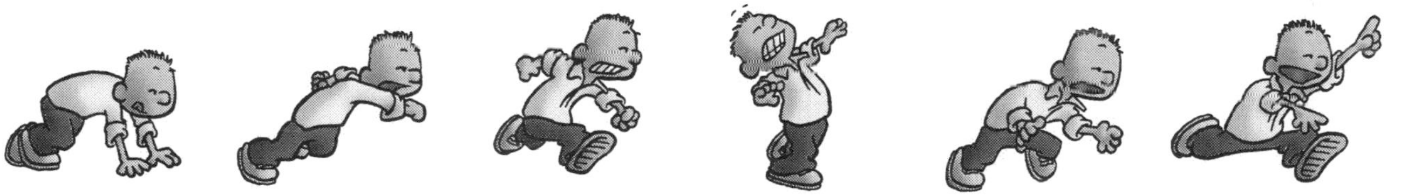

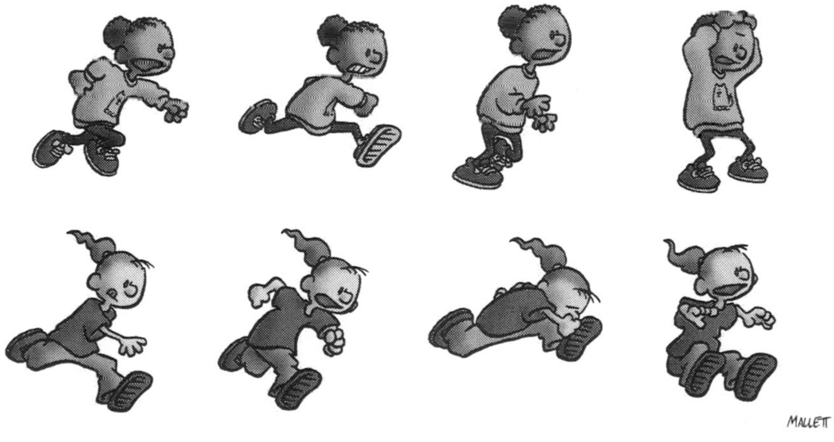
MALLETT

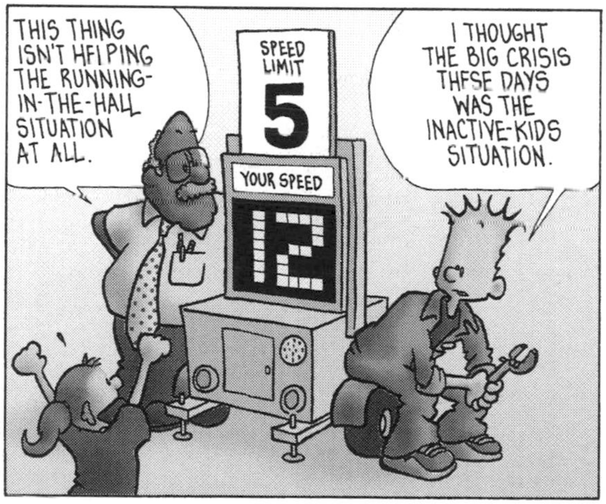
THIS THING ISN'T HELPING THE RUNNING-IN-THE-HALL SITUATION AT ALL.
SPEED LIMIT
5
YOUR SPEED
12
I THOUGHT THE BIG CRISIS THESE DAYS WAS THE INACTIVE-KIDS SITUATION.

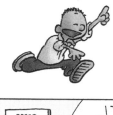

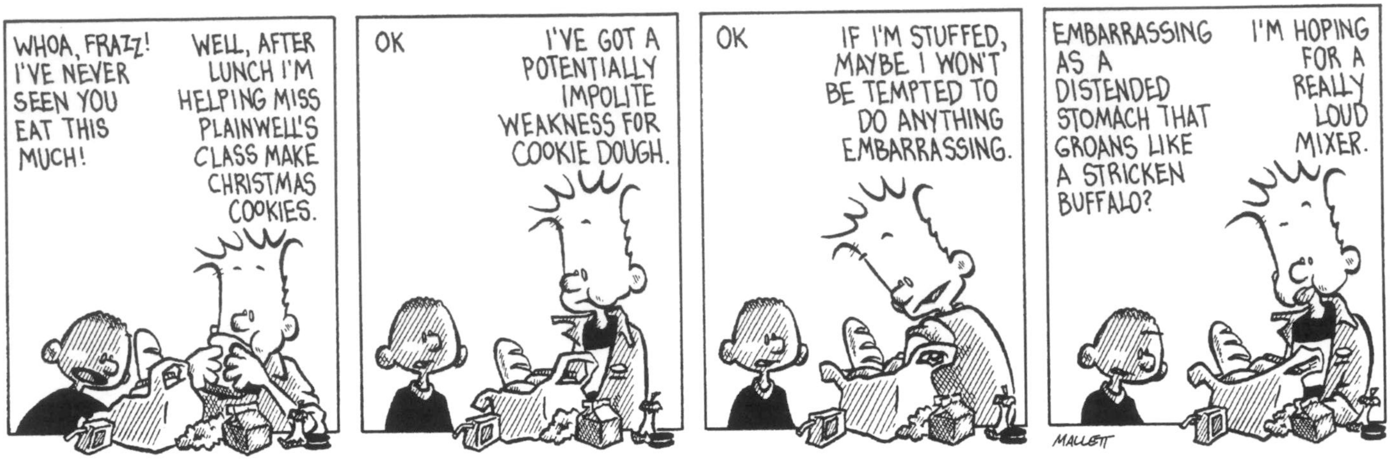
WHOA, FRAZZ! I'VE NEVER SEEN YOU EAT THIS MUCH!
WELL, AFTER LUNCH I'M HELPING MISS PLAINWELL'S CLASS MAKE CHRISTMAS COOKIES.
OK
I'VE GOT A POTENTIALLY IMPOLITE WEAKNESS FOR COOKIE DOUGH.
OK
IF I'M STUFFED, MAYBE I WON'T BE TEMPTED TO DO ANYTHING EMBARRASSING.
EMBARRASSING AS A DISTENDED STOMACH THAT GROANS LIKE A STRICKEN BUFFALO?
I'M HOPING FOR A REALLY LOUD MIXER.
MALLETT

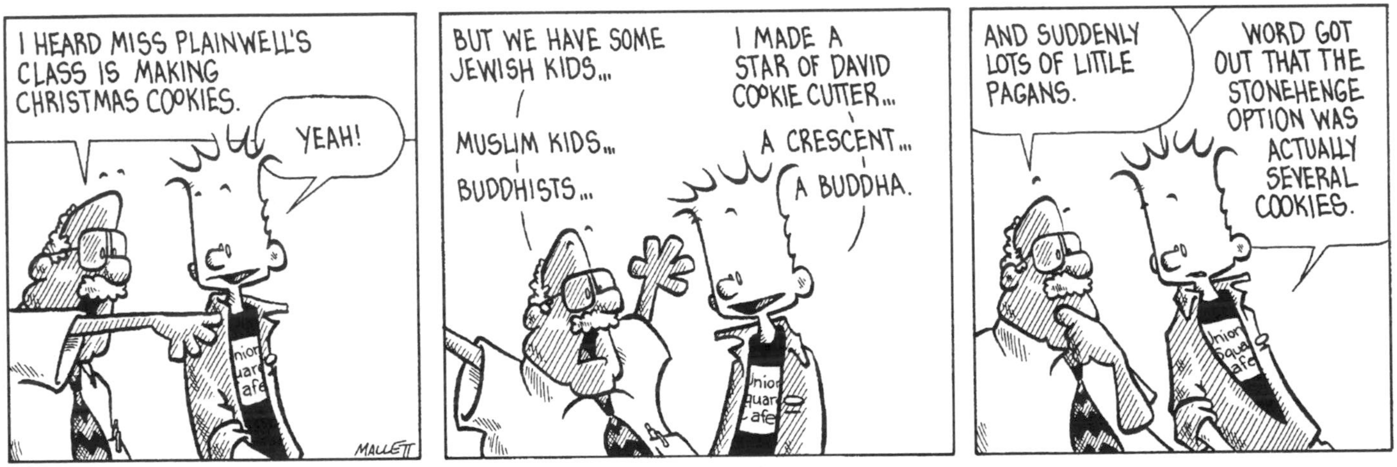
I HEARD MISS PLAINWELL'S CLASS IS MAKING CHRISTMAS COOKIES.
YEAH!
MALLETT
BUT WE HAVE SOME JEWISH KIDS...
MUSLIM KIDS...
BUDDHISTS...
I MADE A STAR OF DAVID COOKIE CUTTER...
A CRESCENT...
A BUDDHA.
AND SUDDENLY LOTS OF LITTLE PAGANS.
WORD GOT OUT THAT THE STONEHENGE OPTION WAS ACTUALLY SEVERAL COOKIES.

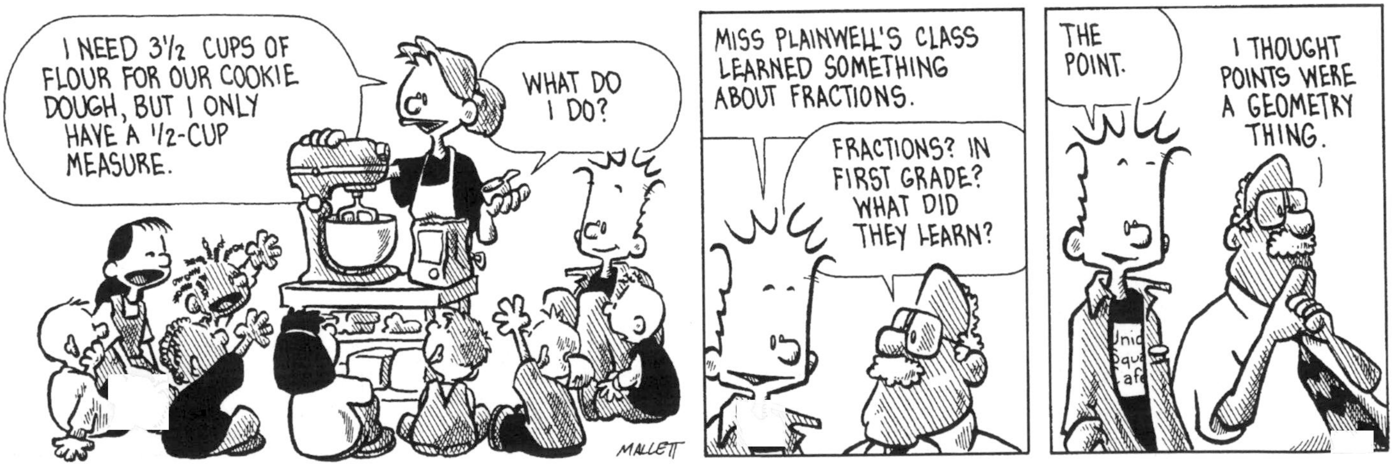
I NEED 3½ CUPS OF FLOUR FOR OUR COOKIE DOUGH, BUT I ONLY HAVE A ½-CUP MEASURE.
WHAT DO I DO?
MALLETT
MISS PLAINWELL'S CLASS LEARNED SOMETHING ABOUT FRACTIONS.
FRACTIONS? IN FIRST GRADE? WHAT DID THEY LEARN?
THE POINT.
I THOUGHT POINTS WERE A GEOMETRY THING.

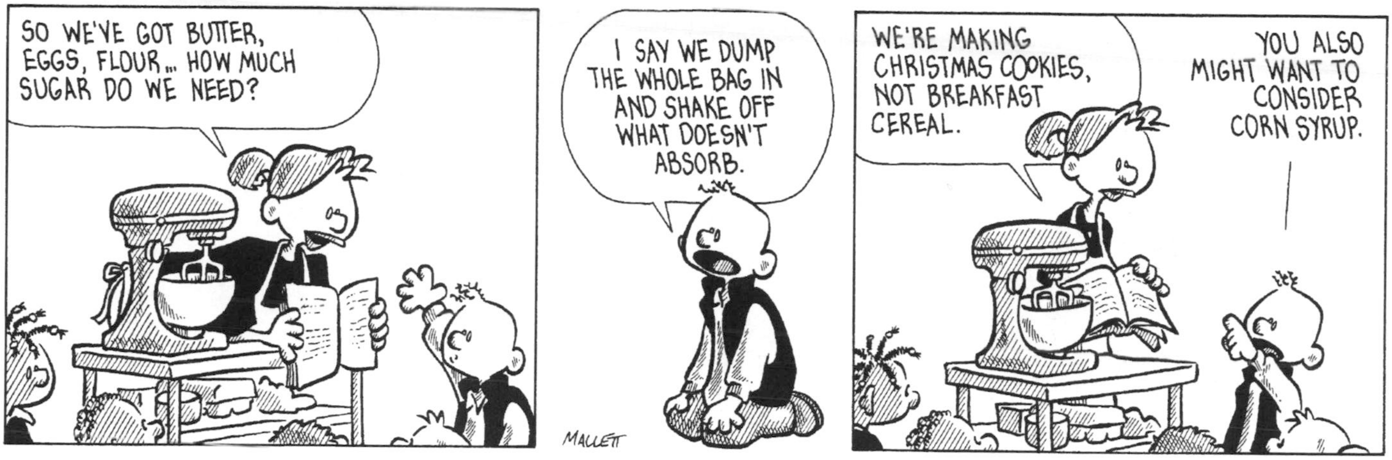
SO WE'VE GOT BUTTER, EGGS, FLOUR... HOW MUCH SUGAR DO WE NEED?
I SAY WE DUMP THE WHOLE BAG IN AND SHAKE OFF WHAT DOESN'T ABSORB.
WE'RE MAKING CHRISTMAS COOKIES, NOT BREAKFAST CEREAL.
YOU ALSO MIGHT WANT TO CONSIDER CORN SYRUP.
MALLETT

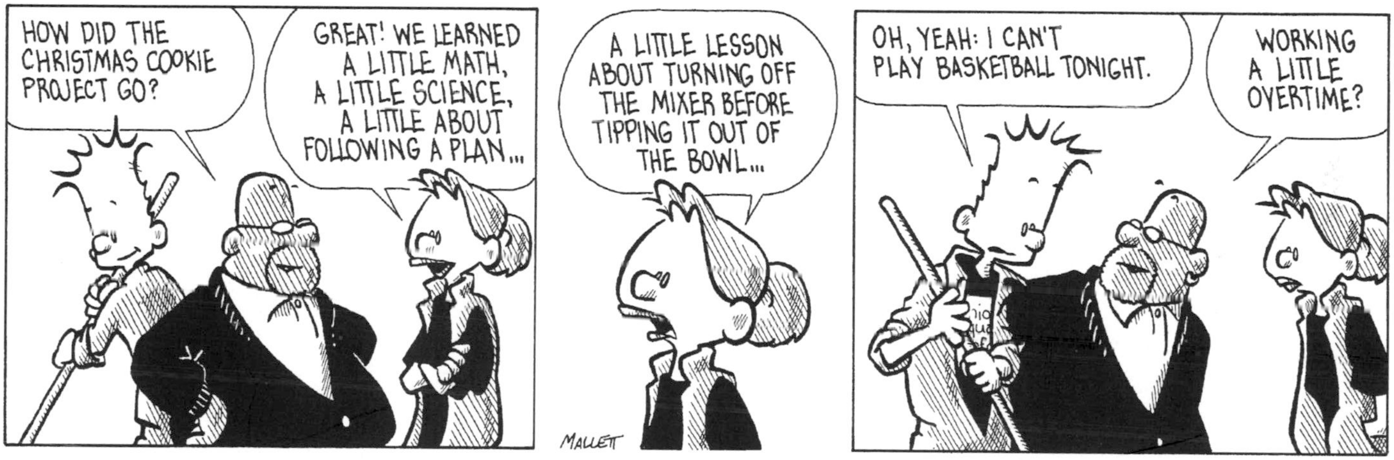
HOW DID THE CHRISTMAS COOKIE PROJECT GO?
GREAT! WE LEARNED A LITTLE MATH, A LITTLE SCIENCE, A LITTLE ABOUT FOLLOWING A PLAN...
A LITTLE LESSON ABOUT TURNING OFF THE MIXER BEFORE TIPPING IT OUT OF THE BOWL...
OH, YEAH: I CAN'T PLAY BASKETBALL TONIGHT.
WORKING A LITTLE OVERTIME?
MALLETT

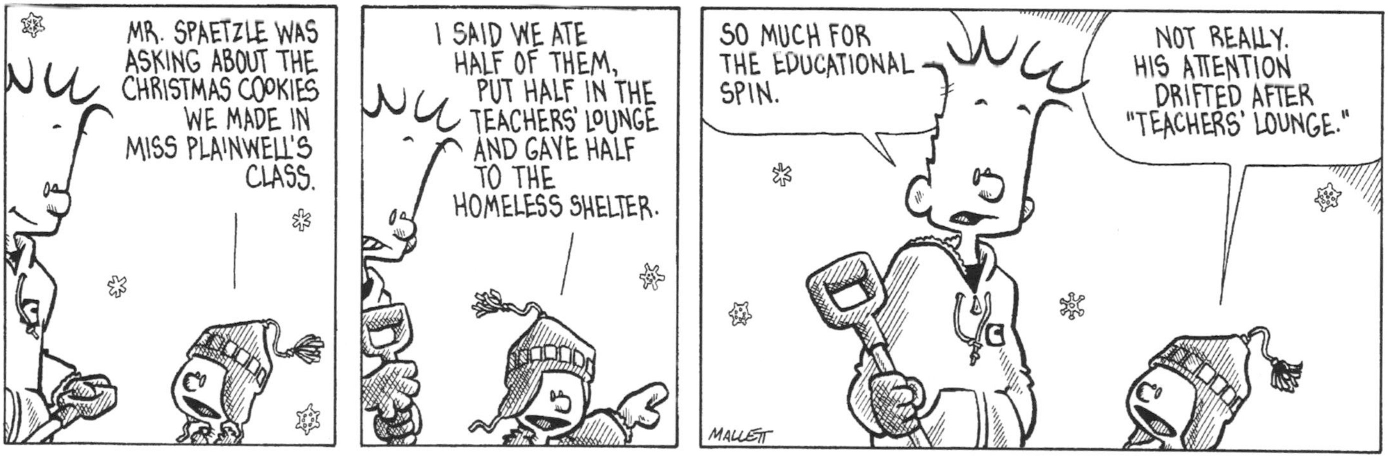
MR. SPAETZLE WAS ASKING ABOUT THE CHRISTMAS COOKIES WE MADE IN MISS PLAINWELL'S CLASS.
I SAID WE ATE HALF OF THEM, PUT HALF IN THE TEACHERS' LOUNGE AND GAVE HALF TO THE HOMELESS SHELTER.
SO MUCH FOR THE EDUCATIONAL SPIN.
NOT REALLY. HIS ATTENTION DRIFTED AFTER "TEACHERS' LOUNGE."
MALLETT

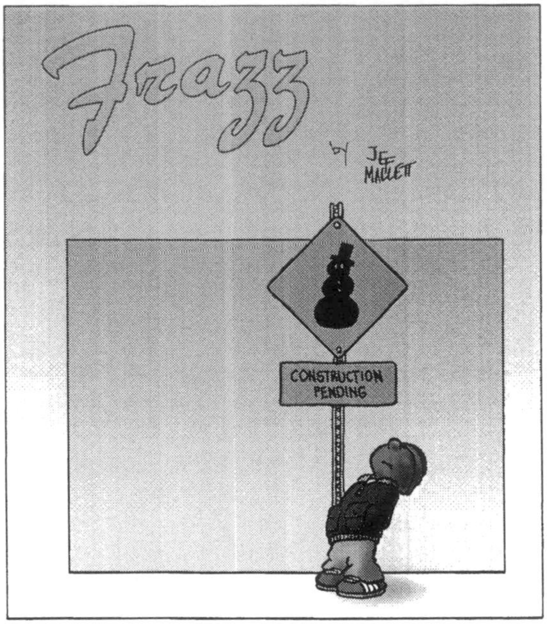
Frazz
by JEF MALLETT
CONSTRUCTION PENDING

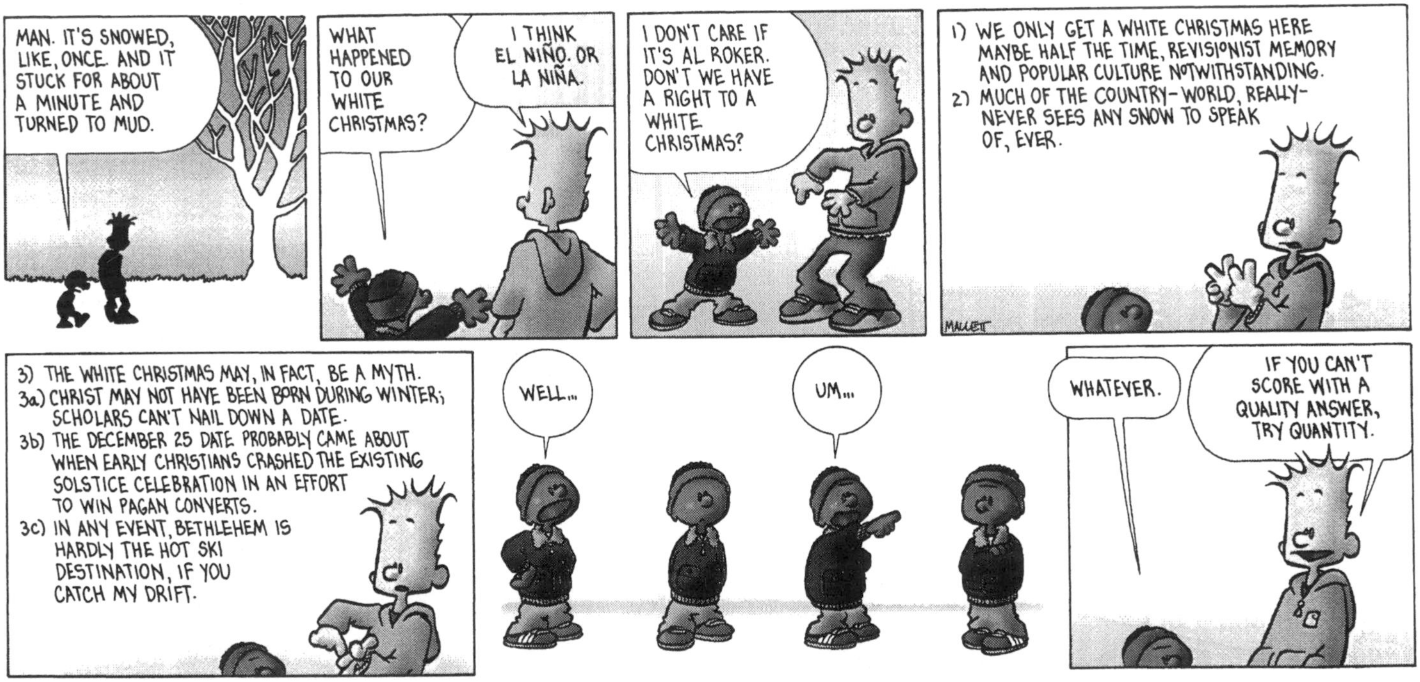
MAN. IT'S SNOWED, LIKE, ONCE. AND IT STUCK FOR ABOUT A MINUTE AND TURNED TO MUD.
WHAT HAPPENED TO OUR WHITE CHRISTMAS?
I THINK EL NIÑO. OR LA NIÑA.
I DON'T CARE IF IT'S AL ROKER. DON'T WE HAVE A RIGHT TO A WHITE CHRISTMAS?
1) WE ONLY GET A WHITE CHRISTMAS HERE MAYBE HALF THE TIME, REVISIONIST MEMORY AND POPULAR CULTURE NOTWITHSTANDING.
2) MUCH OF THE COUNTRY–WORLD, REALLY–NEVER SEES ANY SNOW TO SPEAK OF, EVER.
MALLETT
3) THE WHITE CHRISTMAS MAY, IN FACT, BE A MYTH.
3a) CHRIST MAY NOT HAVE BEEN BORN DURING WINTER; SCHOLARS CAN'T NAIL DOWN A DATE.
3b) THE DECEMBER 25 DATE PROBABLY CAME ABOUT WHEN EARLY CHRISTIANS CRASHED THE EXISTING SOLSTICE CELEBRATION IN AN EFFORT TO WIN PAGAN CONVERTS.
3c) IN ANY EVENT, BETHLEHEM IS HARDLY THE HOT SKI DESTINATION, IF YOU CATCH MY DRIFT.
WELL...
UM...
WHATEVER.
IF YOU CAN'T SCORE WITH A QUALITY ANSWER, TRY QUANTITY.

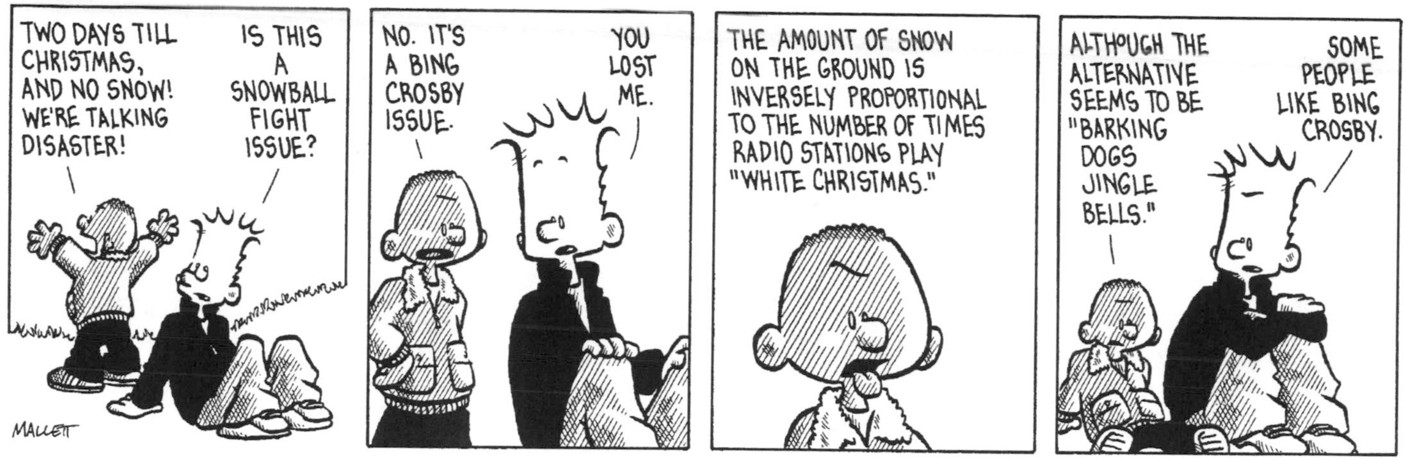
TWO DAYS TILL CHRISTMAS, AND NO SNOW! WE'RE TALKING DISASTER!
IS THIS A SNOWBALL FIGHT ISSUE?
NO. IT'S A BING CROSBY ISSUE.
YOU LOST ME.
THE AMOUNT OF SNOW ON THE GROUND IS INVERSELY PROPORTIONAL TO THE NUMBER OF TIMES RADIO STATIONS PLAY "WHITE CHRISTMAS."
ALTHOUGH THE ALTERNATIVE SEEMS TO BE "BARKING DOGS JINGLE BELLS."
SOME PEOPLE LIKE BING CROSBY.
MALLETT

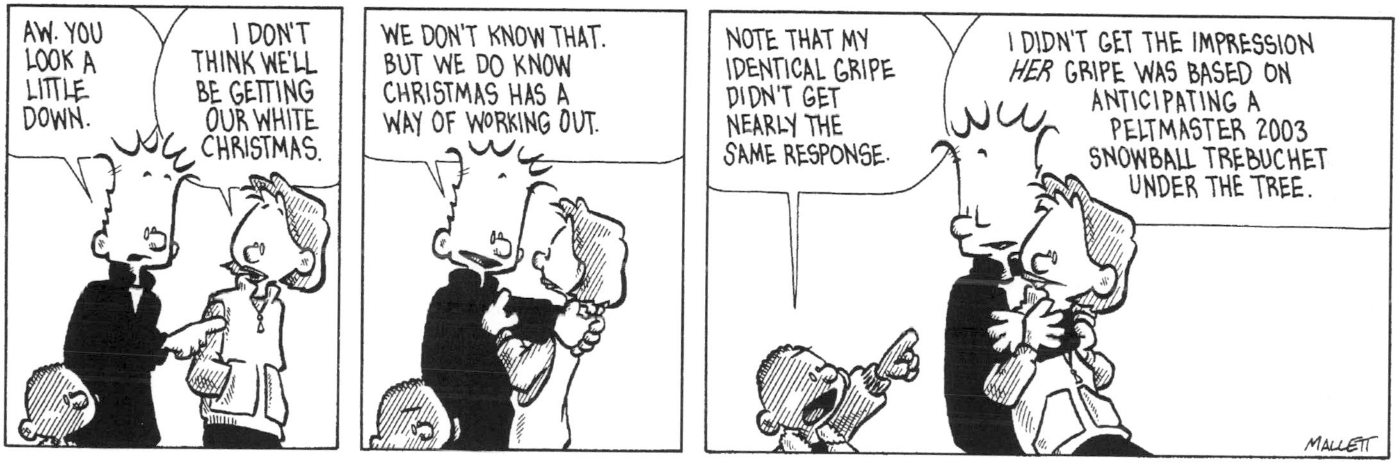
AW. YOU LOOK A LITTLE DOWN.
I DON'T THINK WE'LL BE GETTING OUR WHITE CHRISTMAS.
WE DON'T KNOW THAT. BUT WE DO KNOW CHRISTMAS HAS A WAY OF WORKING OUT.
NOTE THAT MY IDENTICAL GRIPE DIDN'T GET NEARLY THE SAME RESPONSE.
I DIDN'T GET THE IMPRESSION *HER* GRIPE WAS BASED ON ANTICIPATING A PELTMASTER 2003 SNOWBALL TREBUCHET UNDER THE TREE.
MALLETT

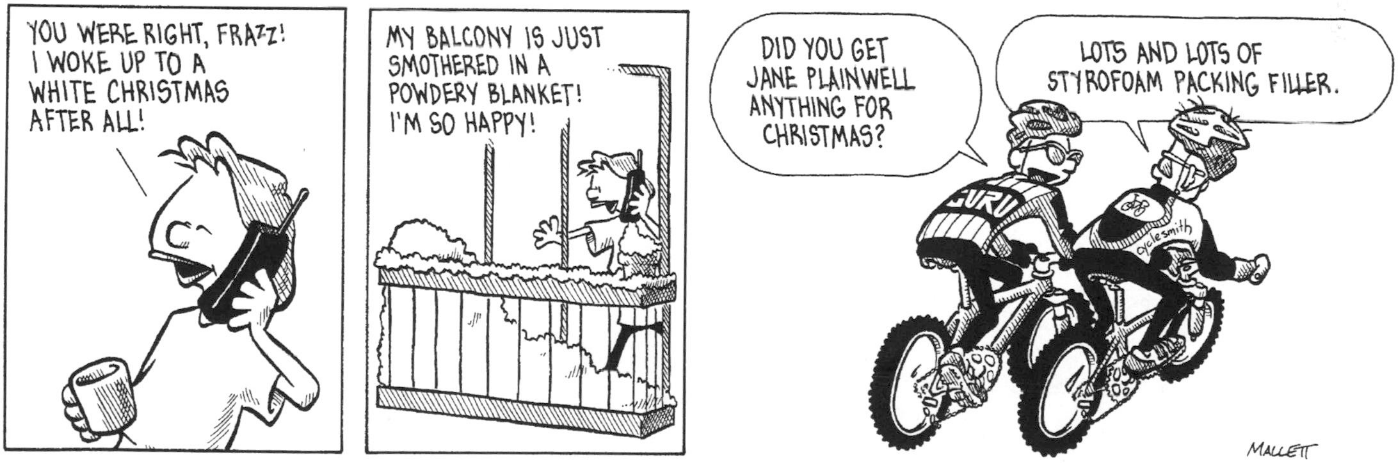
YOU WERE RIGHT, FRAZZ! I WOKE UP TO A WHITE CHRISTMAS AFTER ALL!
MY BALCONY IS JUST SMOTHERED IN A POWDERY BLANKET! I'M SO HAPPY!
DID YOU GET JANE PLAINWELL ANYTHING FOR CHRISTMAS?
LOTS AND LOTS OF STYROFOAM PACKING FILLER.
GURU
cyclesmith
MALLETT

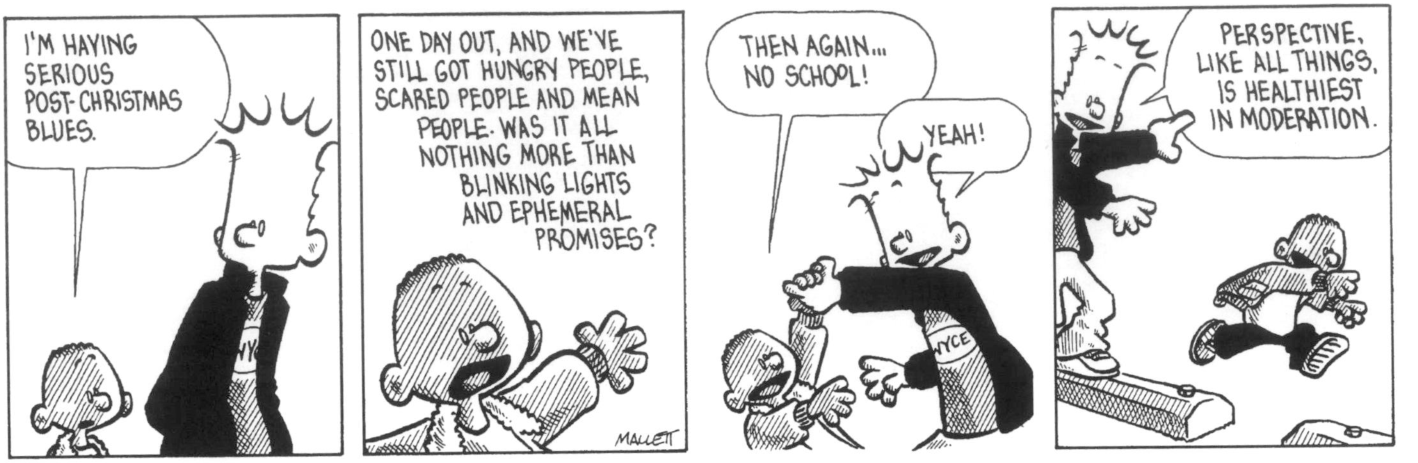
I'M HAVING SERIOUS POST-CHRISTMAS BLUES.
ONE DAY OUT, AND WE'VE STILL GOT HUNGRY PEOPLE, SCARED PEOPLE AND MEAN PEOPLE. WAS IT ALL NOTHING MORE THAN BLINKING LIGHTS AND EPHEMERAL PROMISES?
MALLETT
THEN AGAIN... NO SCHOOL!
YEAH!
NYCE
PERSPECTIVE, LIKE ALL THINGS, IS HEALTHIEST IN MODERATION.

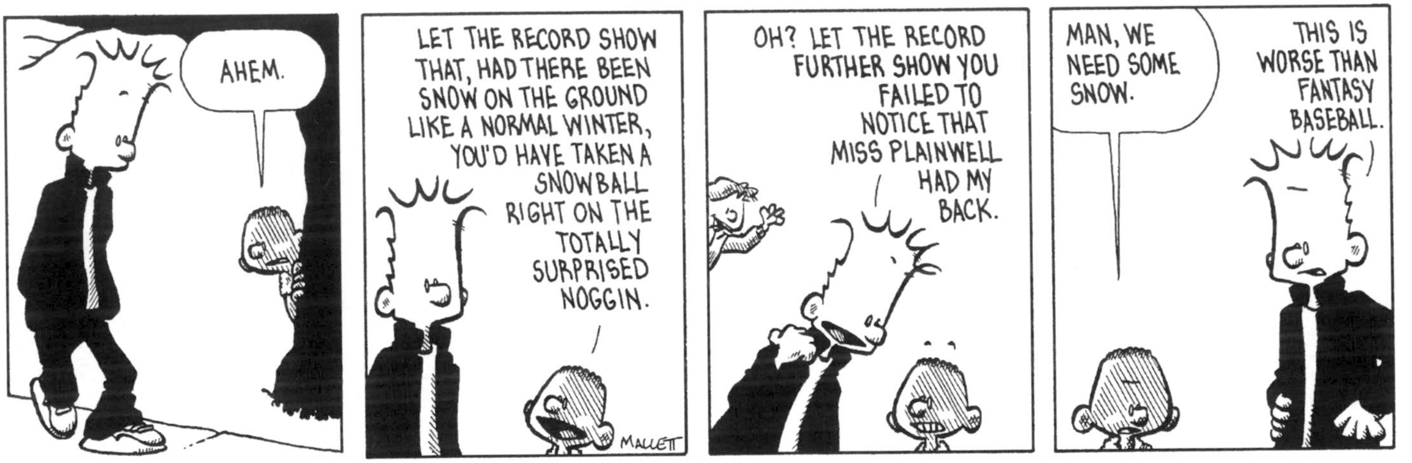
AHEM.
LET THE RECORD SHOW THAT, HAD THERE BEEN SNOW ON THE GROUND LIKE A NORMAL WINTER, YOU'D HAVE TAKEN A SNOWBALL RIGHT ON THE TOTALLY SURPRISED NOGGIN.
MALLETT
OH? LET THE RECORD FURTHER SHOW YOU FAILED TO NOTICE THAT MISS PLAINWELL HAD MY BACK.
MAN, WE NEED SOME SNOW.
THIS IS WORSE THAN FANTASY BASEBALL.

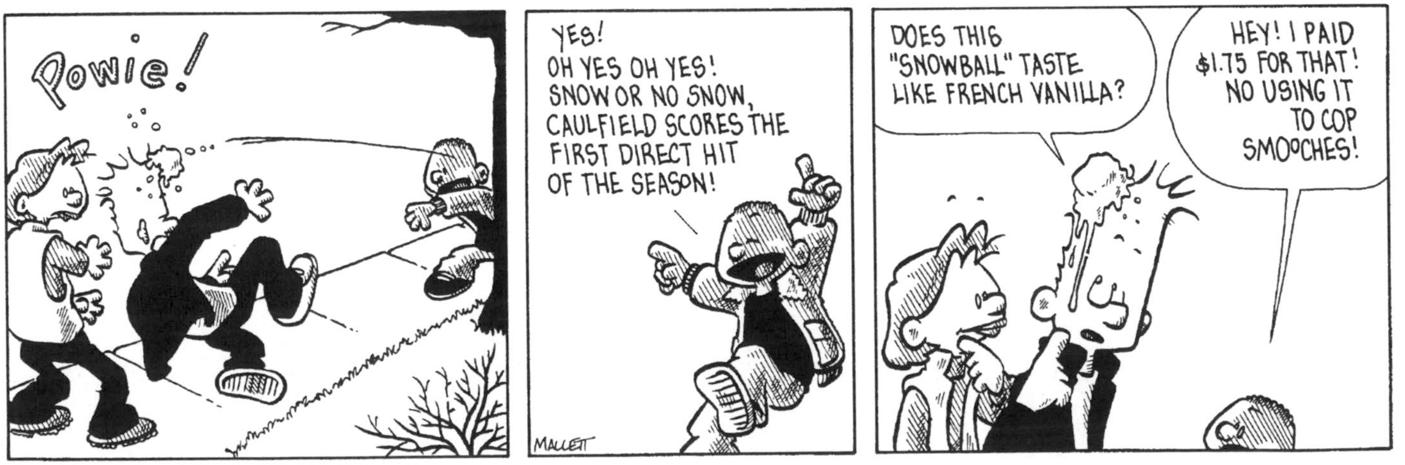
Powie!
YES! OH YES OH YES! SNOW OR NO SNOW, CAULFIELD SCORES THE FIRST DIRECT HIT OF THE SEASON!
MALLETT
DOES THIS "SNOWBALL" TASTE LIKE FRENCH VANILLA?
HEY! I PAID $1.75 FOR THAT! NO USING IT TO COP SMOOCHES!

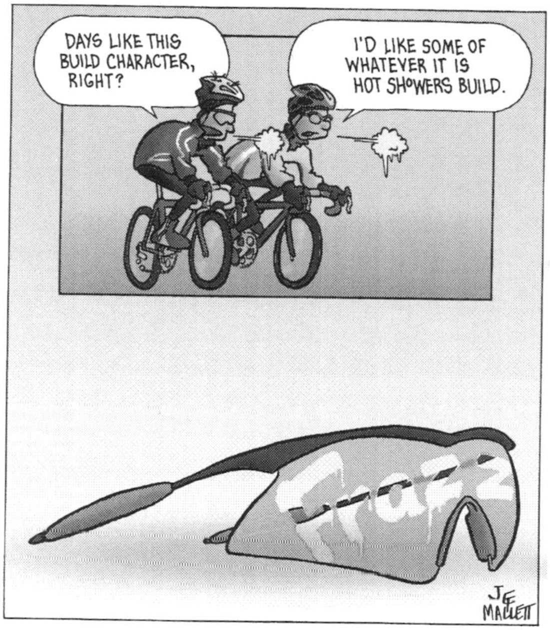
DAYS LIKE THIS BUILD CHARACTER, RIGHT?
I'D LIKE SOME OF WHATEVER IT IS HOT SHOWERS BUILD.
JEFF MALLETT

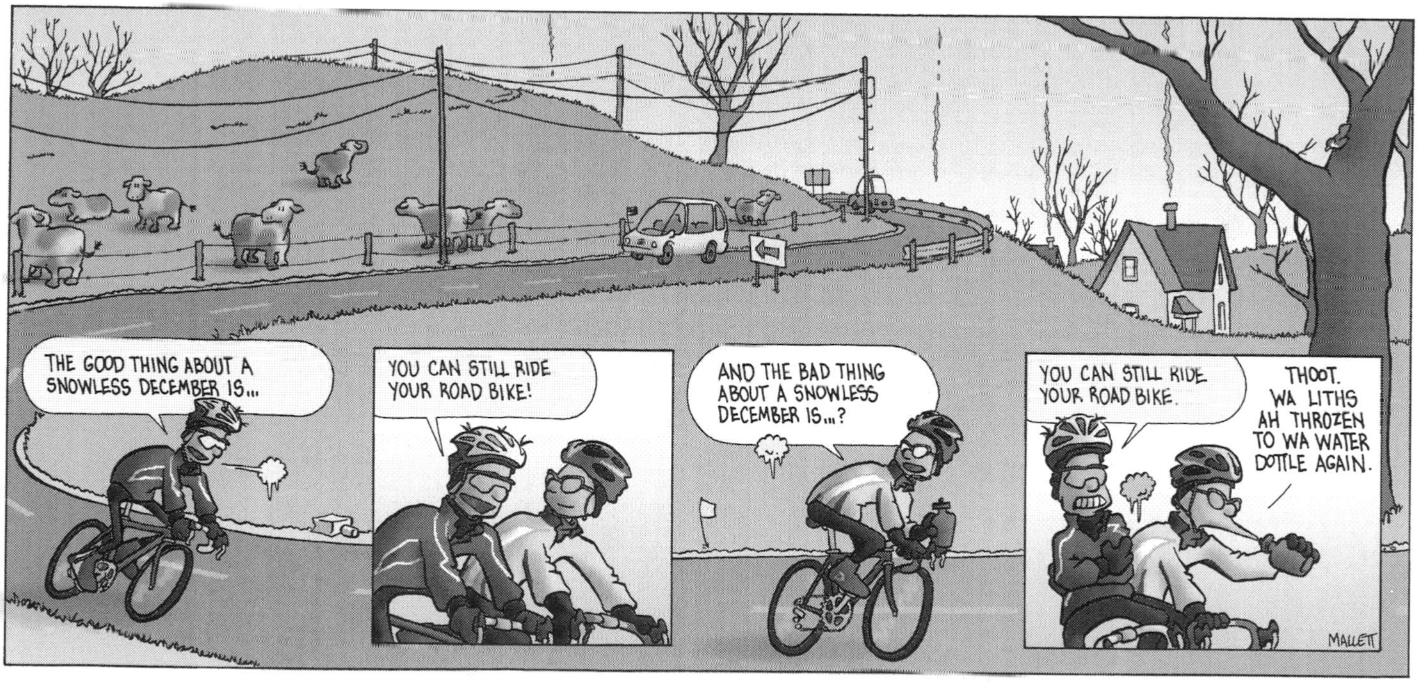
THE GOOD THING ABOUT A SNOWLESS DECEMBER IS...
YOU CAN STILL RIDE YOUR ROAD BIKE!
AND THE BAD THING ABOUT A SNOWLESS DECEMBER IS...?
YOU CAN STILL RIDE YOUR ROAD BIKE.
THOOT. WA LITHS AH THROZEN TO WA WATER DOTTLE AGAIN.
MALLETT

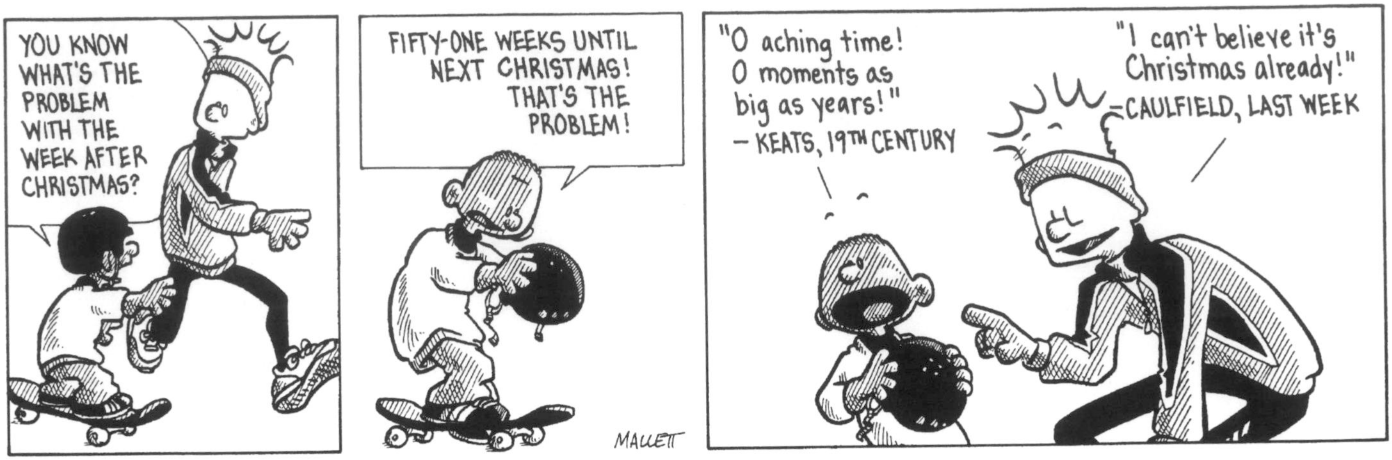
YOU KNOW WHAT'S THE PROBLEM WITH THE WEEK AFTER CHRISTMAS?
FIFTY-ONE WEEKS UNTIL NEXT CHRISTMAS! THAT'S THE PROBLEM!
MALLETT
"O aching time! O moments as big as years!" – KEATS, 19TH CENTURY
"I can't believe it's Christmas already!" –CAULFIELD, LAST WEEK

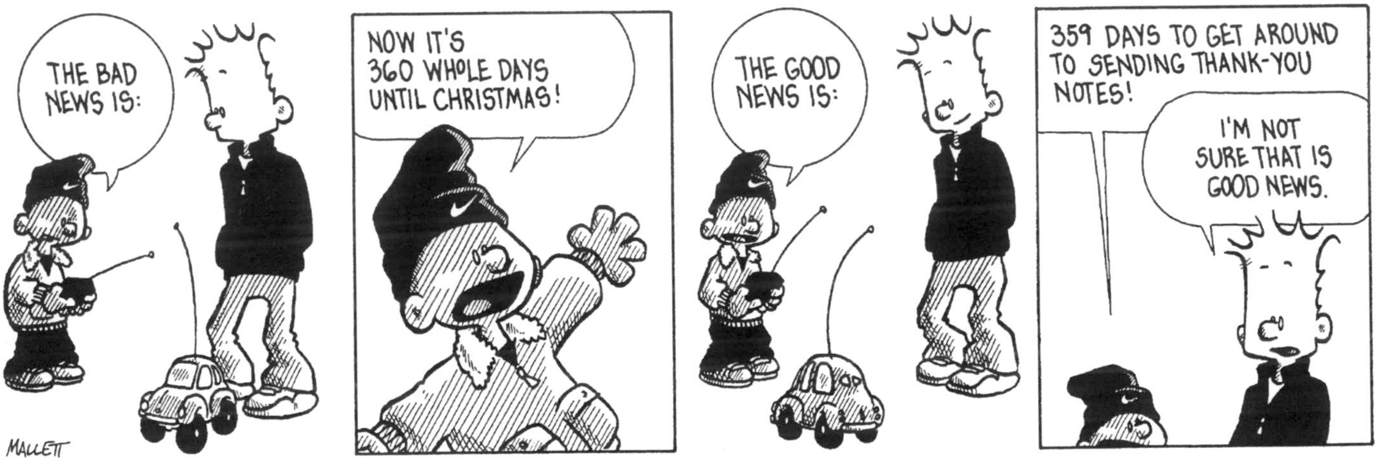
THE BAD NEWS IS:
MALLETT
NOW IT'S 360 WHOLE DAYS UNTIL CHRISTMAS!
THE GOOD NEWS IS:
359 DAYS TO GET AROUND TO SENDING THANK-YOU NOTES!
I'M NOT SURE THAT IS GOOD NEWS.

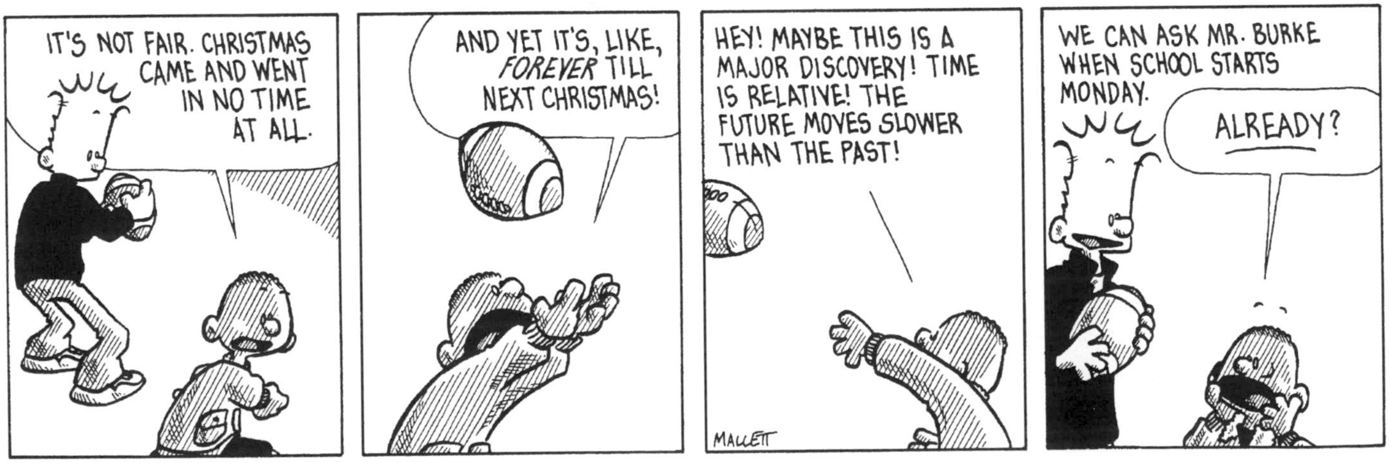
IT'S NOT FAIR. CHRISTMAS CAME AND WENT IN NO TIME AT ALL.
AND YET IT'S, LIKE, FOREVER TILL NEXT CHRISTMAS!
HEY! MAYBE THIS IS A MAJOR DISCOVERY! TIME IS RELATIVE! THE FUTURE MOVES SLOWER THAN THE PAST!
MALLETT
WE CAN ASK MR. BURKE WHEN SCHOOL STARTS MONDAY.
ALREADY?

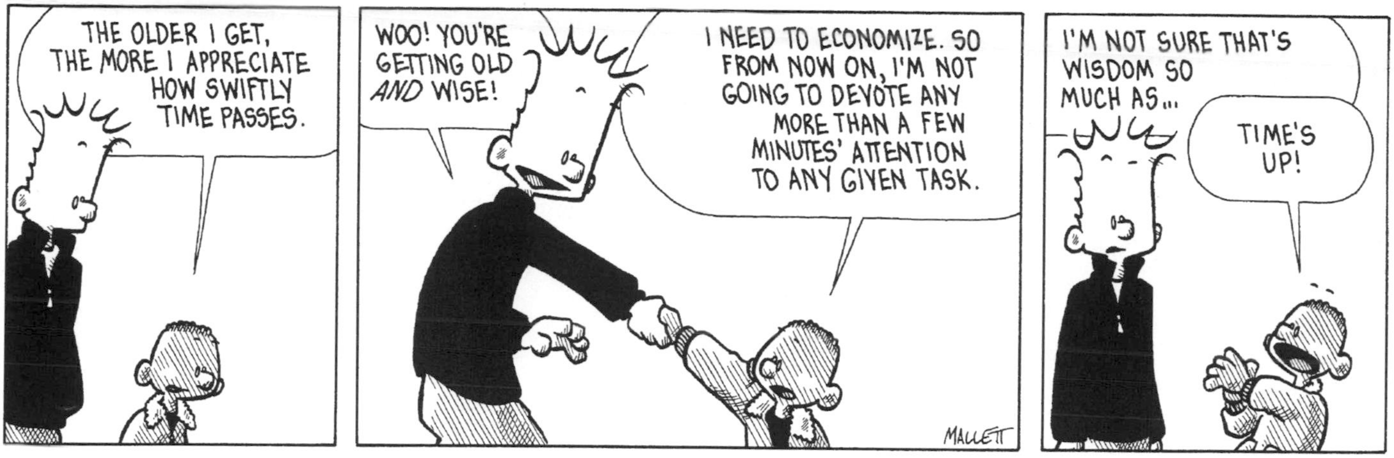
THE OLDER I GET, THE MORE I APPRECIATE HOW SWIFTLY TIME PASSES.
WOO! YOU'RE GETTING OLD *AND* WISE!
I NEED TO ECONOMIZE. SO FROM NOW ON, I'M NOT GOING TO DEVOTE ANY MORE THAN A FEW MINUTES' ATTENTION TO ANY GIVEN TASK.
MALLETT
I'M NOT SURE THAT'S WISDOM SO MUCH AS...
TIME'S UP!

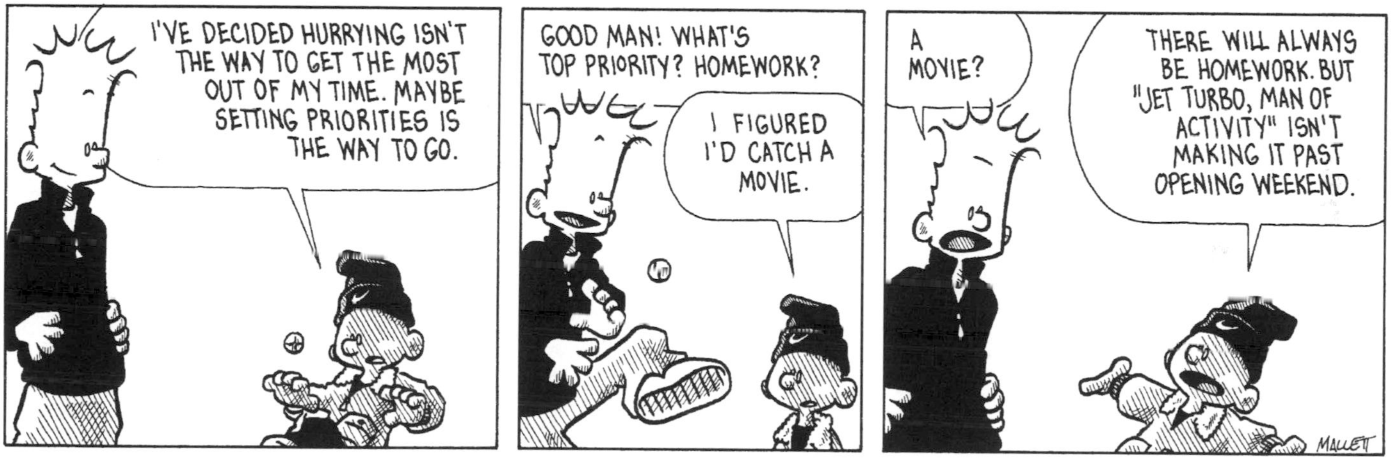
I'VE DECIDED HURRYING ISN'T THE WAY TO GET THE MOST OUT OF MY TIME. MAYBE SETTING PRIORITIES IS THE WAY TO GO.
GOOD MAN! WHAT'S TOP PRIORITY? HOMEWORK?
I FIGURED I'D CATCH A MOVIE.
A MOVIE?
THERE WILL ALWAYS BE HOMEWORK. BUT "JET TURBO, MAN OF ACTIVITY" ISN'T MAKING IT PAST OPENING WEEKEND.
MALLETT

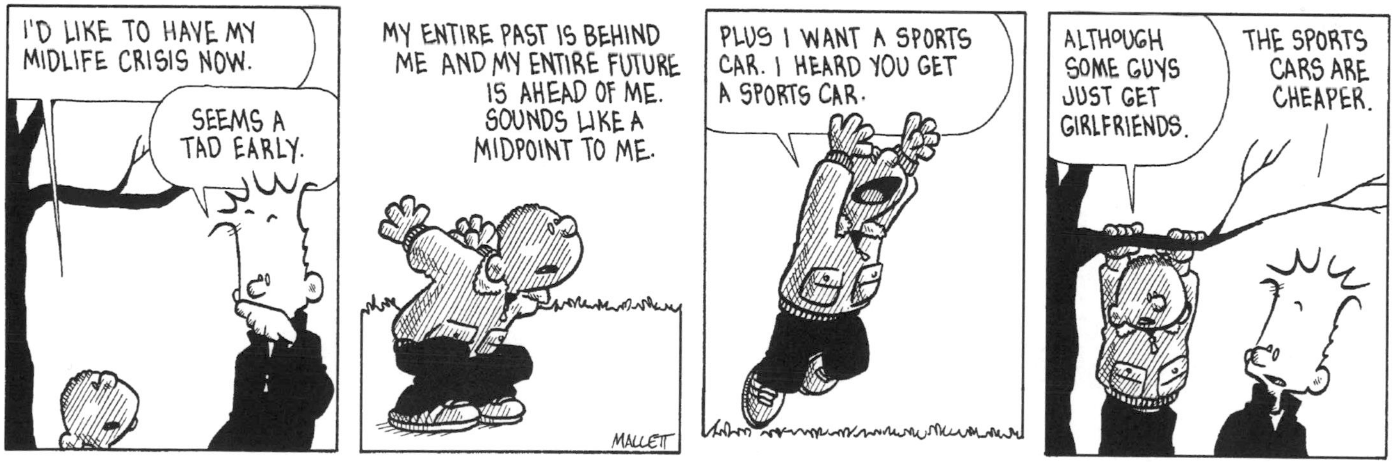
I'D LIKE TO HAVE MY MIDLIFE CRISIS NOW.
SEEMS A TAD EARLY.
MY ENTIRE PAST IS BEHIND ME AND MY ENTIRE FUTURE IS AHEAD OF ME. SOUNDS LIKE A MIDPOINT TO ME.
MALLETT
PLUS I WANT A SPORTS CAR. I HEARD YOU GET A SPORTS CAR.
ALTHOUGH SOME GUYS JUST GET GIRLFRIENDS.
THE SPORTS CARS ARE CHEAPER.

Frazz

by Jef Mallett

MAN! JANUARY 5TH, AND STILL NO SNOW!
THE SNOW GODS HAVE FORSAKEN ME!
HARSH WORDS, BROTHER CAULFIELD.
WELL?! I'VE TRIED BESEECHMENT, SUPPLICATION AND RECRUITING FOLLOWERS! I'VE TRIED CEREMONY AND RITUAL DANCE! I EVEN SACRIFICED A SNO-CONE TO THE SIDEWALK, THOUGH NOT ENTIRELY ON PURPOSE.
WHY ARE THEY IGNORING ME?
MAYBE BECAUSE YOUR REQUEST IS FOUNDED ON SNOWBALL WARFARE, WATCHING CARS SLIDE INTO THE DITCH AND THE HOPE THAT MR. SPAETZLE WILL CANCEL CLASSES.
OLIVER T
SNOW GODS CAN CHECK ON YOUR MOTIVES?
I THOUGHT THEY WERE TOO FAR DOWN THE GOD BUREAUCRACY FOR THAT KIND OF CLEARANCE.
THERE YOU GO. YOUR REQUEST IS JUST TIED UP IN PAPERWORK.
MALLETT

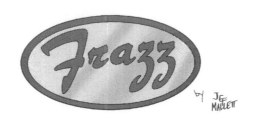

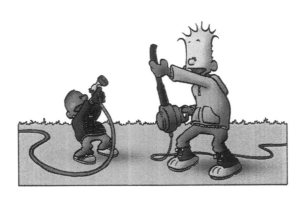

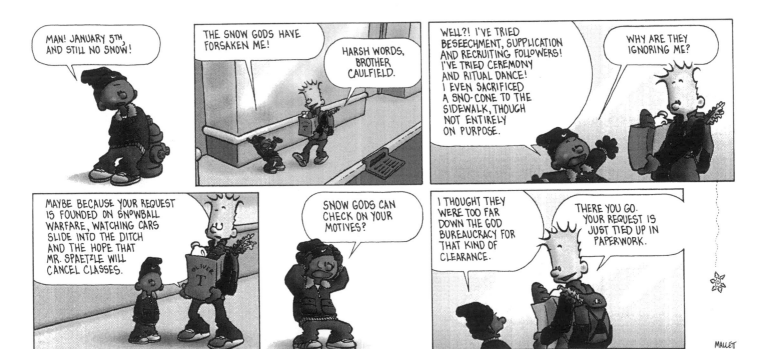

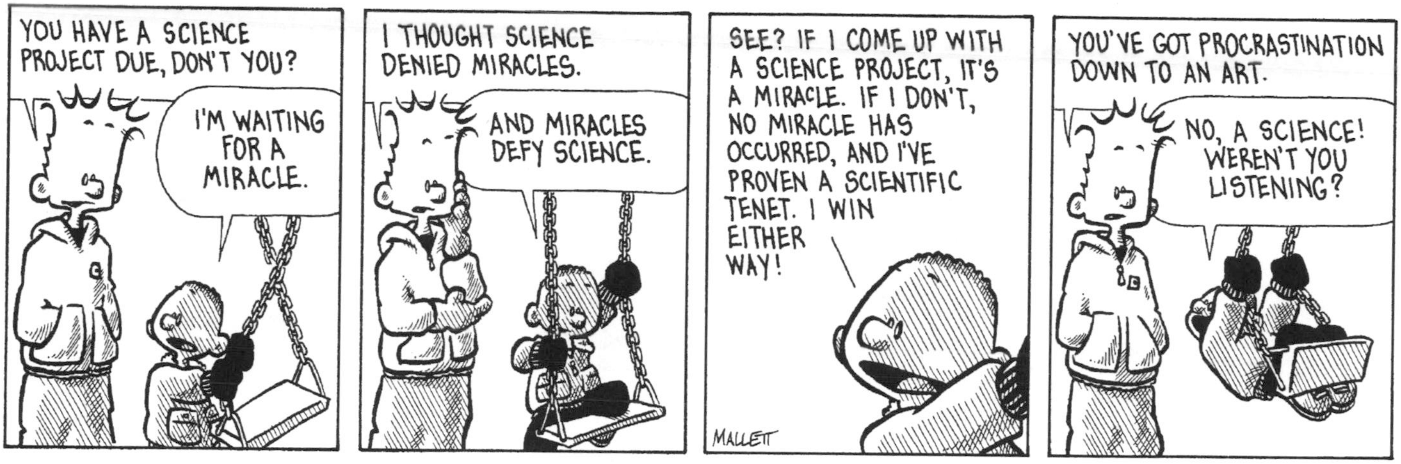
YOU HAVE A SCIENCE PROJECT DUE, DON'T YOU?
I'M WAITING FOR A MIRACLE.
I THOUGHT SCIENCE DENIED MIRACLES.
AND MIRACLES DEFY SCIENCE.
SEE? IF I COME UP WITH A SCIENCE PROJECT, IT'S A MIRACLE. IF I DON'T, NO MIRACLE HAS OCCURRED, AND I'VE PROVEN A SCIENTIFIC TENET. I WIN EITHER WAY!
MALLETT
YOU'VE GOT PROCRASTINATION DOWN TO AN ART.
NO, A SCIENCE! WEREN'T YOU LISTENING?

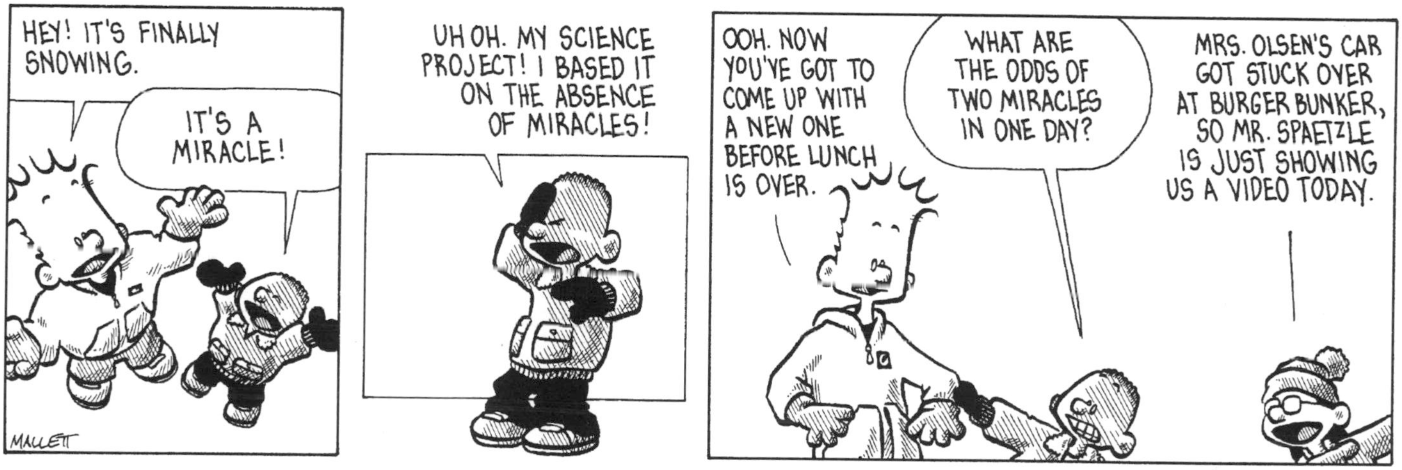
HEY! IT'S FINALLY SNOWING.
IT'S A MIRACLE!
MALLETT
UH OH. MY SCIENCE PROJECT! I BASED IT ON THE ABSENCE OF MIRACLES!
OOH. NOW YOU'VE GOT TO COME UP WITH A NEW ONE BEFORE LUNCH IS OVER.
WHAT ARE THE ODDS OF TWO MIRACLES IN ONE DAY?
MRS. OLSEN'S CAR GOT STUCK OVER AT BURGER BUNKER, SO MR. SPAETZLE IS JUST SHOWING US A VIDEO TODAY.

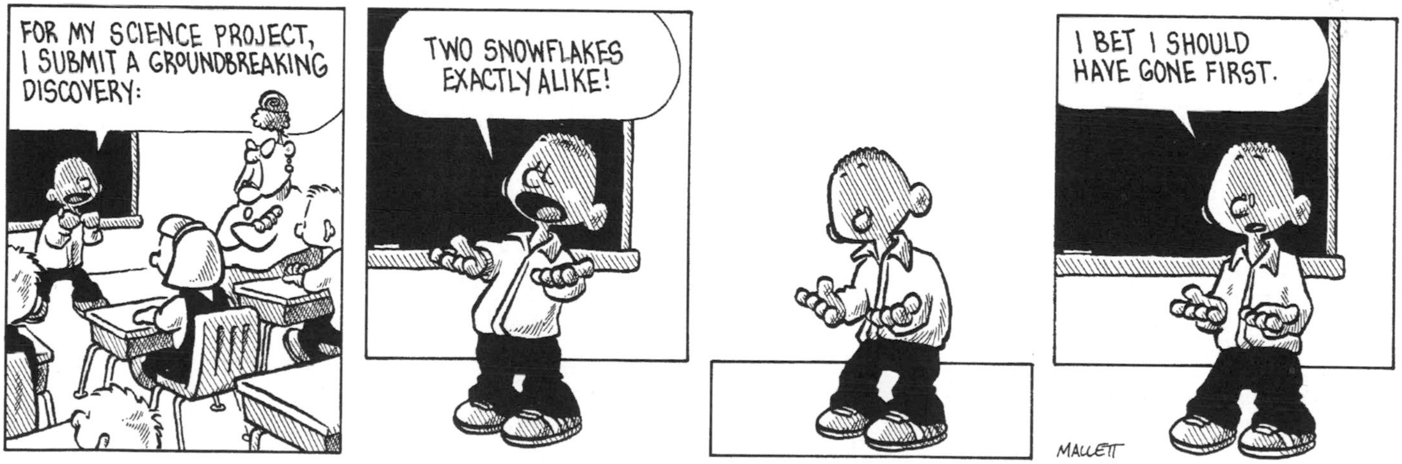
FOR MY SCIENCE PROJECT, I SUBMIT A GROUNDBREAKING DISCOVERY:
TWO SNOWFLAKES EXACTLY ALIKE!
I BET I SHOULD HAVE GONE FIRST.
MALLETT

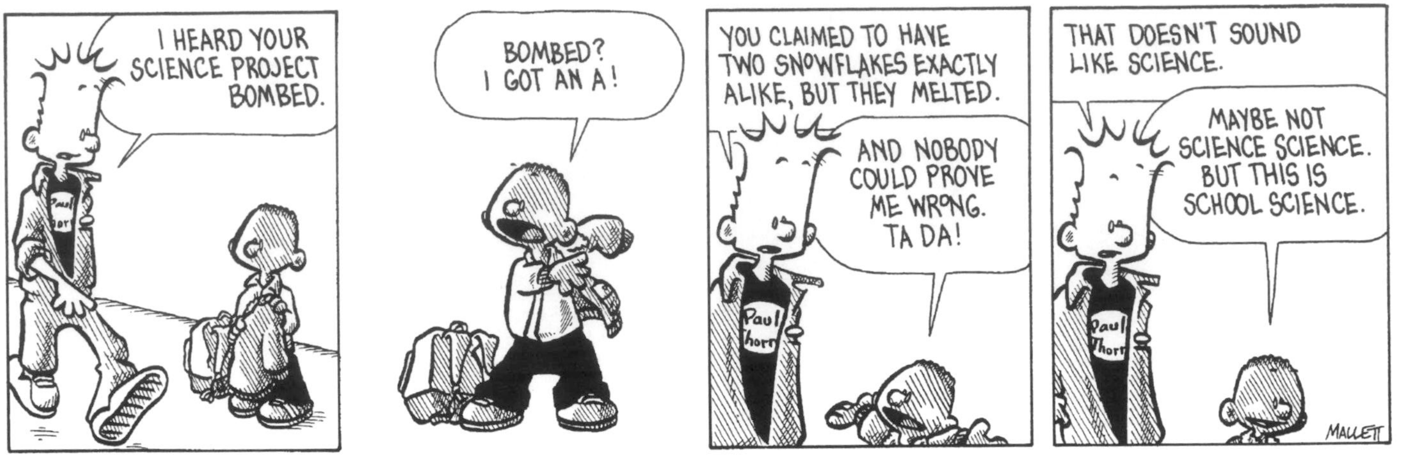
I HEARD YOUR SCIENCE PROJECT BOMBED.
BOMBED? I GOT AN A!
YOU CLAIMED TO HAVE TWO SNOWFLAKES EXACTLY ALIKE, BUT THEY MELTED.
AND NOBODY COULD PROVE ME WRONG. TA DA!
THAT DOESN'T SOUND LIKE SCIENCE.
MAYBE NOT SCIENCE SCIENCE. BUT THIS IS SCHOOL SCIENCE.
MALLETT

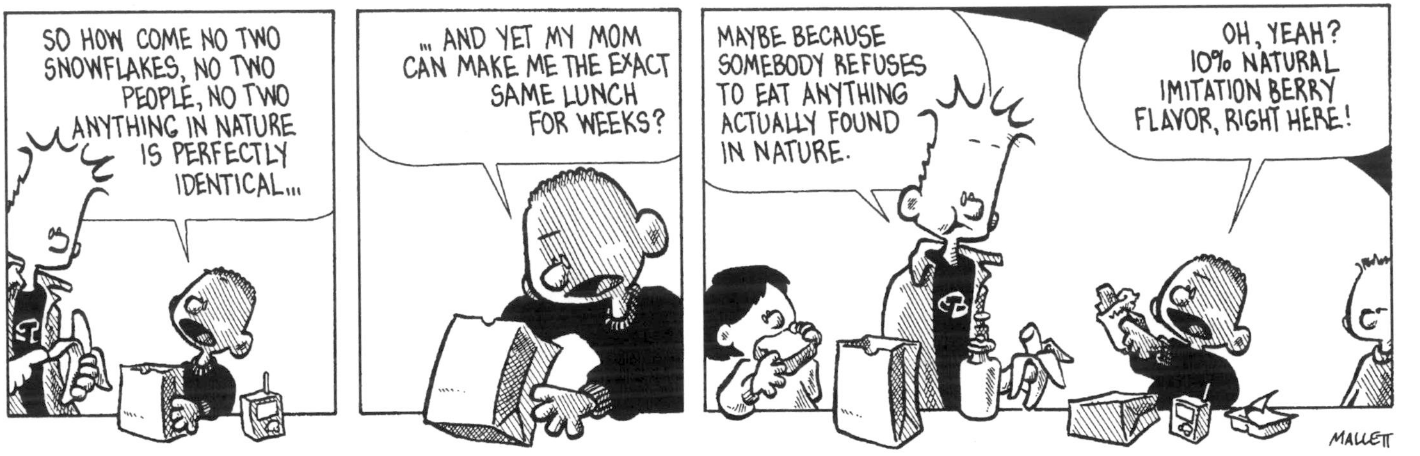
SO HOW COME NO TWO SNOWFLAKES, NO TWO PEOPLE, NO TWO ANYTHING IN NATURE IS PERFECTLY IDENTICAL...
... AND YET MY MOM CAN MAKE ME THE EXACT SAME LUNCH FOR WEEKS?
MAYBE BECAUSE SOMEBODY REFUSES TO EAT ANYTHING ACTUALLY FOUND IN NATURE.
OH, YEAH? 10% NATURAL IMITATION BERRY FLAVOR, RIGHT HERE!
MALLETT

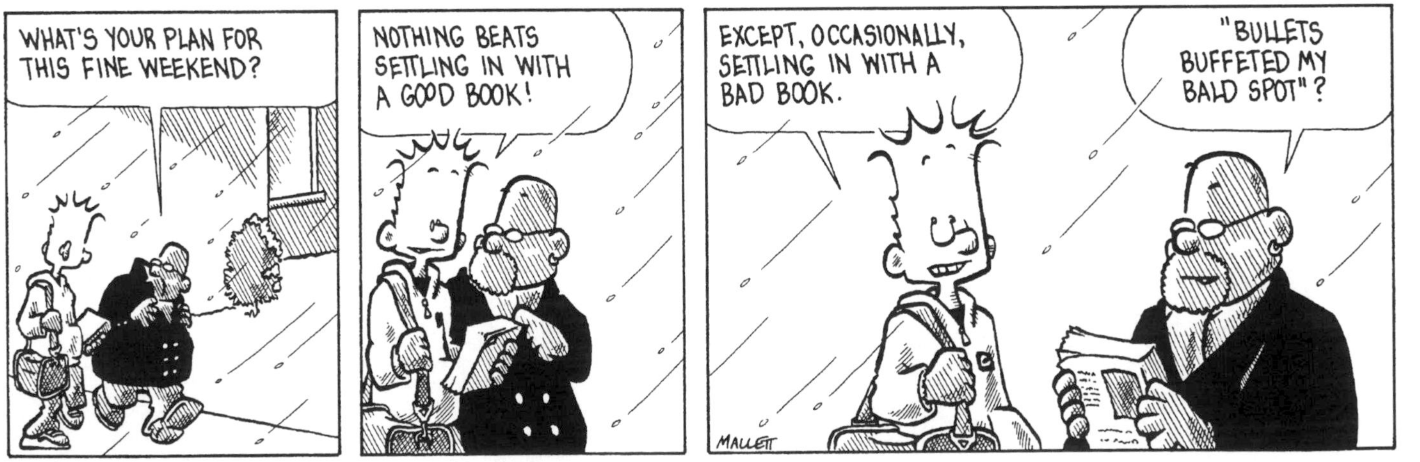
WHAT'S YOUR PLAN FOR THIS FINE WEEKEND?
NOTHING BEATS SETTLING IN WITH A GOOD BOOK!
EXCEPT, OCCASIONALLY, SETTLING IN WITH A BAD BOOK.
"BULLETS BUFFETED MY BALD SPOT"?
MALLETT

Frazz

by Jef Mallett

Auntie drives a Cadillac
and Grandpa rides the bus.
But Grammar don't go noplace
'less we takes her there with us.

... AND TODAY'S STORY IS ENTITLED...
SHE MEANS "TITLED."
ENTITLED MEANS TO POSSESS A RIGHT OR CLAIM TO SOMETHING.
MALLETT
AS IN, WE'RE ENTITLED TO A TEACHER WHO KNOWS A DICTIONARY FROM A DOORKNOB...
UH OH. WHERE'S KRISTIN?
HOW'D YOU END UP IN DETENTION AGAIN?
I WAS ENTATTLED.

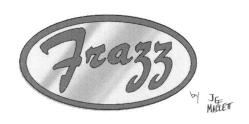

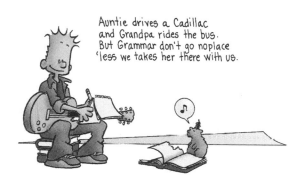

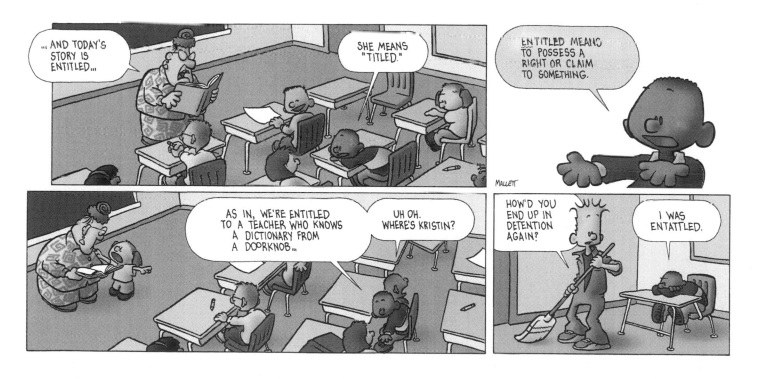

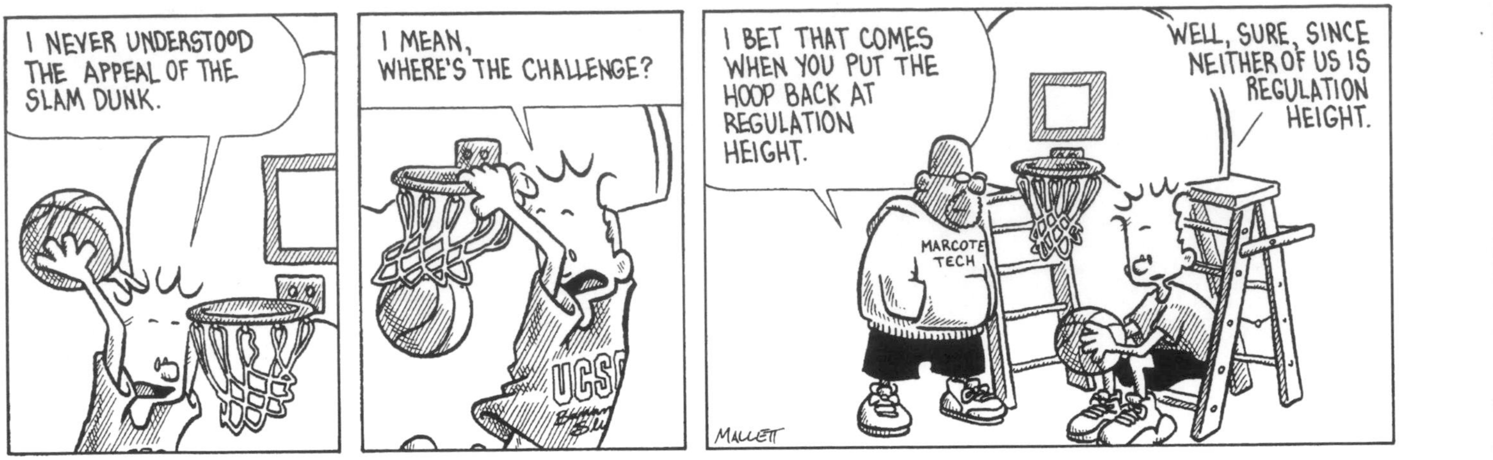
I NEVER UNDERSTOOD THE APPEAL OF THE SLAM DUNK.
I MEAN, WHERE'S THE CHALLENGE?
I BET THAT COMES WHEN YOU PUT THE HOOP BACK AT REGULATION HEIGHT.
WELL, SURE, SINCE NEITHER OF US IS REGULATION HEIGHT.
MARCOTE TECH
MALLETT

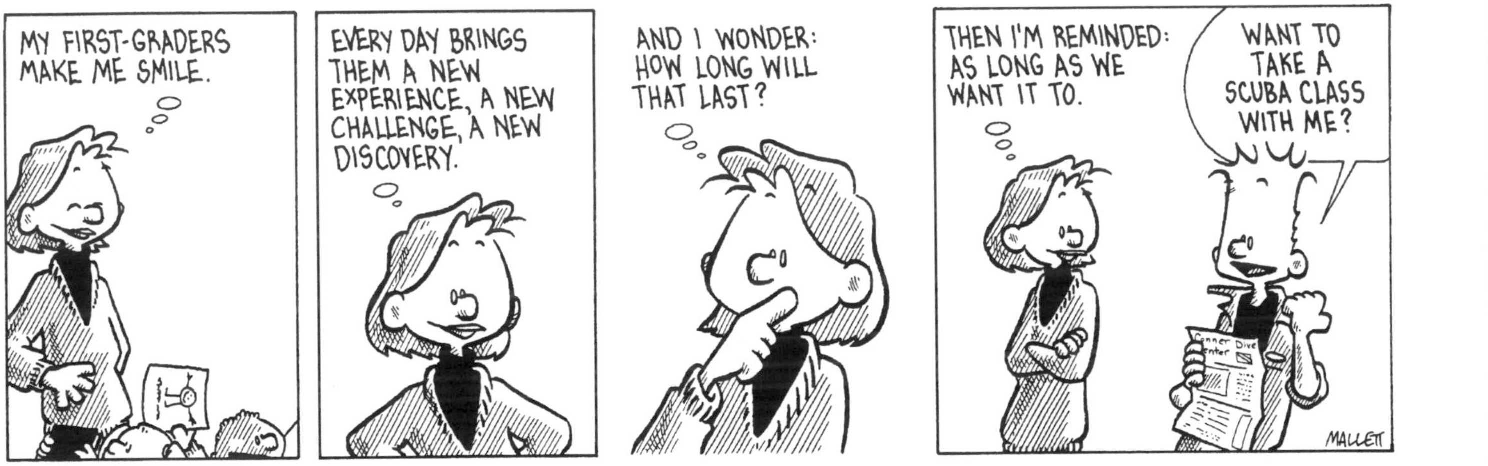
MY FIRST-GRADERS MAKE ME SMILE.
EVERY DAY BRINGS THEM A NEW EXPERIENCE, A NEW CHALLENGE, A NEW DISCOVERY.
AND I WONDER: HOW LONG WILL THAT LAST?
THEN I'M REMINDED: AS LONG AS WE WANT IT TO.
WANT TO TAKE A SCUBA CLASS WITH ME?
MALLETT

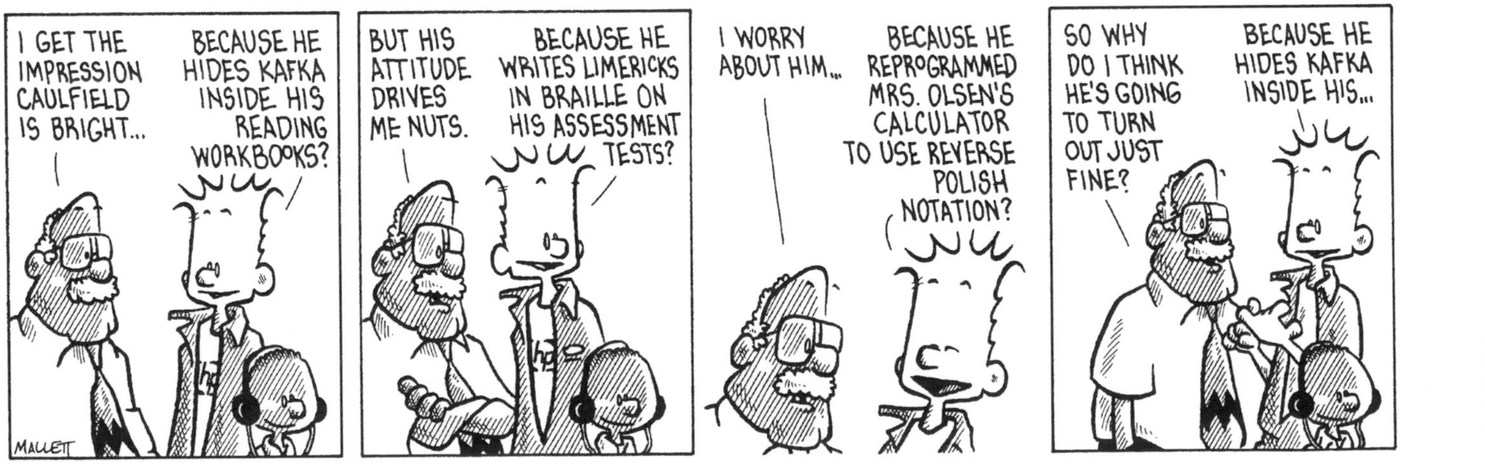
I GET THE IMPRESSION CAULFIELD IS BRIGHT...
BECAUSE HE HIDES KAFKA INSIDE HIS READING WORKBOOKS?
BUT HIS ATTITUDE DRIVES ME NUTS.
BECAUSE HE WRITES LIMERICKS IN BRAILLE ON HIS ASSESSMENT TESTS?
I WORRY ABOUT HIM...
BECAUSE HE REPROGRAMMED MRS. OLSEN'S CALCULATOR TO USE REVERSE POLISH NOTATION?
SO WHY DO I THINK HE'S GOING TO TURN OUT JUST FINE?
BECAUSE HE HIDES KAFKA INSIDE HIS...
MALLETT

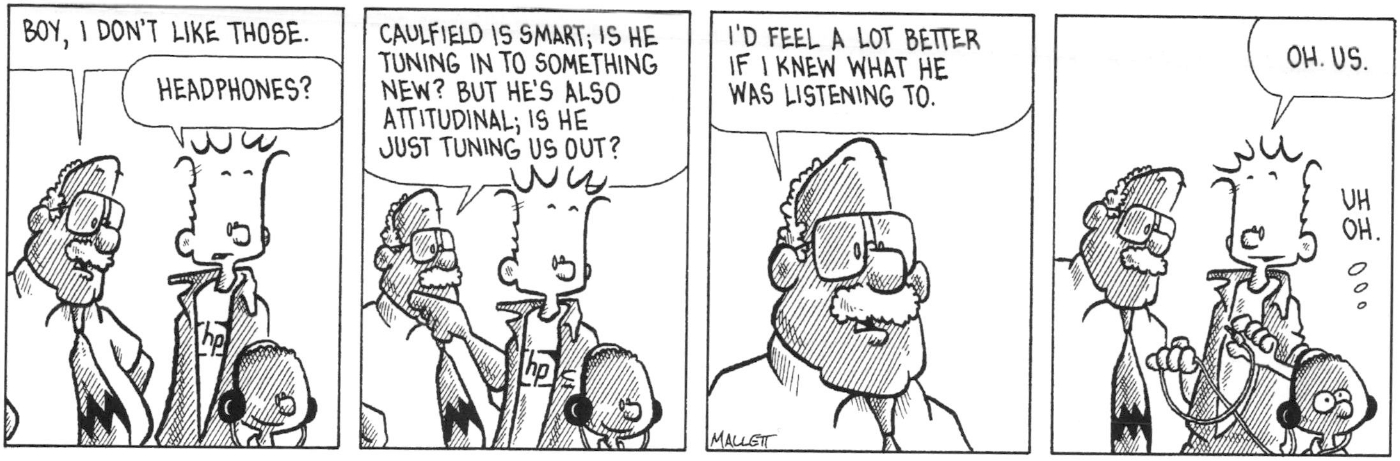
BOY, I DON'T LIKE THOSE.
HEADPHONES?
CAULFIELD IS SMART; IS HE TUNING IN TO SOMETHING NEW? BUT HE'S ALSO ATTITUDINAL; IS HE JUST TUNING US OUT?
I'D FEEL A LOT BETTER IF I KNEW WHAT HE WAS LISTENING TO.
MALLETT
OH. US.
UH OH.

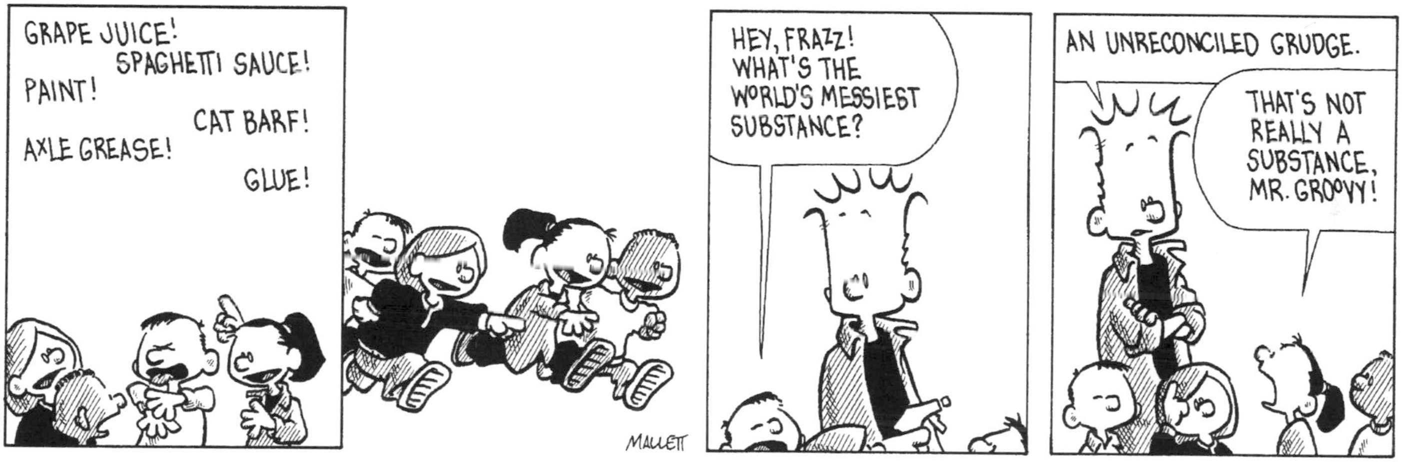
GRAPE JUICE!
SPAGHETTI SAUCE!
PAINT!
CAT BARF!
AXLE GREASE!
GLUE!
MALLETT
HEY, FRAZZ! WHAT'S THE WORLD'S MESSIEST SUBSTANCE?
AN UNRECONCILED GRUDGE.
THAT'S NOT REALLY A SUBSTANCE, MR. GROOVY!

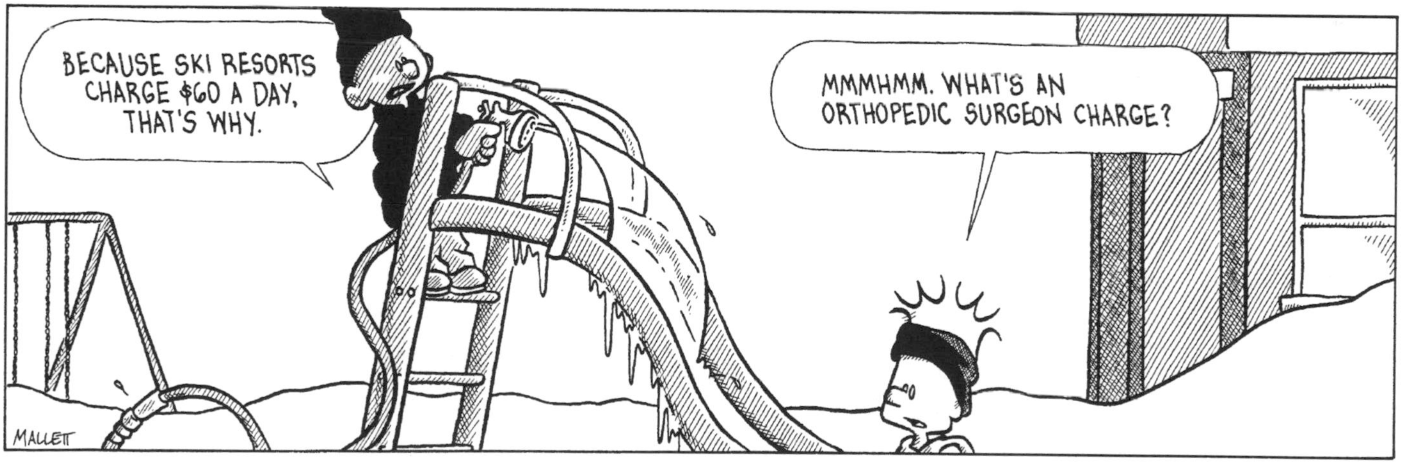
BECAUSE SKI RESORTS CHARGE $60 A DAY, THAT'S WHY.
MMMHMM. WHAT'S AN ORTHOPEDIC SURGEON CHARGE?
MALLETT

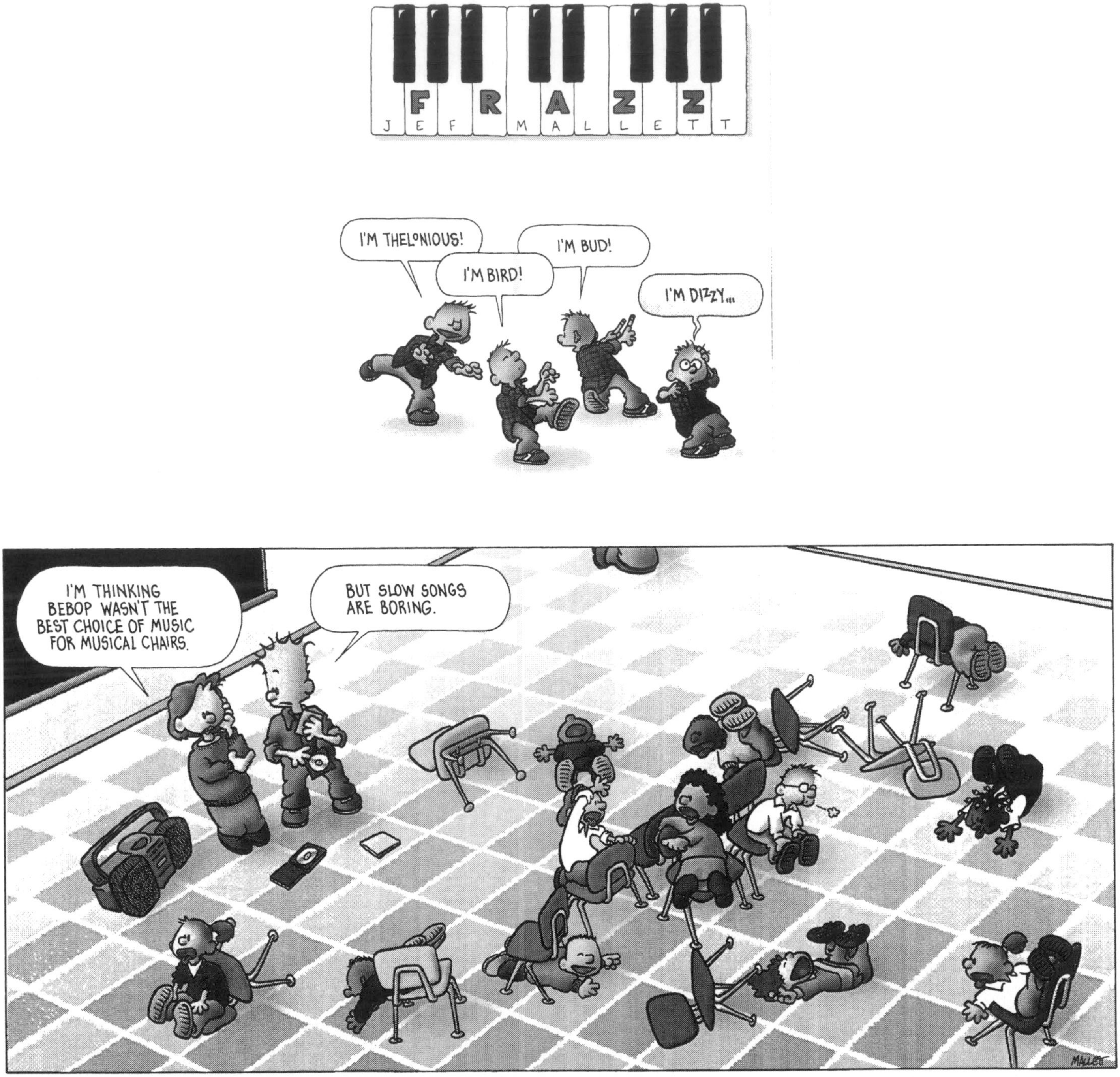
FRAZZ
JEFF MALLETT
I'M THELONIOUS!
I'M BIRD!
I'M BUD!
I'M DIZZY...
I'M THINKING BEBOP WASN'T THE BEST CHOICE OF MUSIC FOR MUSICAL CHAIRS.
BUT SLOW SONGS ARE BORING.
MALLETT

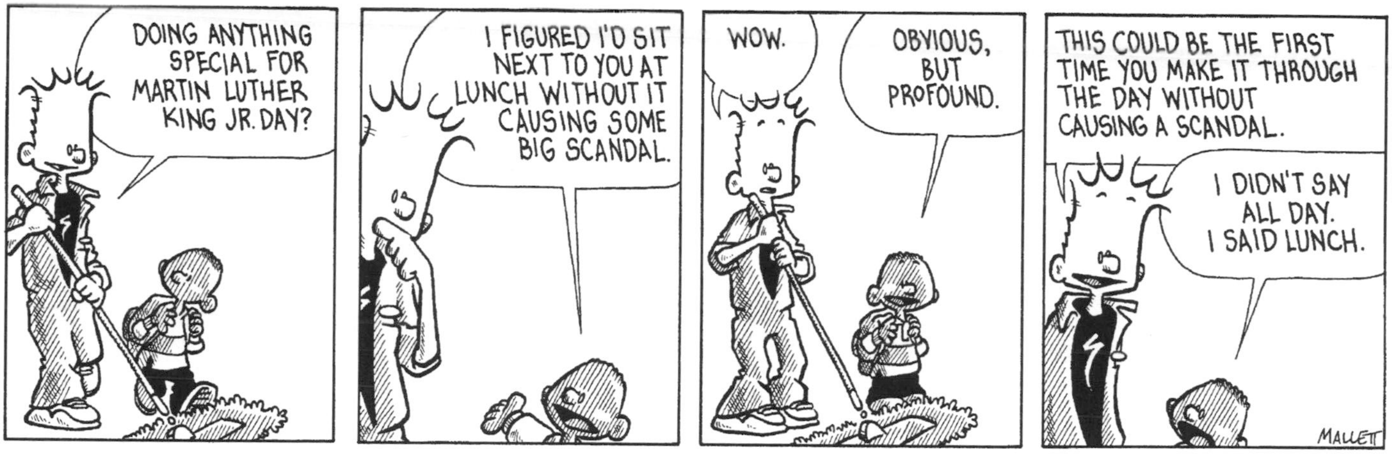
DOING ANYTHING SPECIAL FOR MARTIN LUTHER KING JR. DAY?
I FIGURED I'D SIT NEXT TO YOU AT LUNCH WITHOUT IT CAUSING SOME BIG SCANDAL.
WOW.
OBVIOUS, BUT PROFOUND.
THIS COULD BE THE FIRST TIME YOU MAKE IT THROUGH THE DAY WITHOUT CAUSING A SCANDAL.
I DIDN'T SAY ALL DAY. I SAID LUNCH.
MALLETT

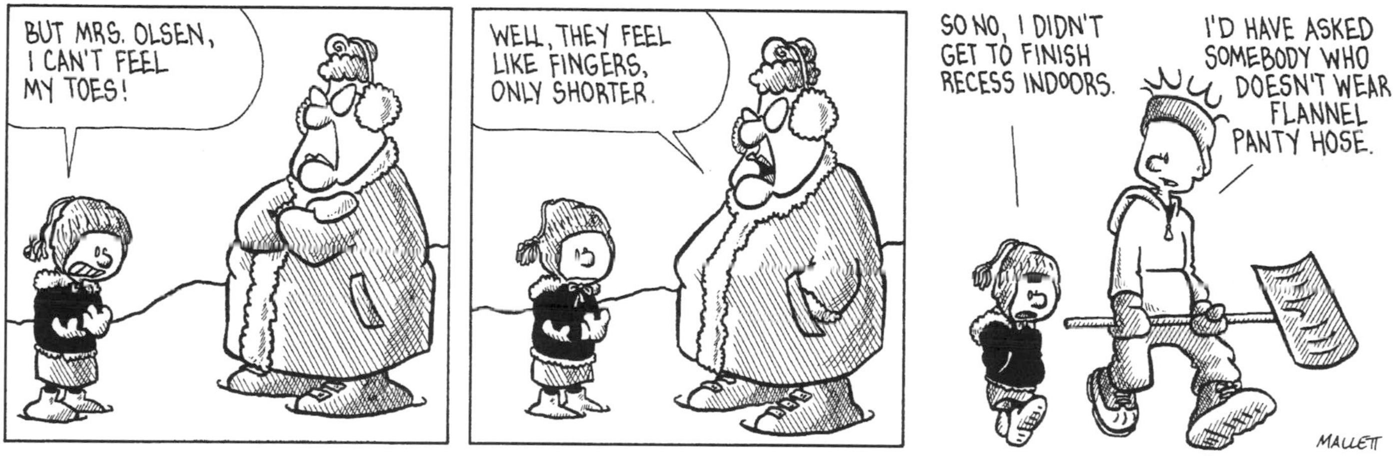
BUT MRS. OLSEN, I CAN'T FEEL MY TOES!
WELL, THEY FEEL LIKE FINGERS, ONLY SHORTER.
SO NO, I DIDN'T GET TO FINISH RECESS INDOORS.
I'D HAVE ASKED SOMEBODY WHO DOESN'T WEAR FLANNEL PANTY HOSE.
MALLETT

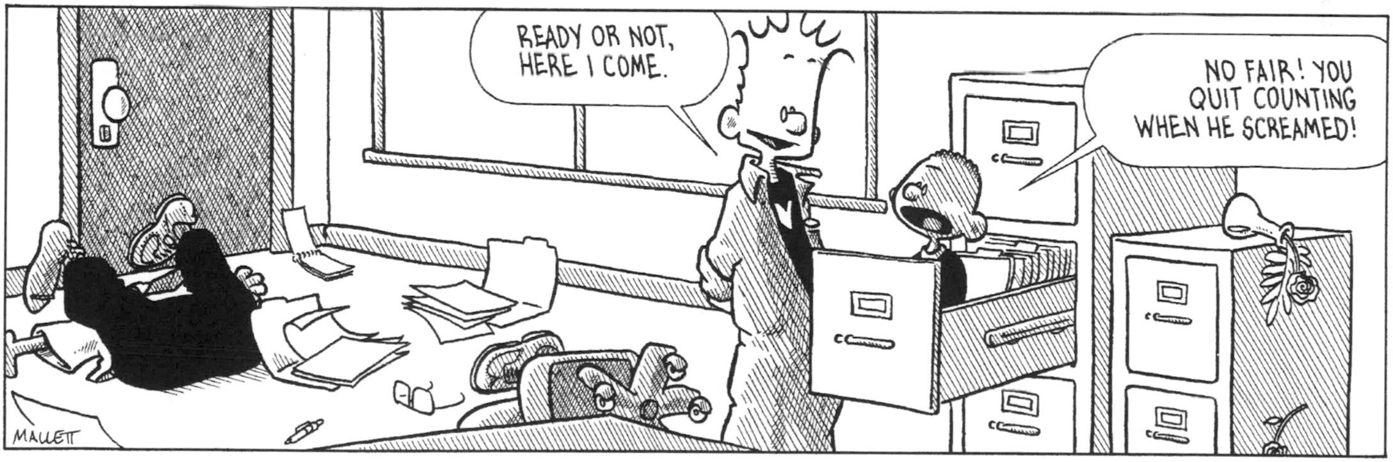
READY OR NOT, HERE I COME.
NO FAIR! YOU QUIT COUNTING WHEN HE SCREAMED!
MALLETT

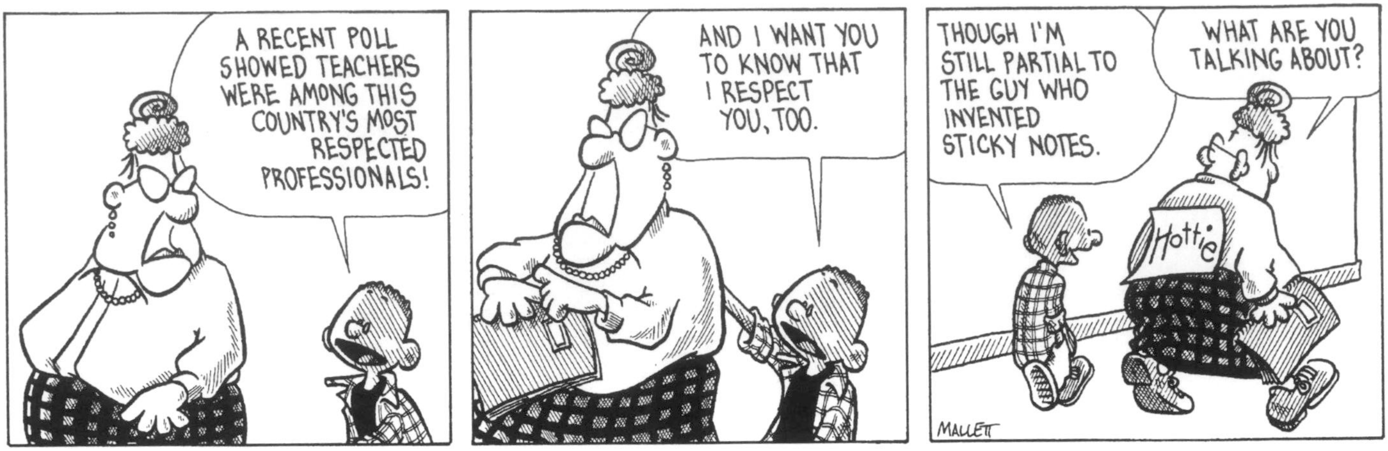
A RECENT POLL SHOWED TEACHERS WERE AMONG THIS COUNTRY'S MOST RESPECTED PROFESSIONALS!
AND I WANT YOU TO KNOW THAT I RESPECT YOU, TOO.
THOUGH I'M STILL PARTIAL TO THE GUY WHO INVENTED STICKY NOTES.
WHAT ARE YOU TALKING ABOUT?
Hottie
MALLETT

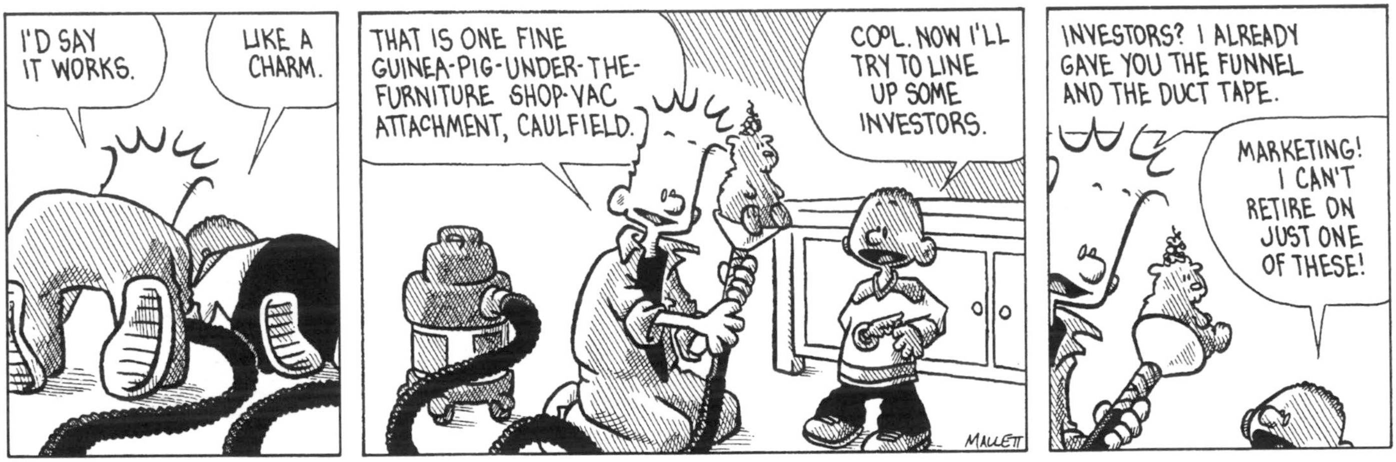
I'D SAY IT WORKS.
LIKE A CHARM.
THAT IS ONE FINE GUINEA-PIG-UNDER-THE-FURNITURE SHOP-VAC ATTACHMENT, CAULFIELD.
COOL. NOW I'LL TRY TO LINE UP SOME INVESTORS.
INVESTORS? I ALREADY GAVE YOU THE FUNNEL AND THE DUCT TAPE.
MARKETING! I CAN'T RETIRE ON JUST ONE OF THESE!
MALLETT

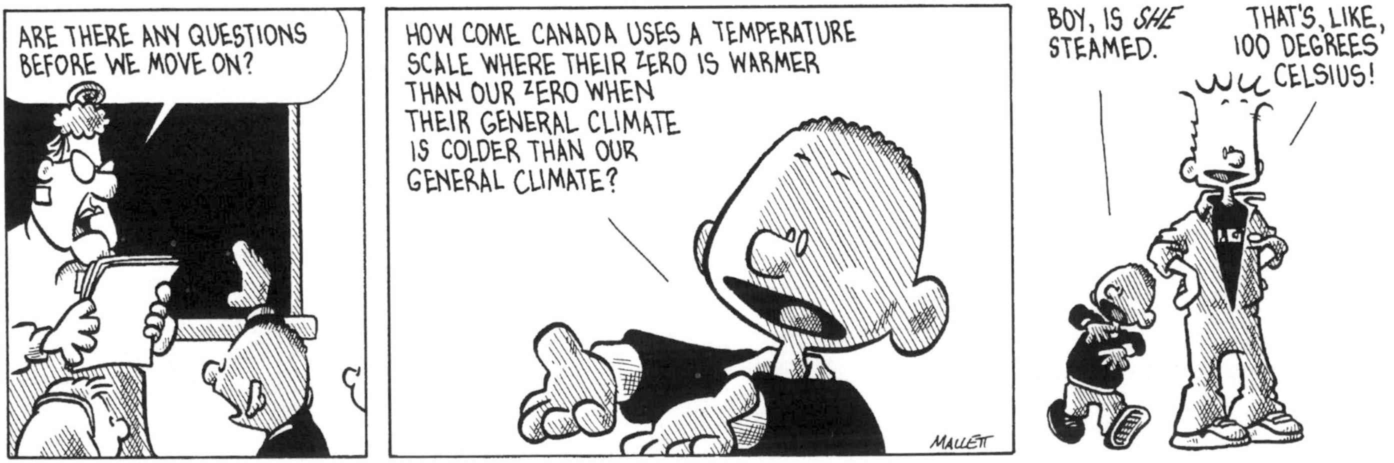
ARE THERE ANY QUESTIONS BEFORE WE MOVE ON?
HOW COME CANADA USES A TEMPERATURE SCALE WHERE THEIR ZERO IS WARMER THAN OUR ZERO WHEN THEIR GENERAL CLIMATE IS COLDER THAN OUR GENERAL CLIMATE?
BOY, IS *SHE* STEAMED.
THAT'S, LIKE, 100 DEGREES CELSIUS!
MALLETT

FRAZZ

by Jef Mallett

Lose 10 pounds fast!
Ask me how

JUST HOW MANY POUNDS OF STUFF DO YOU CARRY IN THAT BACKPACK?
I DON'T KNOW! JUST HELP ME BACK UP BEFORE I MISS MY BUS!
MALLETT

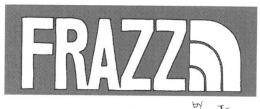

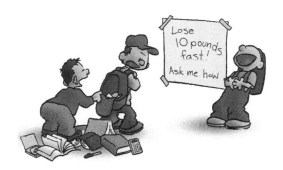

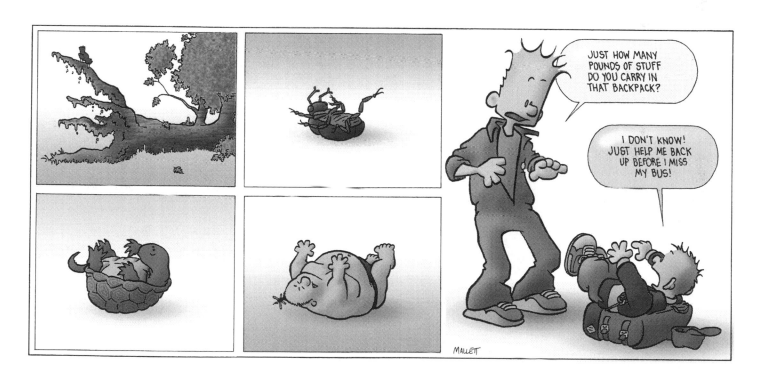

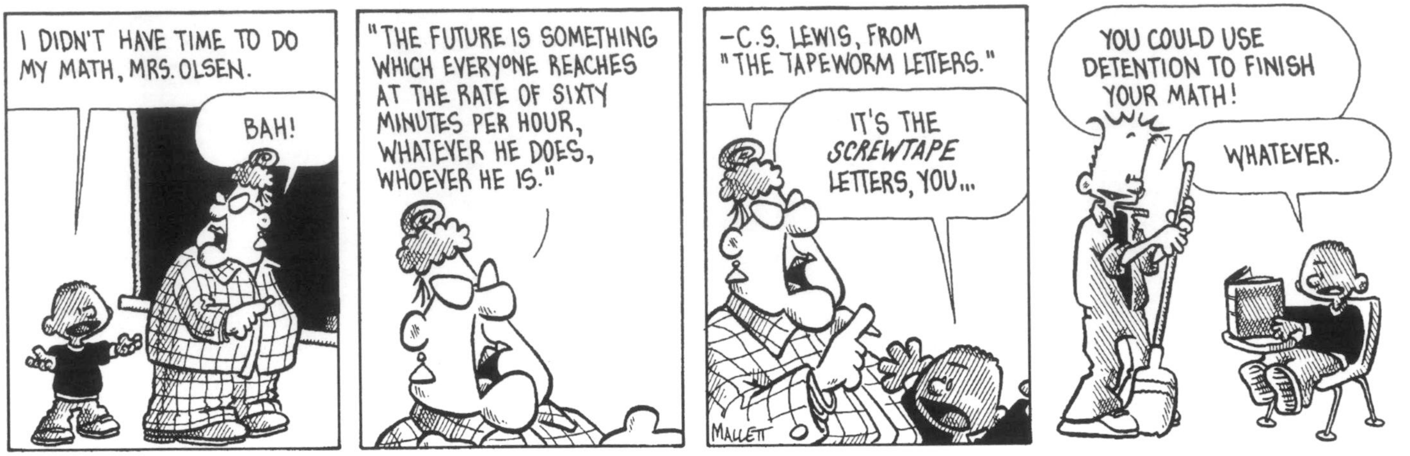
I DIDN'T HAVE TIME TO DO MY MATH, MRS. OLSEN.
BAH!
"THE FUTURE IS SOMETHING WHICH EVERYONE REACHES AT THE RATE OF SIXTY MINUTES PER HOUR, WHATEVER HE DOES, WHOEVER HE IS."
–C.S. LEWIS, FROM "THE TAPEWORM LETTERS."
IT'S THE *SCREWTAPE* LETTERS, YOU...
MALLETT
YOU COULD USE DETENTION TO FINISH YOUR MATH!
WHATEVER.

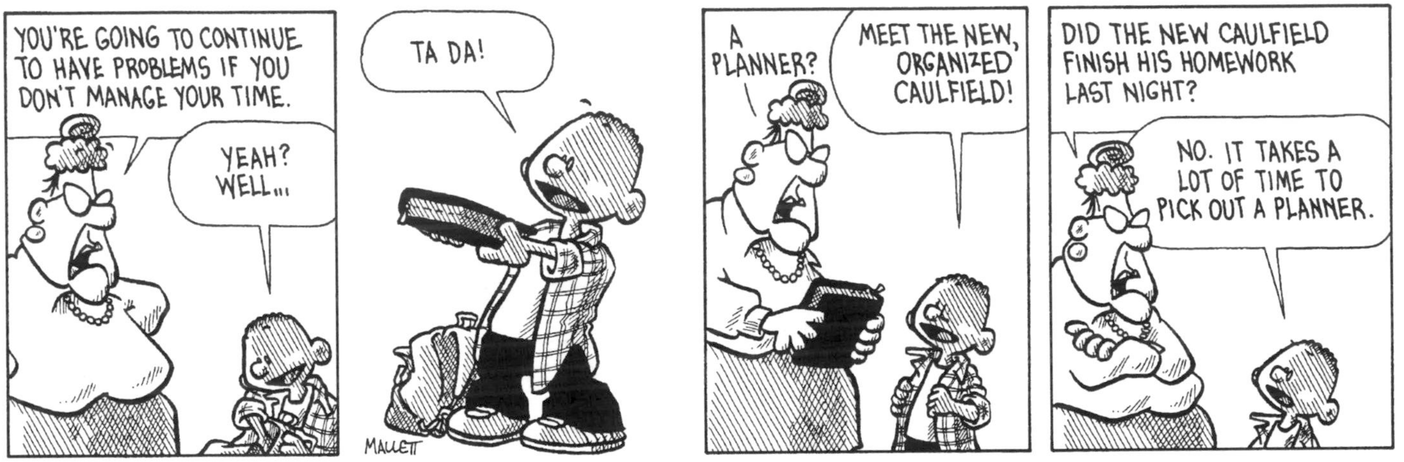
YOU'RE GOING TO CONTINUE TO HAVE PROBLEMS IF YOU DON'T MANAGE YOUR TIME.
YEAH? WELL...
TA DA!
MALLETT
A PLANNER?
MEET THE NEW, ORGANIZED CAULFIELD!
DID THE NEW CAULFIELD FINISH HIS HOMEWORK LAST NIGHT?
NO. IT TAKES A LOT OF TIME TO PICK OUT A PLANNER.

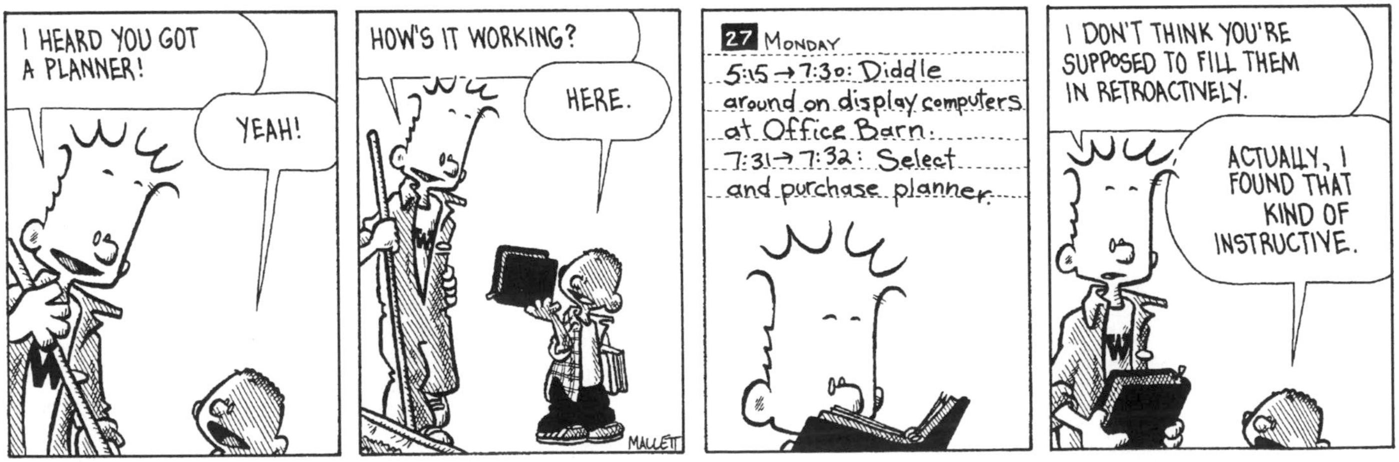
I HEARD YOU GOT A PLANNER!
YEAH!
HOW'S IT WORKING?
HERE.
MALLETT
27 MONDAY
5:15 → 7:30: Diddle around on display computers at Office Barn.
7:31 → 7:32: Select and purchase planner.
I DON'T THINK YOU'RE SUPPOSED TO FILL THEM IN RETROACTIVELY.
ACTUALLY, I FOUND THAT KIND OF INSTRUCTIVE.

Panel 1: HAVE YOU FILLED IN YOUR NEW PLANNER YET?

Panel 2: SORT OF. I DID THE BATTLE OF THE BULGE ON JANUARY 13-19.

6 THURSDAY

17 FRIDAY

Panel 3: ISN'T THE WHOLE POINT OF THESE THINGS TO HELP YOU USE YOUR TIME MORE CONSTRUCTIVELY?

Panel 4: YOU PLAY SOLITAIRE ON YOUR PERSONAL ELECTRONIC ASSISTANT THINGIE.

BUT ONLY WHEN IT TELLS ME I CAN.

MALLETT

Panel 5: THESE PLANNERS WOULD MAKE MORE SENSE IF YOU DIDN'T HAVE TO WASTE TIME FILLING THEM OUT.

Panel 6: I SHOULD DO LIKE MR. HACKER.

Panel 7: HE BUYS A NEW ONE EVERY WEEK, ALL FILLED OUT.

?

MALLETT

Panel 8: THAT'S A TV GUIDE.

OF COURSE, I'D HAVE TO CHANGE MY LIFESTYLE.

Panel 9: WHAT DO YOU LIKE BEST ABOUT YOUR PLANNER?

IT'S FUNNY!

Panel 10: SEE? THE VERSION I GOT HAS A "FAR SIDE" CARTOON ON EVERY PAGE.

Panel 11: I WONDER WHAT THE "FAR SIDE" CARTOONIST HAS IN HIS PLANNER.

Panel 12: AT THIS POINT, I'M GUESSING, ANYTHING HE WANTS.

SEE, THAT'S THE KIND OF SCHEDULE I'D LIKE.

MALLETT

Frazz

by Jef Mallett

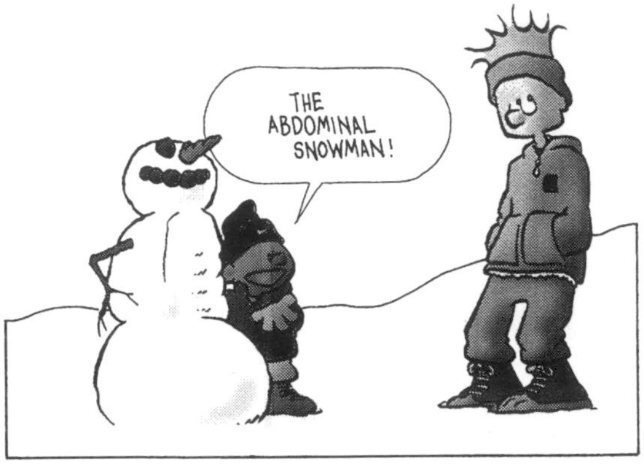
THE ABDOMINAL SNOWMAN!

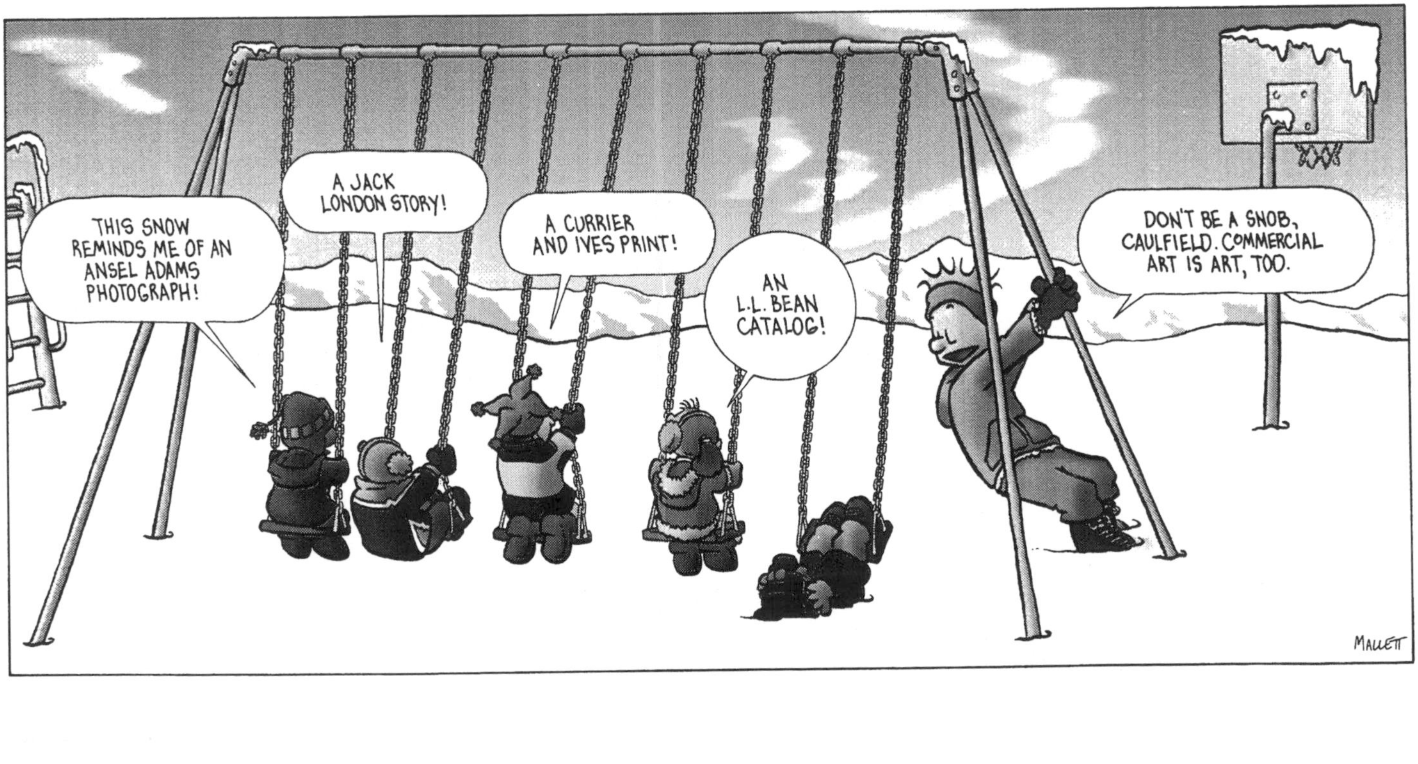
THIS SNOW REMINDS ME OF AN ANSEL ADAMS PHOTOGRAPH!
A JACK LONDON STORY!
A CURRIER AND IVES PRINT!
AN L.L. BEAN CATALOG!
DON'T BE A SNOB, CAULFIELD. COMMERCIAL ART IS ART, TOO.
MALLETT

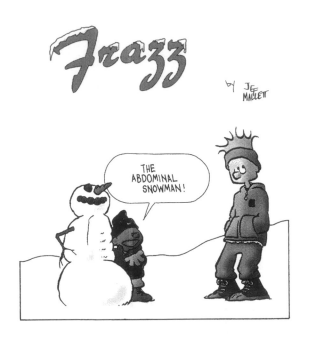

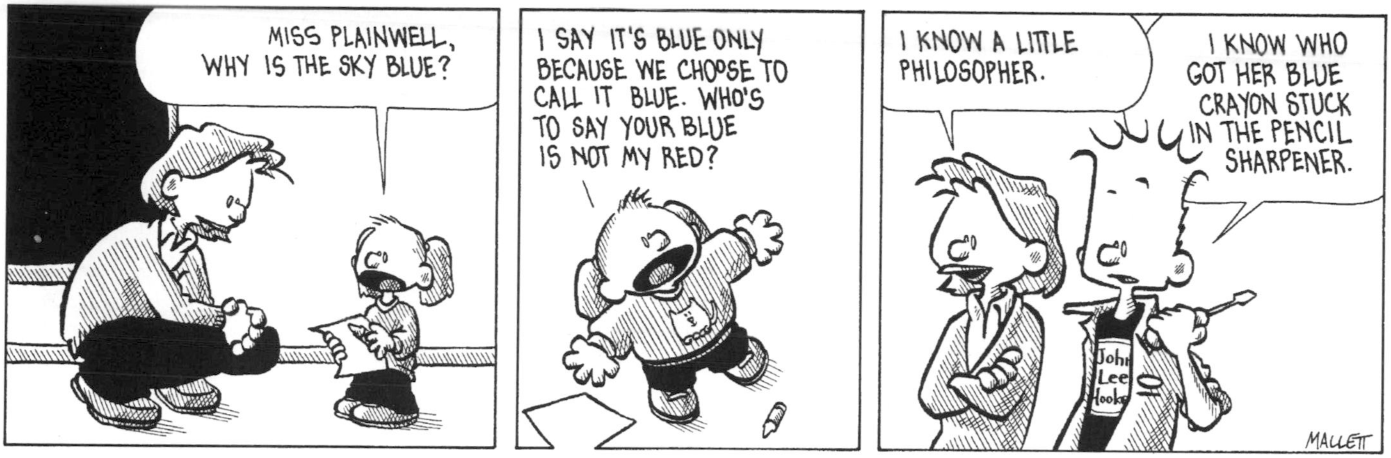
MISS PLAINWELL, WHY IS THE SKY BLUE?
I SAY IT'S BLUE ONLY BECAUSE WE CHOOSE TO CALL IT BLUE. WHO'S TO SAY YOUR BLUE IS NOT MY RED?
I KNOW A LITTLE PHILOSOPHER.
I KNOW WHO GOT HER BLUE CRAYON STUCK IN THE PENCIL SHARPENER.
MALLETT

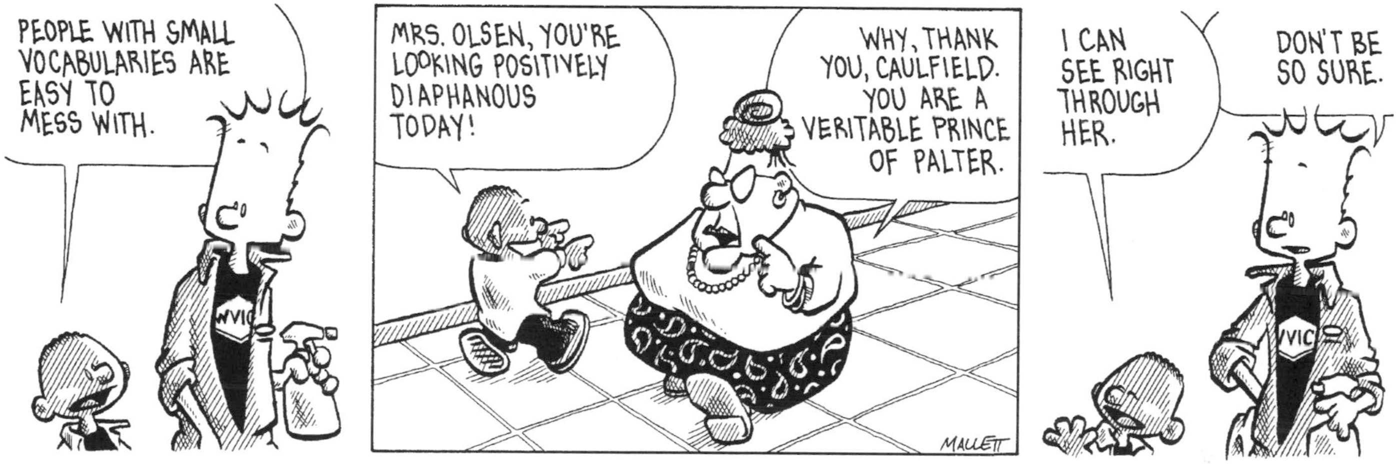
PEOPLE WITH SMALL VOCABULARIES ARE EASY TO MESS WITH.
MRS. OLSEN, YOU'RE LOOKING POSITIVELY DIAPHANOUS TODAY!
WHY, THANK YOU, CAULFIELD. YOU ARE A VERITABLE PRINCE OF PALTER.
I CAN SEE RIGHT THROUGH HER.
DON'T BE SO SURE.
MALLETT

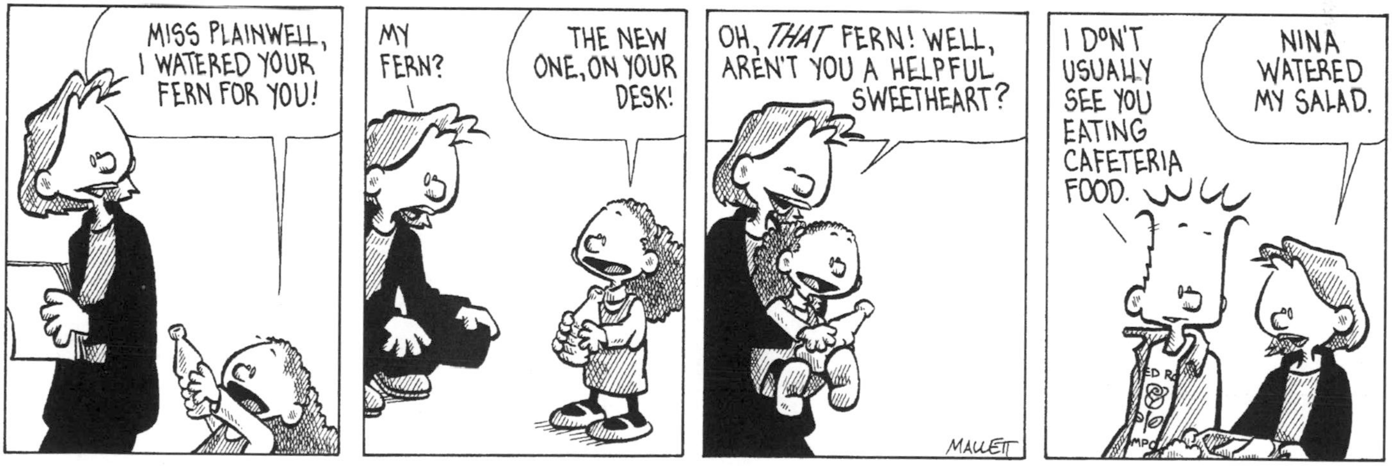
MISS PLAINWELL, I WATERED YOUR FERN FOR YOU!
MY FERN?
THE NEW ONE, ON YOUR DESK!
OH, *THAT* FERN! WELL, AREN'T YOU A HELPFUL SWEETHEART?
I DON'T USUALLY SEE YOU EATING CAFETERIA FOOD.
NINA WATERED MY SALAD.
MALLETT

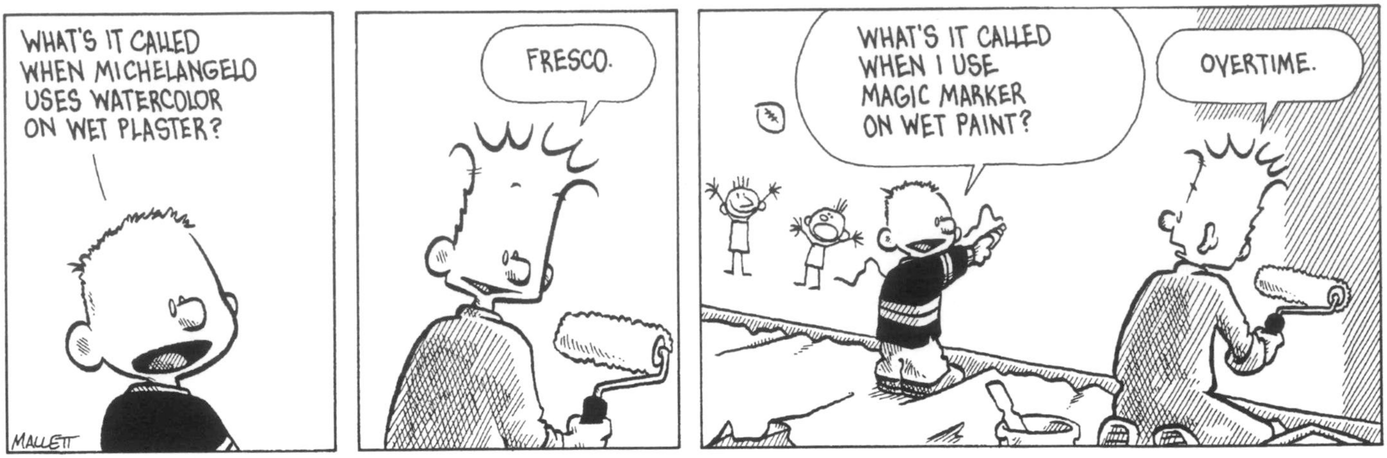
WHAT'S IT CALLED WHEN MICHELANGELO USES WATERCOLOR ON WET PLASTER?
FRESCO.
WHAT'S IT CALLED WHEN I USE MAGIC MARKER ON WET PAINT?
OVERTIME.
MALLETT

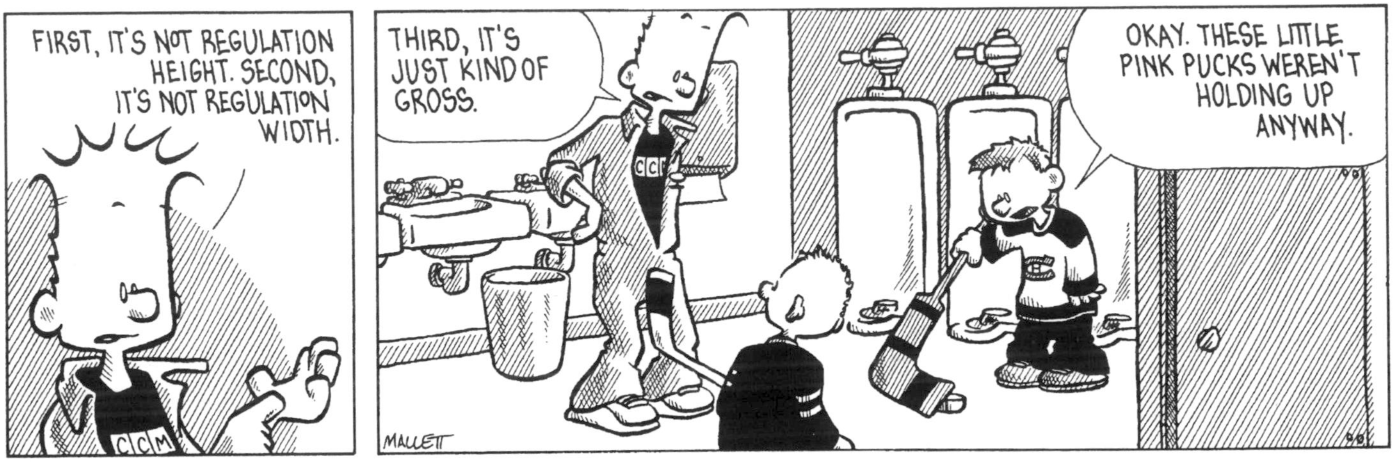
FIRST, IT'S NOT REGULATION HEIGHT. SECOND, IT'S NOT REGULATION WIDTH.
THIRD, IT'S JUST KIND OF GROSS.
OKAY. THESE LITTLE PINK PUCKS WEREN'T HOLDING UP ANYWAY.
CCM
MALLETT

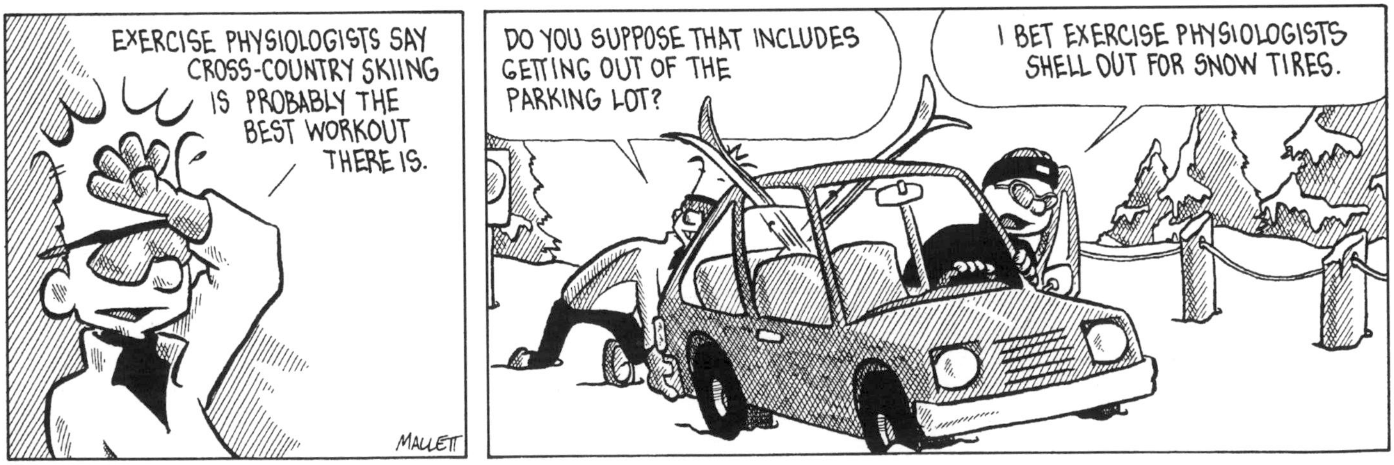
EXERCISE PHYSIOLOGISTS SAY CROSS-COUNTRY SKIING IS PROBABLY THE BEST WORKOUT THERE IS.
DO YOU SUPPOSE THAT INCLUDES GETTING OUT OF THE PARKING LOT?
I BET EXERCISE PHYSIOLOGISTS SHELL OUT FOR SNOW TIRES.
MALLETT

NOTE THAT I SPILLED MY GRAPE JUICE WHERE THERE WAS ALREADY A BIG COFFEE STAIN.
LESSER DEFENSES HAVE WORKED IN HIGHER COURTS.

GREAT.
FIVE MINUTES AFTER I SCOLD SOME KIDS FOR EATING IN THE HALL, I BLOOP SOME JELLY ON THE CARPET.
IF I'M SEEN CLEANING IT UP, I'LL LOOK LIKE A HYPOCRITE.
BUT IF I JUST LEAVE IT, I REALLY AM A HYPOCRITE.
MALLETT

I WONDER WHAT FRAZZ WOULD DO?
HARD TO SAY, SINCE FRAZZ HARDLY EVER EATS JELLY DONUTS.
I WONDER IF FRAZZ CAN TALK TO HIMSELF WITHOUT MOVING HIS LIPS...
HE CAN.

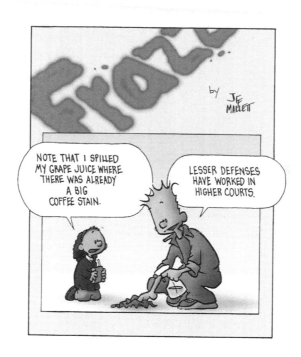

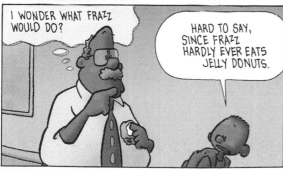

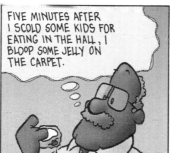

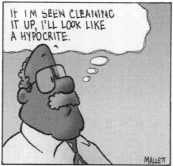

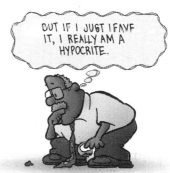

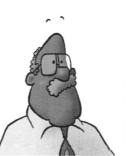

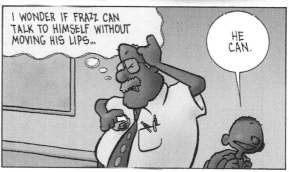

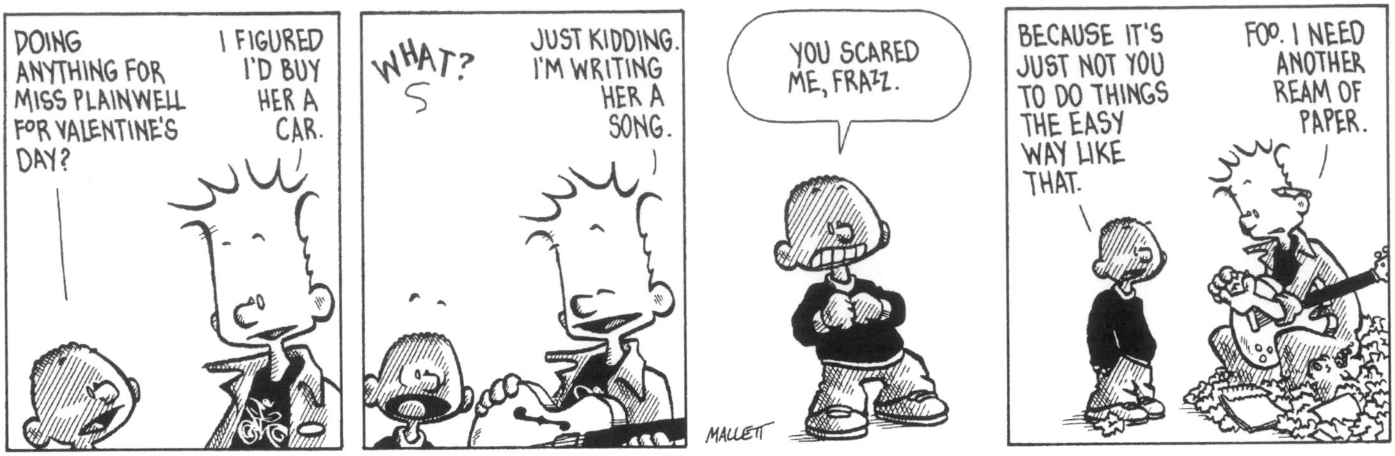
DOING ANYTHING FOR MISS PLAINWELL FOR VALENTINE'S DAY?
I FIGURED I'D BUY HER A CAR.
WHAT?
JUST KIDDING. I'M WRITING HER A SONG.
YOU SCARED ME, FRAZZ.
MALLETT
BECAUSE IT'S JUST NOT YOU TO DO THINGS THE EASY WAY LIKE THAT.
FOO. I NEED ANOTHER REAM OF PAPER.

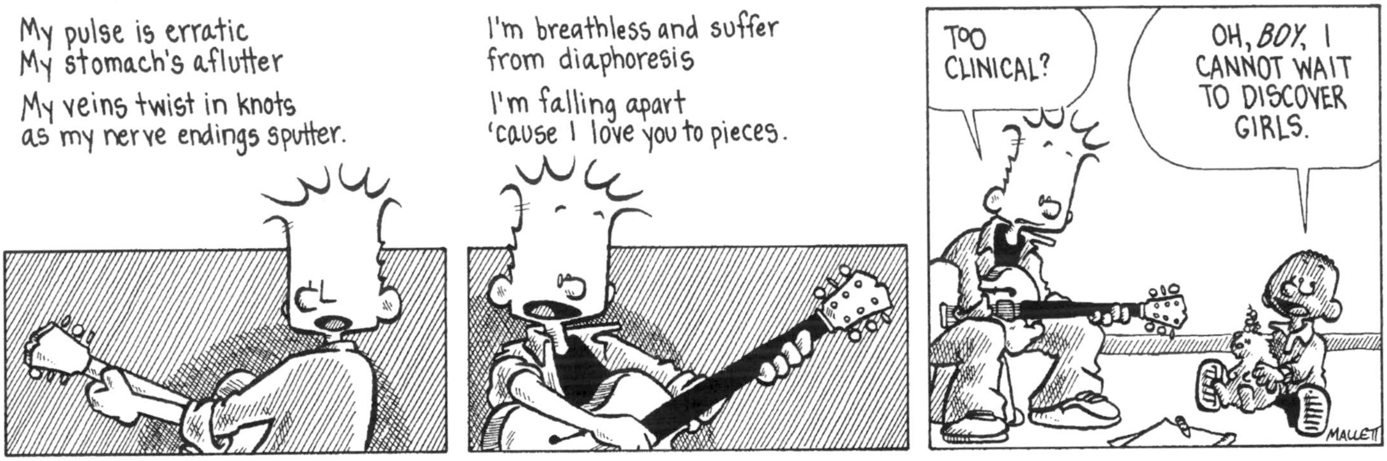
My pulse is erratic
My stomach's aflutter
My veins twist in knots
as my nerve endings sputter.
I'm breathless and suffer
from diaphoresis
I'm falling apart
'cause I love you to pieces.
TOO CLINICAL?
OH, *BOY*, I CANNOT WAIT TO DISCOVER GIRLS.
MALLETT

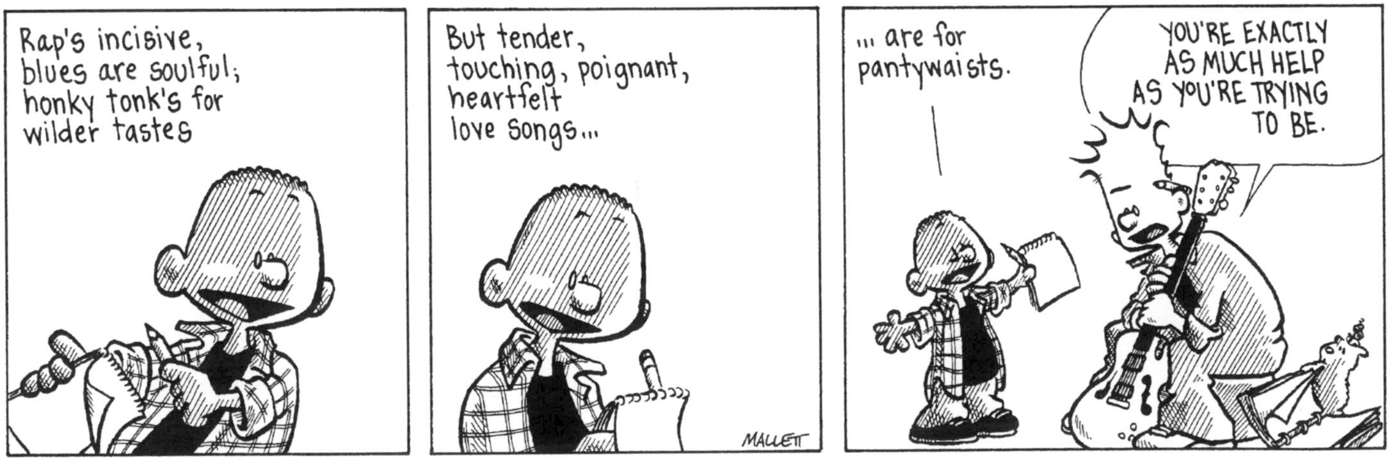
Rap's incisive, blues are soulful; honky tonk's for wilder tastes
But tender, touching, poignant, heartfelt love songs...
MALLETT
... are for pantywaists.
YOU'RE EXACTLY AS MUCH HELP AS YOU'RE TRYING TO BE.

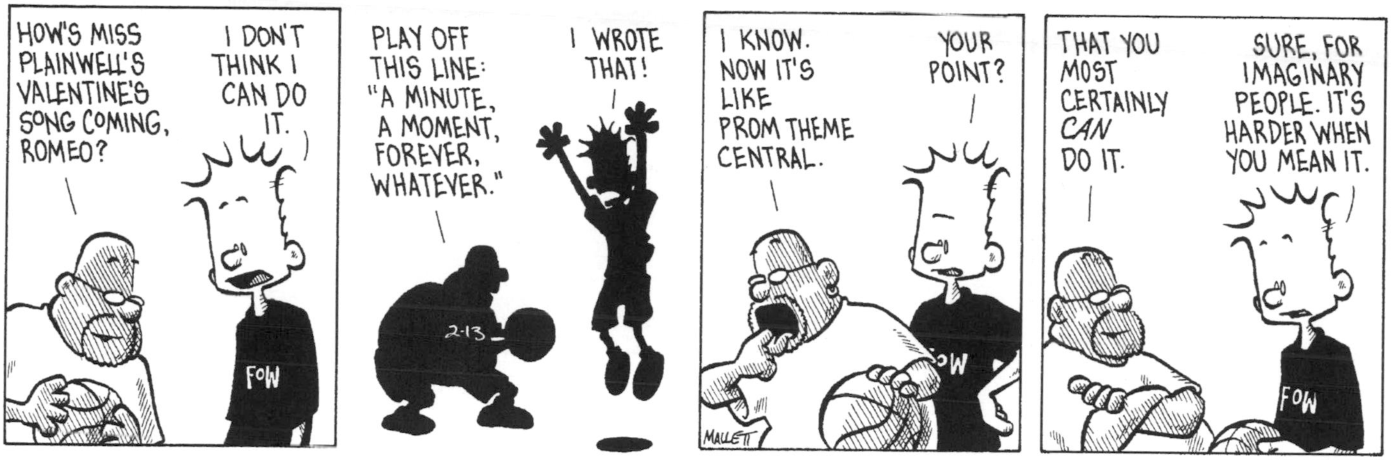
HOW'S MISS PLAINWELL'S VALENTINE'S SONG COMING, ROMEO?
I DON'T THINK I CAN DO IT.
PLAY OFF THIS LINE: "A MINUTE, A MOMENT, FOREVER, WHATEVER."
I WROTE THAT!
2-13
I KNOW. NOW IT'S LIKE PROM THEME CENTRAL.
YOUR POINT?
MALLETT
THAT YOU MOST CERTAINLY *CAN* DO IT.
SURE, FOR IMAGINARY PEOPLE. IT'S HARDER WHEN YOU MEAN IT.

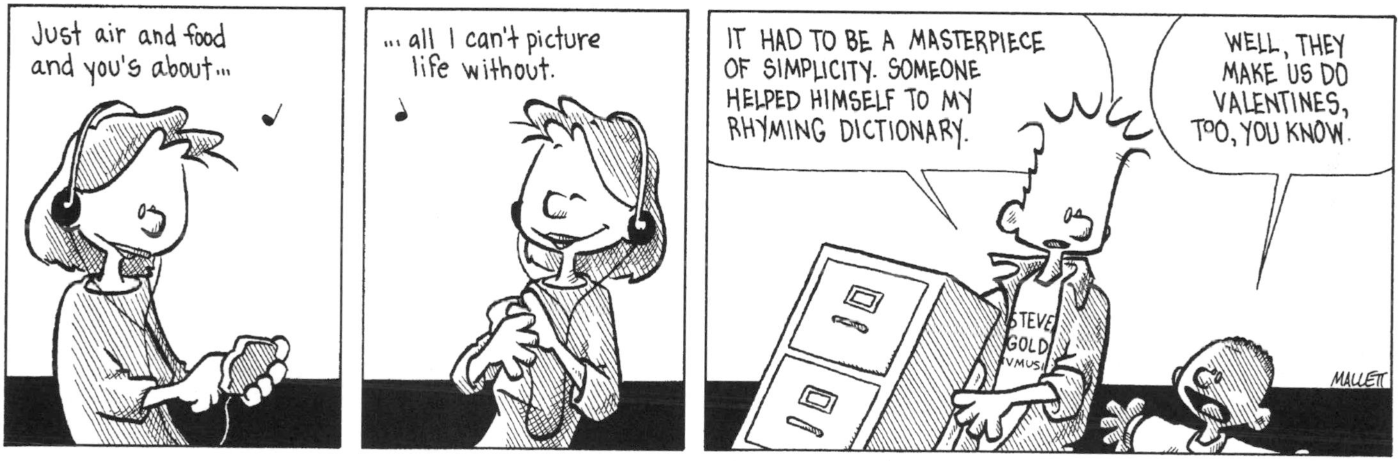
Just air and food and you's about...
... all I can't picture life without.
IT HAD TO BE A MASTERPIECE OF SIMPLICITY. SOMEONE HELPED HIMSELF TO MY RHYMING DICTIONARY.
WELL, THEY MAKE US DO VALENTINES, TOO, YOU KNOW.
MALLETT

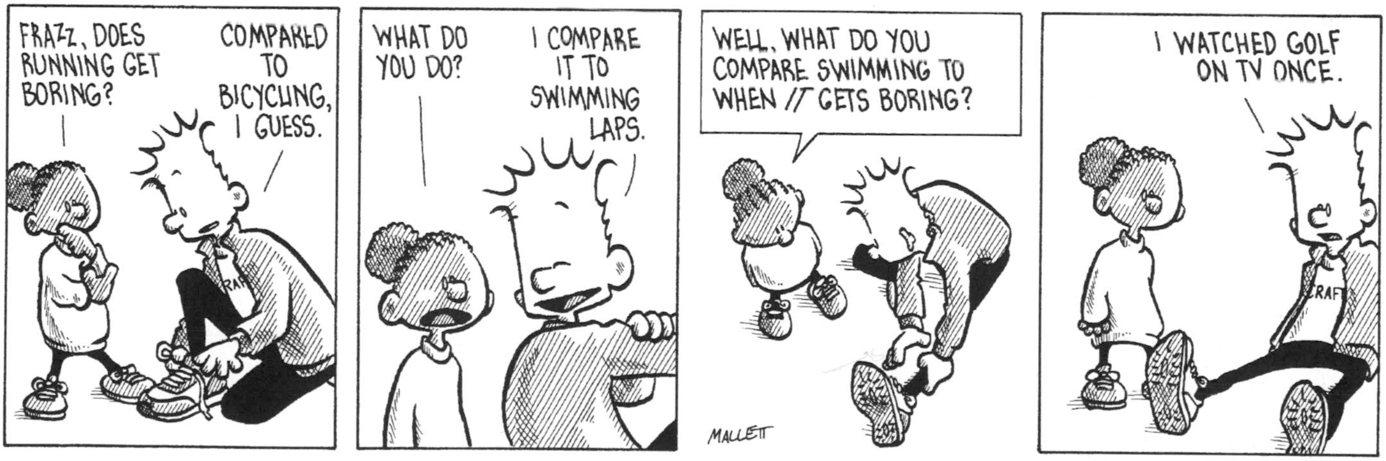
FRAZZ, DOES RUNNING GET BORING?
COMPARED TO BICYCLING, I GUESS.
WHAT DO YOU DO?
I COMPARE IT TO SWIMMING LAPS.
WELL, WHAT DO YOU COMPARE SWIMMING TO WHEN *IT* GETS BORING?
MALLETT
I WATCHED GOLF ON TV ONCE.

"I'm open!"
I'm open!"
shouted the flea.

The point guard knew a flea can jump 20 times its own height:
Dunk city!

So he fired a smart pass to his teammate the flea...

and...

the flea was once again placed on injured reserve.

Proving:
a) fleas are nature's best jumpers.

b) versatility is more important than ability.

c) NBA careers can be distressingly short.

d) teamwork is dumb.

MALLETT

THERE ARE MORE RIGHT ANSWERS THAN WRONG ANSWERS!

I LIKE MY TEST QUESTIONS TO MIRROR REAL LIFE.

INASMUCH AS A FLEA PLAYING BASKETBALL MIRRORS LIFE.

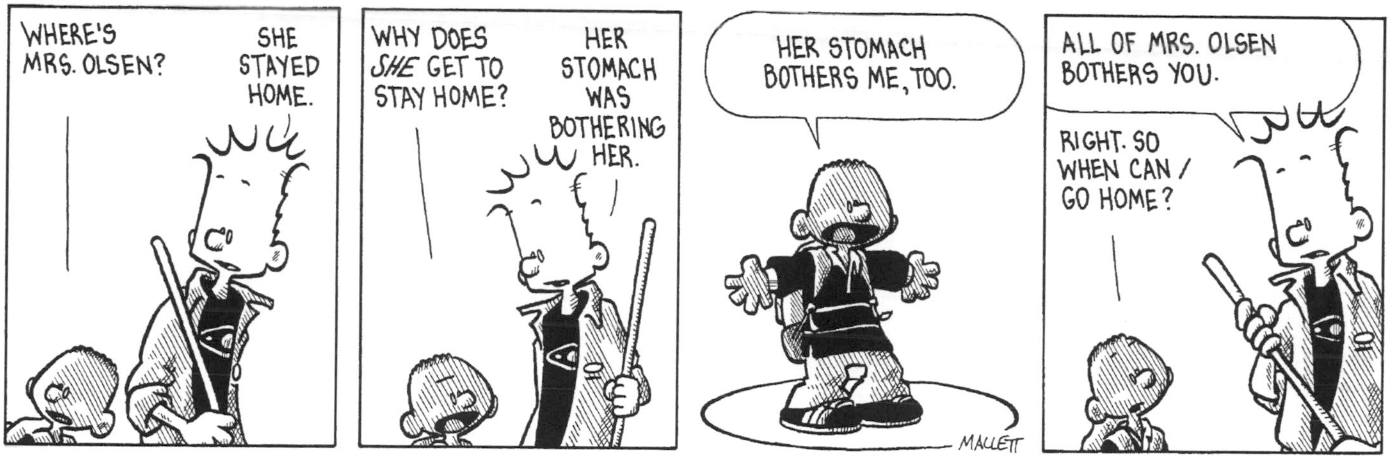
WHERE'S MRS. OLSEN?
SHE STAYED HOME.
WHY DOES *SHE* GET TO STAY HOME?
HER STOMACH WAS BOTHERING HER.
HER STOMACH BOTHERS ME, TOO.
MALLETT
ALL OF MRS. OLSEN BOTHERS YOU.
RIGHT. SO WHEN CAN I GO HOME?

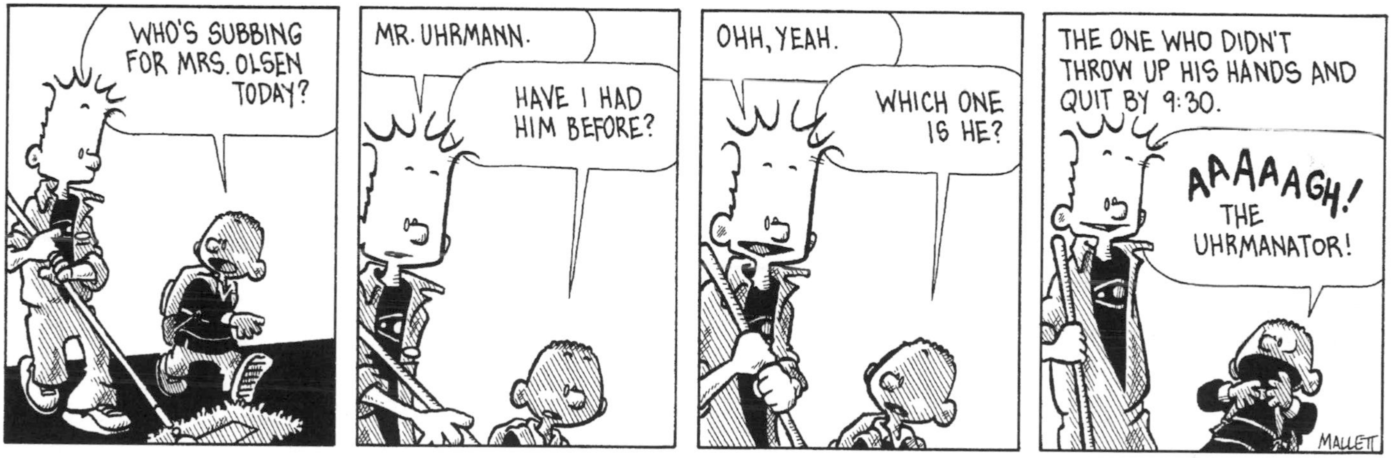
WHO'S SUBBING FOR MRS. OLSEN TODAY?
MR. UHRMANN.
HAVE I HAD HIM BEFORE?
OHH, YEAH.
WHICH ONE IS HE?
THE ONE WHO DIDN'T THROW UP HIS HANDS AND QUIT BY 9:30.
AAAAAGH! THE UHRMANATOR!
MALLETT

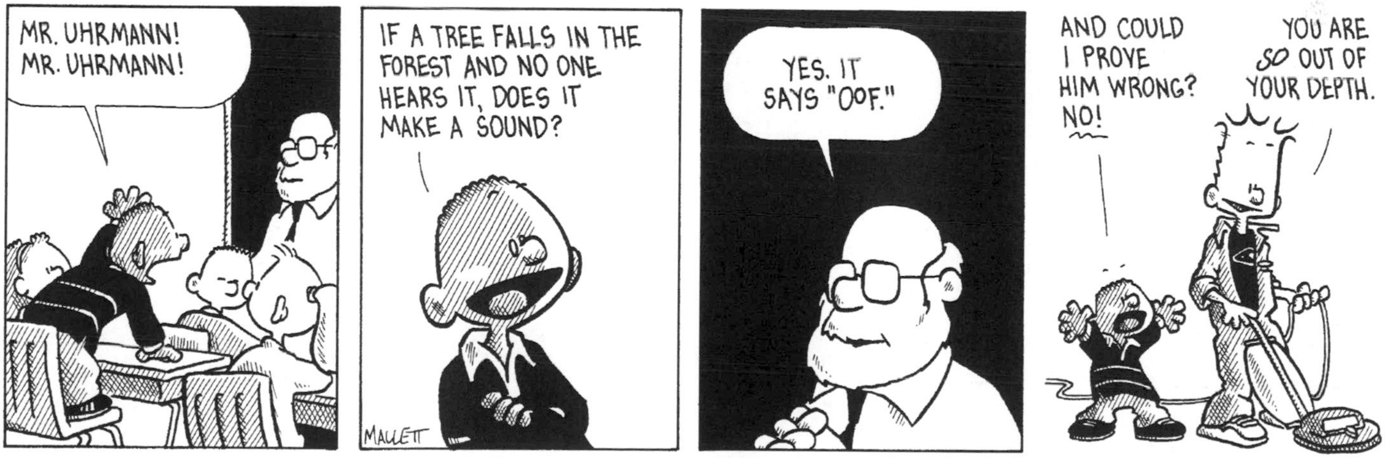
MR. UHRMANN! MR. UHRMANN!
MALLETT
IF A TREE FALLS IN THE FOREST AND NO ONE HEARS IT, DOES IT MAKE A SOUND?
YES. IT SAYS "OOF."
AND COULD I PROVE HIM WRONG? NO!
YOU ARE *SO* OUT OF YOUR DEPTH.

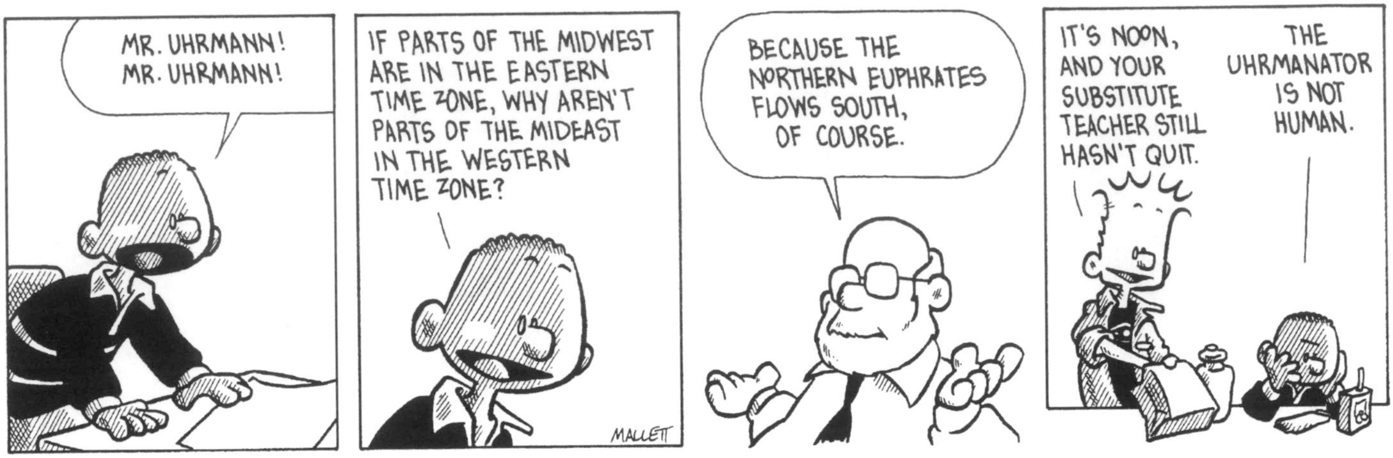
MR. UHRMANN! MR. UHRMANN!
IF PARTS OF THE MIDWEST ARE IN THE EASTERN TIME ZONE, WHY AREN'T PARTS OF THE MIDEAST IN THE WESTERN TIME ZONE?
MALLETT
BECAUSE THE NORTHERN EUPHRATES FLOWS SOUTH, OF COURSE.
IT'S NOON, AND YOUR SUBSTITUTE TEACHER STILL HASN'T QUIT.
THE UHRMANATOR IS NOT HUMAN.

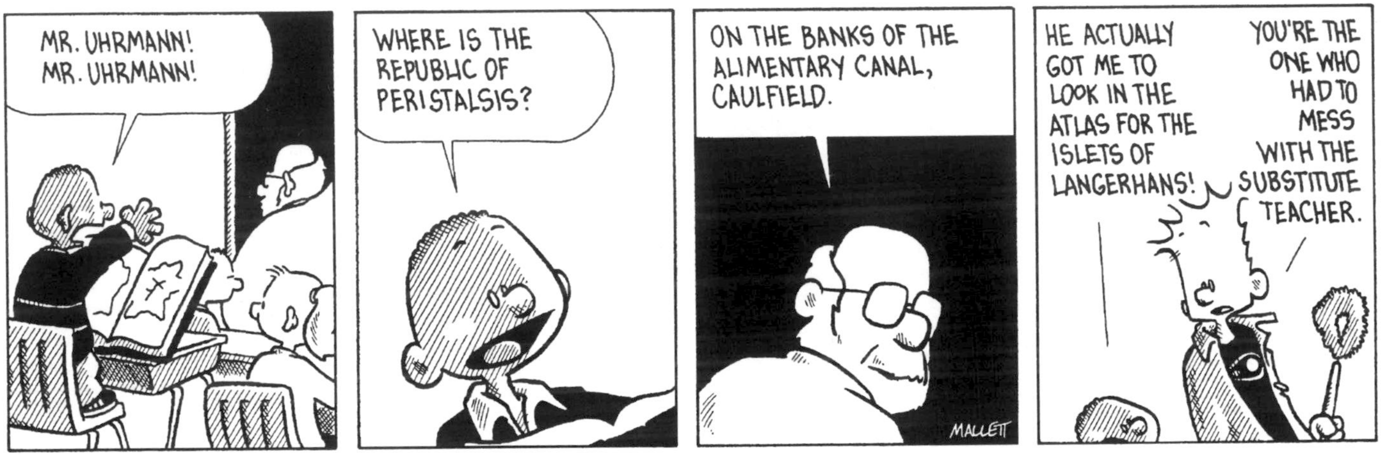
MR. UHRMANN! MR. UHRMANN!
WHERE IS THE REPUBLIC OF PERISTALSIS?
ON THE BANKS OF THE ALIMENTARY CANAL, CAULFIELD.
MALLETT
HE ACTUALLY GOT ME TO LOOK IN THE ATLAS FOR THE ISLETS OF LANGERHANS!
YOU'RE THE ONE WHO HAD TO MESS WITH THE SUBSTITUTE TEACHER.

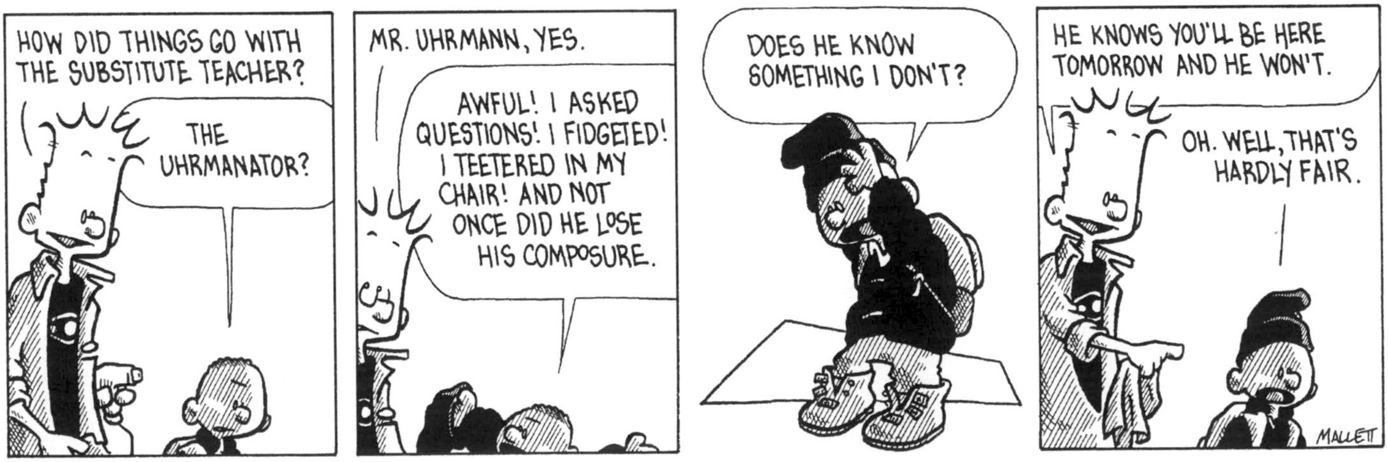
HOW DID THINGS GO WITH THE SUBSTITUTE TEACHER?
THE UHRMANATOR?
MR. UHRMANN, YES.
AWFUL! I ASKED QUESTIONS! I FIDGETED! I TEETERED IN MY CHAIR! AND NOT ONCE DID HE LOSE HIS COMPOSURE.
DOES HE KNOW SOMETHING I DON'T?
HE KNOWS YOU'LL BE HERE TOMORROW AND HE WON'T.
OH. WELL, THAT'S HARDLY FAIR.
MALLETT

Frazz
by JEF MALLETT
Spelling test tommorow.
I WONDER IF THIS IS A GOOD SIGN OR A BAD SIGN.

NICE MURAL.
THIS BABY'S GOING TO GET SCHOOL CANCELED TOMORROW!
WE'LL DRAW SIX BIG PANELS OF WINTER-STORM CARNAGE...
SPLICE THEM TOGETHER ONTO A GIANT SHEET OF PARTICLE BOARD...
MALLETT
MARCH THE WHOLE THING ACROSS TOWN...
AND HOLD IT UP IN FRONT OF MR. SPAETZLE'S BEDROOM WINDOW!
AT FIVE IN THE MORNING.
WHO KNEW AVOIDING WORK COULD BE SO MUCH WORK?
MY DAD SAYS HALF THE PhD CANDIDATES AT STATE.

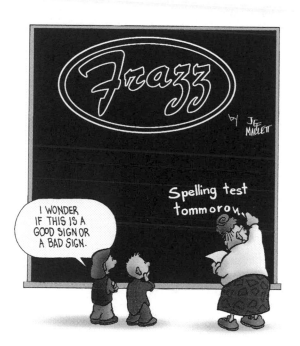

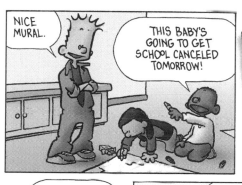

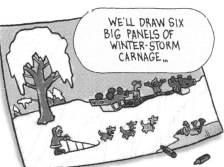

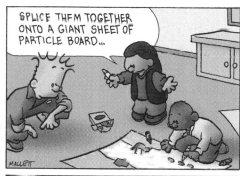

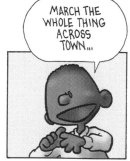

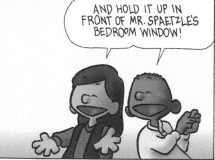

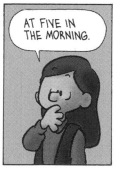

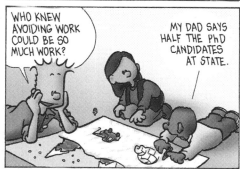

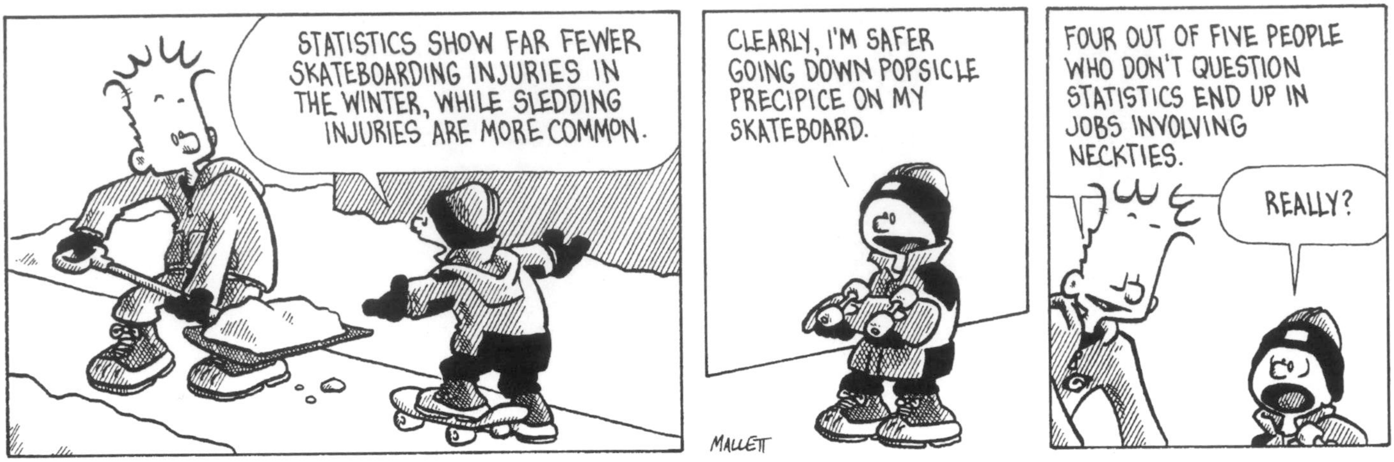
STATISTICS SHOW FAR FEWER SKATEBOARDING INJURIES IN THE WINTER, WHILE SLEDDING INJURIES ARE MORE COMMON.
CLEARLY, I'M SAFER GOING DOWN POPSICLE PRECIPICE ON MY SKATEBOARD.
MALLETT
FOUR OUT OF FIVE PEOPLE WHO DON'T QUESTION STATISTICS END UP IN JOBS INVOLVING NECKTIES.
REALLY?

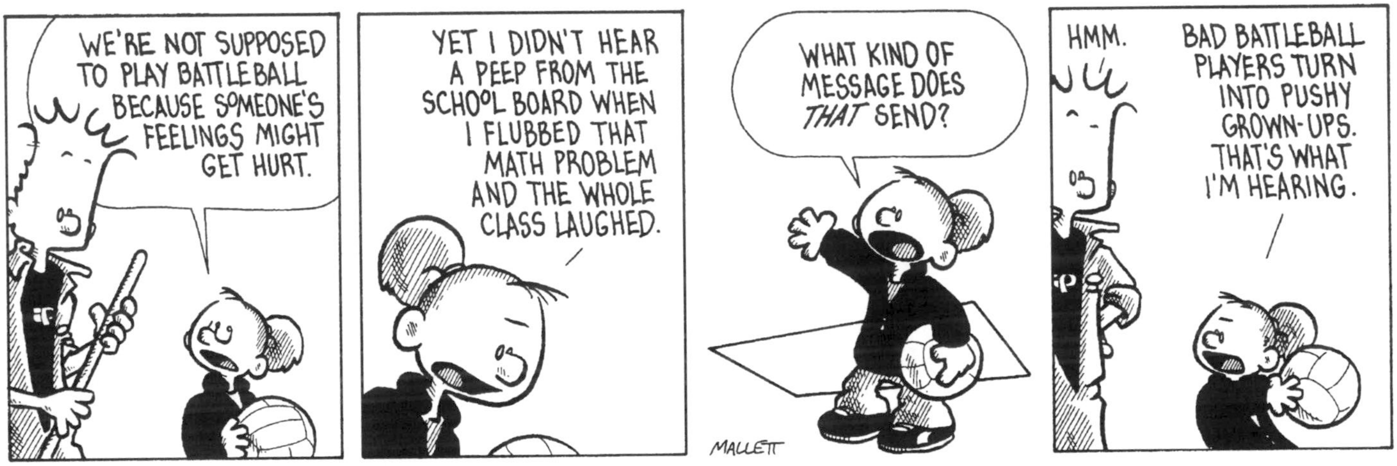
WE'RE NOT SUPPOSED TO PLAY BATTLEBALL BECAUSE SOMEONE'S FEELINGS MIGHT GET HURT.
YET I DIDN'T HEAR A PEEP FROM THE SCHOOL BOARD WHEN I FLUBBED THAT MATH PROBLEM AND THE WHOLE CLASS LAUGHED.
WHAT KIND OF MESSAGE DOES *THAT* SEND?
MALLETT
HMM.
BAD BATTLEBALL PLAYERS TURN INTO PUSHY GROWN-UPS. THAT'S WHAT I'M HEARING.

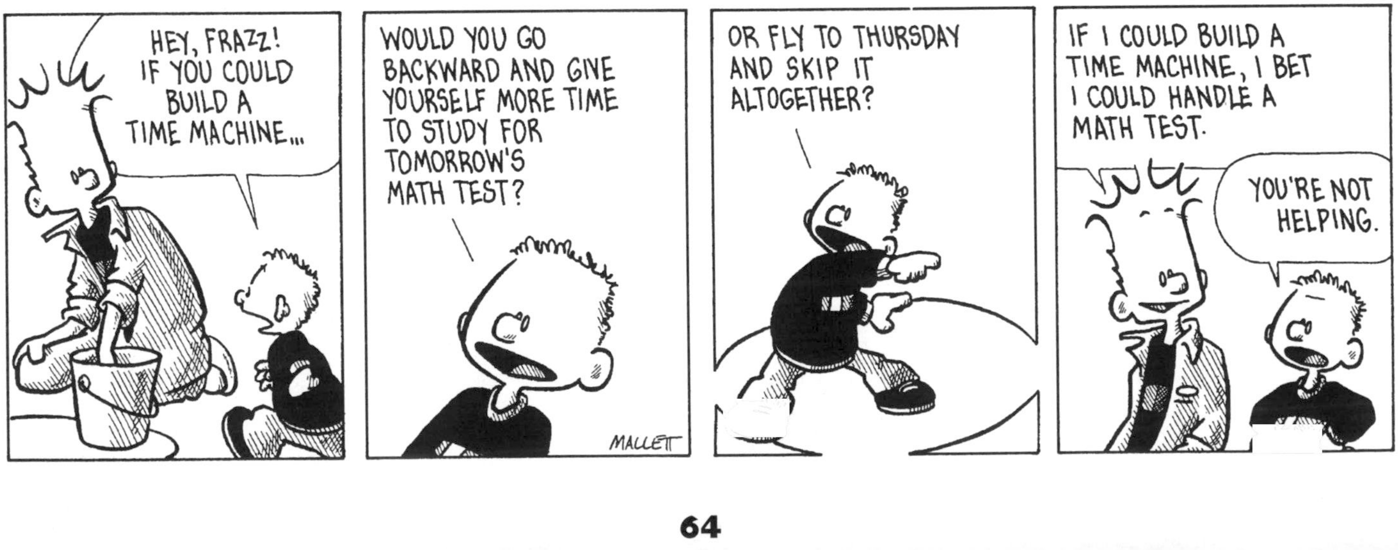
HEY, FRAZZ! IF YOU COULD BUILD A TIME MACHINE...
WOULD YOU GO BACKWARD AND GIVE YOURSELF MORE TIME TO STUDY FOR TOMORROW'S MATH TEST?
MALLETT
OR FLY TO THURSDAY AND SKIP IT ALTOGETHER?
IF I COULD BUILD A TIME MACHINE, I BET I COULD HANDLE A MATH TEST.
YOU'RE NOT HELPING.

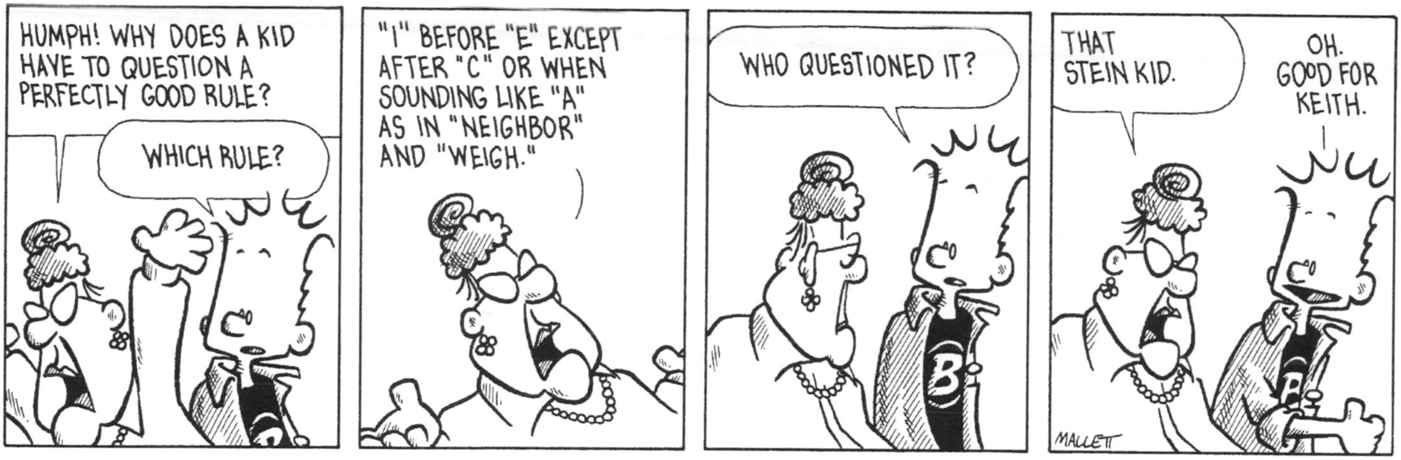
HUMPH! WHY DOES A KID HAVE TO QUESTION A PERFECTLY GOOD RULE?
WHICH RULE?
"I" BEFORE "E" EXCEPT AFTER "C" OR WHEN SOUNDING LIKE "A" AS IN "NEIGHBOR" AND "WEIGH."
WHO QUESTIONED IT?
THAT STEIN KID.
OH. GOOD FOR KEITH.
MALLETT

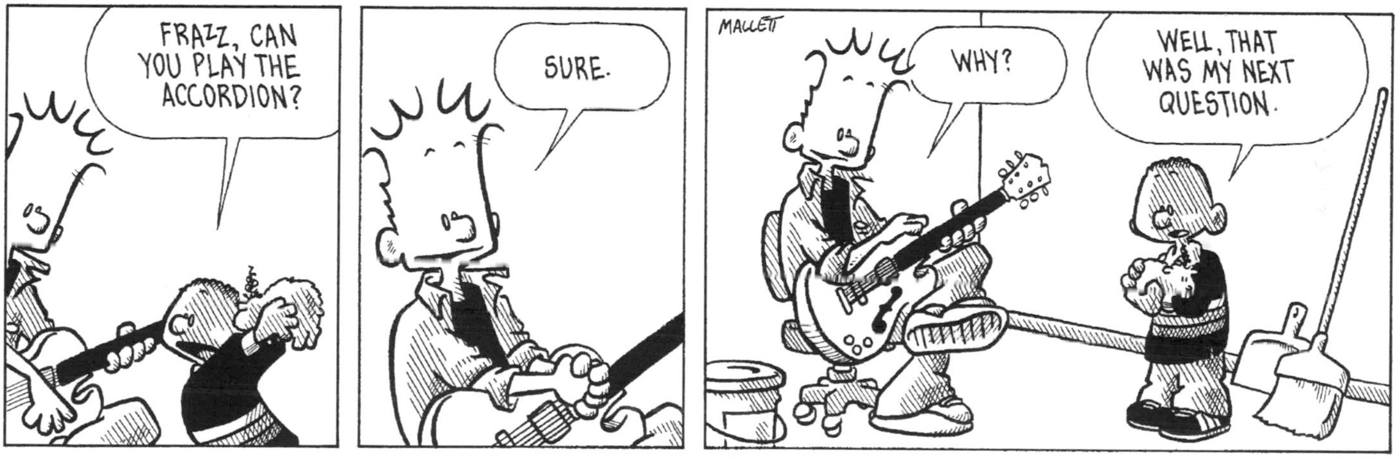
FRAZZ, CAN YOU PLAY THE ACCORDION?
SURE.
MALLETT
WHY?
WELL, THAT WAS MY NEXT QUESTION.

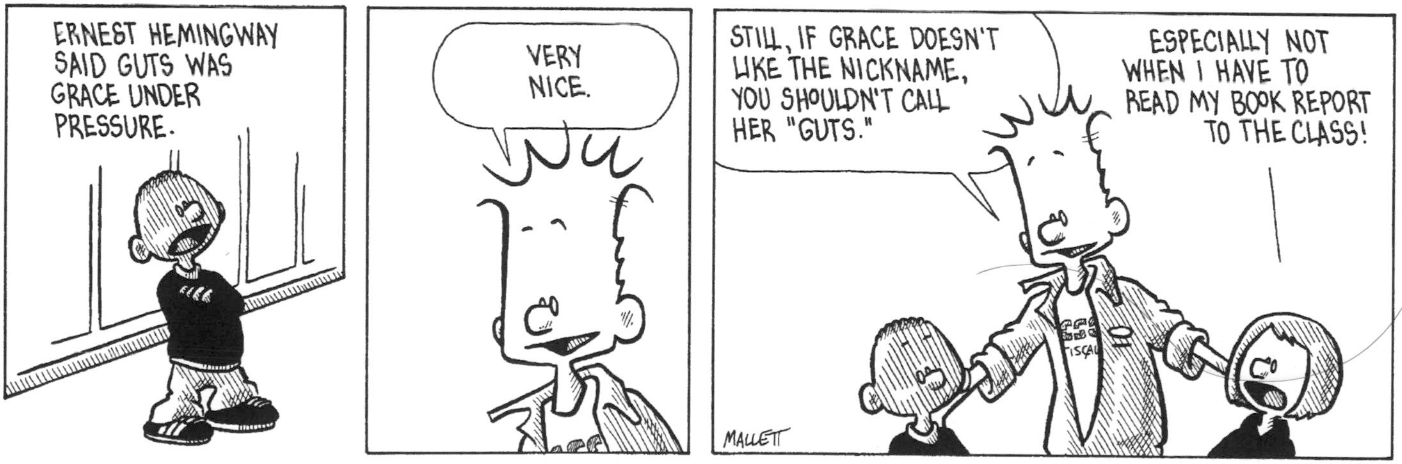
ERNEST HEMINGWAY SAID GUTS WAS GRACE UNDER PRESSURE.
VERY NICE.
STILL, IF GRACE DOESN'T LIKE THE NICKNAME, YOU SHOULDN'T CALL HER "GUTS."
ESPECIALLY NOT WHEN I HAVE TO READ MY BOOK REPORT TO THE CLASS!
MALLETT

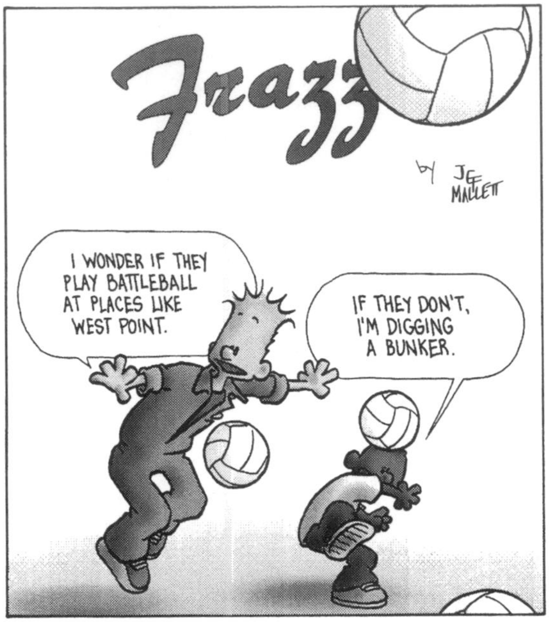
Frazz
by JEF MALLETT
I WONDER IF THEY PLAY BATTLEBALL AT PLACES LIKE WEST POINT.
IF THEY DON'T, I'M DIGGING A BUNKER.

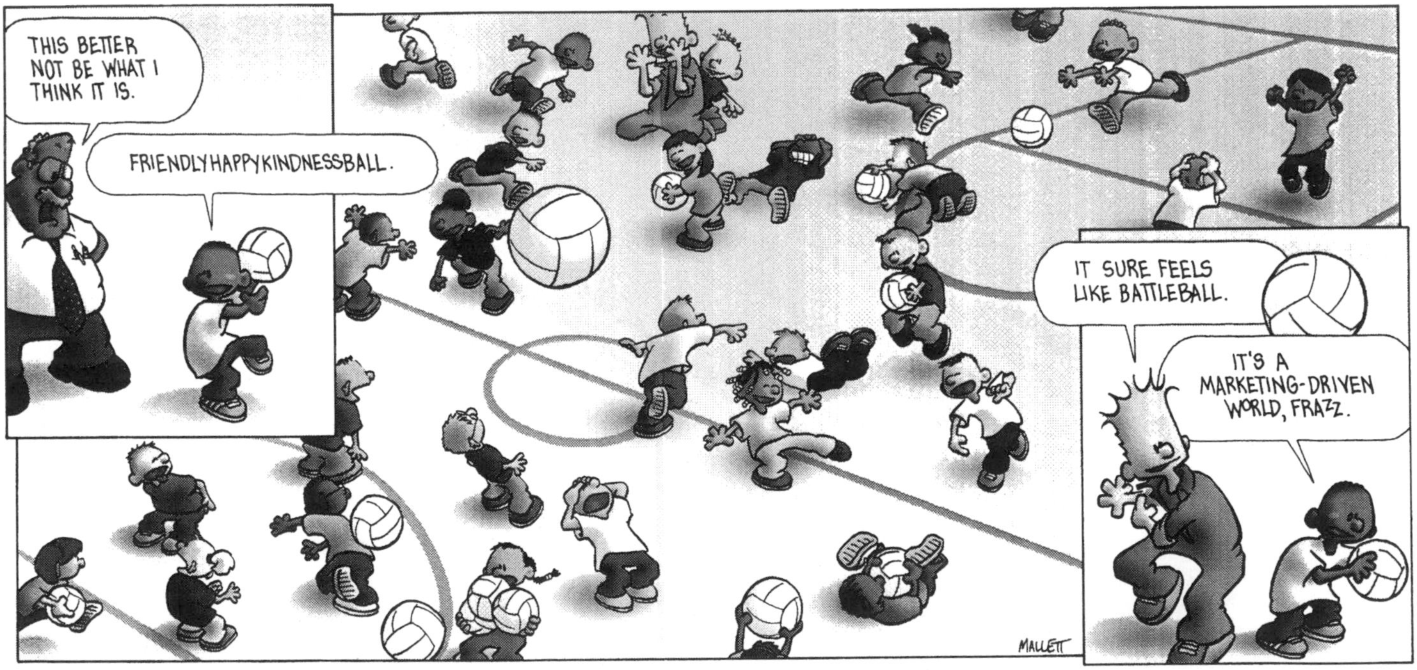
THIS BETTER NOT BE WHAT I THINK IT IS.
FRIENDLYHAPPYKINDNESSBALL.
IT SURE FEELS LIKE BATTLEBALL.
IT'S A MARKETING-DRIVEN WORLD, FRAZZ.
MALLETT

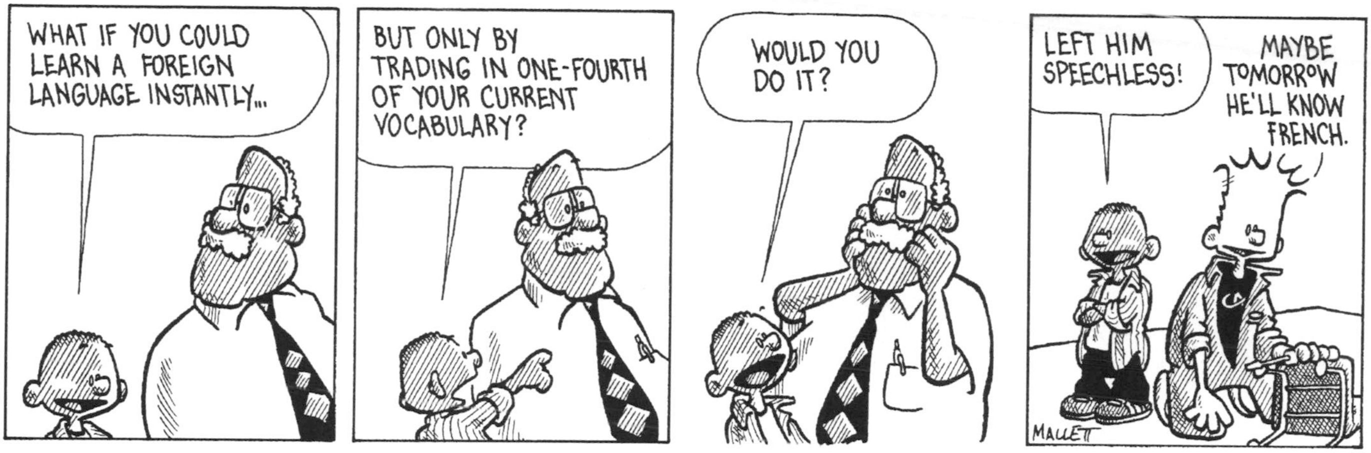
WHAT IF YOU COULD LEARN A FOREIGN LANGUAGE INSTANTLY...
BUT ONLY BY TRADING IN ONE-FOURTH OF YOUR CURRENT VOCABULARY?
WOULD YOU DO IT?
LEFT HIM SPEECHLESS!
MAYBE TOMORROW HE'LL KNOW FRENCH.
MALLETT

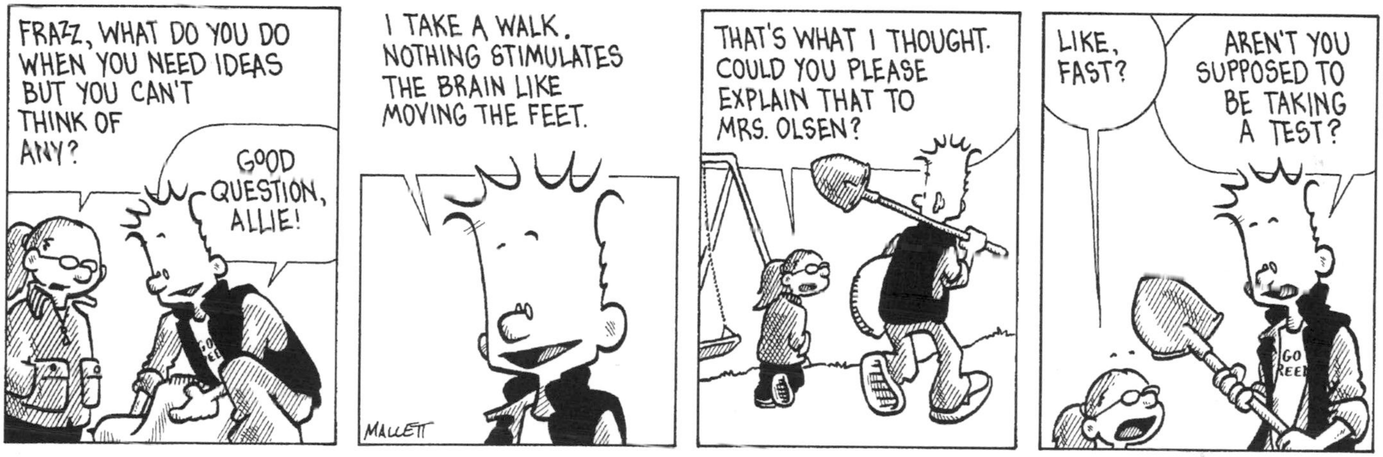
FRAZZ, WHAT DO YOU DO WHEN YOU NEED IDEAS BUT YOU CAN'T THINK OF ANY?
GOOD QUESTION, ALLIE!
I TAKE A WALK. NOTHING STIMULATES THE BRAIN LIKE MOVING THE FEET.
MALLETT
THAT'S WHAT I THOUGHT. COULD YOU PLEASE EXPLAIN THAT TO MRS. OLSEN?
AREN'T YOU SUPPOSED TO BE TAKING A TEST?
LIKE, FAST?

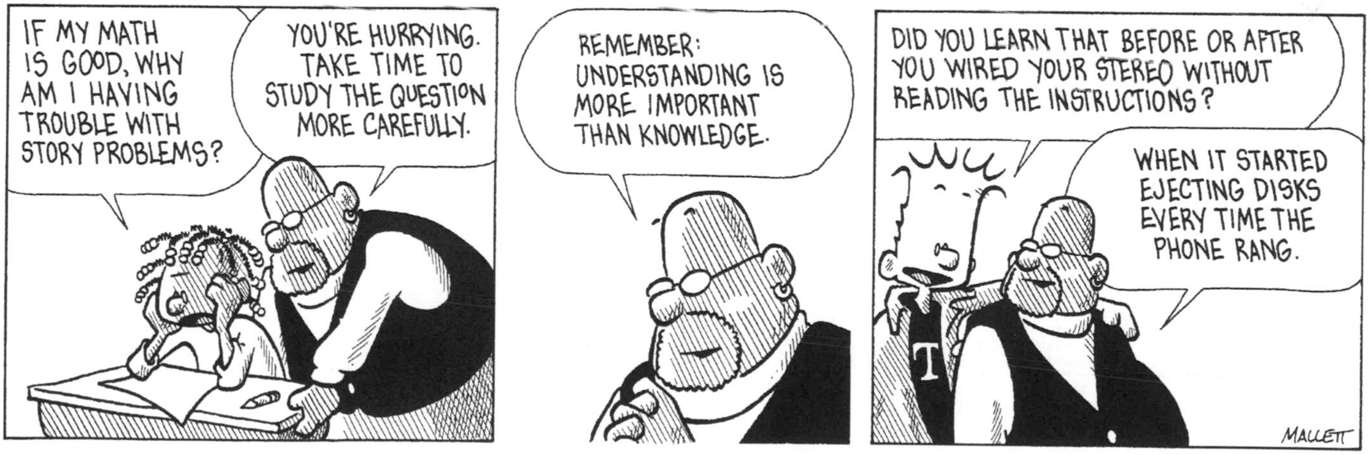
IF MY MATH IS GOOD, WHY AM I HAVING TROUBLE WITH STORY PROBLEMS?
YOU'RE HURRYING. TAKE TIME TO STUDY THE QUESTION MORE CAREFULLY.
REMEMBER: UNDERSTANDING IS MORE IMPORTANT THAN KNOWLEDGE.
DID YOU LEARN THAT BEFORE OR AFTER YOU WIRED YOUR STEREO WITHOUT READING THE INSTRUCTIONS?
WHEN IT STARTED EJECTING DISKS EVERY TIME THE PHONE RANG.
MALLETT

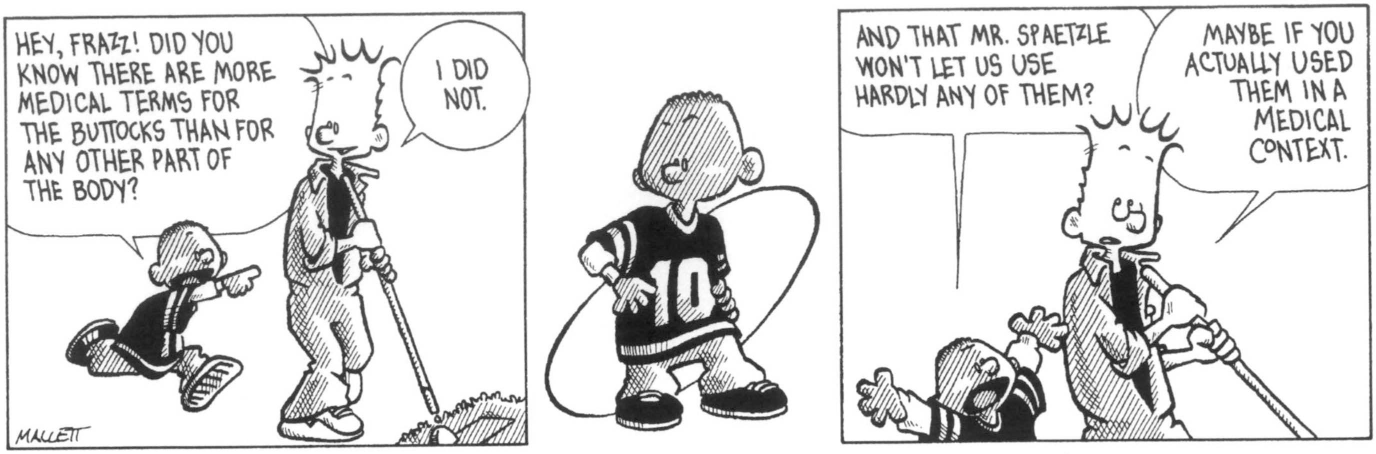
HEY, FRAZZ! DID YOU KNOW THERE ARE MORE MEDICAL TERMS FOR THE BUTTOCKS THAN FOR ANY OTHER PART OF THE BODY?
I DID NOT.
MALLETT
10
AND THAT MR. SPAETZLE WON'T LET US USE HARDLY ANY OF THEM?
MAYBE IF YOU ACTUALLY USED THEM IN A MEDICAL CONTEXT.

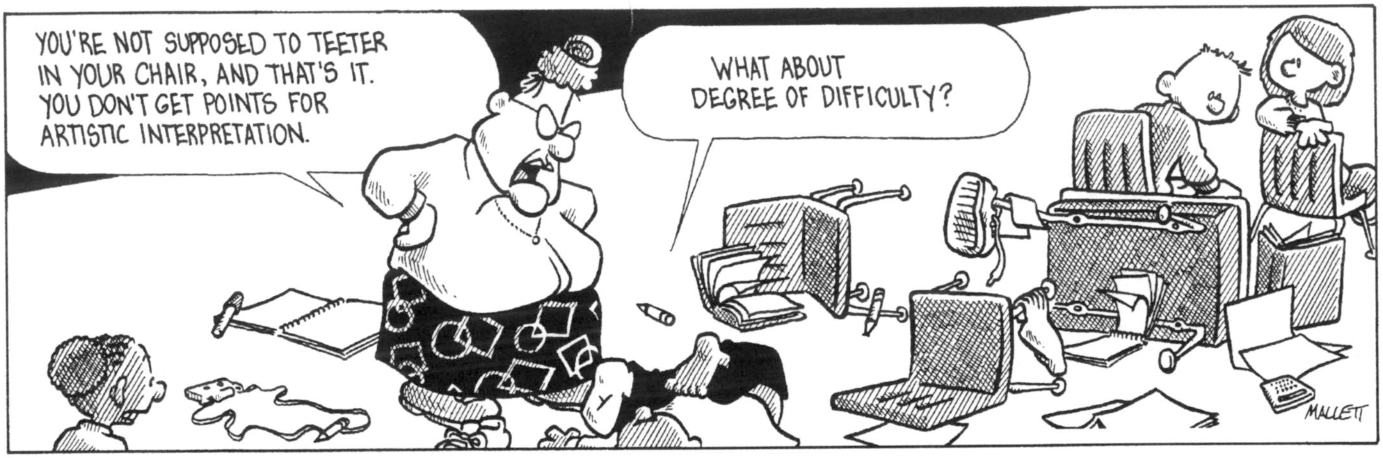
YOU'RE NOT SUPPOSED TO TEETER IN YOUR CHAIR, AND THAT'S IT. YOU DON'T GET POINTS FOR ARTISTIC INTERPRETATION.
WHAT ABOUT DEGREE OF DIFFICULTY?
MALLETT

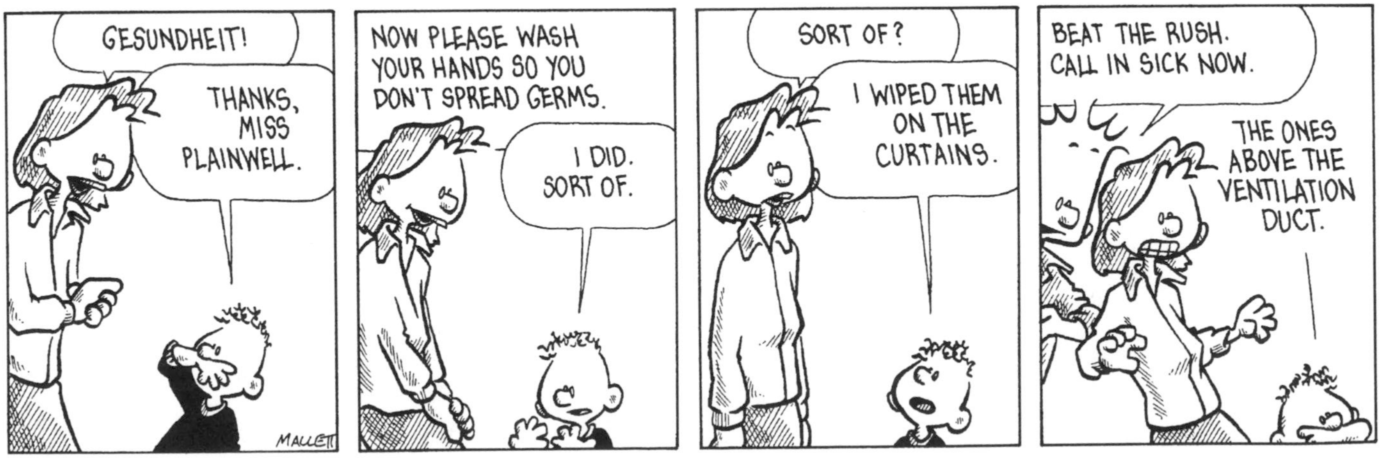
GESUNDHEIT!
THANKS, MISS PLAINWELL.
MALLETT
NOW PLEASE WASH YOUR HANDS SO YOU DON'T SPREAD GERMS.
I DID. SORT OF.
SORT OF?
I WIPED THEM ON THE CURTAINS.
BEAT THE RUSH. CALL IN SICK NOW.
THE ONES ABOVE THE VENTILATION DUCT.

Frazz
by JEF MALLETT
SOME SCHOOLS HAVE BELLS. BRYSON ELEMENTARY HAS A FOGHORN.

CAULFIELD! RECESS IS OVER!
YOU'RE SUPPOSED TO BE INSIDE DOING YOUR SOCIAL STUDIES WORKSHEET.
MRS. OLSEN.
WHEN I'M DONE WITH HIGH SCHOOL, DONE WITH COLLEGE AND HALFWAY UP THE LADDER IN CUBICLE WORLD SOMEWHERE, WHAT WILL I WISH I REMEMBERED?
A FLEETING GRASP OF EPHEMERAL SOUTHWEST ASIAN BORDERS?
OR THE FIRST NICE MARCH DAY OF MY THIRD-GRADE YEAR?
ALL THE SAME, SOCIAL STUDIES ARE IMPORTANT.
PSYCHOLOGY IS SOCIAL STUDIES.
MALLETT

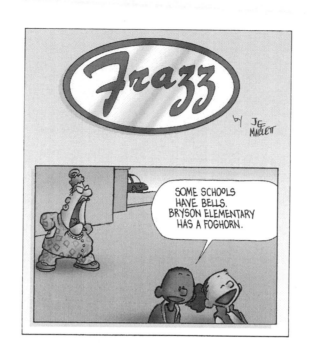

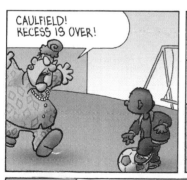

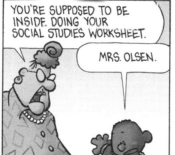

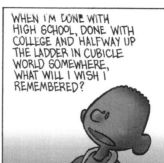

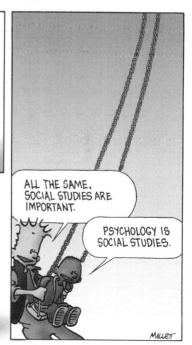

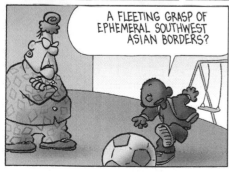

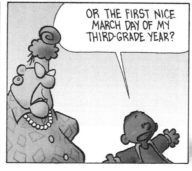

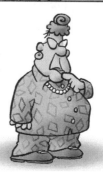

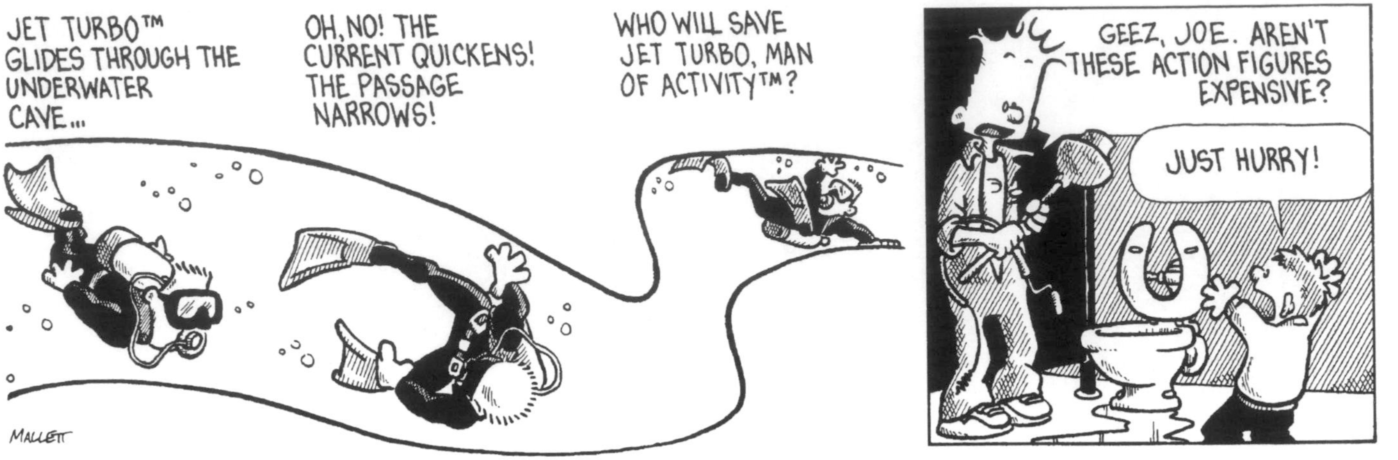
JET TURBO™ GLIDES THROUGH THE UNDERWATER CAVE...
OH, NO! THE CURRENT QUICKENS! THE PASSAGE NARROWS!
WHO WILL SAVE JET TURBO, MAN OF ACTIVITY™?
GEEZ, JOE. AREN'T THESE ACTION FIGURES EXPENSIVE?
JUST HURRY!
MALLETT

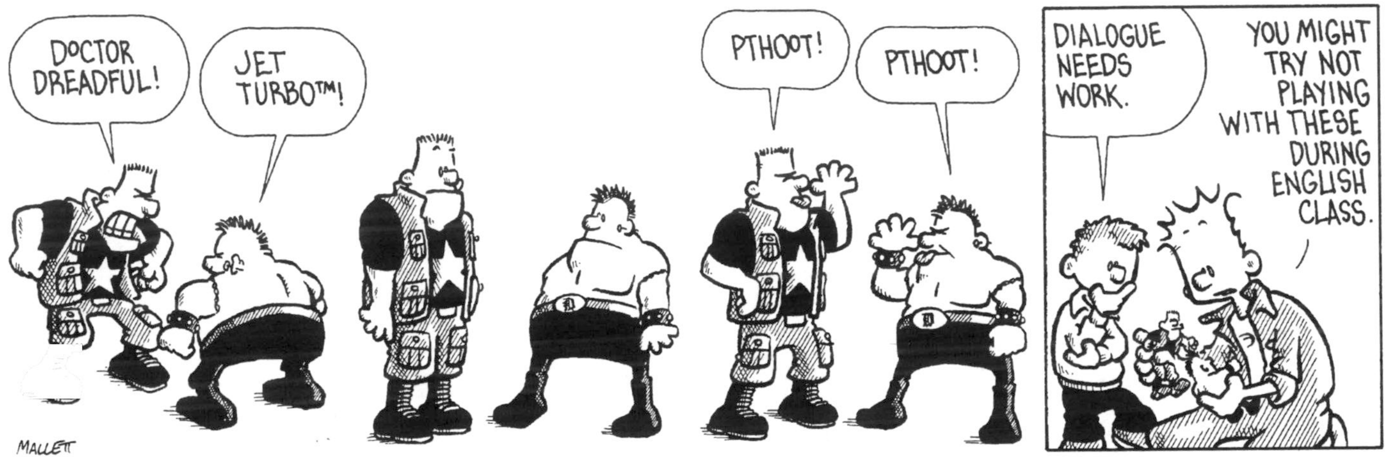
DOCTOR DREADFUL!
JET TURBO™!
PTHOOT!
PTHOOT!
DIALOGUE NEEDS WORK.
YOU MIGHT TRY NOT PLAYING WITH THESE DURING ENGLISH CLASS.
MALLETT

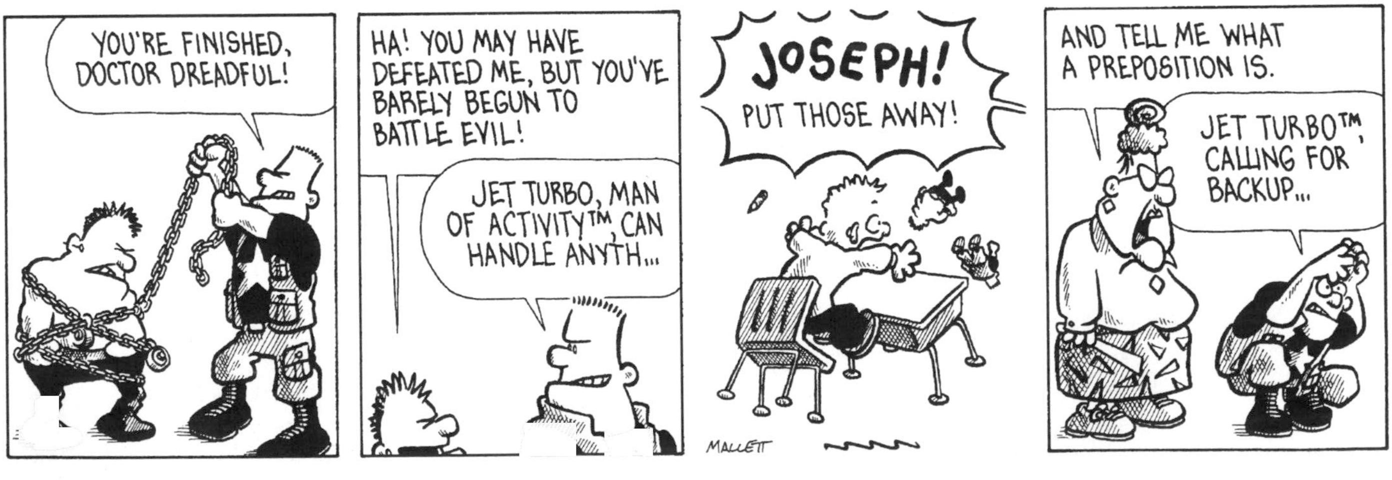
YOU'RE FINISHED, DOCTOR DREADFUL!
HA! YOU MAY HAVE DEFEATED ME, BUT YOU'VE BARELY BEGUN TO BATTLE EVIL!
JET TURBO, MAN OF ACTIVITY™, CAN HANDLE ANYTH...
JOSEPH!
PUT THOSE AWAY!
AND TELL ME WHAT A PREPOSITION IS.
JET TURBO™, CALLING FOR BACKUP...
MALLETT

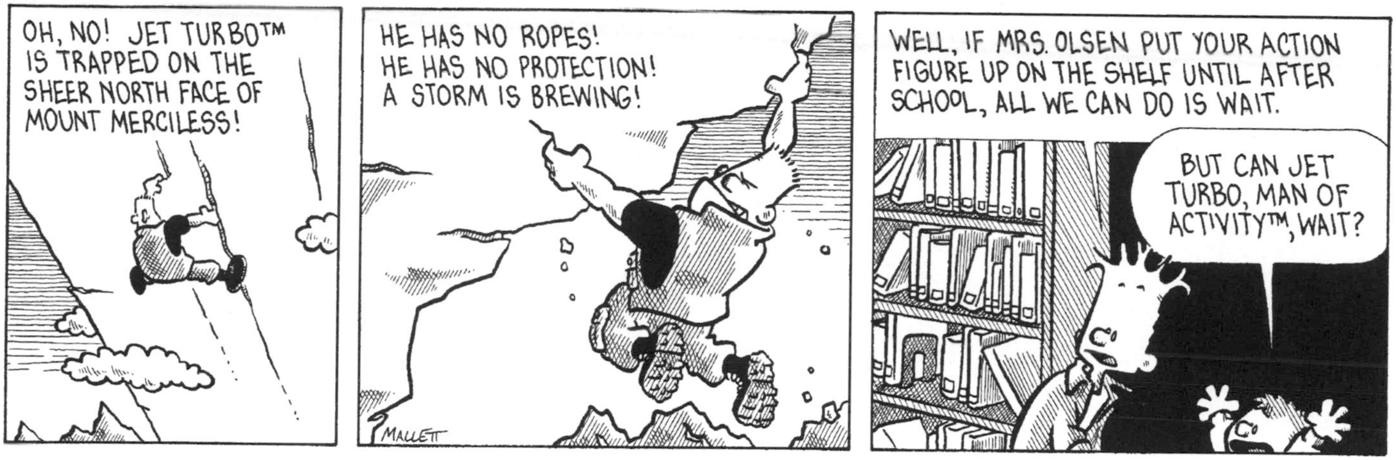
OH, NO! JET TURBO™ IS TRAPPED ON THE SHEER NORTH FACE OF MOUNT MERCILESS!
HE HAS NO ROPES! HE HAS NO PROTECTION! A STORM IS BREWING!
MALLETT
WELL, IF MRS. OLSEN PUT YOUR ACTION FIGURE UP ON THE SHELF UNTIL AFTER SCHOOL, ALL WE CAN DO IS WAIT.
BUT CAN JET TURBO, MAN OF ACTIVITY™, WAIT?

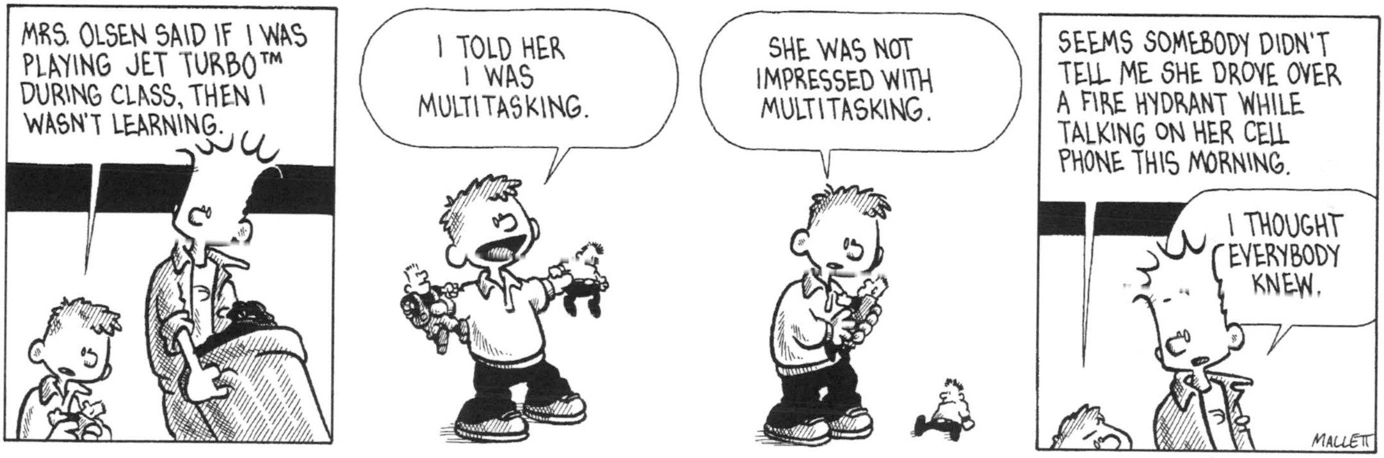
MRS. OLSEN SAID IF I WAS PLAYING JET TURBO™ DURING CLASS, THEN I WASN'T LEARNING.
I TOLD HER I WAS MULTITASKING.
SHE WAS NOT IMPRESSED WITH MULTITASKING.
SEEMS SOMEBODY DIDN'T TELL ME SHE DROVE OVER A FIRE HYDRANT WHILE TALKING ON HER CELL PHONE THIS MORNING.
I THOUGHT EVERYBODY KNEW.
MALLETT

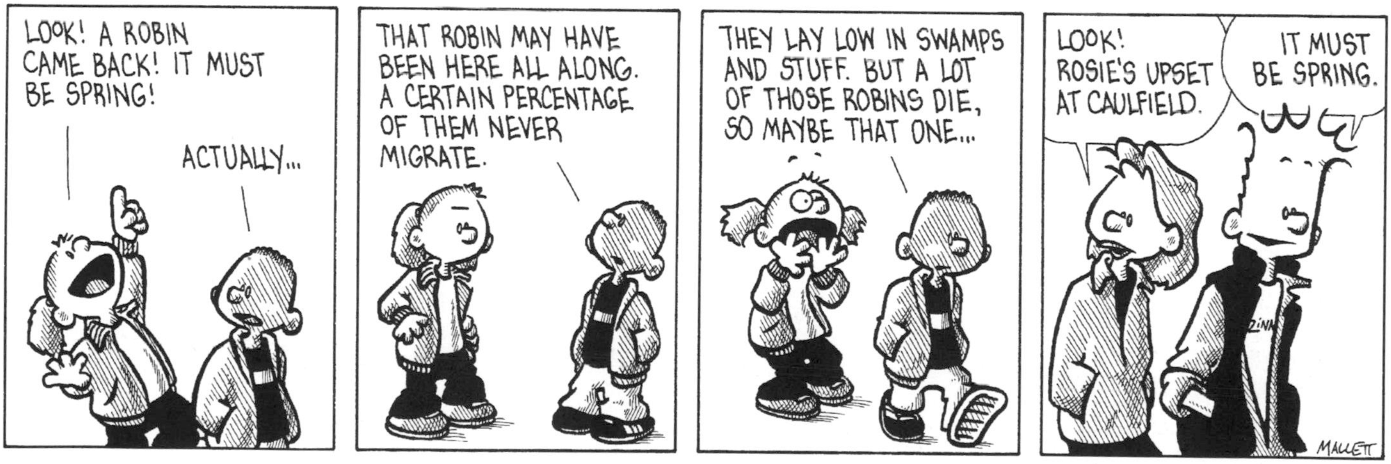
LOOK! A ROBIN CAME BACK! IT MUST BE SPRING!
ACTUALLY...
THAT ROBIN MAY HAVE BEEN HERE ALL ALONG. A CERTAIN PERCENTAGE OF THEM NEVER MIGRATE.
THEY LAY LOW IN SWAMPS AND STUFF. BUT A LOT OF THOSE ROBINS DIE, SO MAYBE THAT ONE...
LOOK! ROSIE'S UPSET AT CAULFIELD.
IT MUST BE SPRING.
MALLETT

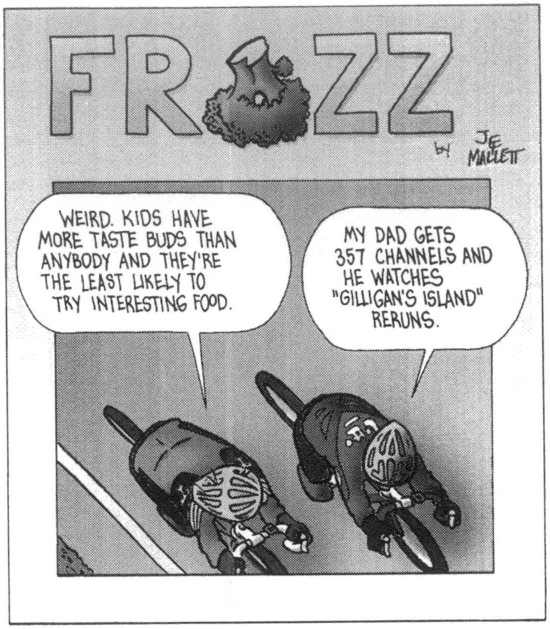
FROZZ
by JEF MALLETT
WEIRD. KIDS HAVE MORE TASTE BUDS THAN ANYBODY AND THEY'RE THE LEAST LIKELY TO TRY INTERESTING FOOD.
MY DAD GETS 357 CHANNELS AND HE WATCHES "GILLIGAN'S ISLAND" RERUNS.

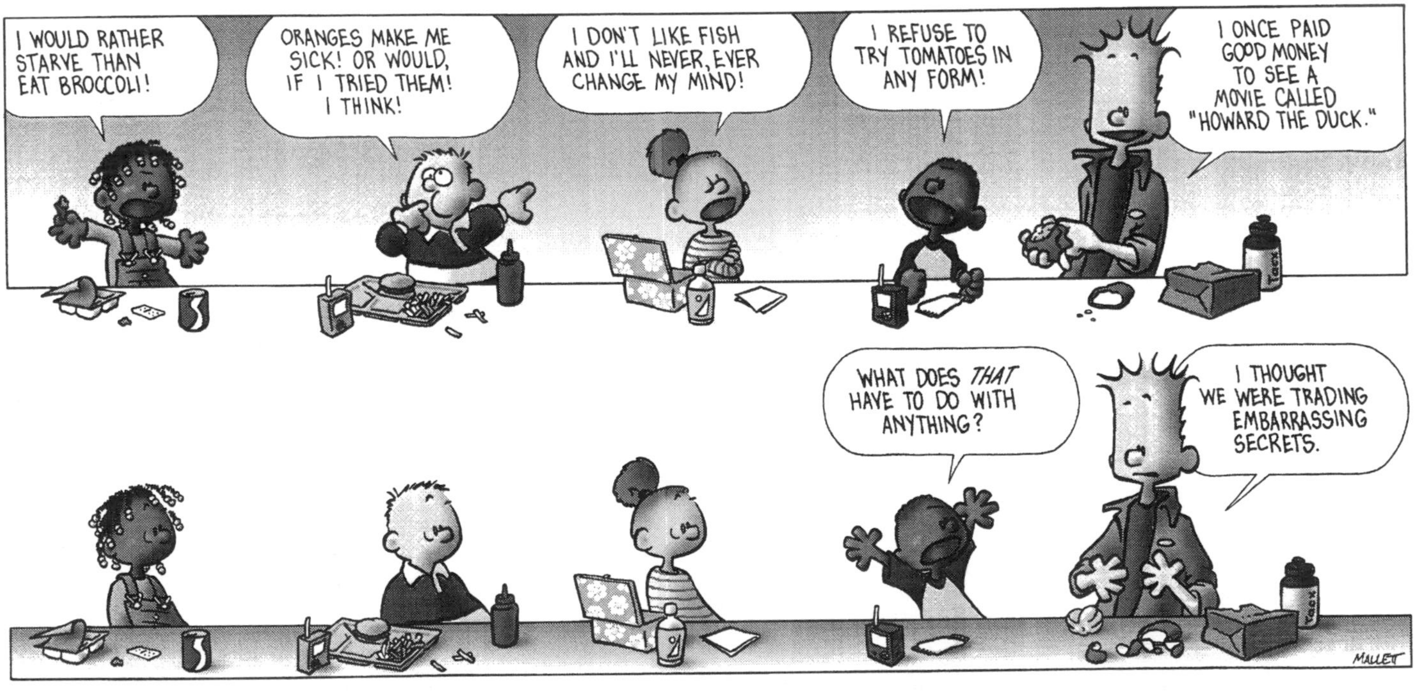
I WOULD RATHER STARVE THAN EAT BROCCOLI!
ORANGES MAKE ME SICK! OR WOULD, IF I TRIED THEM! I THINK!
I DON'T LIKE FISH AND I'LL NEVER, EVER CHANGE MY MIND!
I REFUSE TO TRY TOMATOES IN ANY FORM!
I ONCE PAID GOOD MONEY TO SEE A MOVIE CALLED "HOWARD THE DUCK."
WHAT DOES *THAT* HAVE TO DO WITH ANYTHING?
I THOUGHT WE WERE TRADING EMBARRASSING SECRETS.
MALLETT

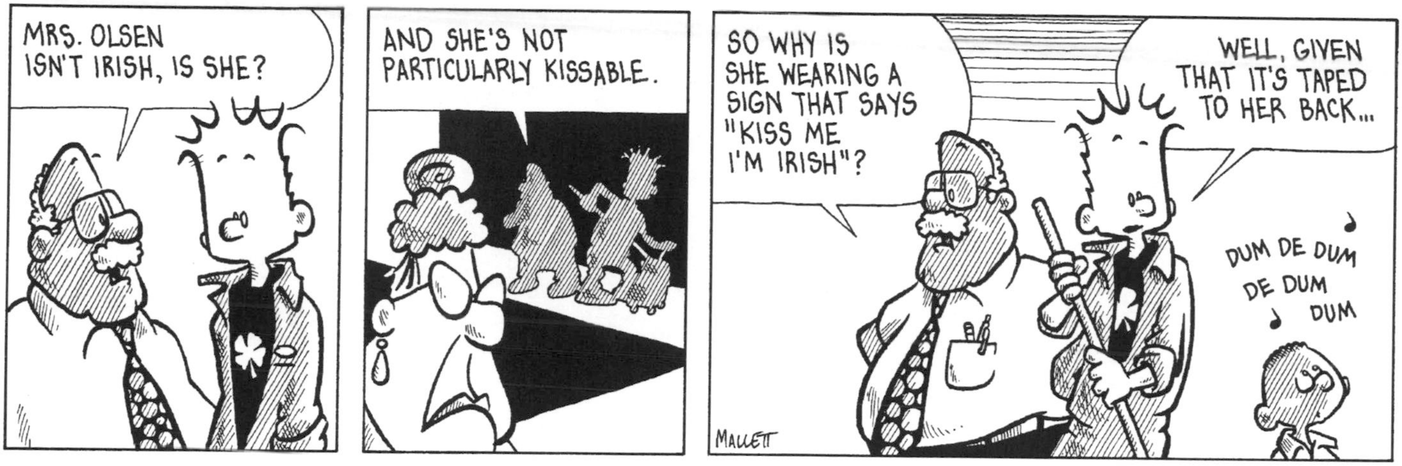
MRS. OLSEN ISN'T IRISH, IS SHE?
AND SHE'S NOT PARTICULARLY KISSABLE.
SO WHY IS SHE WEARING A SIGN THAT SAYS "KISS ME I'M IRISH"?
WELL, GIVEN THAT IT'S TAPED TO HER BACK...
DUM DE DUM DE DUM DUM
MALLETT

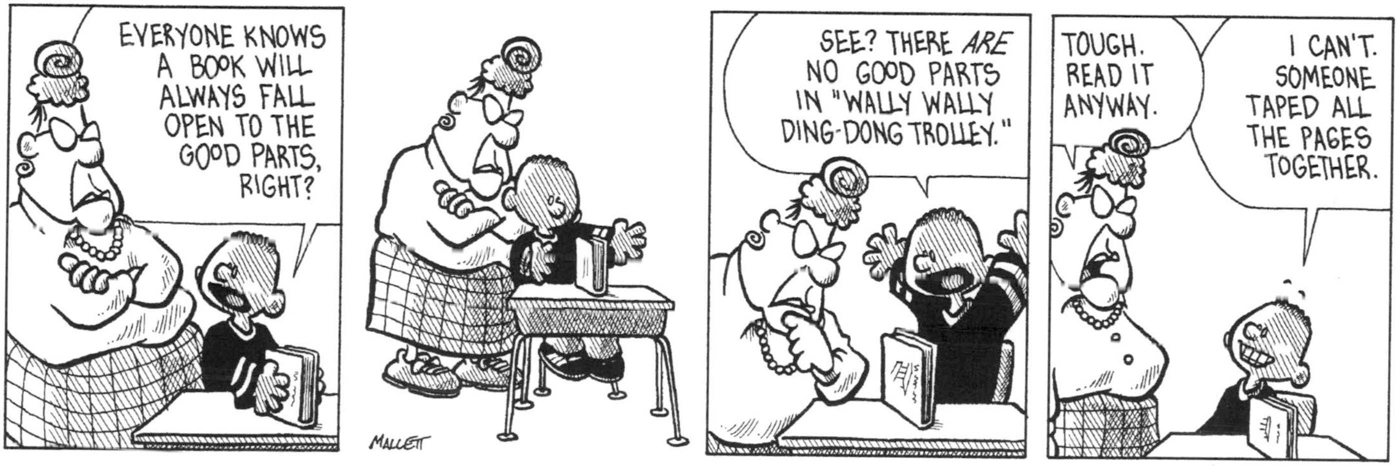
EVERYONE KNOWS A BOOK WILL ALWAYS FALL OPEN TO THE GOOD PARTS, RIGHT?
MALLETT
SEE? THERE *ARE* NO GOOD PARTS IN "WALLY WALLY DING-DONG TROLLEY."
TOUGH. READ IT ANYWAY.
I CAN'T. SOMEONE TAPED ALL THE PAGES TOGETHER.

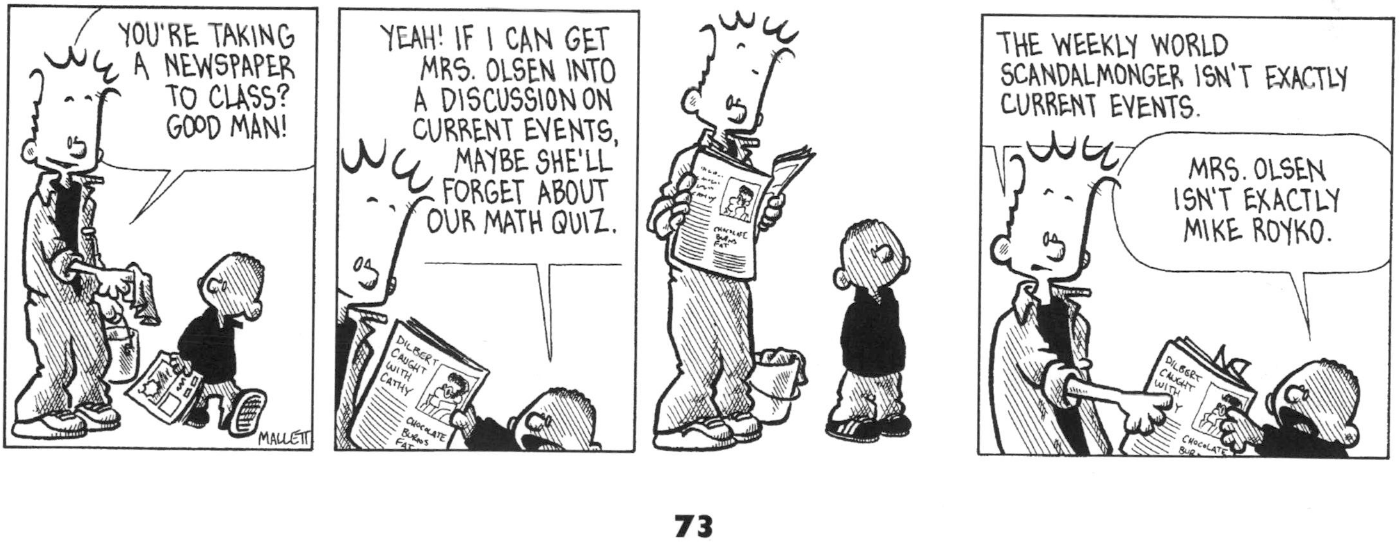
YOU'RE TAKING A NEWSPAPER TO CLASS? GOOD MAN!
MALLETT
YEAH! IF I CAN GET MRS. OLSEN INTO A DISCUSSION ON CURRENT EVENTS, MAYBE SHE'LL FORGET ABOUT OUR MATH QUIZ.
DILBERT CAUGHT WITH CATHY
CHOCOLATE BURNS FAT
THE WEEKLY WORLD SCANDALMONGER ISN'T EXACTLY CURRENT EVENTS.
MRS. OLSEN ISN'T EXACTLY MIKE ROYKO.

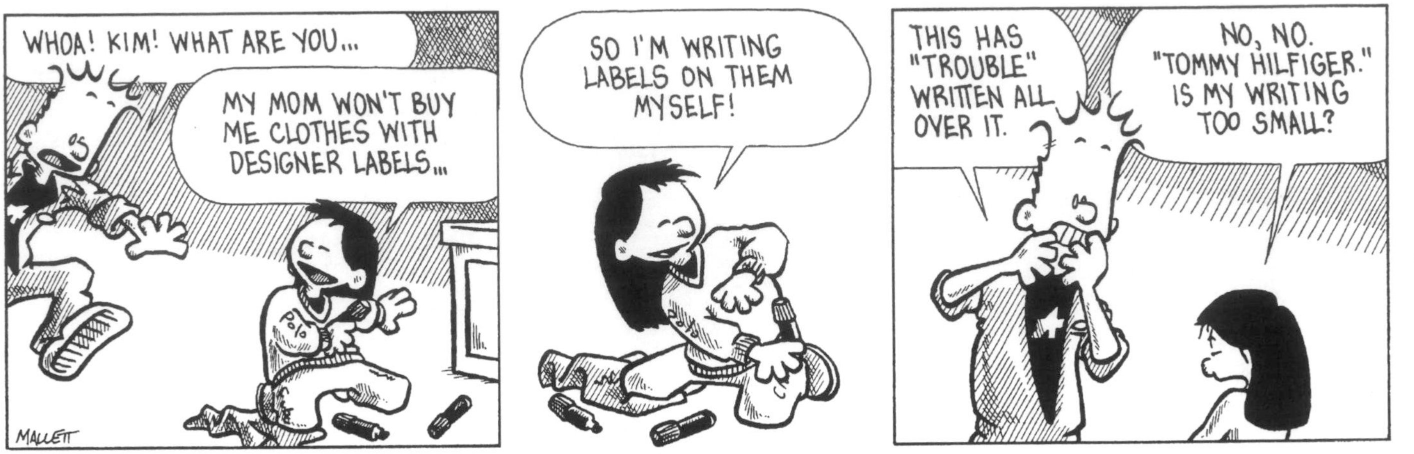
WHOA! KIM! WHAT ARE YOU...
MY MOM WON'T BUY ME CLOTHES WITH DESIGNER LABELS...
MALLETT
SO I'M WRITING LABELS ON THEM MYSELF!
THIS HAS "TROUBLE" WRITTEN ALL OVER IT.
NO, NO. "TOMMY HILFIGER." IS MY WRITING TOO SMALL?

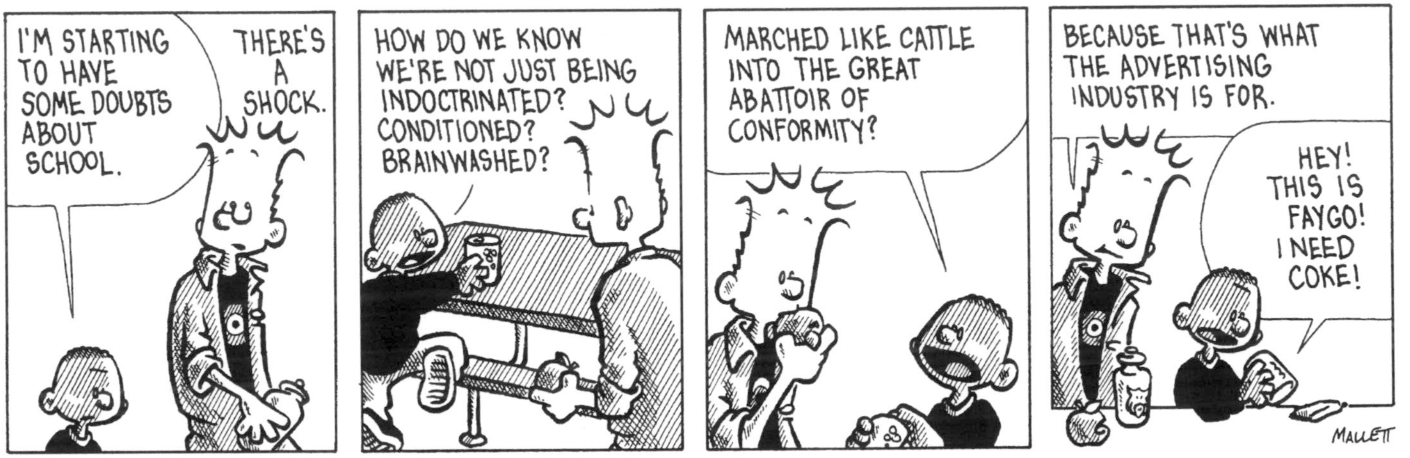
I'M STARTING TO HAVE SOME DOUBTS ABOUT SCHOOL.
THERE'S A SHOCK.
HOW DO WE KNOW WE'RE NOT JUST BEING INDOCTRINATED? CONDITIONED? BRAINWASHED?
MARCHED LIKE CATTLE INTO THE GREAT ABATTOIR OF CONFORMITY?
BECAUSE THAT'S WHAT THE ADVERTISING INDUSTRY IS FOR.
HEY! THIS IS FAYGO! I NEED COKE!
MALLETT

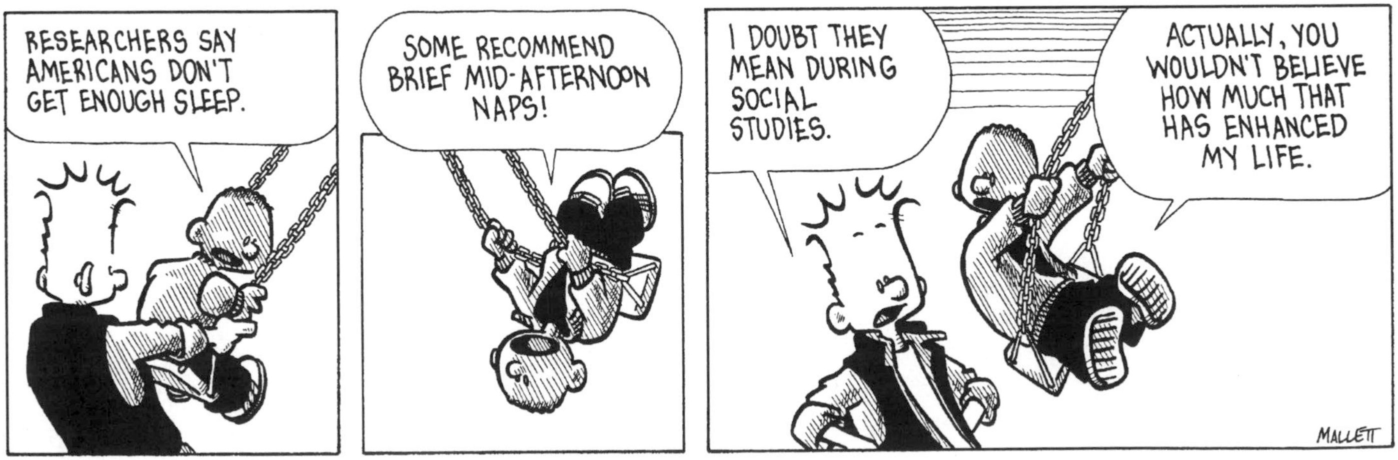
RESEARCHERS SAY AMERICANS DON'T GET ENOUGH SLEEP.
SOME RECOMMEND BRIEF MID-AFTERNOON NAPS!
I DOUBT THEY MEAN DURING SOCIAL STUDIES.
ACTUALLY, YOU WOULDN'T BELIEVE HOW MUCH THAT HAS ENHANCED MY LIFE.
MALLETT

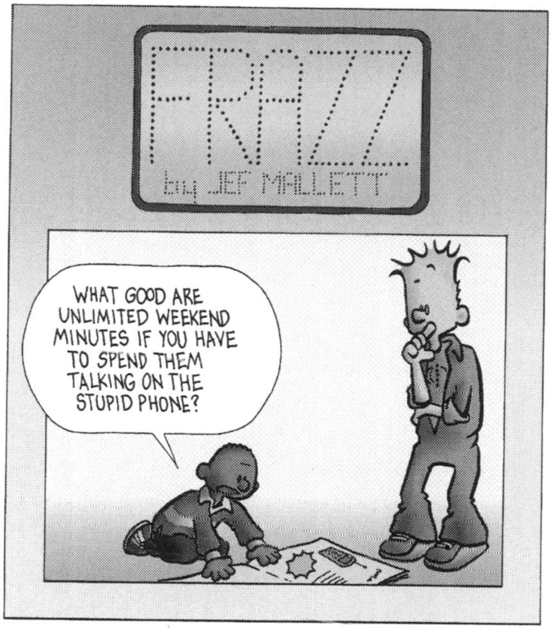
FRAZZ
by JEF MALLETT
WHAT GOOD ARE UNLIMITED WEEKEND MINUTES IF YOU HAVE TO SPEND THEM TALKING ON THE STUPID PHONE?

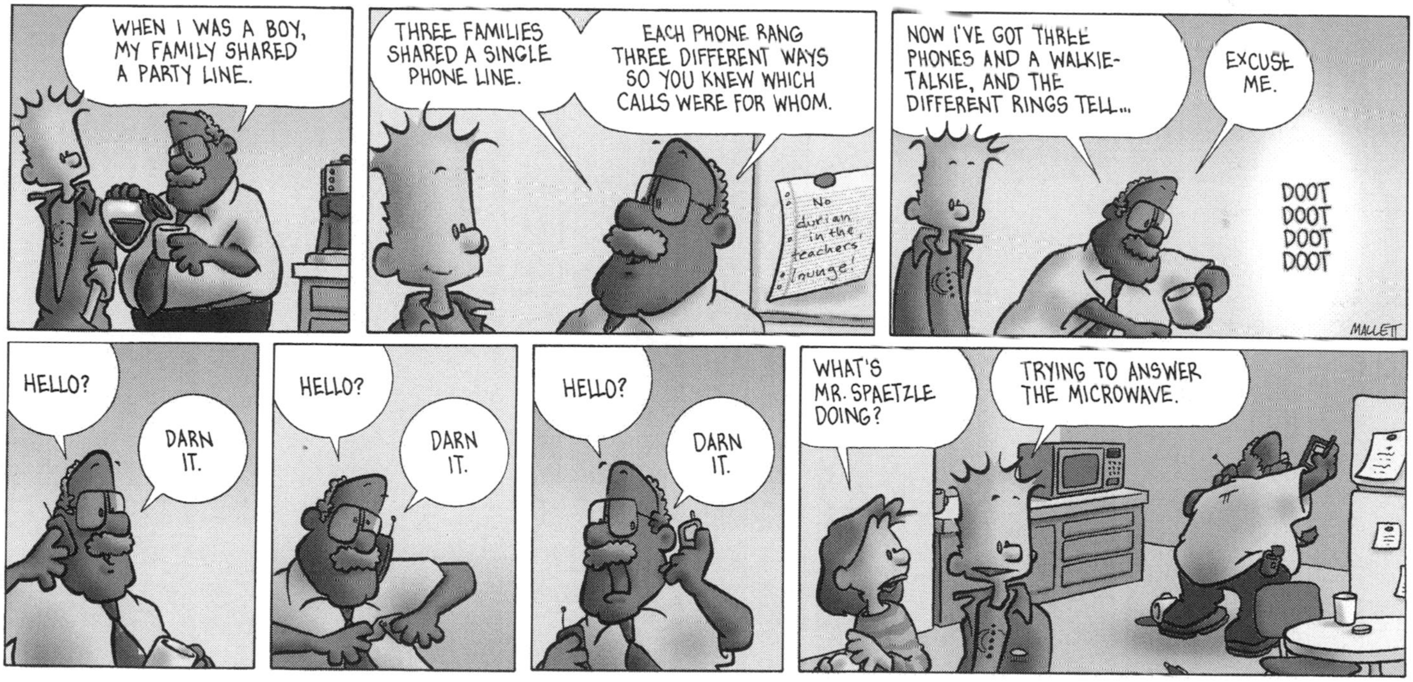
WHEN I WAS A BOY, MY FAMILY SHARED A PARTY LINE.
THREE FAMILIES SHARED A SINGLE PHONE LINE.
EACH PHONE RANG THREE DIFFERENT WAYS SO YOU KNEW WHICH CALLS WERE FOR WHOM.
No durian in the teachers' lounge!
NOW I'VE GOT THREE PHONES AND A WALKIE-TALKIE, AND THE DIFFERENT RINGS TELL...
EXCUSE ME.
DOOT DOOT DOOT DOOT
MALLETT
HELLO?
DARN IT.
HELLO?
DARN IT.
HELLO?
DARN IT.
WHAT'S MR. SPAETZLE DOING?
TRYING TO ANSWER THE MICROWAVE.

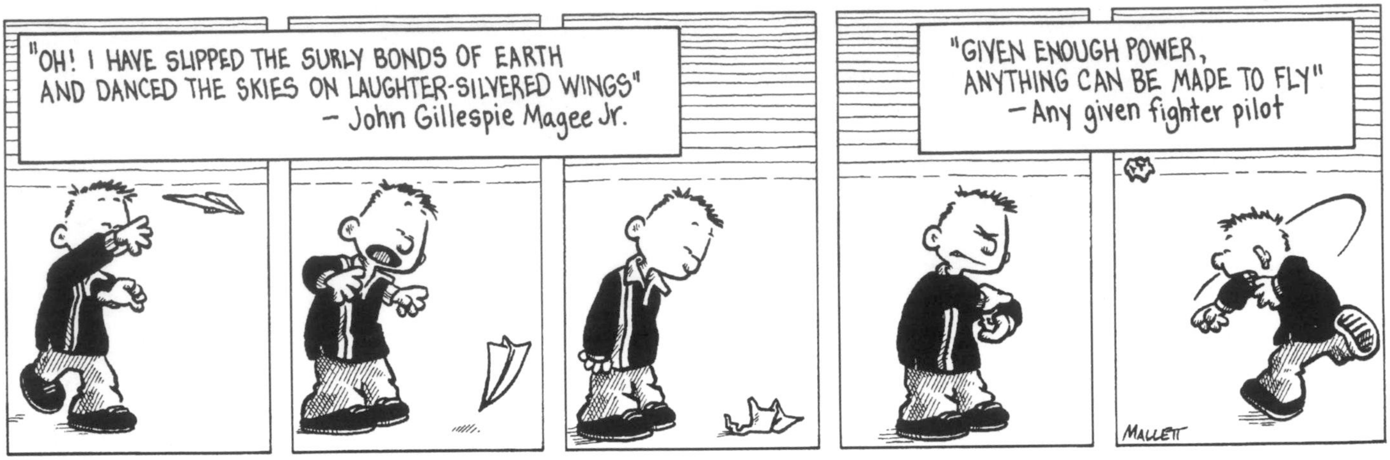
"OH! I HAVE SLIPPED THE SURLY BONDS OF EARTH AND DANCED THE SKIES ON LAUGHTER-SILVERED WINGS"
– John Gillespie Magee Jr.
"GIVEN ENOUGH POWER, ANYTHING CAN BE MADE TO FLY"
– Any given fighter pilot
MALLETT

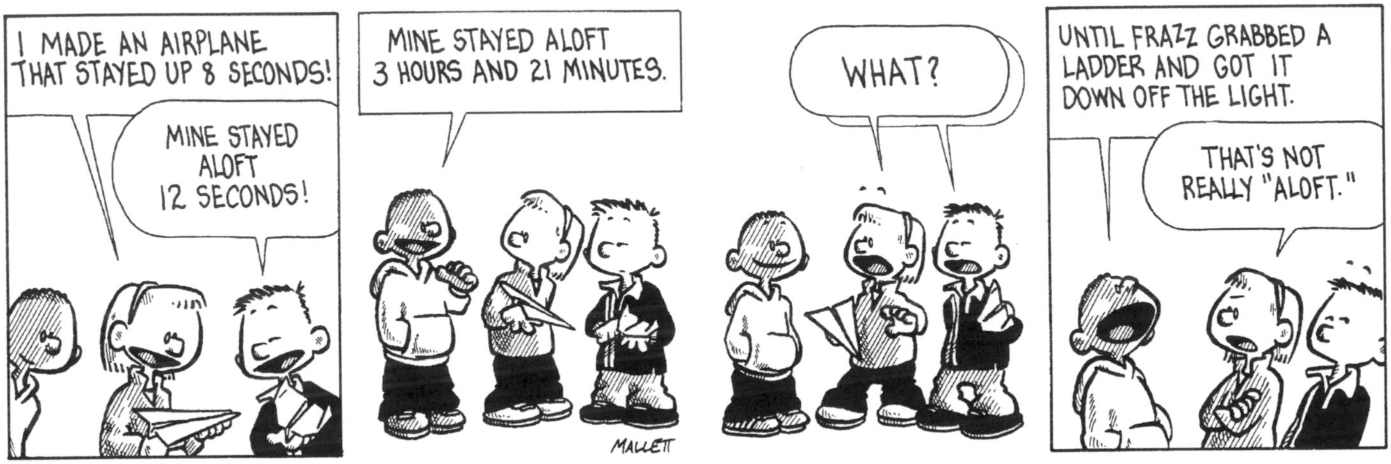
I MADE AN AIRPLANE THAT STAYED UP 8 SECONDS!
MINE STAYED ALOFT 12 SECONDS!
MINE STAYED ALOFT 3 HOURS AND 21 MINUTES.
MALLETT
WHAT?
UNTIL FRAZZ GRABBED A LADDER AND GOT IT DOWN OFF THE LIGHT.
THAT'S NOT REALLY "ALOFT."

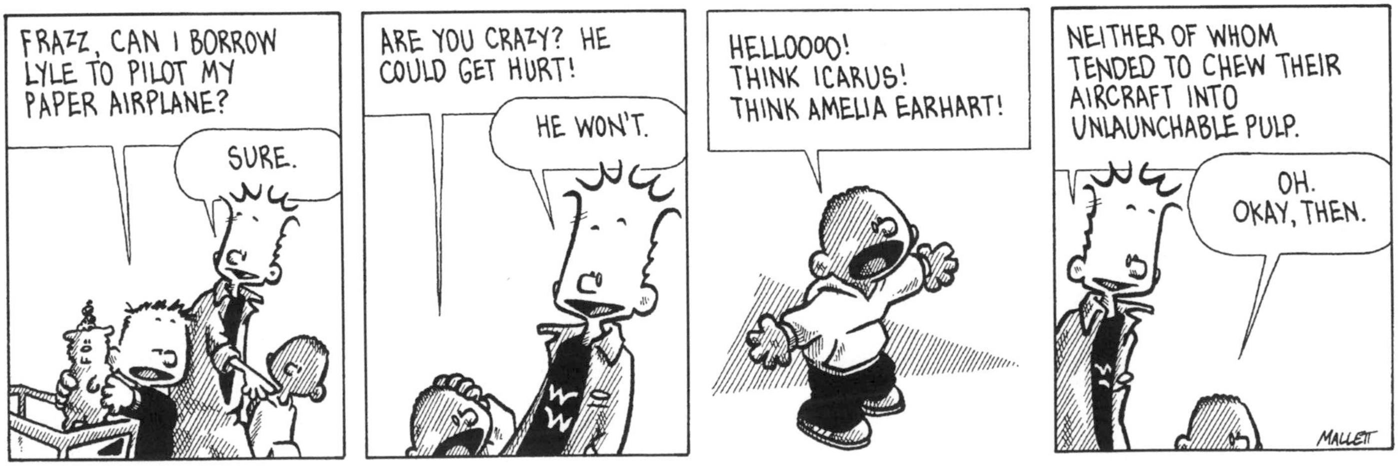
FRAZZ, CAN I BORROW LYLE TO PILOT MY PAPER AIRPLANE?
SURE.
ARE YOU CRAZY? HE COULD GET HURT!
HE WON'T.
HELLOOOO! THINK ICARUS! THINK AMELIA EARHART!
NEITHER OF WHOM TENDED TO CHEW THEIR AIRCRAFT INTO UNLAUNCHABLE PULP.
OH. OKAY, THEN.
MALLETT

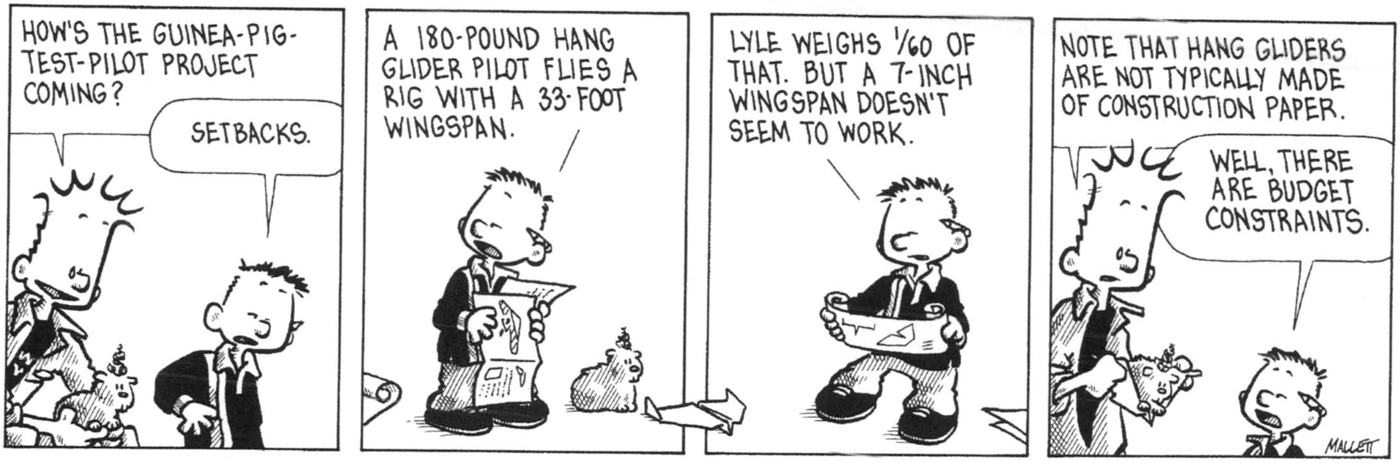
HOW'S THE GUINEA-PIG-TEST-PILOT PROJECT COMING?
SETBACKS.
A 180-POUND HANG GLIDER PILOT FLIES A RIG WITH A 33-FOOT WINGSPAN.
LYLE WEIGHS 1/60 OF THAT. BUT A 7-INCH WINGSPAN DOESN'T SEEM TO WORK.
NOTE THAT HANG GLIDERS ARE NOT TYPICALLY MADE OF CONSTRUCTION PAPER.
WELL, THERE ARE BUDGET CONSTRAINTS.
MALLETT

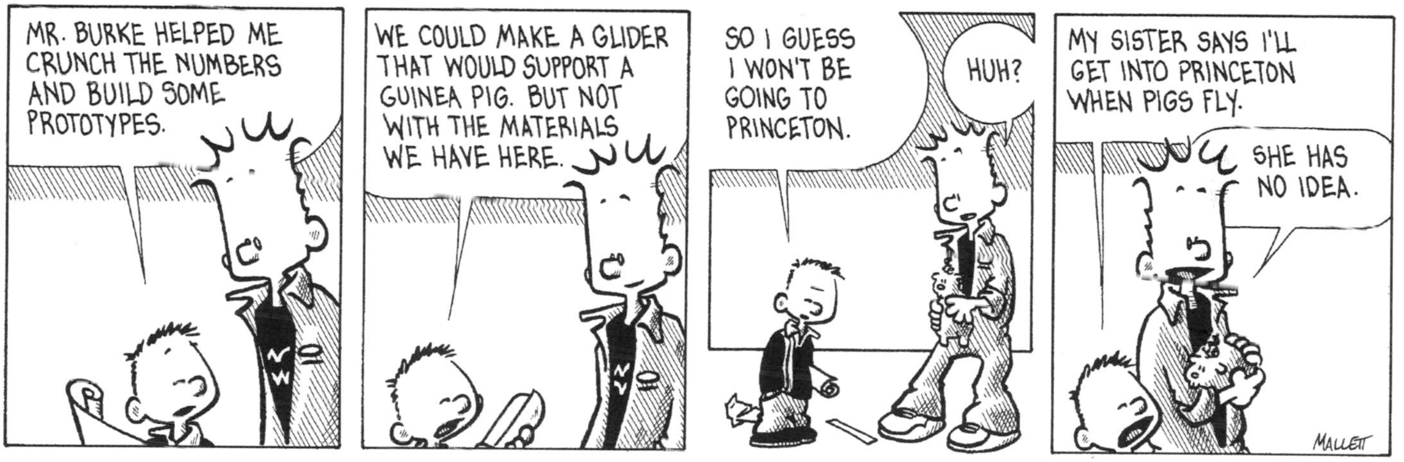
MR. BURKE HELPED ME CRUNCH THE NUMBERS AND BUILD SOME PROTOTYPES.
WE COULD MAKE A GLIDER THAT WOULD SUPPORT A GUINEA PIG. BUT NOT WITH THE MATERIALS WE HAVE HERE.
SO I GUESS I WON'T BE GOING TO PRINCETON.
HUH?
MY SISTER SAYS I'LL GET INTO PRINCETON WHEN PIGS FLY.
SHE HAS NO IDEA.
MALLETT

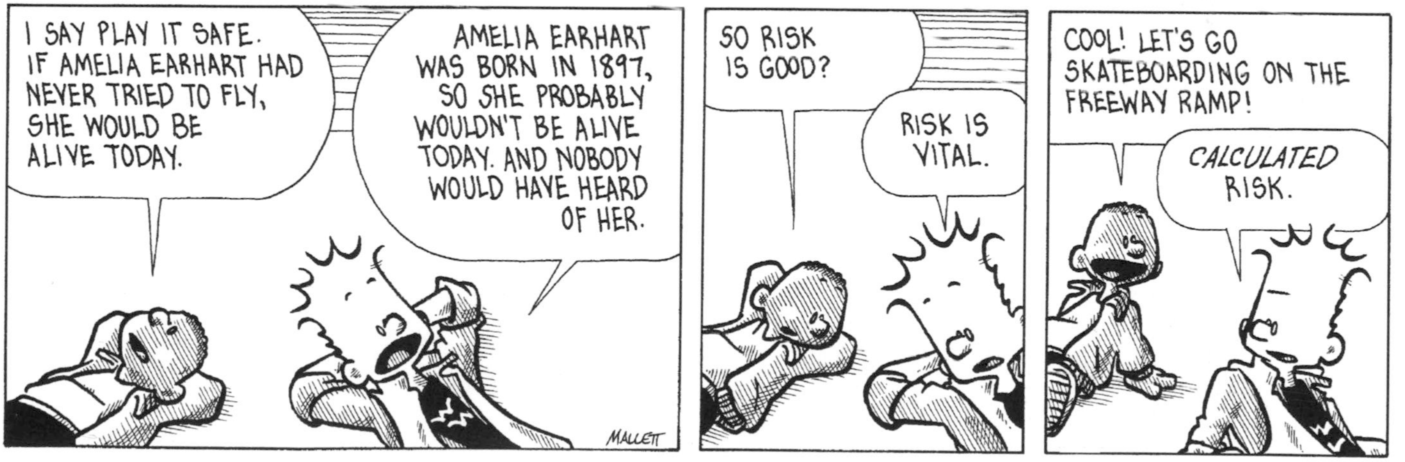
I SAY PLAY IT SAFE. IF AMELIA EARHART HAD NEVER TRIED TO FLY, SHE WOULD BE ALIVE TODAY.
AMELIA EARHART WAS BORN IN 1897, SO SHE PROBABLY WOULDN'T BE ALIVE TODAY. AND NOBODY WOULD HAVE HEARD OF HER.
MALLETT
SO RISK IS GOOD?
RISK IS VITAL.
COOL! LET'S GO SKATEBOARDING ON THE FREEWAY RAMP!
CALCULATED RISK.

FRAZZ
BY JEF MALLETT
I SAY IT'S AN ELOQUENT COMPROMISE BETWEEN THE SEAT-OF-THE-PANTS APPROACH AND THE BY-THE-BOOK APPROACH.
I SAY IT'S TEMPTING FATE TO FOLD YOUR AIRPLANE OUT OF THE CHECKLIST.

©2003 Jef Mallett
YOU KNOW, JUST COLORING IT BLACK DOESN'T MAKE IT A STEALTH FIGHTER.
WELL, THEN NO WONDER THEY COST A BAZILLION DOLLARS.
I will not thro
I will not thro
I will not thro
I will not t

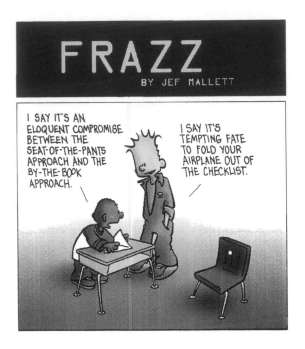

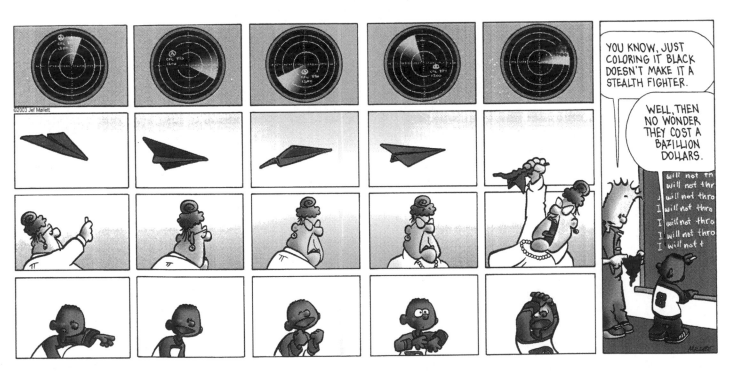

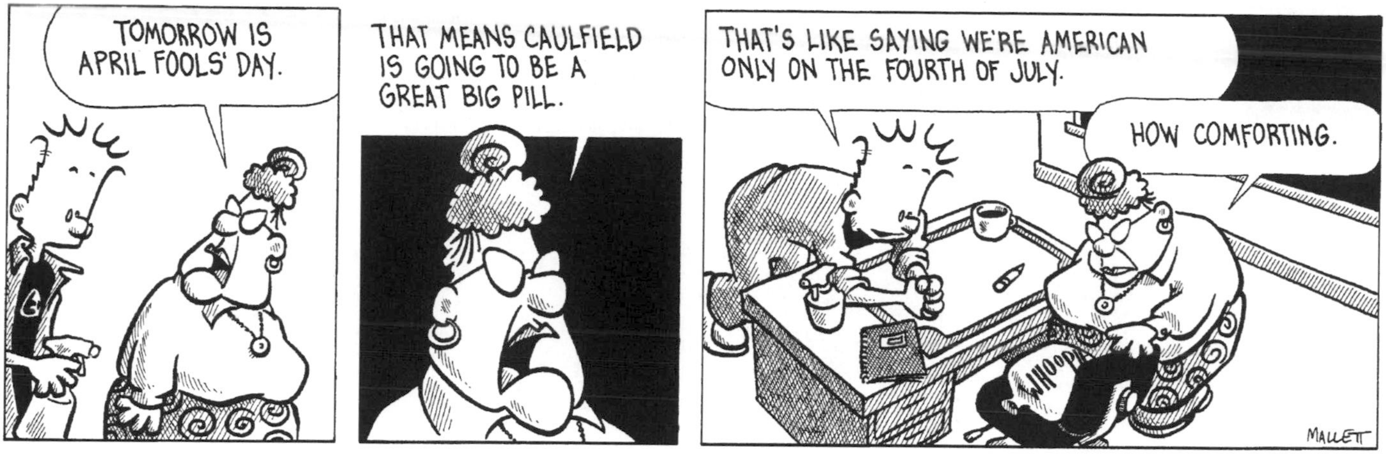
TOMORROW IS APRIL FOOLS' DAY.
THAT MEANS CAULFIELD IS GOING TO BE A GREAT BIG PILL.
THAT'S LIKE SAYING WE'RE AMERICAN ONLY ON THE FOURTH OF JULY.
HOW COMFORTING.
MALLETT

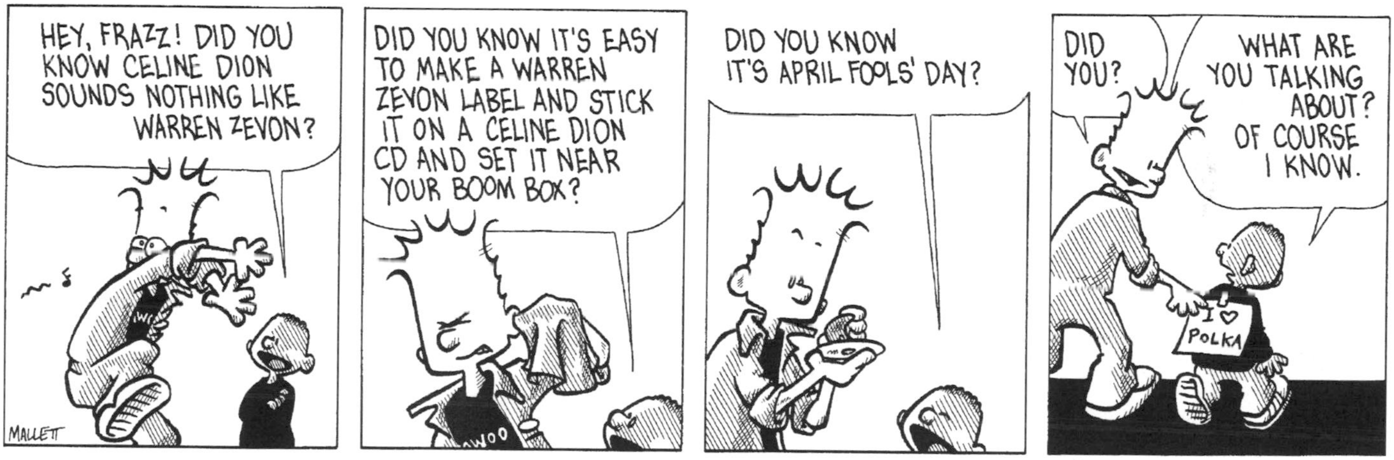
HEY, FRAZZ! DID YOU KNOW CELINE DION SOUNDS NOTHING LIKE WARREN ZEVON?
MALLETT
DID YOU KNOW IT'S EASY TO MAKE A WARREN ZEVON LABEL AND STICK IT ON A CELINE DION CD AND SET IT NEAR YOUR BOOM BOX?
DID YOU KNOW IT'S APRIL FOOLS' DAY?
DID YOU?
WHAT ARE YOU TALKING ABOUT? OF COURSE I KNOW.
I ♥ POLKA

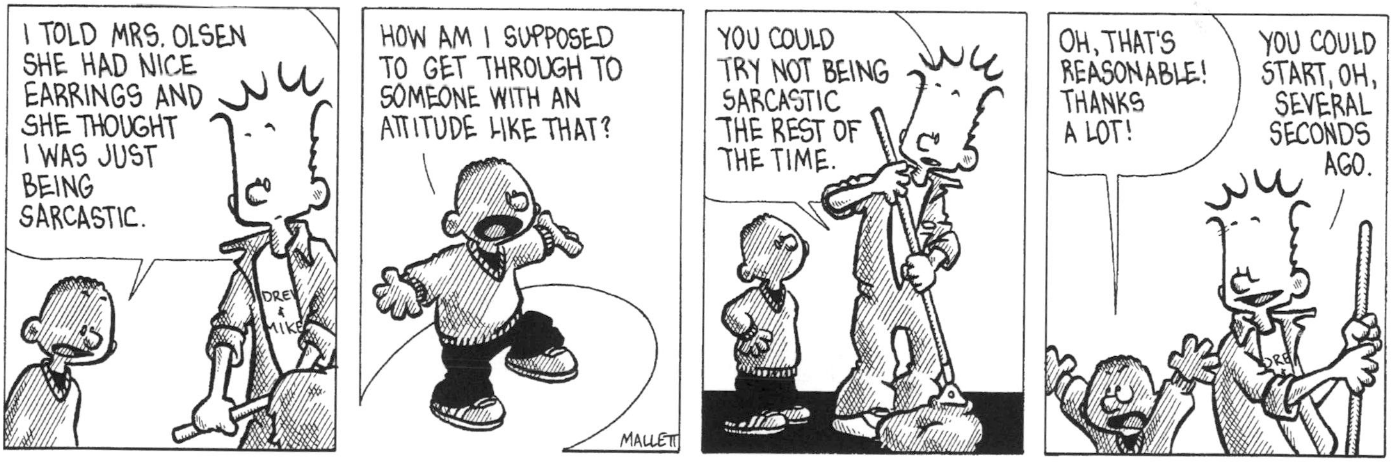
I TOLD MRS. OLSEN SHE HAD NICE EARRINGS AND SHE THOUGHT I WAS JUST BEING SARCASTIC.
HOW AM I SUPPOSED TO GET THROUGH TO SOMEONE WITH AN ATTITUDE LIKE THAT?
MALLETT
YOU COULD TRY NOT BEING SARCASTIC THE REST OF THE TIME.
OH, THAT'S REASONABLE! THANKS A LOT!
YOU COULD START, OH, SEVERAL SECONDS AGO.

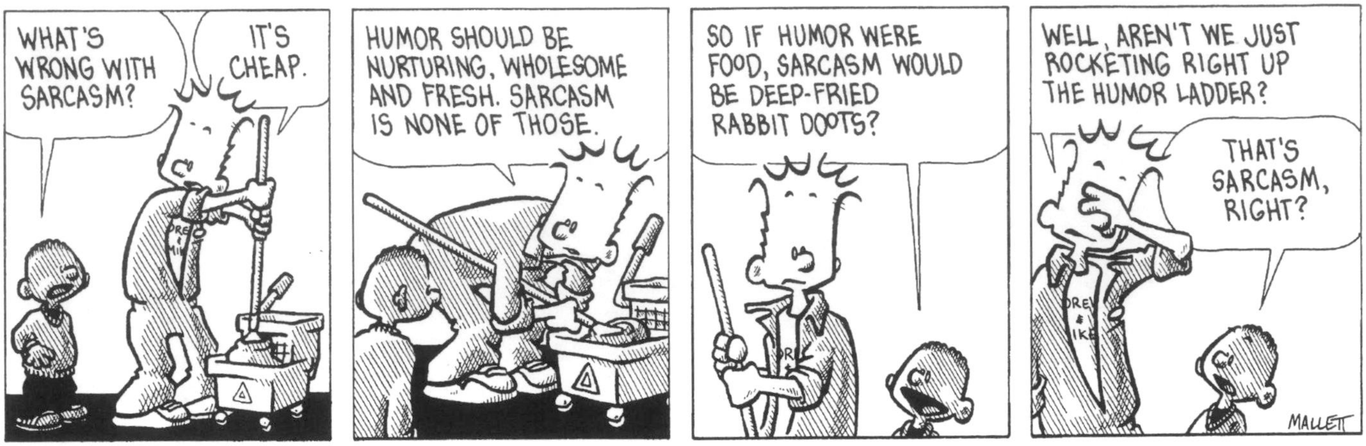
WHAT'S WRONG WITH SARCASM?
IT'S CHEAP.
HUMOR SHOULD BE NURTURING, WHOLESOME AND FRESH. SARCASM IS NONE OF THOSE.
SO IF HUMOR WERE FOOD, SARCASM WOULD BE DEEP-FRIED RABBIT DOOTS?
WELL, AREN'T WE JUST ROCKETING RIGHT UP THE HUMOR LADDER?
THAT'S SARCASM, RIGHT?
MALLETT

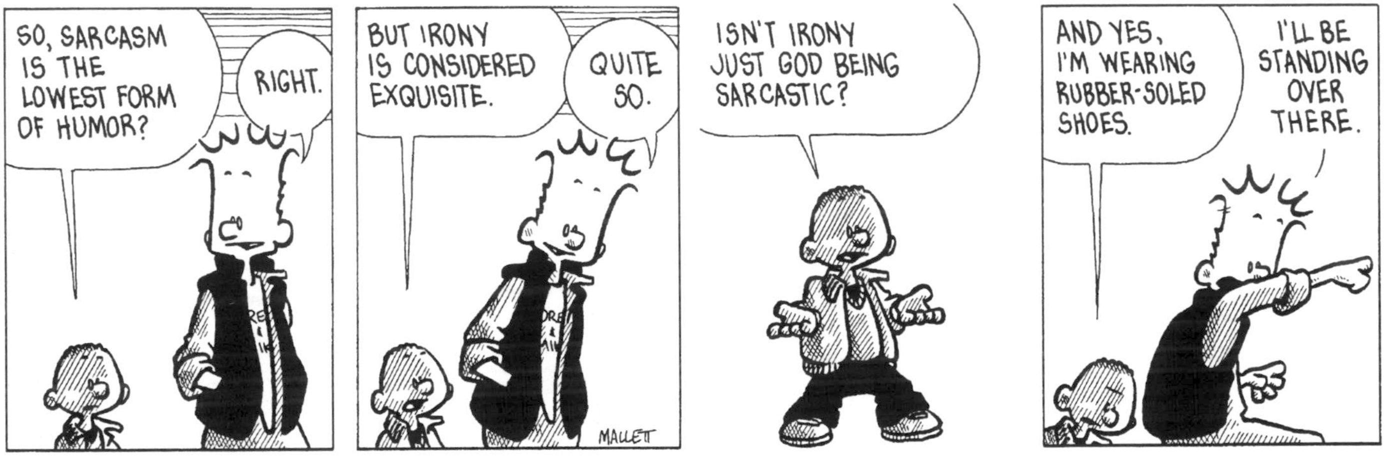
SO, SARCASM IS THE LOWEST FORM OF HUMOR?
RIGHT.
BUT IRONY IS CONSIDERED EXQUISITE.
QUITE SO.
MALLETT
ISN'T IRONY JUST GOD BEING SARCASTIC?
AND YES, I'M WEARING RUBBER-SOLED SHOES.
I'LL BE STANDING OVER THERE.

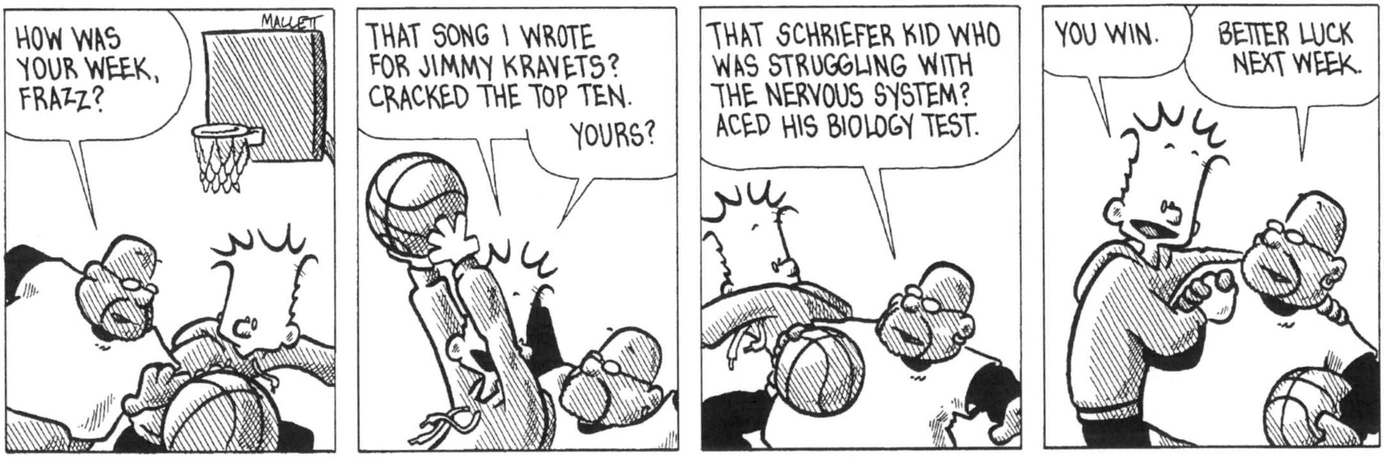
HOW WAS YOUR WEEK, FRAZZ?
MALLETT
THAT SONG I WROTE FOR JIMMY KRAVETS? CRACKED THE TOP TEN.
YOURS?
THAT SCHRIEFER KID WHO WAS STRUGGLING WITH THE NERVOUS SYSTEM? ACED HIS BIOLOGY TEST.
YOU WIN.
BETTER LUCK NEXT WEEK.

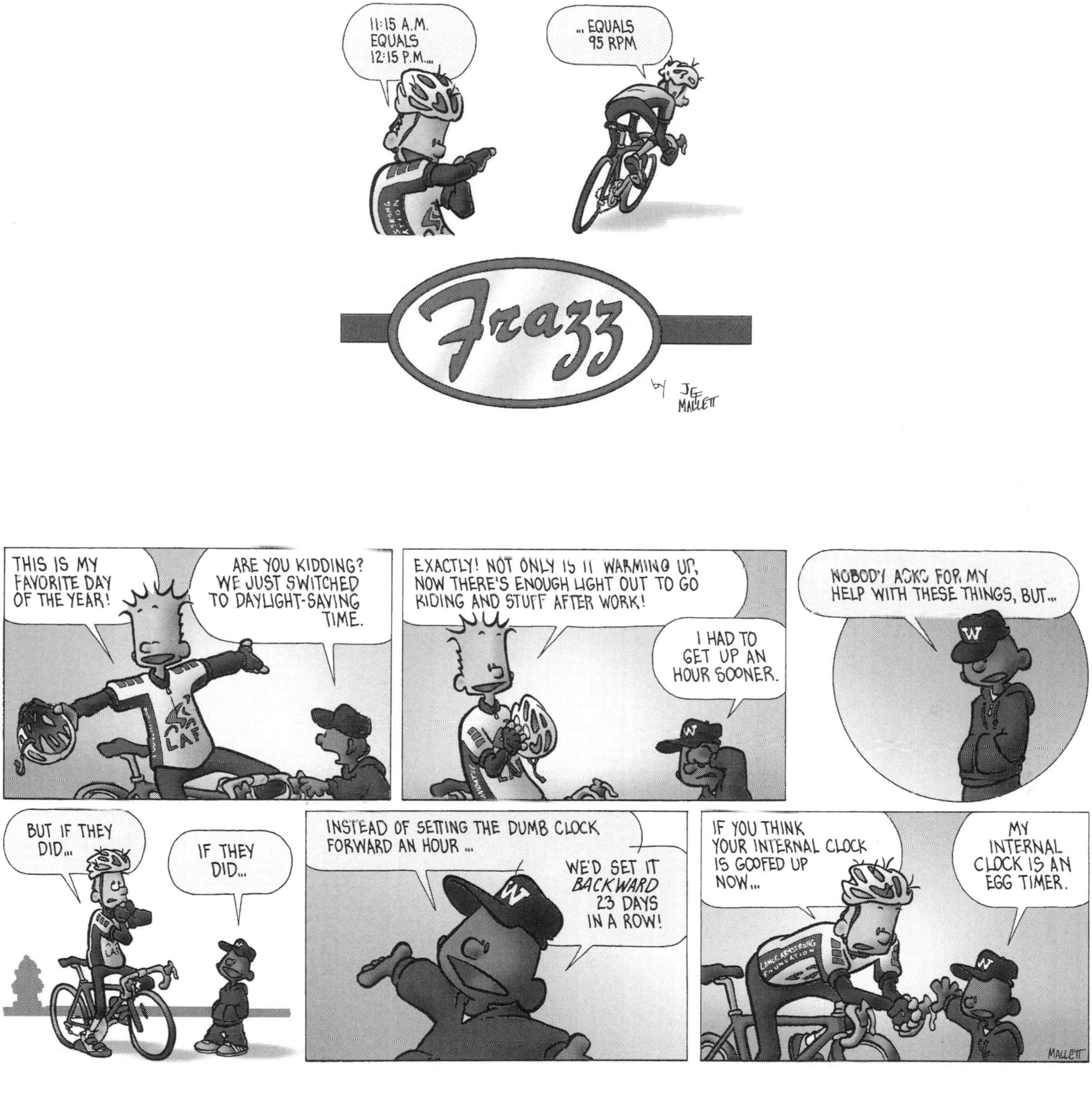
11:15 A.M. EQUALS 12:15 P.M...
... EQUALS 95 RPM
Frazz
by JEF MALLETT
THIS IS MY FAVORITE DAY OF THE YEAR!
ARE YOU KIDDING? WE JUST SWITCHED TO DAYLIGHT-SAVING TIME.
EXACTLY! NOT ONLY IS IT WARMING UP, NOW THERE'S ENOUGH LIGHT OUT TO GO RIDING AND STUFF AFTER WORK!
I HAD TO GET UP AN HOUR SOONER.
NOBODY ASKS FOR MY HELP WITH THESE THINGS, BUT...
BUT IF THEY DID...
IF THEY DID...
INSTEAD OF SETTING THE DUMB CLOCK FORWARD AN HOUR ...
WE'D SET IT *BACKWARD* 23 DAYS IN A ROW!
IF YOU THINK YOUR INTERNAL CLOCK IS GOOFED UP NOW...
MY INTERNAL CLOCK IS AN EGG TIMER.
MALLETT

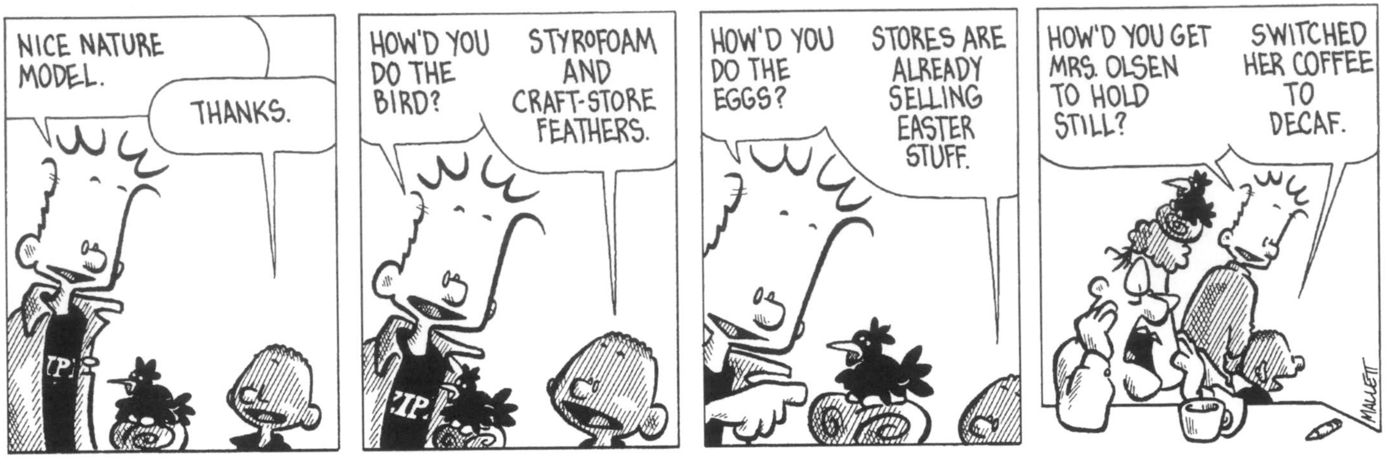
NICE NATURE MODEL.
THANKS.
HOW'D YOU DO THE BIRD?
STYROFOAM AND CRAFT-STORE FEATHERS.
HOW'D YOU DO THE EGGS?
STORES ARE ALREADY SELLING EASTER STUFF.
HOW'D YOU GET MRS. OLSEN TO HOLD STILL?
SWITCHED HER COFFEE TO DECAF.
MALLETT

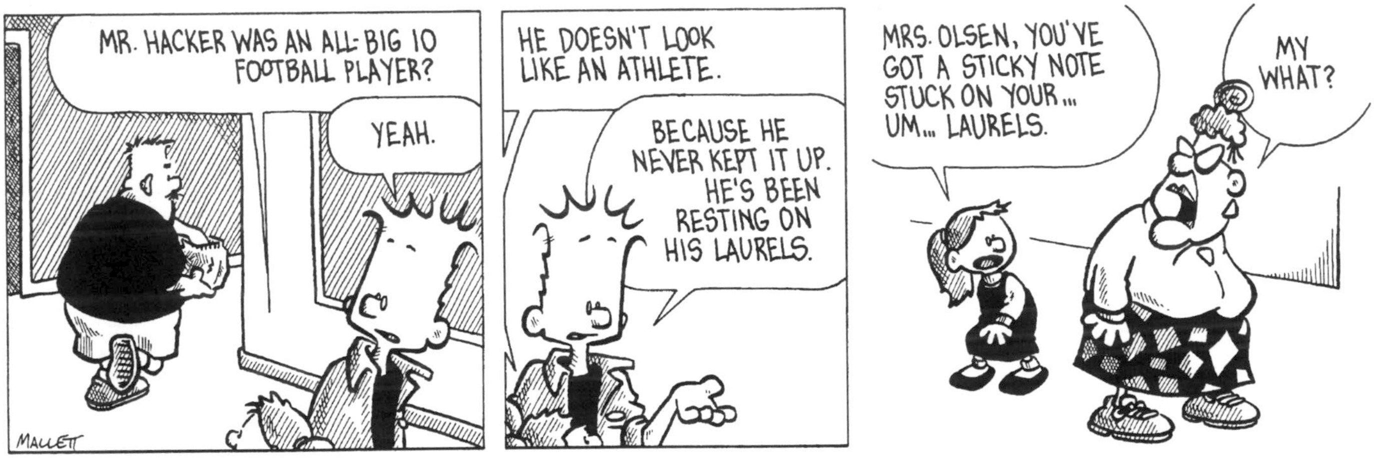
MR. HACKER WAS AN ALL-BIG 10 FOOTBALL PLAYER?
YEAH.
MALLETT
HE DOESN'T LOOK LIKE AN ATHLETE.
BECAUSE HE NEVER KEPT IT UP. HE'S BEEN RESTING ON HIS LAURELS.
MRS. OLSEN, YOU'VE GOT A STICKY NOTE STUCK ON YOUR... UM... LAURELS.
MY WHAT?

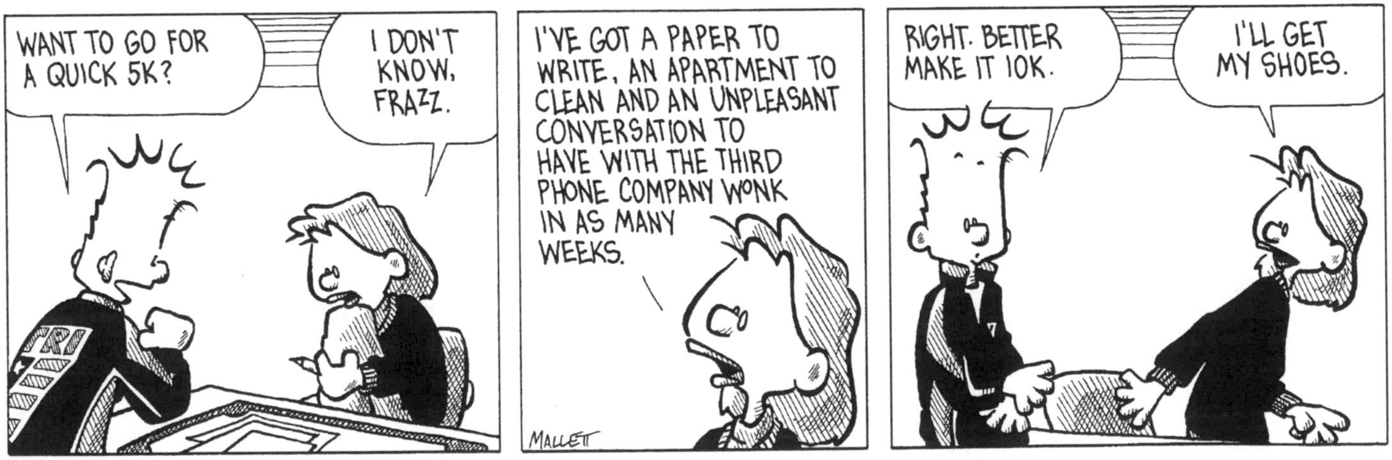
WANT TO GO FOR A QUICK 5K?
I DON'T KNOW, FRAZZ.
I'VE GOT A PAPER TO WRITE, AN APARTMENT TO CLEAN AND AN UNPLEASANT CONVERSATION TO HAVE WITH THE THIRD PHONE COMPANY WONK IN AS MANY WEEKS.
MALLETT
RIGHT. BETTER MAKE IT 10K.
I'LL GET MY SHOES.

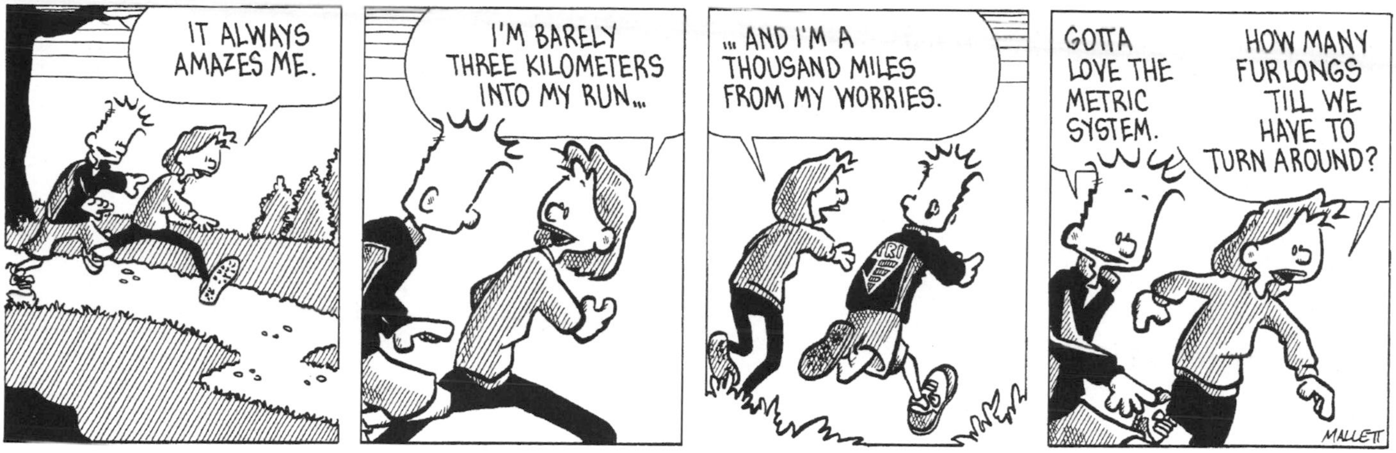
IT ALWAYS AMAZES ME.
I'M BARELY THREE KILOMETERS INTO MY RUN...
... AND I'M A THOUSAND MILES FROM MY WORRIES.
GOTTA LOVE THE METRIC SYSTEM.
HOW MANY FURLONGS TILL WE HAVE TO TURN AROUND?
MALLETT

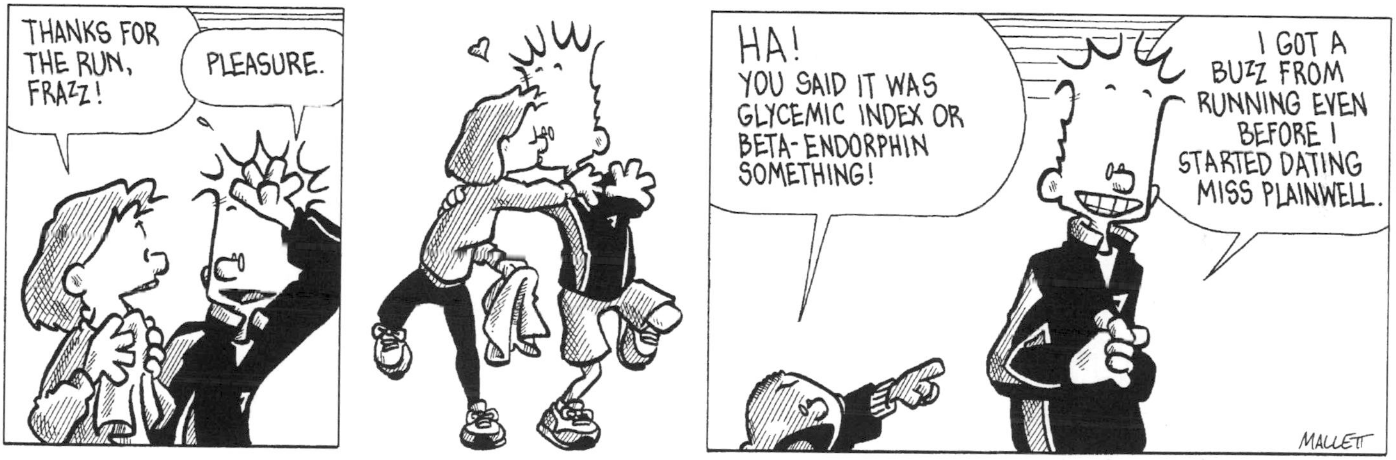
THANKS FOR THE RUN, FRAZZ!
PLEASURE.
HA! YOU SAID IT WAS GLYCEMIC INDEX OR BETA-ENDORPHIN SOMETHING!
I GOT A BUZZ FROM RUNNING EVEN BEFORE I STARTED DATING MISS PLAINWELL.
MALLETT

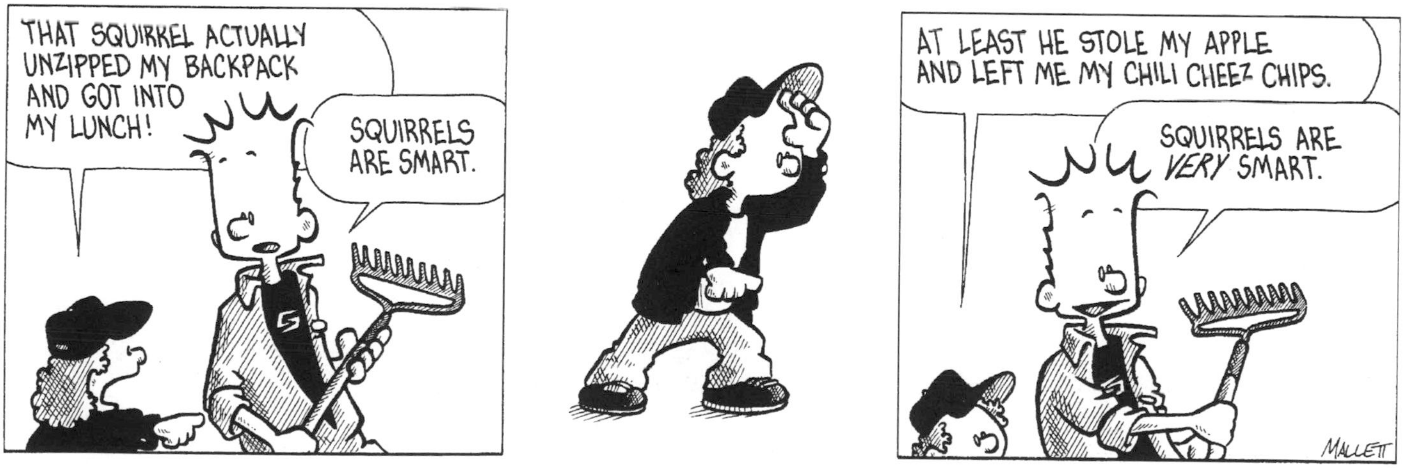
THAT SQUIRREL ACTUALLY UNZIPPED MY BACKPACK AND GOT INTO MY LUNCH!
SQUIRRELS ARE SMART.
AT LEAST HE STOLE MY APPLE AND LEFT ME MY CHILI CHEEZ CHIPS.
SQUIRRELS ARE *VERY* SMART.
MALLETT

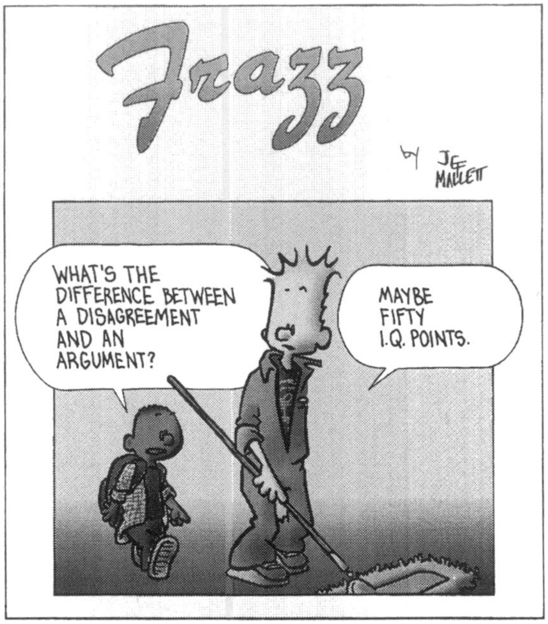
Frazz
by Jef Mallett
WHAT'S THE DIFFERENCE BETWEEN A DISAGREEMENT AND AN ARGUMENT?
MAYBE FIFTY I.Q. POINTS.

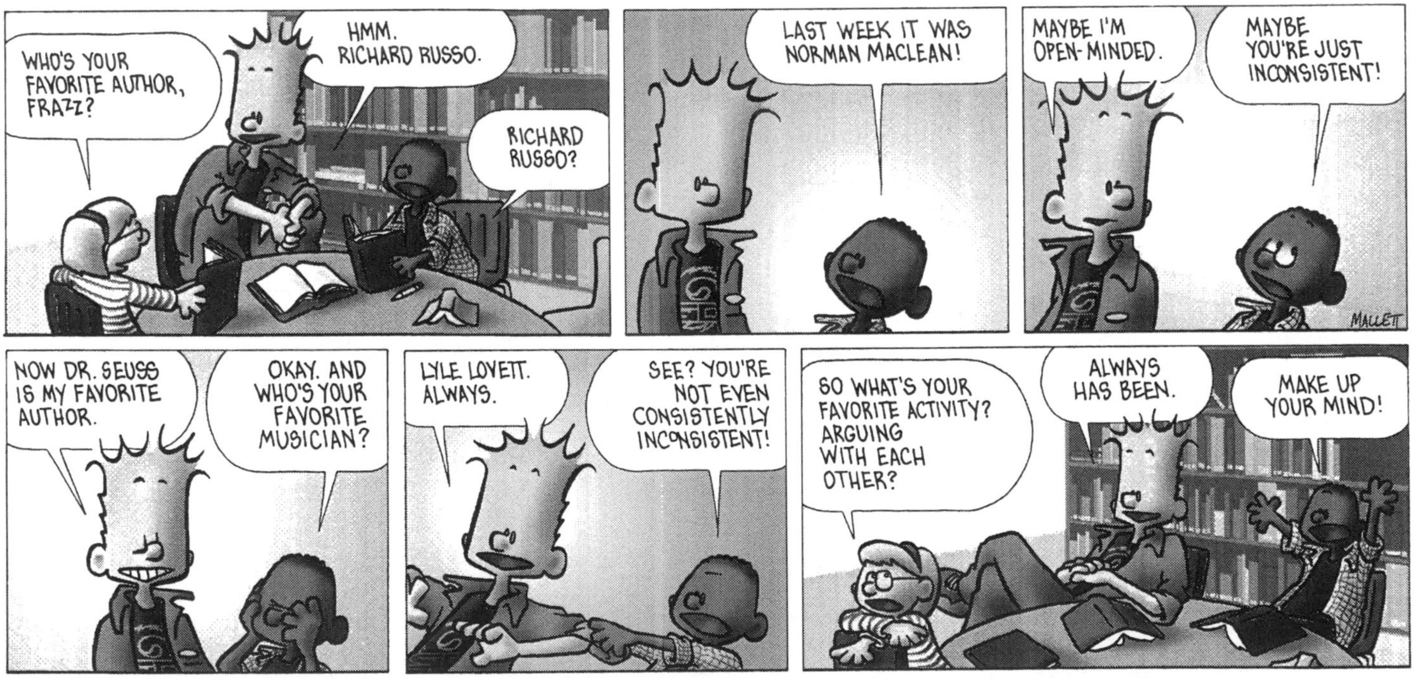
WHO'S YOUR FAVORITE AUTHOR, FRAZZ?
HMM. RICHARD RUSSO.
RICHARD RUSSO?
LAST WEEK IT WAS NORMAN MACLEAN!
MAYBE I'M OPEN-MINDED.
MAYBE YOU'RE JUST INCONSISTENT!
MALLETT
NOW DR. SEUSS IS MY FAVORITE AUTHOR.
OKAY. AND WHO'S YOUR FAVORITE MUSICIAN?
LYLE LOVETT. ALWAYS.
SEE? YOU'RE NOT EVEN CONSISTENTLY INCONSISTENT!
SO WHAT'S YOUR FAVORITE ACTIVITY? ARGUING WITH EACH OTHER?
ALWAYS HAS BEEN.
MAKE UP YOUR MIND!

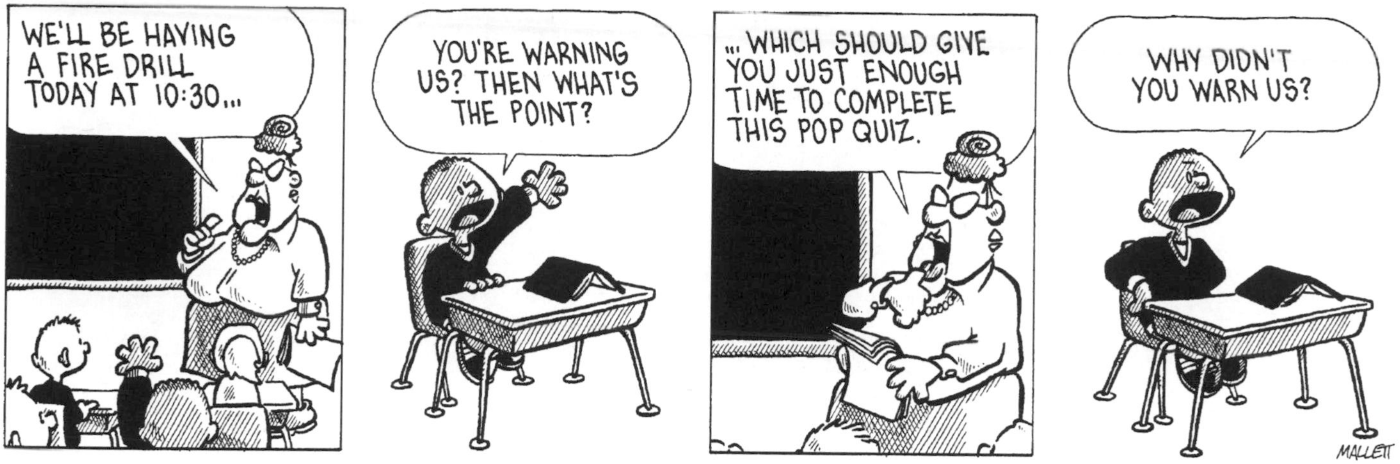
WE'LL BE HAVING A FIRE DRILL TODAY AT 10:30...
YOU'RE WARNING US? THEN WHAT'S THE POINT?
... WHICH SHOULD GIVE YOU JUST ENOUGH TIME TO COMPLETE THIS POP QUIZ.
WHY DIDN'T YOU WARN US?
MALLETT

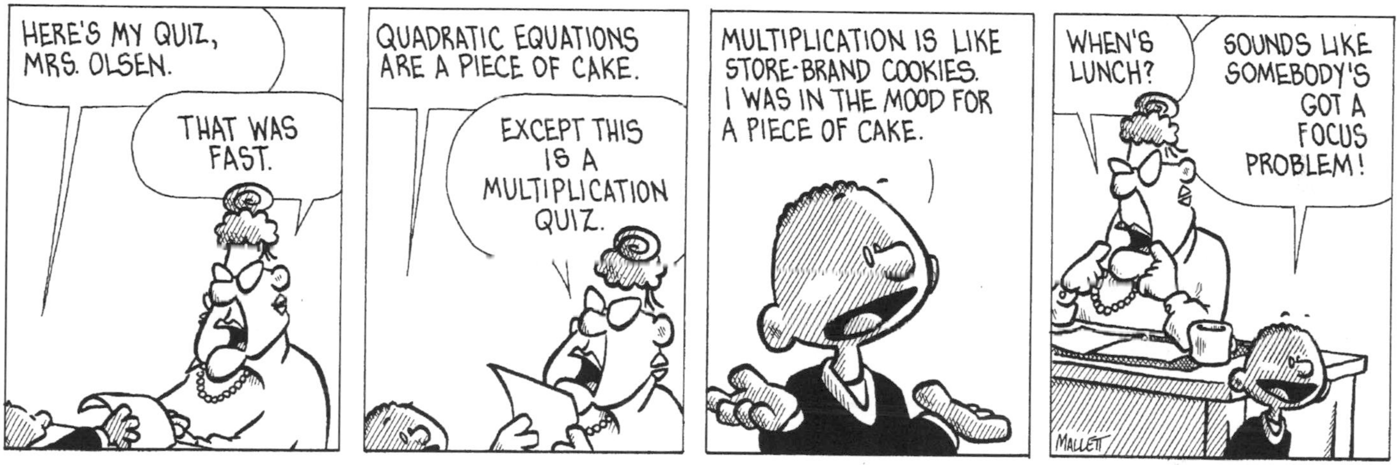
HERE'S MY QUIZ, MRS. OLSEN.
THAT WAS FAST.
QUADRATIC EQUATIONS ARE A PIECE OF CAKE.
EXCEPT THIS IS A MULTIPLICATION QUIZ.
MULTIPLICATION IS LIKE STORE-BRAND COOKIES. I WAS IN THE MOOD FOR A PIECE OF CAKE.
WHEN'S LUNCH?
SOUNDS LIKE SOMEBODY'S GOT A FOCUS PROBLEM!
MALLETT

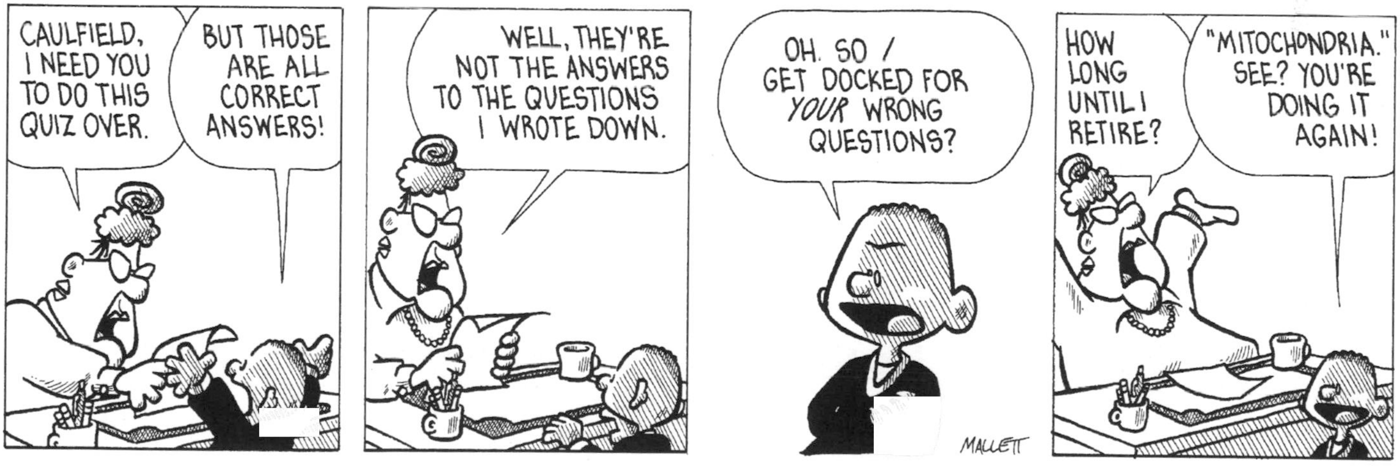
CAULFIELD, I NEED YOU TO DO THIS QUIZ OVER.
BUT THOSE ARE ALL CORRECT ANSWERS!
WELL, THEY'RE NOT THE ANSWERS TO THE QUESTIONS I WROTE DOWN.
OH. SO I GET DOCKED FOR YOUR WRONG QUESTIONS?
MALLETT
HOW LONG UNTIL I RETIRE?
"MITOCHONDRIA." SEE? YOU'RE DOING IT AGAIN!

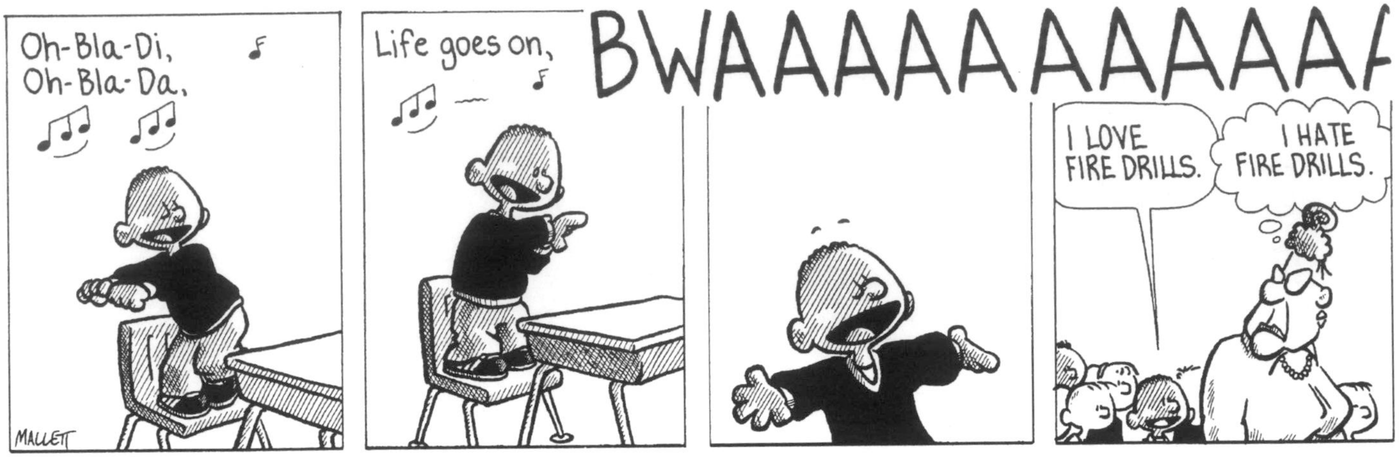
Oh-Bla-Di,
Oh-Bla-Da,
Life goes on,
BWAAAAAAAAAAA
I LOVE FIRE DRILLS.
I HATE FIRE DRILLS.
MALLETT

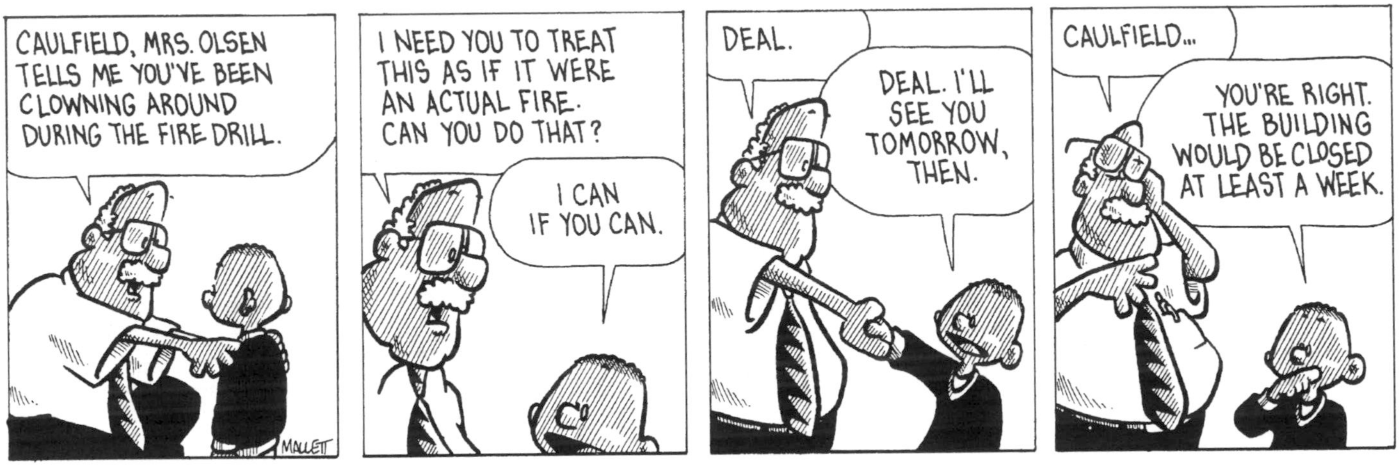
CAULFIELD, MRS. OLSEN TELLS ME YOU'VE BEEN CLOWNING AROUND DURING THE FIRE DRILL.
MALLETT
I NEED YOU TO TREAT THIS AS IF IT WERE AN ACTUAL FIRE. CAN YOU DO THAT?
I CAN IF YOU CAN.
DEAL.
DEAL. I'LL SEE YOU TOMORROW, THEN.
CAULFIELD...
YOU'RE RIGHT. THE BUILDING WOULD BE CLOSED AT LEAST A WEEK.

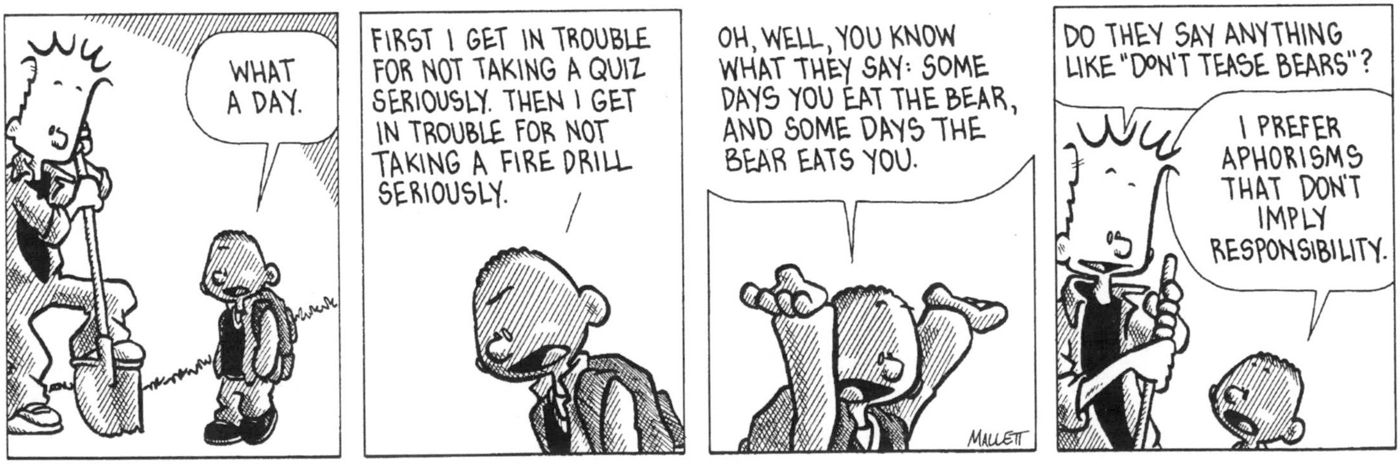
WHAT A DAY.
FIRST I GET IN TROUBLE FOR NOT TAKING A QUIZ SERIOUSLY. THEN I GET IN TROUBLE FOR NOT TAKING A FIRE DRILL SERIOUSLY.
OH, WELL, YOU KNOW WHAT THEY SAY: SOME DAYS YOU EAT THE BEAR, AND SOME DAYS THE BEAR EATS YOU.
MALLETT
DO THEY SAY ANYTHING LIKE "DON'T TEASE BEARS"?
I PREFER APHORISMS THAT DON'T IMPLY RESPONSIBILITY.

Frazz
by JEF MALLETT
SEE? THE MICROWAVE MAKES THEM ALL HUGE AND MUSHY.
MY MOM SAYS THE REFRIGERATOR IS WHAT DOES THAT TO HER.

MAN, EASTER WHIPS BY FAST.
OH, I DON'T KNOW.
SOME ASPECTS OF EASTER LAST AND LAST AND LAST.
LIKE REDEMPTION AND STUFF?
LIKE A TENACIOUSLY STICKY YELLOW RESIDUE IN THE TEACHERS-LOUNGE MICROWAVE.
MALLETT
NO JOKE! THE QUALITY CONTROL ON THOSE MARSHMALLOW CHICKY THINGS IS AWFUL. TOO MANY OF THEM EXPLODE WITHOUT BLOATING OR...
...ANYTHING. UM.
NOT THAT I WOULD KNOW, OF COURSE.
YOU ARE SO BUSTED.
ABOUT THAT REDEMPTION AND STUFF...
HELP ME CHISEL OUT THE MICROWAVE AND WE'LL CALL IT GOOD.

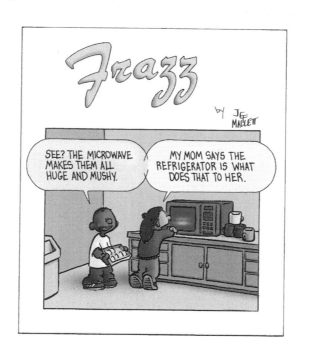

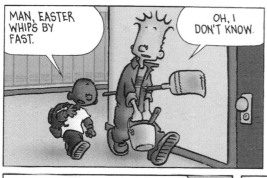

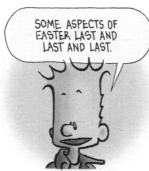

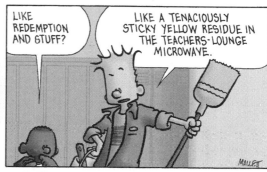

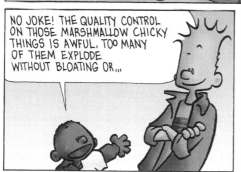

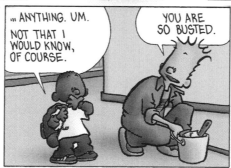

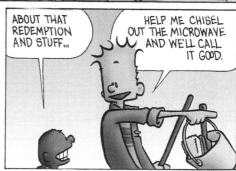

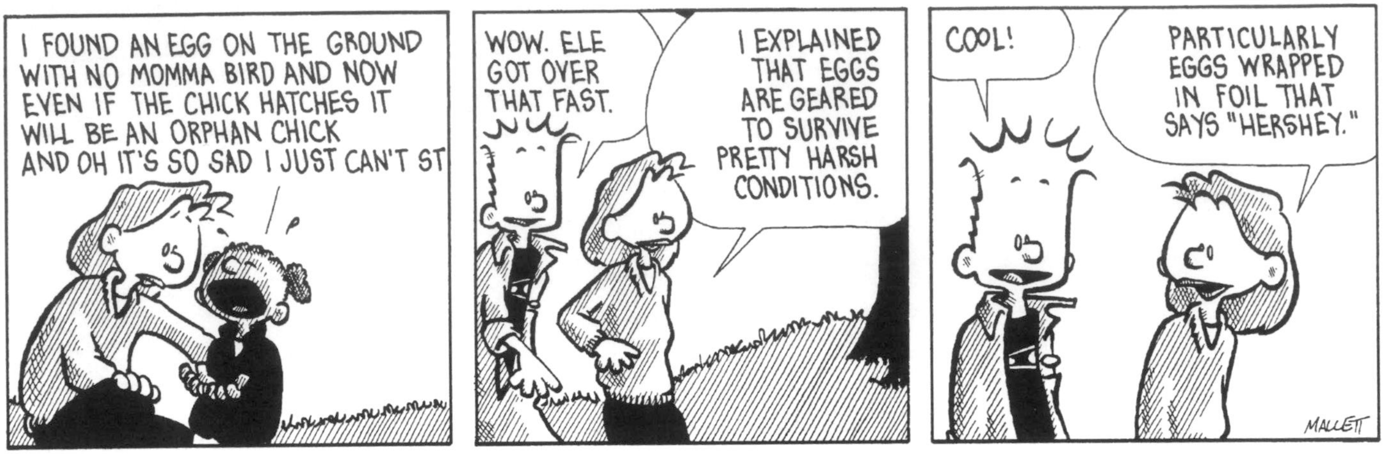
I FOUND AN EGG ON THE GROUND WITH NO MOMMA BIRD AND NOW EVEN IF THE CHICK HATCHES IT WILL BE AN ORPHAN CHICK AND OH IT'S SO SAD I JUST CAN'T ST
WOW. ELE GOT OVER THAT FAST.
I EXPLAINED THAT EGGS ARE GEARED TO SURVIVE PRETTY HARSH CONDITIONS.
COOL!
PARTICULARLY EGGS WRAPPED IN FOIL THAT SAYS "HERSHEY."
MALLETT

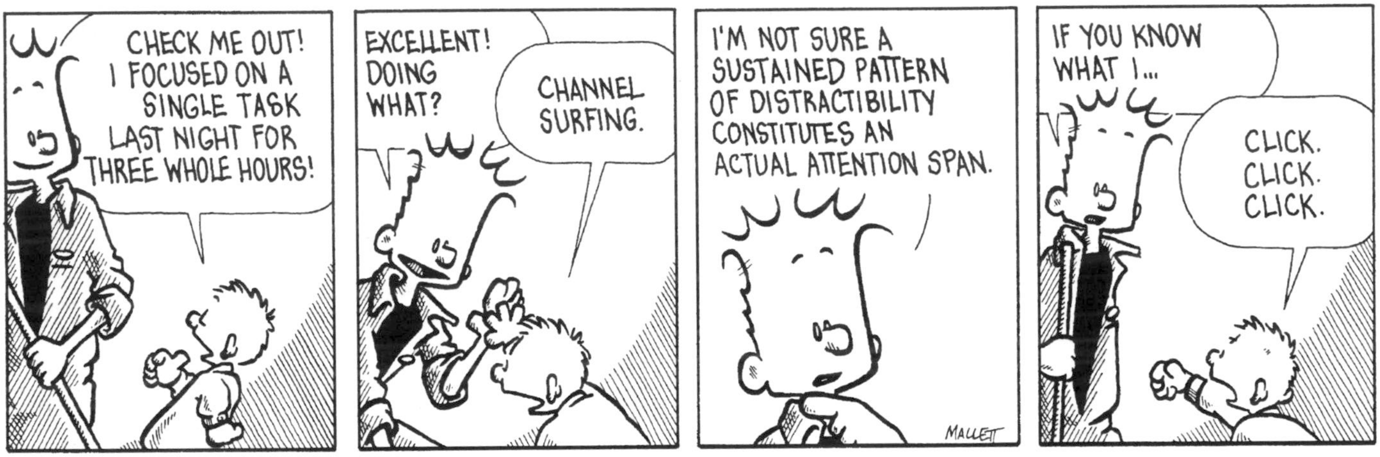
CHECK ME OUT! I FOCUSED ON A SINGLE TASK LAST NIGHT FOR THREE WHOLE HOURS!
EXCELLENT! DOING WHAT?
CHANNEL SURFING.
I'M NOT SURE A SUSTAINED PATTERN OF DISTRACTIBILITY CONSTITUTES AN ACTUAL ATTENTION SPAN.
MALLETT
IF YOU KNOW WHAT I...
CLICK. CLICK. CLICK.

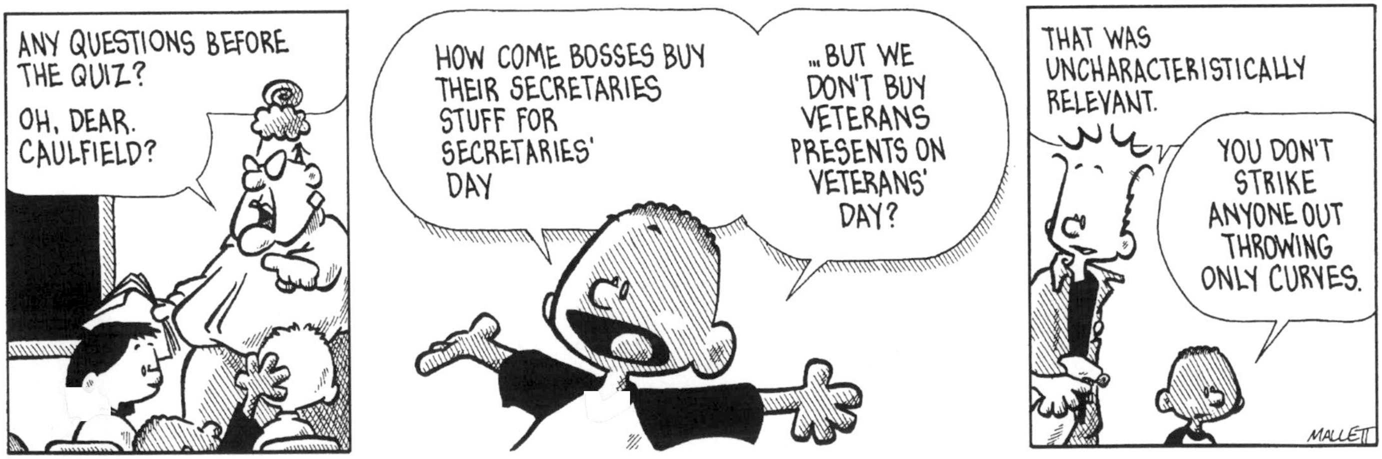
ANY QUESTIONS BEFORE THE QUIZ?
OH, DEAR. CAULFIELD?
HOW COME BOSSES BUY THEIR SECRETARIES STUFF FOR SECRETARIES' DAY
...BUT WE DON'T BUY VETERANS PRESENTS ON VETERANS' DAY?
THAT WAS UNCHARACTERISTICALLY RELEVANT.
YOU DON'T STRIKE ANYONE OUT THROWING ONLY CURVES.
MALLETT

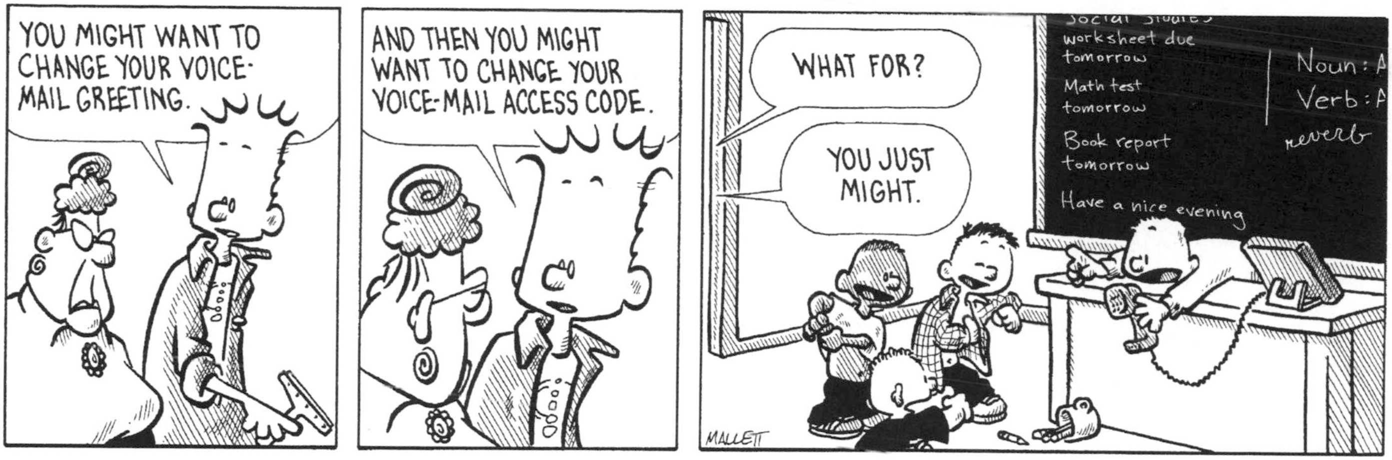
YOU MIGHT WANT TO CHANGE YOUR VOICE-MAIL GREETING.
AND THEN YOU MIGHT WANT TO CHANGE YOUR VOICE-MAIL ACCESS CODE.
WHAT FOR?
YOU JUST MIGHT.
worksheet due tomorrow
Math test tomorrow
Book report tomorrow
Have a nice evening
reverb
MALLETT

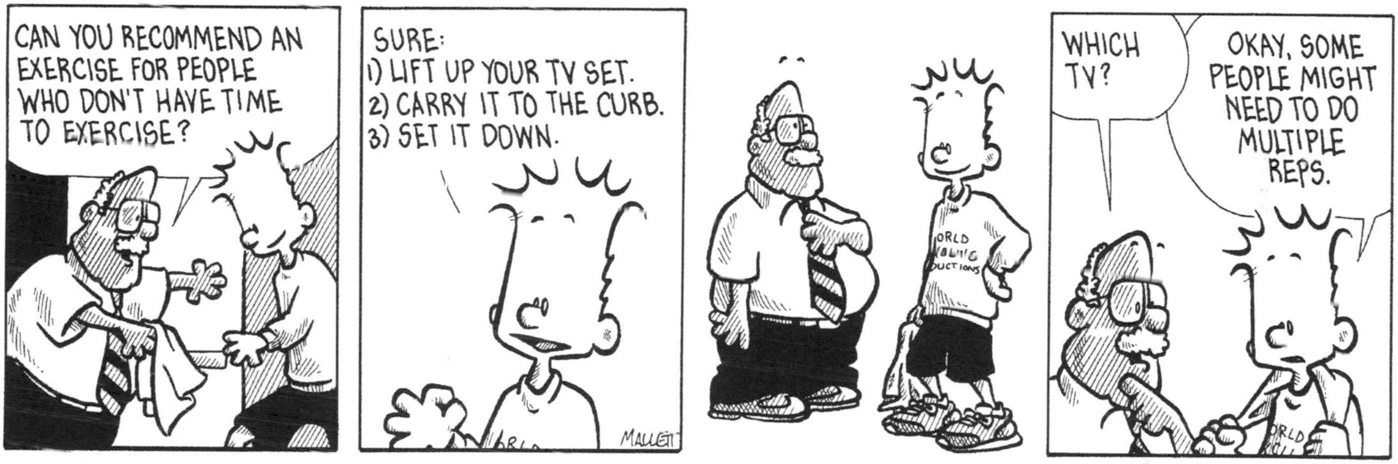
CAN YOU RECOMMEND AN EXERCISE FOR PEOPLE WHO DON'T HAVE TIME TO EXERCISE?
SURE:
1) LIFT UP YOUR TV SET.
2) CARRY IT TO THE CURB.
3) SET IT DOWN.
MALLETT
WHICH TV?
OKAY, SOME PEOPLE MIGHT NEED TO DO MULTIPLE REPS.

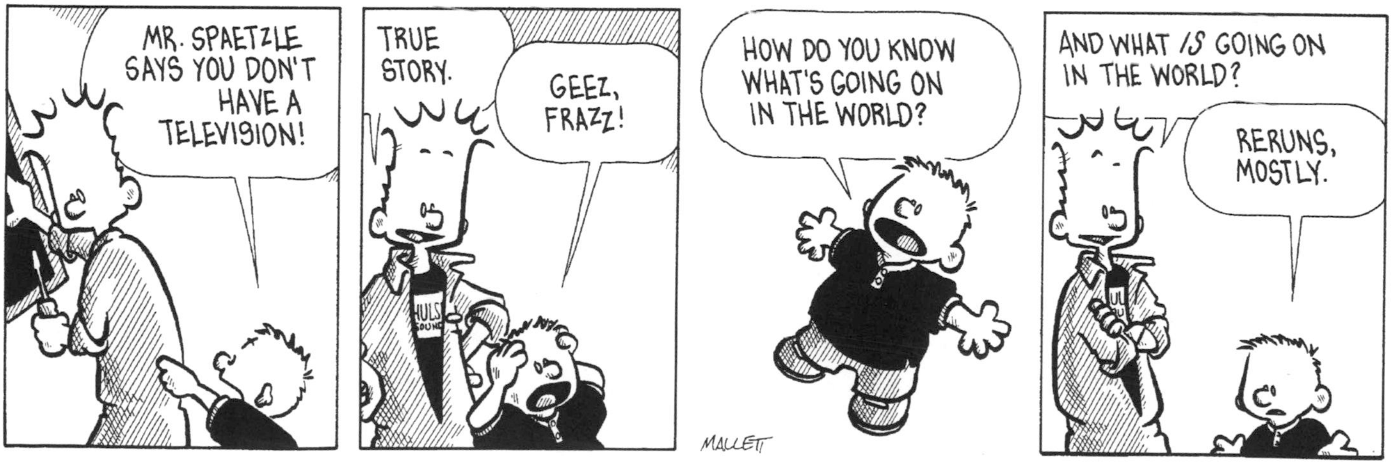
MR. SPAETZLE SAYS YOU DON'T HAVE A TELEVISION!
TRUE STORY.
GEEZ, FRAZZ!
HOW DO YOU KNOW WHAT'S GOING ON IN THE WORLD?
MALLETT
AND WHAT *IS* GOING ON IN THE WORLD?
RERUNS, MOSTLY.

FRAZZ
by JEF MALLETT
NOPE. WE'RE FRESH OUT OF GRAPHING CALCULATORS, AIRCRAFT-GRADE ALUMINUM AND JET FUEL.
SUPPLIES
HOW'S ANYONE SUPPOSED TO GET AN EDUCATION AROUND HERE?

CHARISMATIC CAULFIELD
BOOM!
YES! CAULFIELD BREAKS THE SOUND BARRIER!
WAS THAT THUNDER? THAT DIDN'T QUITE SOUND LIKE THUNDER.
HOW IS IT THAT I'M ALWAYS SHORT ON GARBAGE BAGS WHEN IT RAINS?
MALLETT

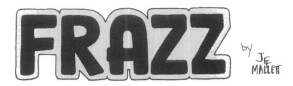

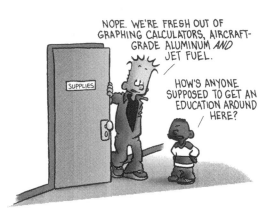

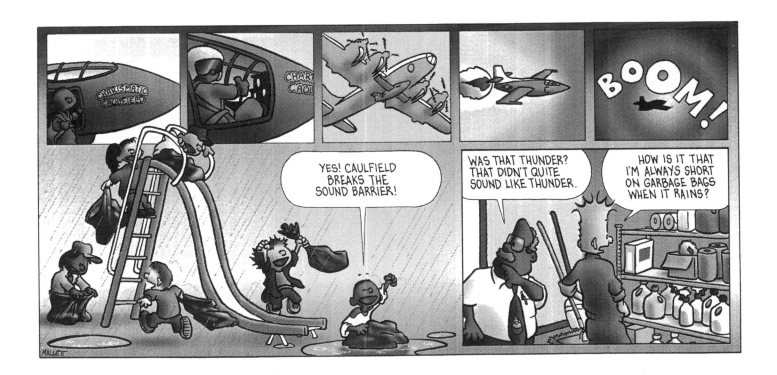

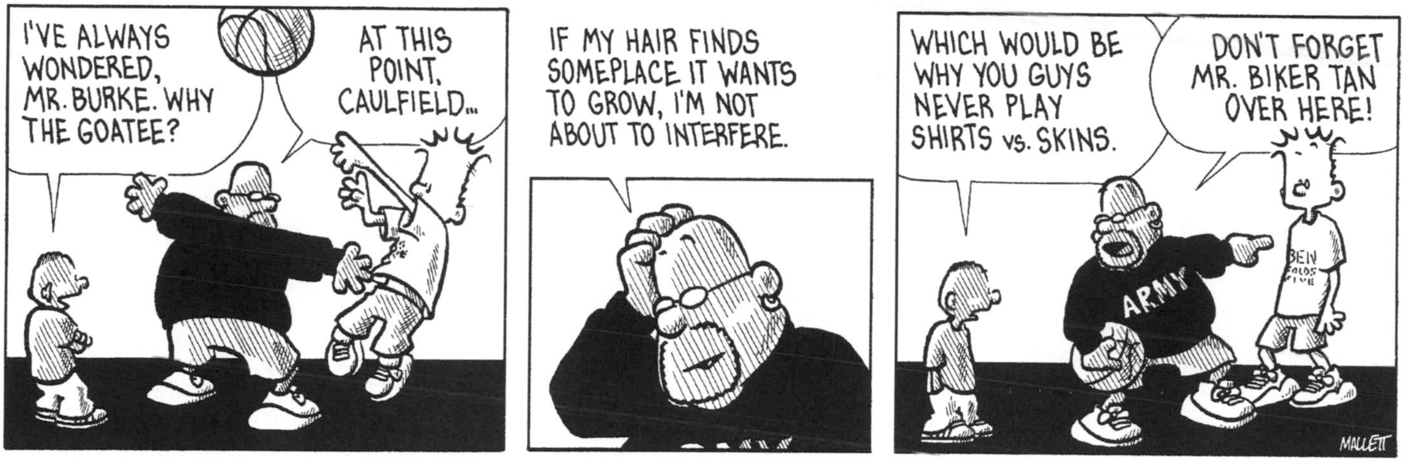
I'VE ALWAYS WONDERED, MR. BURKE. WHY THE GOATEE?
AT THIS POINT, CAULFIELD...
IF MY HAIR FINDS SOMEPLACE IT WANTS TO GROW, I'M NOT ABOUT TO INTERFERE.
WHICH WOULD BE WHY YOU GUYS NEVER PLAY SHIRTS vs. SKINS.
DON'T FORGET MR. BIKER TAN OVER HERE!
ARMY
BEN FOLDS FIVE
MALLETT

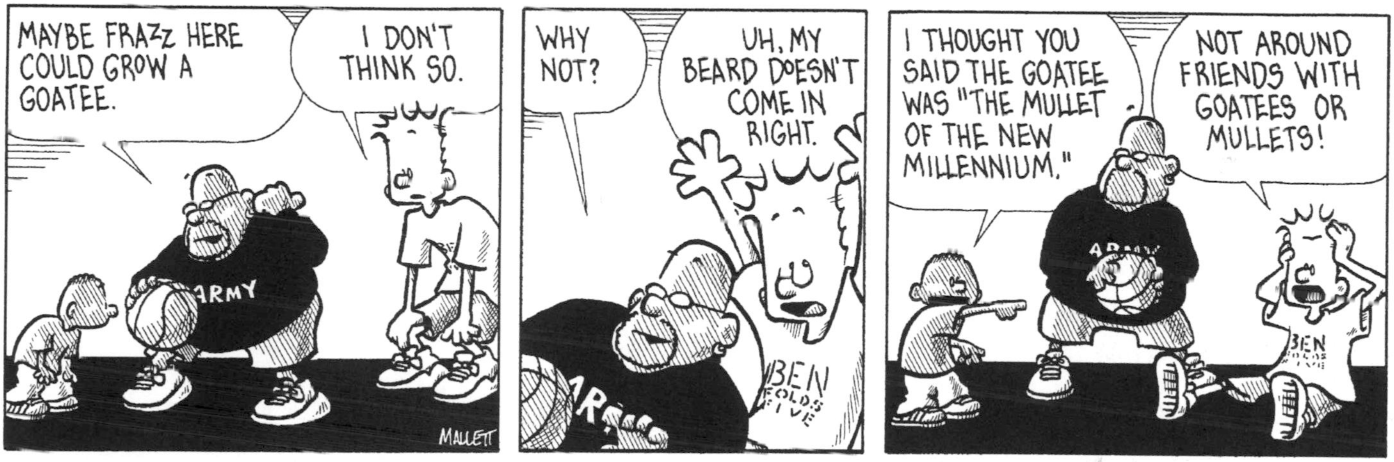
MAYBE FRAZZ HERE COULD GROW A GOATEE.
I DON'T THINK SO.
WHY NOT?
UH, MY BEARD DOESN'T COME IN RIGHT.
I THOUGHT YOU SAID THE GOATEE WAS "THE MULLET OF THE NEW MILLENNIUM."
NOT AROUND FRIENDS WITH GOATEES OR MULLETS!
ARMY
BEN FOLDS FIVE
MALLETT

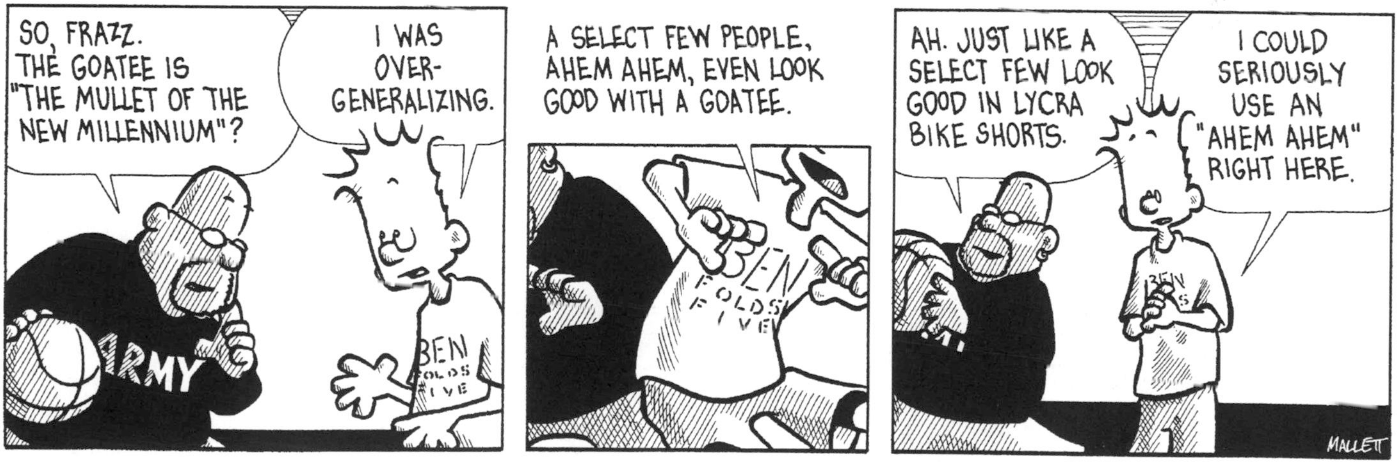
SO, FRAZZ. THE GOATEE IS "THE MULLET OF THE NEW MILLENNIUM"?
I WAS OVER-GENERALIZING.
A SELECT FEW PEOPLE, AHEM AHEM, EVEN LOOK GOOD WITH A GOATEE.
AH. JUST LIKE A SELECT FEW LOOK GOOD IN LYCRA BIKE SHORTS.
I COULD SERIOUSLY USE AN "AHEM AHEM" RIGHT HERE.
ARMY
BEN FOLDS FIVE
MALLETT

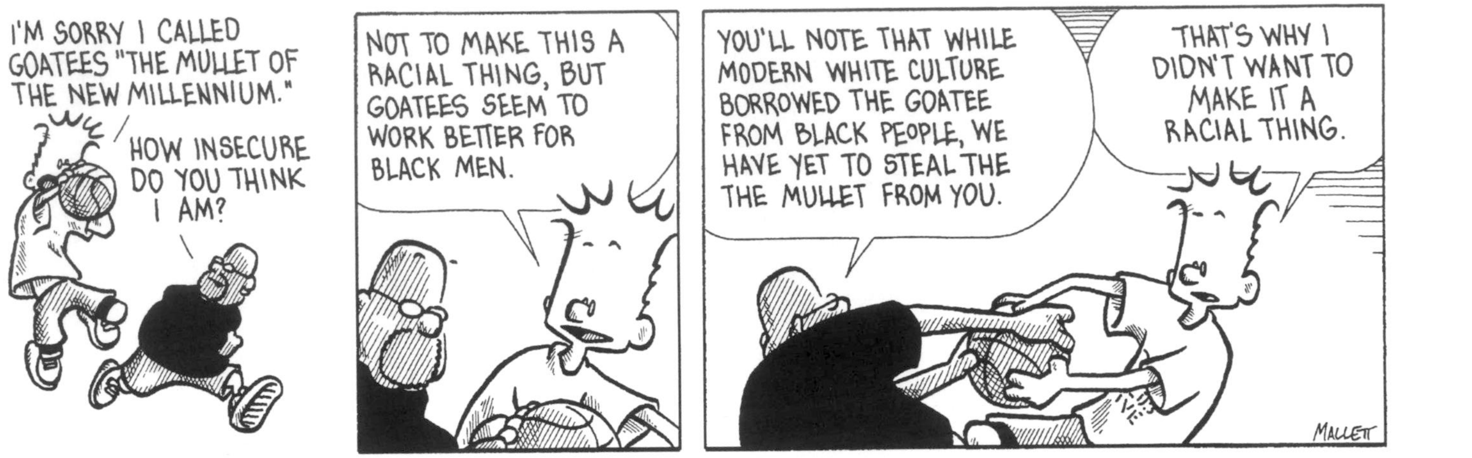
I'M SORRY I CALLED GOATEES "THE MULLET OF THE NEW MILLENNIUM."
HOW INSECURE DO YOU THINK I AM?
NOT TO MAKE THIS A RACIAL THING, BUT GOATEES SEEM TO WORK BETTER FOR BLACK MEN.
YOU'LL NOTE THAT WHILE MODERN WHITE CULTURE BORROWED THE GOATEE FROM BLACK PEOPLE, WE HAVE YET TO STEAL THE THE MULLET FROM YOU.
THAT'S WHY I DIDN'T WANT TO MAKE IT A RACIAL THING.
MALLETT

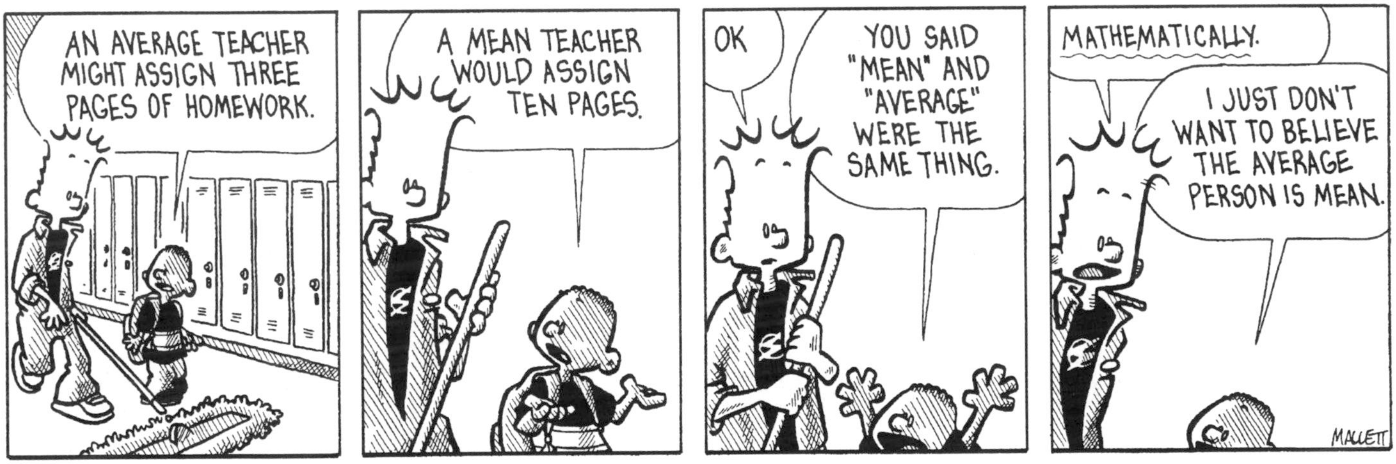
AN AVERAGE TEACHER MIGHT ASSIGN THREE PAGES OF HOMEWORK.
A MEAN TEACHER WOULD ASSIGN TEN PAGES.
OK
YOU SAID "MEAN" AND "AVERAGE" WERE THE SAME THING.
MATHEMATICALLY.
I JUST DON'T WANT TO BELIEVE THE AVERAGE PERSON IS MEAN.
MALLETT

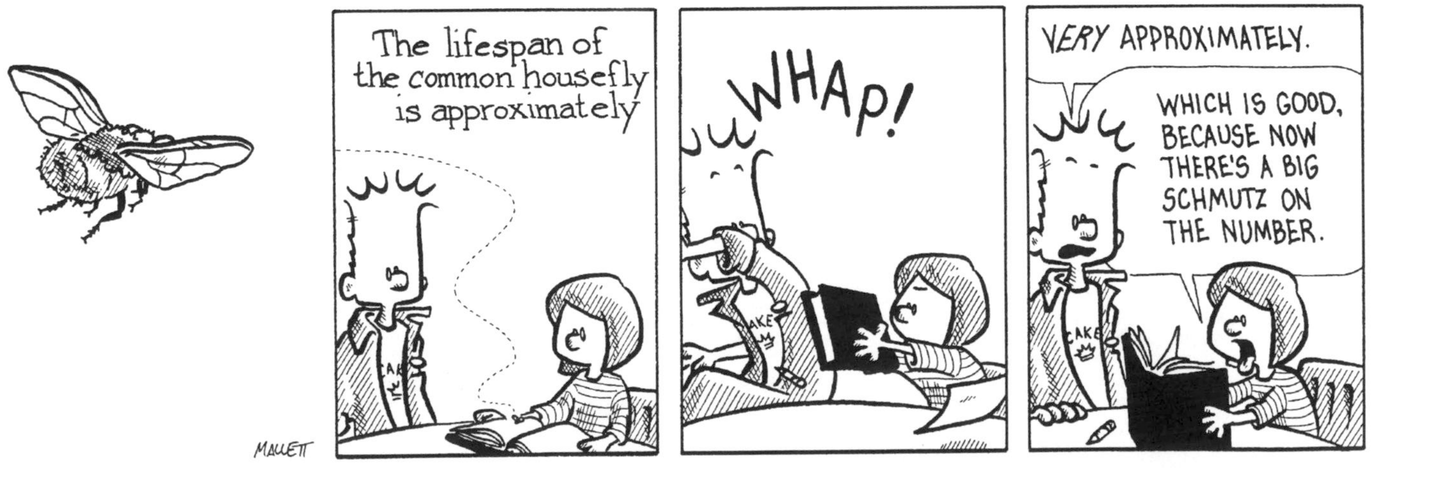
The lifespan of the common housefly is approximately
WHAP!
VERY APPROXIMATELY.
WHICH IS GOOD, BECAUSE NOW THERE'S A BIG SCHMUTZ ON THE NUMBER.
MALLETT

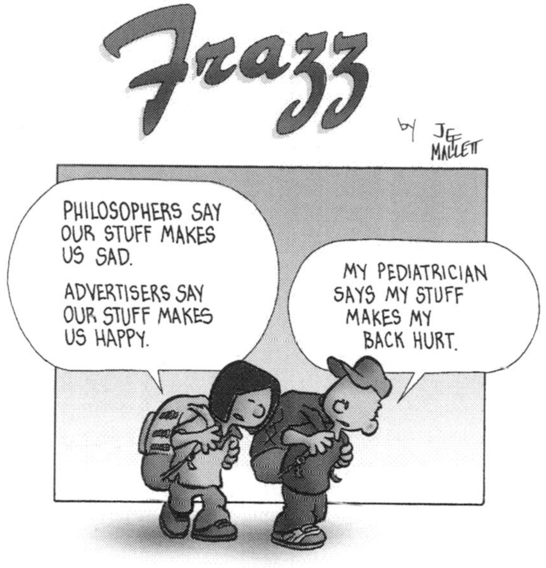
Frazz
by Jeff Mallett
PHILOSOPHERS SAY OUR STUFF MAKES US SAD.
ADVERTISERS SAY OUR STUFF MAKES US HAPPY.
MY PEDIATRICIAN SAYS MY STUFF MAKES MY BACK HURT.

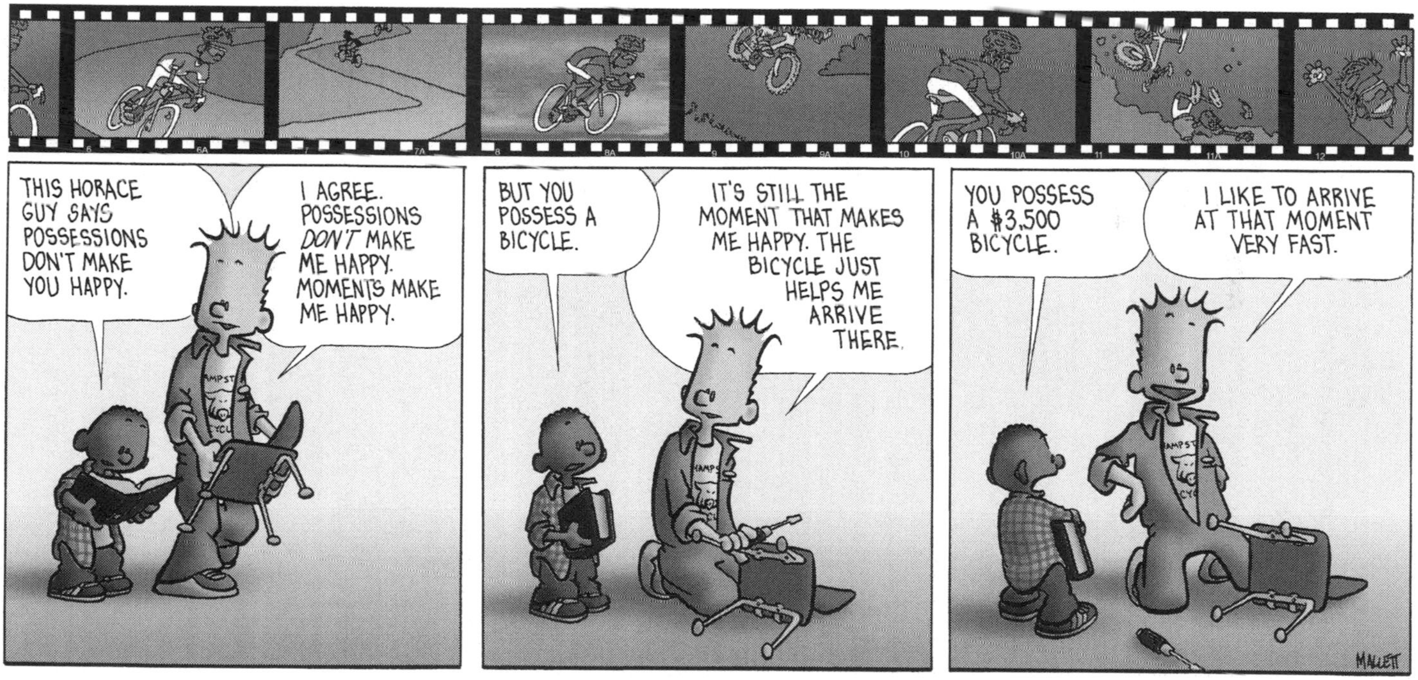
THIS HORACE GUY *SAYS* POSSESSIONS DON'T MAKE YOU HAPPY.
I AGREE. POSSESSIONS *DON'T* MAKE ME HAPPY. MOMENTS MAKE ME HAPPY.
BUT YOU POSSESS A BICYCLE.
IT'S STILL THE MOMENT THAT MAKES ME HAPPY. THE BICYCLE JUST HELPS ME ARRIVE THERE.
YOU POSSESS A $3,500 BICYCLE.
I LIKE TO ARRIVE AT THAT MOMENT VERY FAST.
MALLETT

Panel 1: TODAY IS A GREAT DAY TO BE IN THE SECOND GRADE!

WHY?

Panel 2: EVERY CINCO DE MAYO, MRS. TREVINO COOKS GORDITAS FOR HER CLASS.

Panel 3: IT *IS* GOOD TO BE IN THE SECOND GRADE!

Panel 4: IS THAT WHY MR. HACKER STAYED IN IT FOR THREE YEARS?

ACTUALLY, THAT'S A MYTH.

MALLETT

Panel 5: MRS. TREVINO, WHY DO YOU COOK US GORDITAS FOR CINCO DE MAYO?

Panel 6: TO HELP YOU LEARN ABOUT THE WORLD. FOOD IS AT THE HEART OF CULTURE.

MM!

Panel 7: THIS DOESN'T TASTE LIKE THE MEXICAN FOOD OUT AT THE HUNGRY HEREFORD.

Panel 8: SEE? YOU'RE ALREADY LEARNING SOMETHING.

ABOUT MEXICO, OR ABOUT THE HUNGRY HEREFORD?

MALLETT

Panel 9: MRS. TREVINO, HOW ... UM ... HOW AUTHENTIC IS TODAY'S GORDITA FIESTA?

VERY AUTHENTIC.

MALLETT

Panel 10: REALLY AUTHENTIC?

IT'S SAFE TO DRINK THE WATER, IF THAT'S WHAT YOU'RE GETTING AT.

Panel 11: SURE, THEY REMEMBER *THAT* ABOUT MEXICO.

HEY. WHEN I TRAVEL, THAT'S THE LAST THING I WANT TO FORGET.

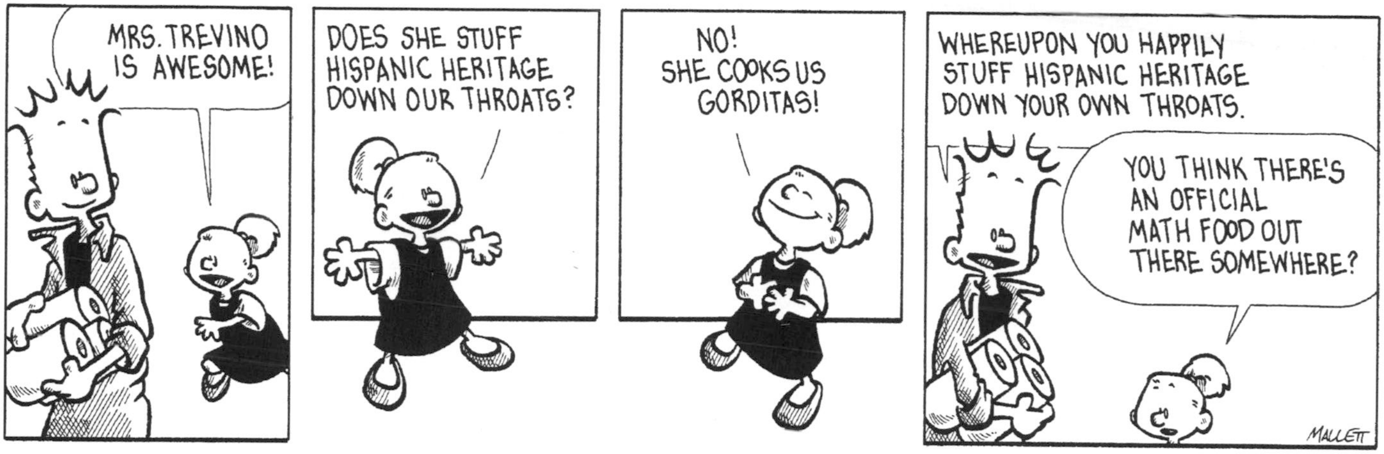
MRS. TREVINO IS AWESOME!
DOES SHE STUFF HISPANIC HERITAGE DOWN OUR THROATS?
NO! SHE COOKS US GORDITAS!
WHEREUPON YOU HAPPILY STUFF HISPANIC HERITAGE DOWN YOUR OWN THROATS.
YOU THINK THERE'S AN OFFICIAL MATH FOOD OUT THERE SOMEWHERE?
MALLETT

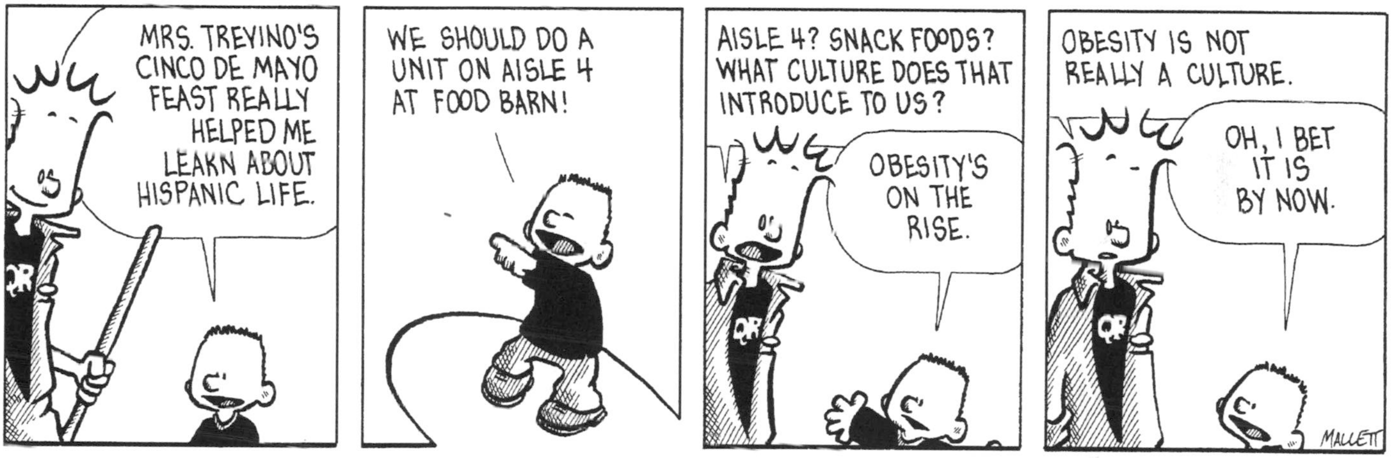
MRS. TREVINO'S CINCO DE MAYO FEAST REALLY HELPED ME LEARN ABOUT HISPANIC LIFE.
WE SHOULD DO A UNIT ON AISLE 4 AT FOOD BARN!
AISLE 4? SNACK FOODS? WHAT CULTURE DOES THAT INTRODUCE TO US?
OBESITY'S ON THE RISE.
OBESITY IS NOT REALLY A CULTURE.
OH, I BET IT IS BY NOW.
MALLETT

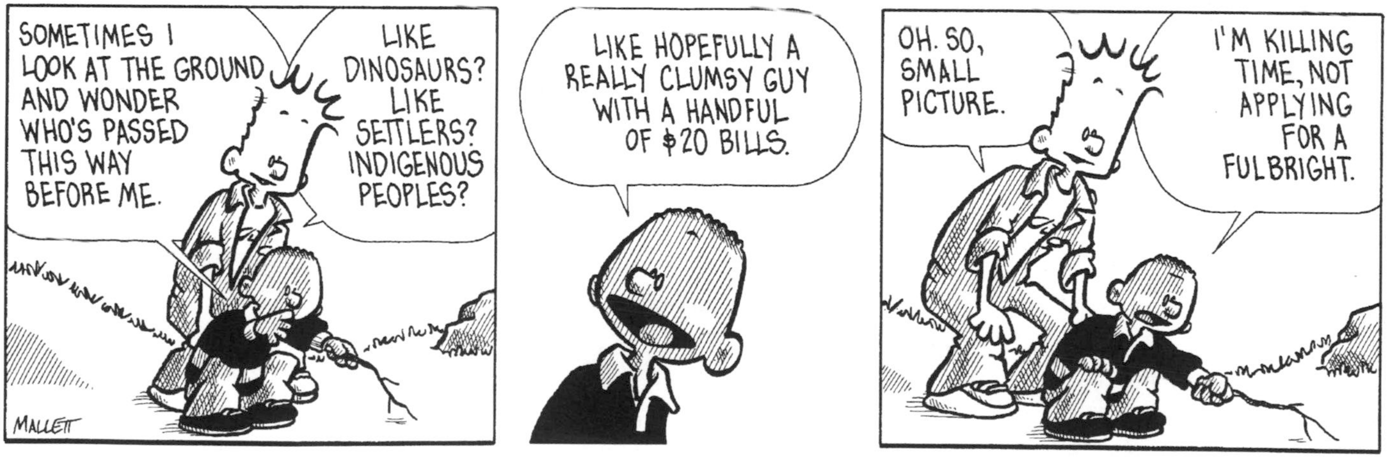
SOMETIMES I LOOK AT THE GROUND AND WONDER WHO'S PASSED THIS WAY BEFORE ME.
LIKE DINOSAURS? LIKE SETTLERS? INDIGENOUS PEOPLES?
MALLETT
LIKE HOPEFULLY A REALLY CLUMSY GUY WITH A HANDFUL OF $20 BILLS.
OH. SO, SMALL PICTURE.
I'M KILLING TIME, NOT APPLYING FOR A FULBRIGHT.

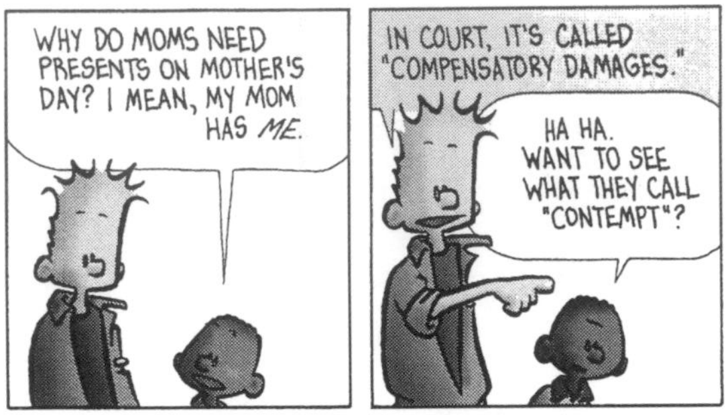
WHY DO MOMS NEED PRESENTS ON MOTHER'S DAY? I MEAN, MY MOM HAS *ME*.
IN COURT, IT'S CALLED "COMPENSATORY DAMAGES."
HA HA. WANT TO SEE WHAT THEY CALL "CONTEMPT"?

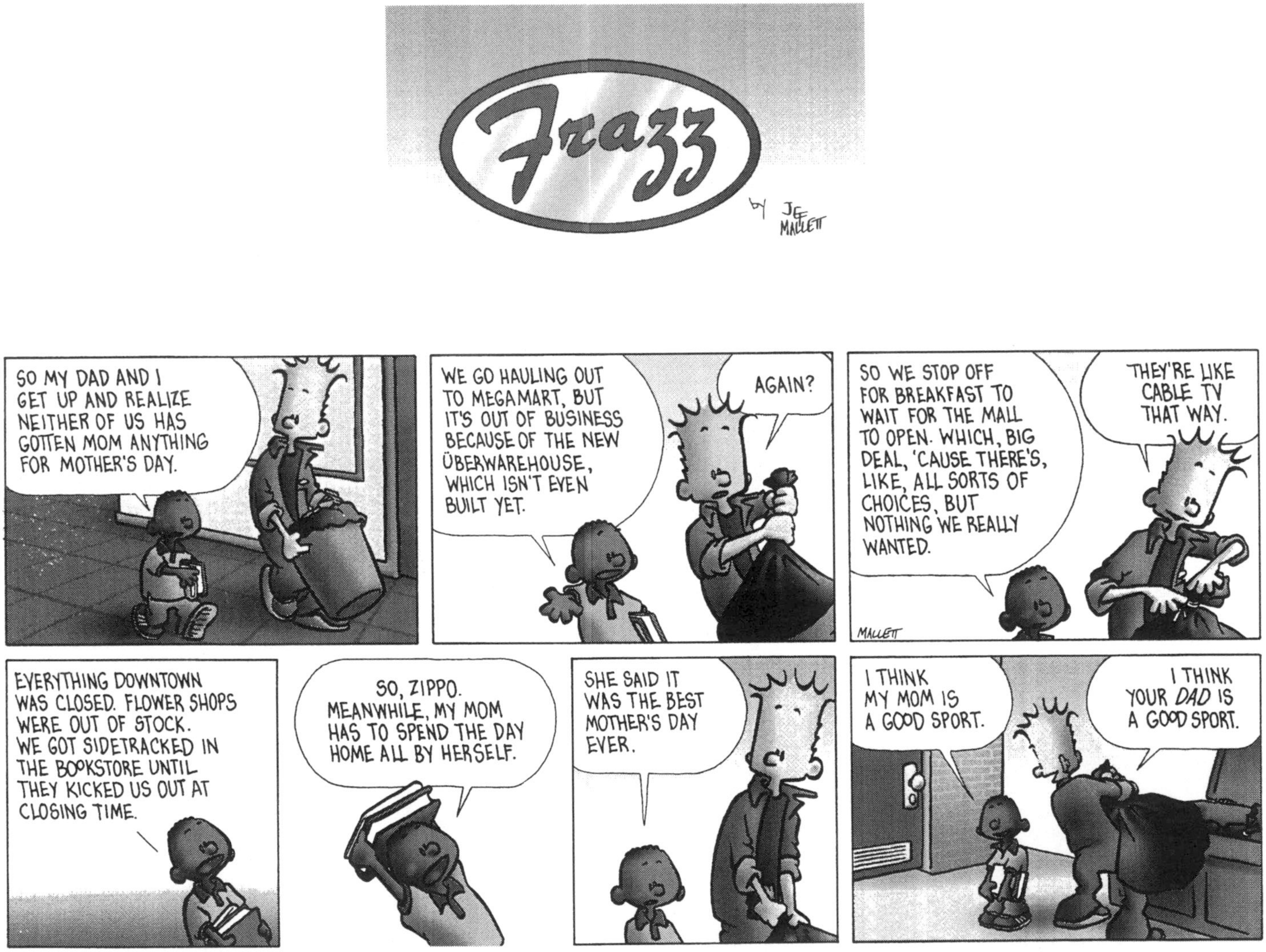
Frazz
by JEFF MALLETT
SO MY DAD AND I GET UP AND REALIZE NEITHER OF US HAS GOTTEN MOM ANYTHING FOR MOTHER'S DAY.
WE GO HAULING OUT TO MEGAMART, BUT IT'S OUT OF BUSINESS BECAUSE OF THE NEW ÜBERWAREHOUSE, WHICH ISN'T EVEN BUILT YET.
AGAIN?
SO WE STOP OFF FOR BREAKFAST TO WAIT FOR THE MALL TO OPEN. WHICH, BIG DEAL, 'CAUSE THERE'S, LIKE, ALL SORTS OF CHOICES, BUT NOTHING WE REALLY WANTED.
THEY'RE LIKE CABLE TV THAT WAY.
MALLETT
EVERYTHING DOWNTOWN WAS CLOSED. FLOWER SHOPS WERE OUT OF STOCK. WE GOT SIDETRACKED IN THE BOOKSTORE UNTIL THEY KICKED US OUT AT CLOSING TIME.
SO, ZIPPO. MEANWHILE, MY MOM HAS TO SPEND THE DAY HOME ALL BY HERSELF.
SHE SAID IT WAS THE BEST MOTHER'S DAY EVER.
I THINK MY MOM IS A GOOD SPORT.
I THINK YOUR *DAD* IS A GOOD SPORT.

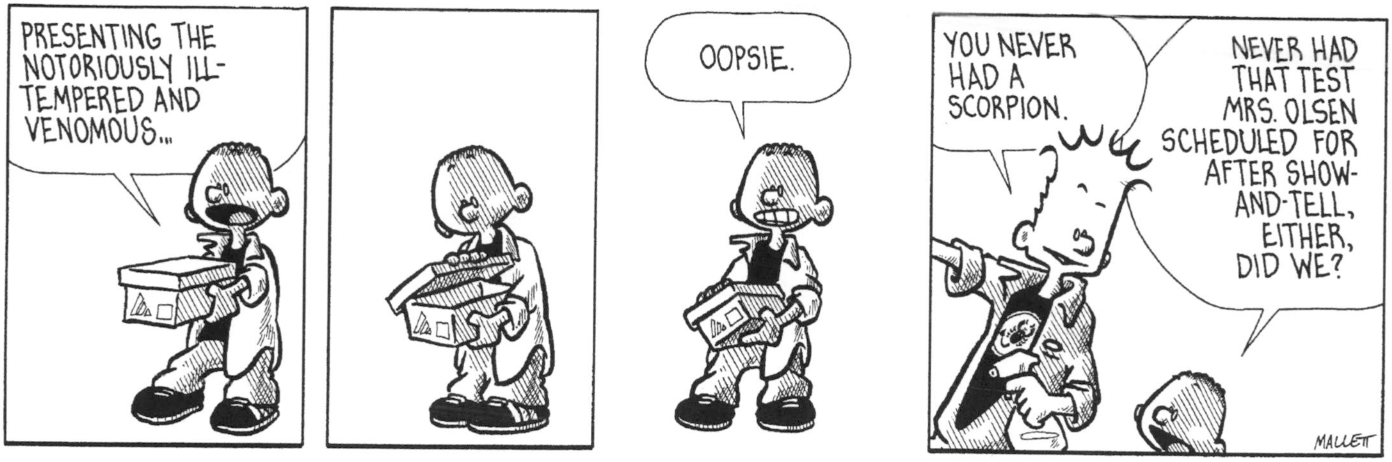
PRESENTING THE NOTORIOUSLY ILL-TEMPERED AND VENOMOUS...
OOPSIE.
YOU NEVER HAD A SCORPION.
NEVER HAD THAT TEST MRS. OLSEN SCHEDULED FOR AFTER SHOW-AND-TELL, EITHER, DID WE?
MALLETT

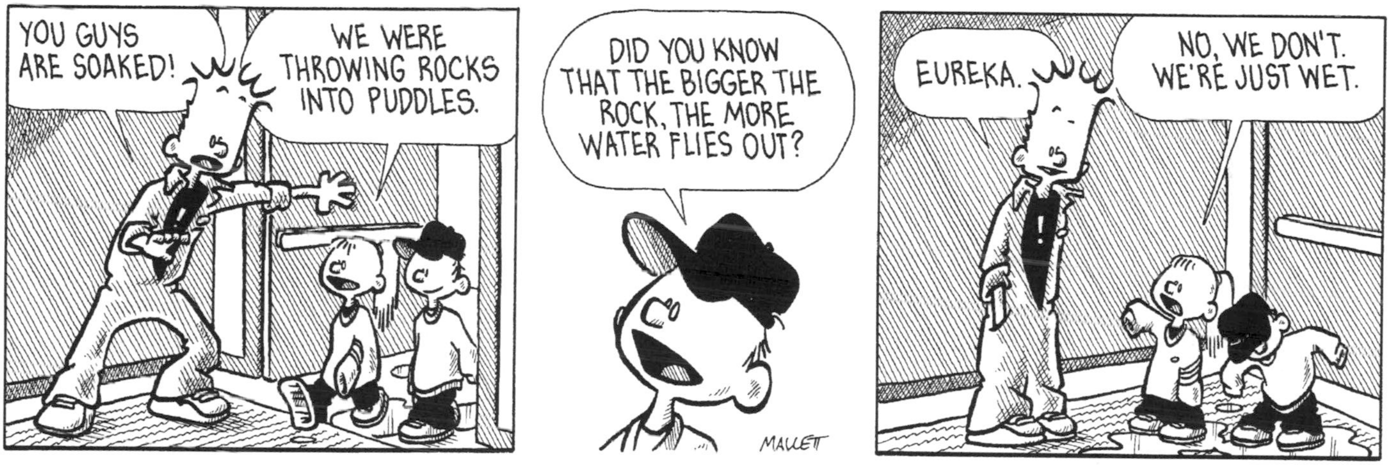
YOU GUYS ARE SOAKED!
WE WERE THROWING ROCKS INTO PUDDLES.
DID YOU KNOW THAT THE BIGGER THE ROCK, THE MORE WATER FLIES OUT?
MALLETT
EUREKA.
NO, WE DON'T. WE'RE JUST WET.

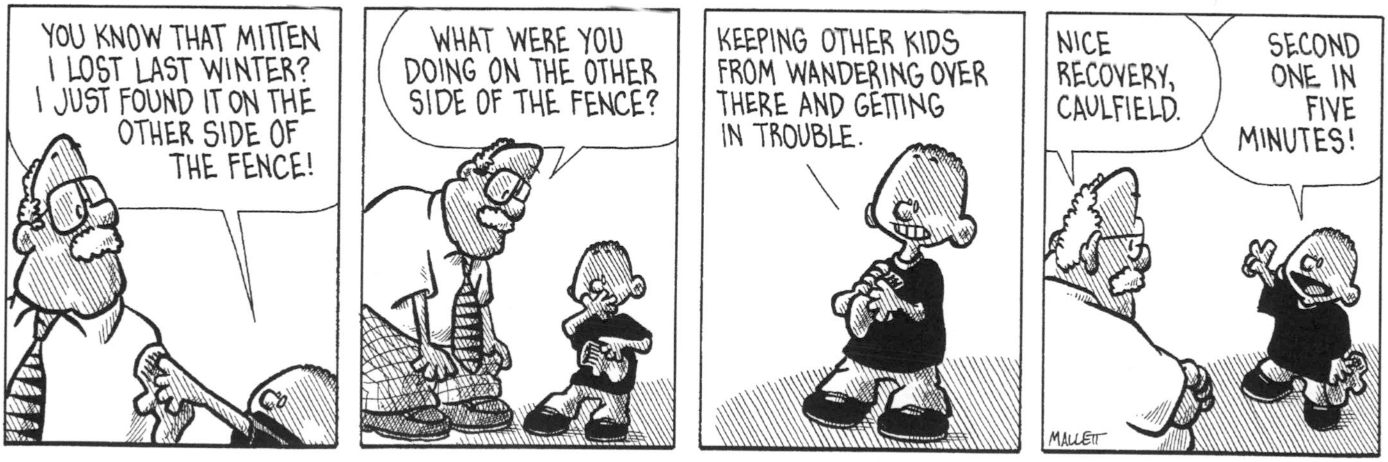
YOU KNOW THAT MITTEN I LOST LAST WINTER? I JUST FOUND IT ON THE OTHER SIDE OF THE FENCE!
WHAT WERE YOU DOING ON THE OTHER SIDE OF THE FENCE?
KEEPING OTHER KIDS FROM WANDERING OVER THERE AND GETTING IN TROUBLE.
NICE RECOVERY, CAULFIELD.
SECOND ONE IN FIVE MINUTES!
MALLETT

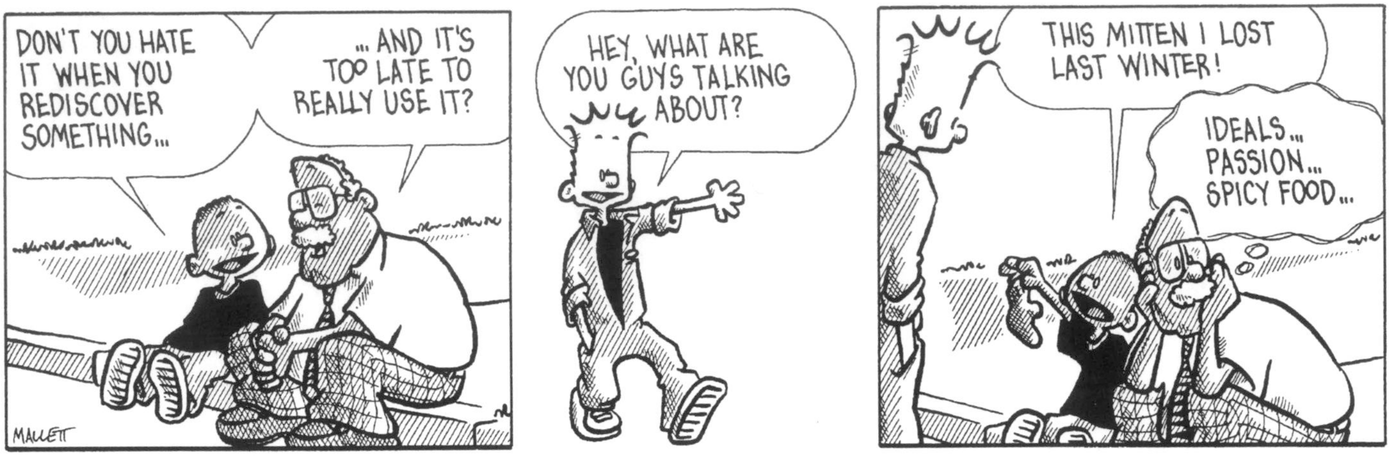
DON'T YOU HATE IT WHEN YOU REDISCOVER SOMETHING...
... AND IT'S TOO LATE TO REALLY USE IT?
HEY, WHAT ARE YOU GUYS TALKING ABOUT?
THIS MITTEN I LOST LAST WINTER!
IDEALS... PASSION... SPICY FOOD...
MALLETT

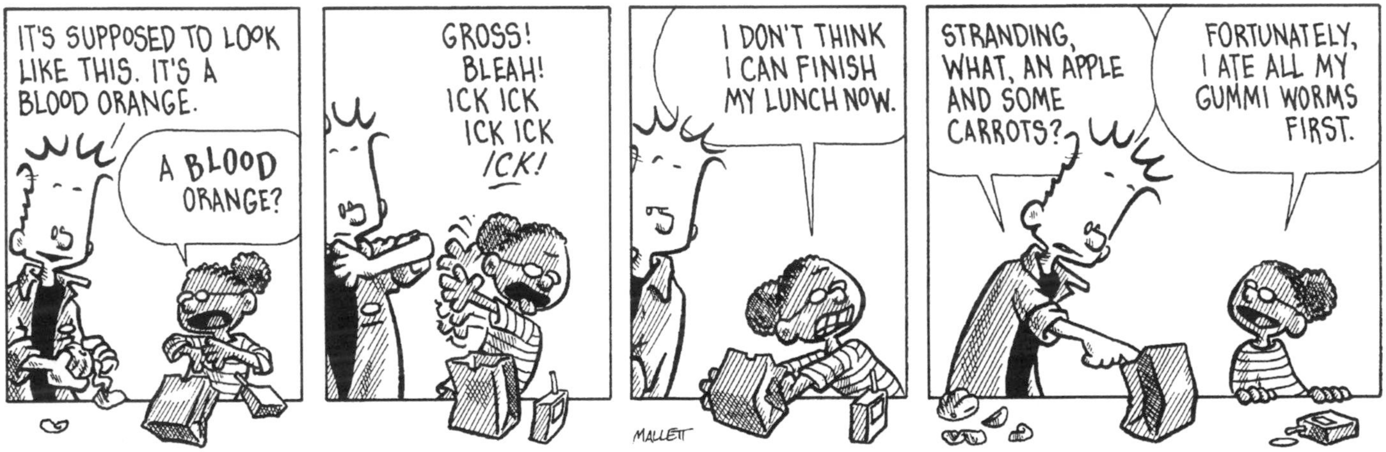
IT'S SUPPOSED TO LOOK LIKE THIS. IT'S A BLOOD ORANGE.
A BLOOD ORANGE?
GROSS! BLEAH! ICK ICK ICK ICK ICK!
I DON'T THINK I CAN FINISH MY LUNCH NOW.
STRANDING, WHAT, AN APPLE AND SOME CARROTS?
FORTUNATELY, I ATE ALL MY GUMMI WORMS FIRST.
MALLETT

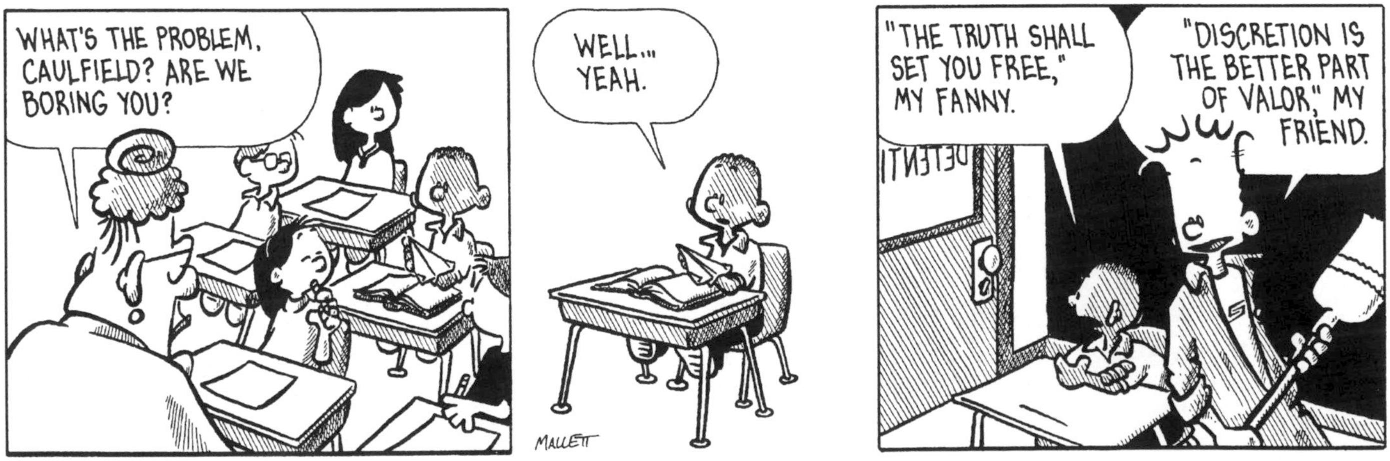
WHAT'S THE PROBLEM, CAULFIELD? ARE WE BORING YOU?
WELL... YEAH.
"THE TRUTH SHALL SET YOU FREE," MY FANNY.
"DISCRETION IS THE BETTER PART OF VALOR," MY FRIEND.
MALLETT

Frazz
by JEF MALLETT
IF TWO WRONGS DON'T MAKE A RIGHT, WHY DO THREE OUTS MAKE AN INNING?
DO FOUR DOWNS MAKE AN UP?
IN DETROIT, FOUR DOWNS MAKE A PUNT.

GOTCHA! YOU'RE OUT!
NOT!
THEN MAYBE YOU SHOULD PLAY IN YOUR UNDIES.
HA HA HA! YOU WISH!
I GOT YOUR LEG!
YOU GOT MY PANT LEG!
YEAH! THEN I COULD AIM FOR THE SPIDER-MAN ON YOUR BUTT.
X-MEN! SPIDER-MAN IS SO 2002!
LIKE I SAID!
MY PANTS ARE NOT ME!
SHOOT. THERE'S THE BELL. WANT HALF OF MY CANDY BAR?
THANKS! WANT A SIP OF MY GRAPE JUICE?
I LOVE RECESS BECAUSE IT MAKES ME THINK OF A WORLD WITHOUT LAWYERS.
I LIKE THE 15-MINUTE STATUTE OF LIMITATIONS.
MALLETT

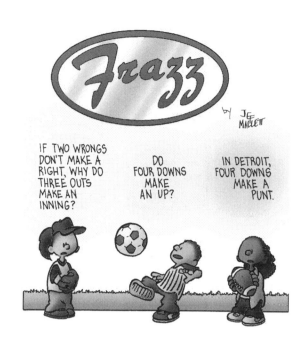

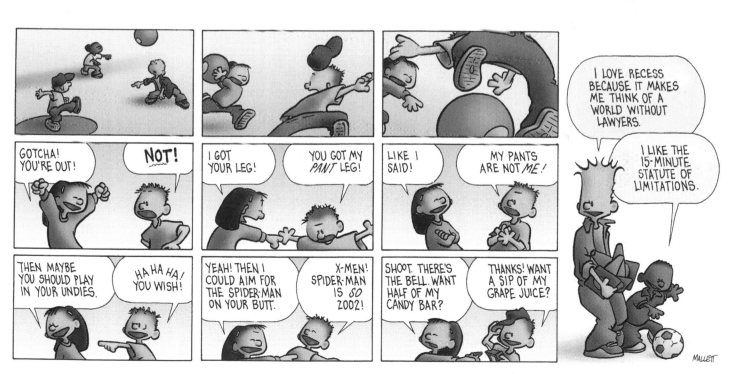

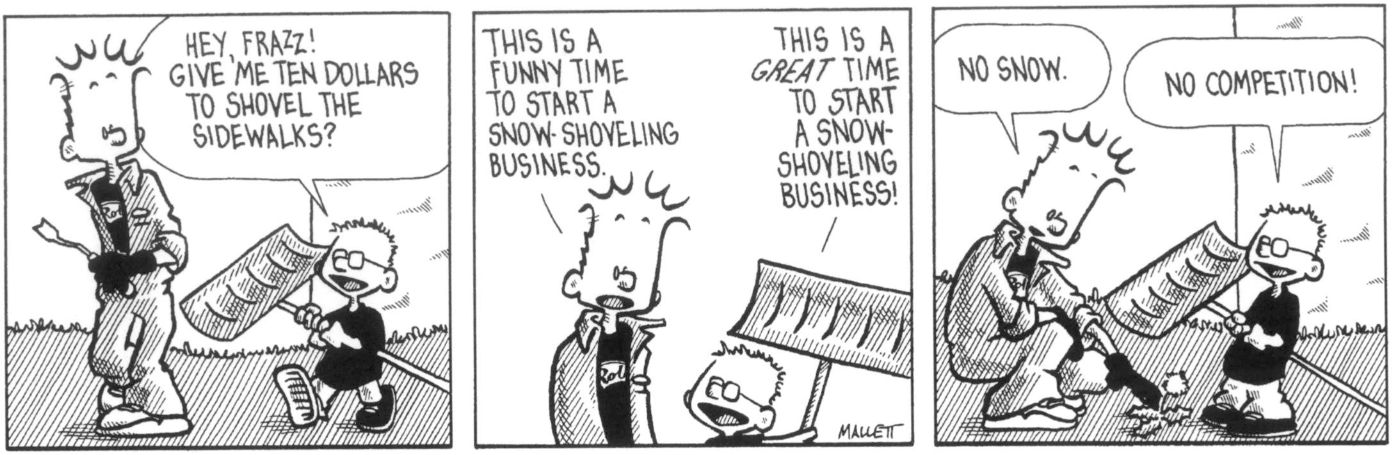
HEY, FRAZZ! GIVE ME TEN DOLLARS TO SHOVEL THE SIDEWALKS?
THIS IS A FUNNY TIME TO START A SNOW-SHOVELING BUSINESS.
THIS IS A *GREAT* TIME TO START A SNOW-SHOVELING BUSINESS!
MALLETT
NO SNOW.
NO COMPETITION!

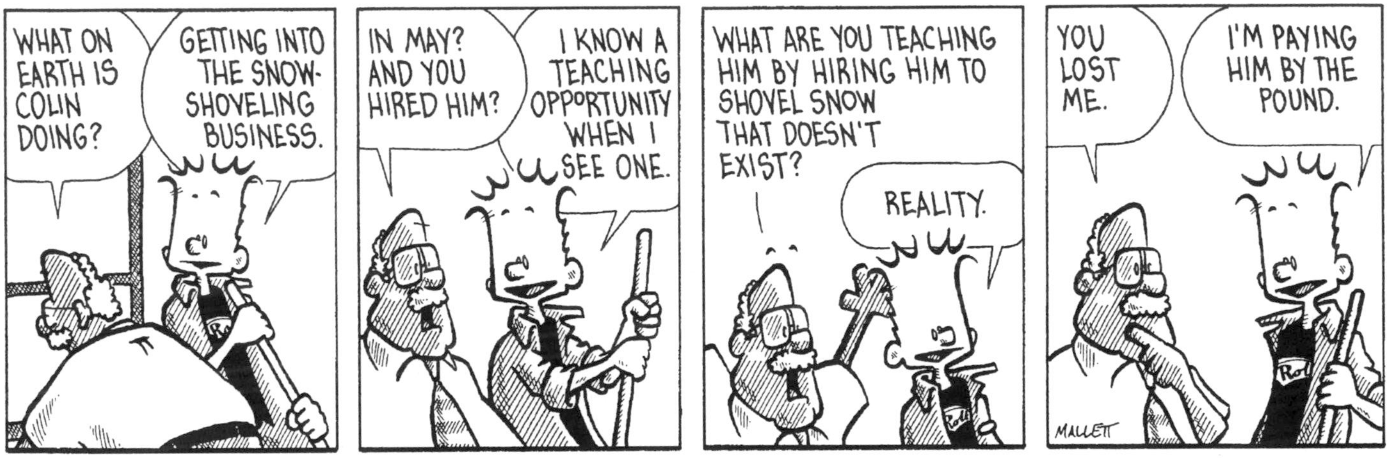
WHAT ON EARTH IS COLIN DOING?
GETTING INTO THE SNOW-SHOVELING BUSINESS.
IN MAY? AND YOU HIRED HIM?
I KNOW A TEACHING OPPORTUNITY WHEN I SEE ONE.
WHAT ARE YOU TEACHING HIM BY HIRING HIM TO SHOVEL SNOW THAT DOESN'T EXIST?
REALITY.
YOU LOST ME.
I'M PAYING HIM BY THE POUND.
MALLETT

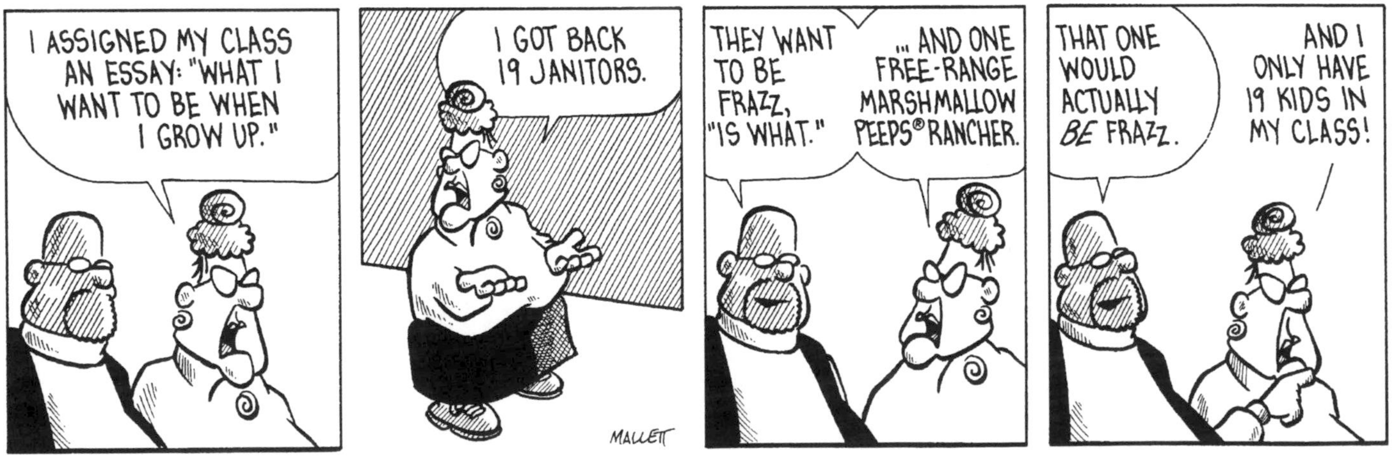
I ASSIGNED MY CLASS AN ESSAY: "WHAT I WANT TO BE WHEN I GROW UP."
I GOT BACK 19 JANITORS.
MALLETT
THEY WANT TO BE FRAZZ, "IS WHAT."
... AND ONE FREE-RANGE MARSHMALLOW PEEPS® RANCHER.
THAT ONE WOULD ACTUALLY *BE* FRAZZ.
AND I ONLY HAVE 19 KIDS IN MY CLASS!

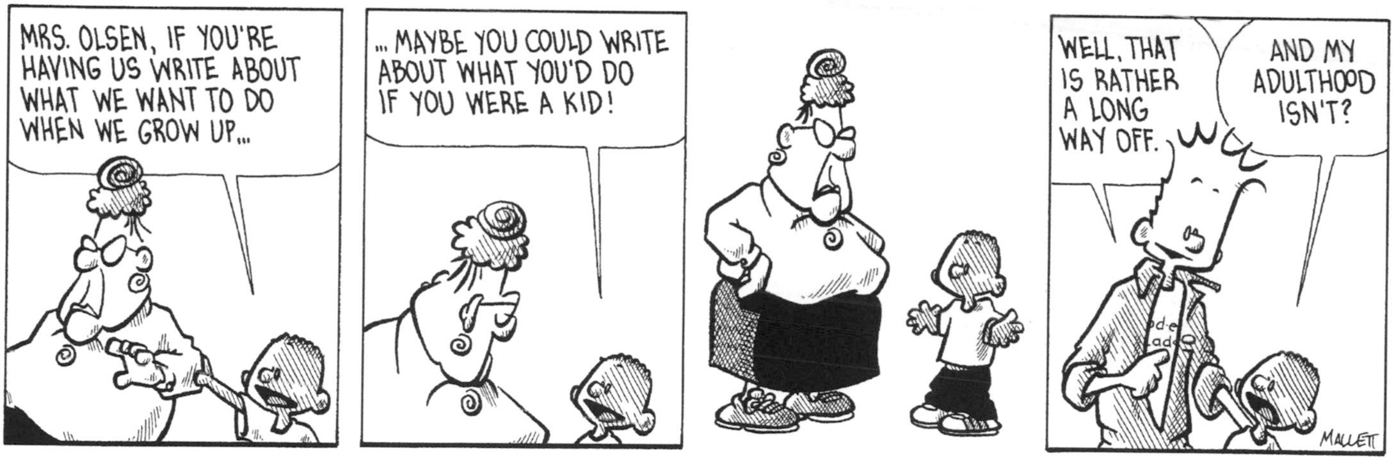
MRS. OLSEN, IF YOU'RE HAVING US WRITE ABOUT WHAT WE WANT TO DO WHEN WE GROW UP...
... MAYBE YOU COULD WRITE ABOUT WHAT YOU'D DO IF YOU WERE A KID!
WELL, THAT IS RATHER A LONG WAY OFF.
AND MY ADULTHOOD ISN'T?
MALLETT

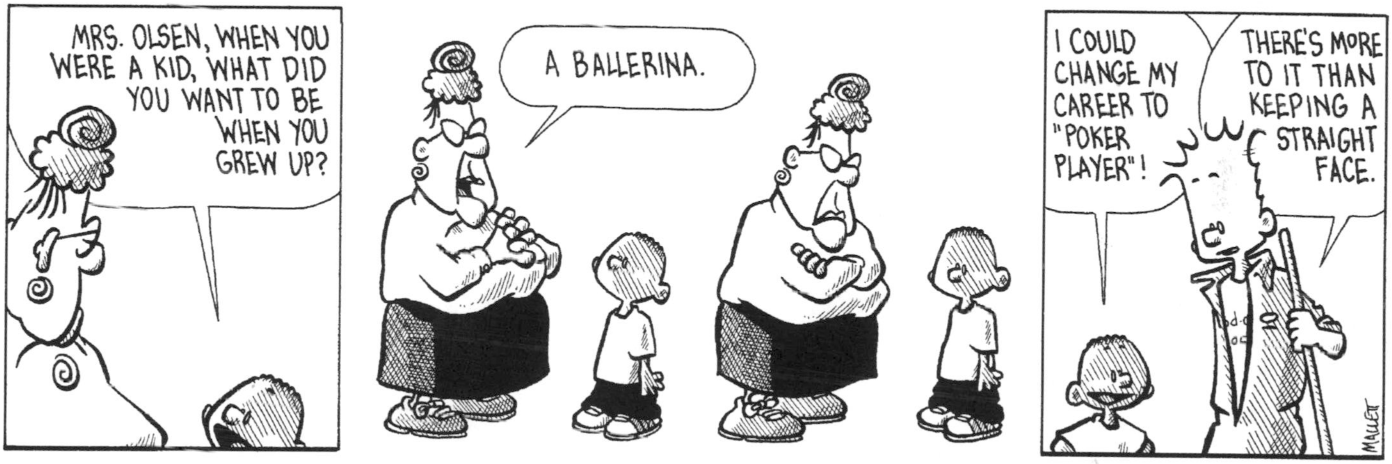
MRS. OLSEN, WHEN YOU WERE A KID, WHAT DID YOU WANT TO BE WHEN YOU GREW UP?
A BALLERINA.
I COULD CHANGE MY CAREER TO "POKER PLAYER"!
THERE'S MORE TO IT THAN KEEPING A STRAIGHT FACE.
MALLETT

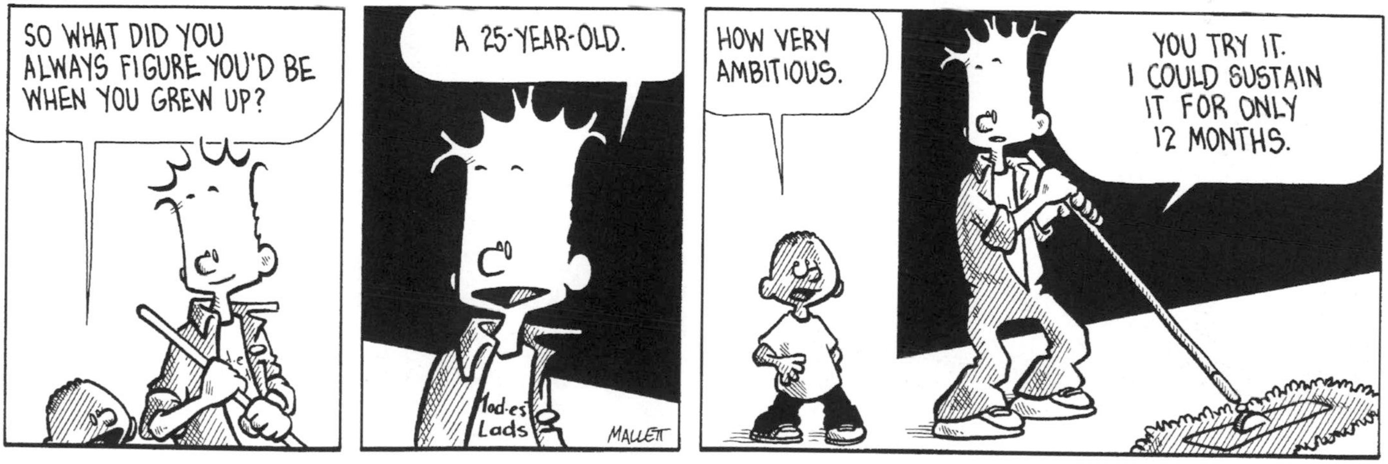
SO WHAT DID YOU ALWAYS FIGURE YOU'D BE WHEN YOU GREW UP?
A 25-YEAR-OLD.
Mod-es Lads
MALLETT
HOW VERY AMBITIOUS.
YOU TRY IT. I COULD SUSTAIN IT FOR ONLY 12 MONTHS.

Frazz

by Jef Mallett

WHY ASK WHY?
HOLD THAT SENTIMENT FOR THE NEXT TIME MATH SEEMS POINTLESS.

NO.
NO?
WHAT IF ICARUS HAD SAID NO? WHAT IF MAGELLAN SAID NO? WHAT IF GEORGE MALLORY SAID NO?
ICARUS CRASHED INTO THE SEA, MAGELLAN WAS MURDERED HALF A WORLD FROM HOME, AND MALLORY NEVER MADE IT OFF EVEREST.
WHAT IF MY GRANDPA, WHO SPENDS 14 HOURS A DAY WATCHING GAME SHOWS, HAD EVER SAID YES?
OKAY, ONE PUSH.
THAT'S ALL I'M ASKING.
MALLETT

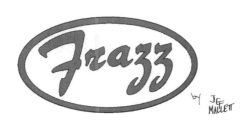

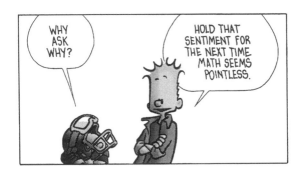

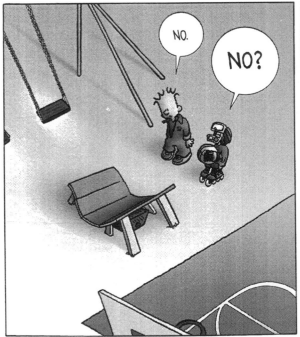

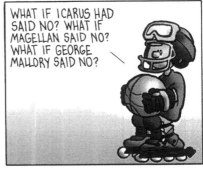

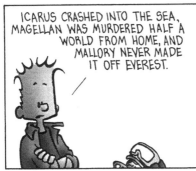

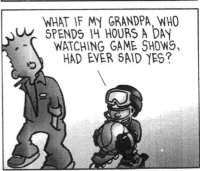

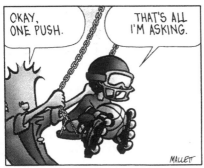

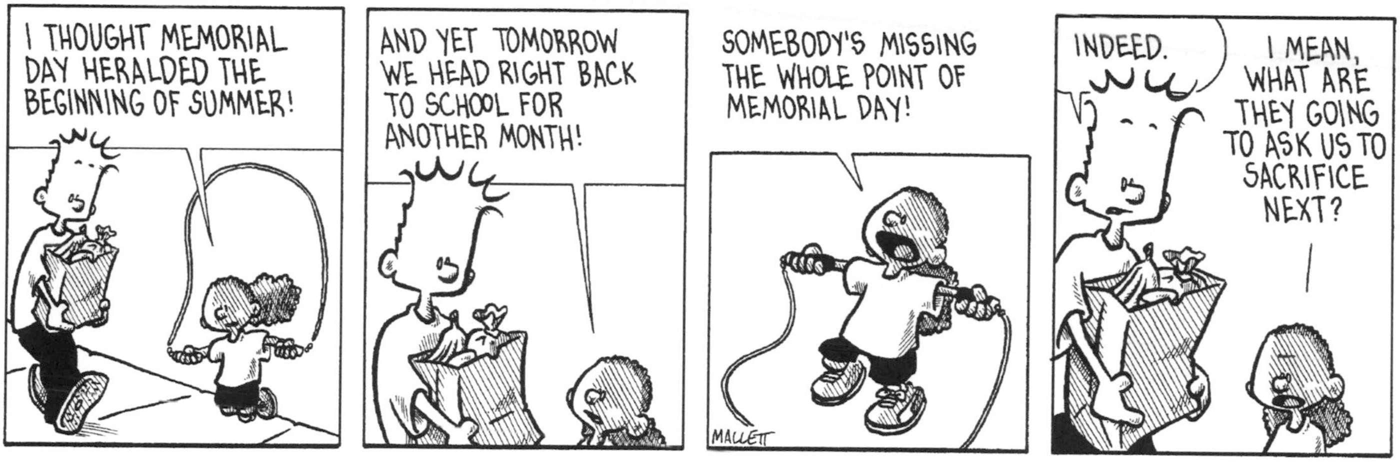
I THOUGHT MEMORIAL DAY HERALDED THE BEGINNING OF SUMMER!
AND YET TOMORROW WE HEAD RIGHT BACK TO SCHOOL FOR ANOTHER MONTH!
SOMEBODY'S MISSING THE WHOLE POINT OF MEMORIAL DAY!
MALLETT
INDEED.
I MEAN, WHAT ARE THEY GOING TO ASK US TO SACRIFICE NEXT?

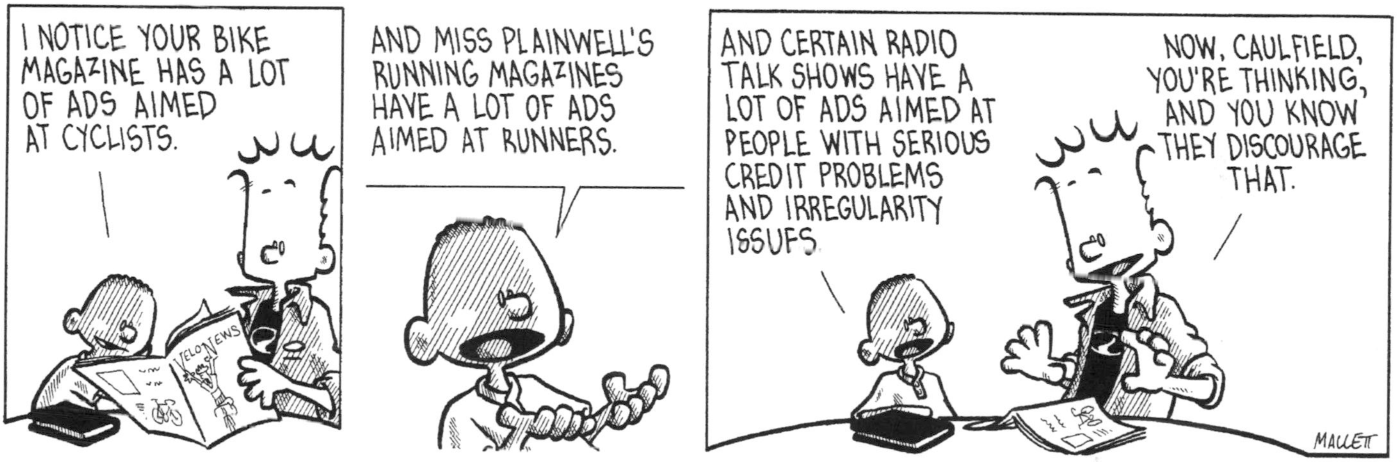
I NOTICE YOUR BIKE MAGAZINE HAS A LOT OF ADS AIMED AT CYCLISTS.
VELO NEWS
AND MISS PLAINWELL'S RUNNING MAGAZINES HAVE A LOT OF ADS AIMED AT RUNNERS.
AND CERTAIN RADIO TALK SHOWS HAVE A LOT OF ADS AIMED AT PEOPLE WITH SERIOUS CREDIT PROBLEMS AND IRREGULARITY ISSUES.
NOW, CAULFIELD, YOU'RE THINKING, AND YOU KNOW THEY DISCOURAGE THAT.
MALLETT

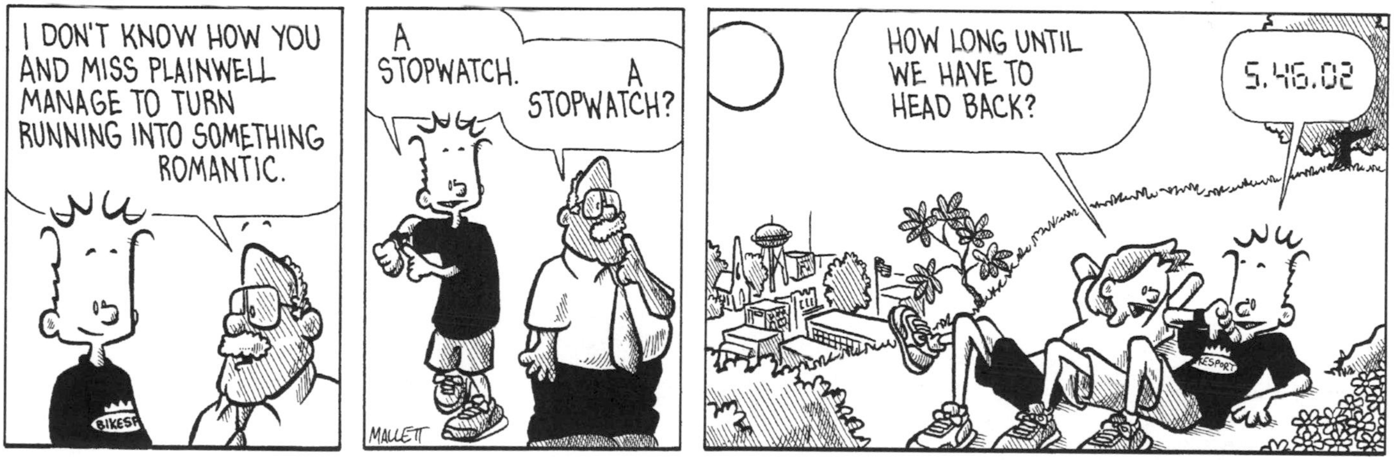
I DON'T KNOW HOW YOU AND MISS PLAINWELL MANAGE TO TURN RUNNING INTO SOMETHING ROMANTIC.
BIKESP
A STOPWATCH.
A STOPWATCH?
MALLETT
HOW LONG UNTIL WE HAVE TO HEAD BACK?
5.46.02

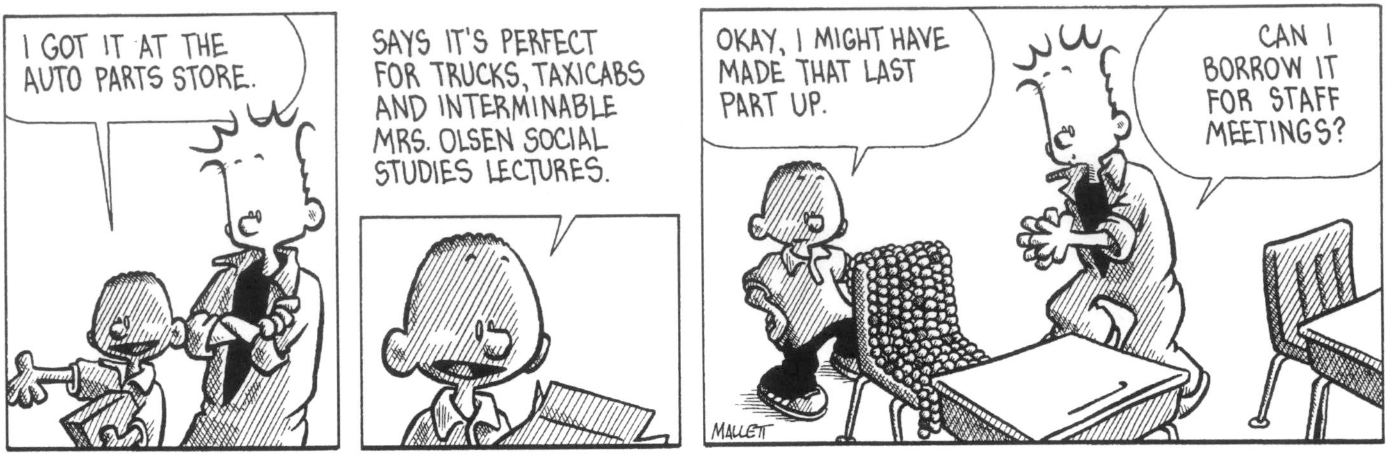

I GOT IT AT THE AUTO PARTS STORE.
SAYS IT'S PERFECT FOR TRUCKS, TAXICABS AND INTERMINABLE MRS. OLSEN SOCIAL STUDIES LECTURES.
OKAY, I MIGHT HAVE MADE THAT LAST PART UP.
CAN I BORROW IT FOR STAFF MEETINGS?
MALLETT

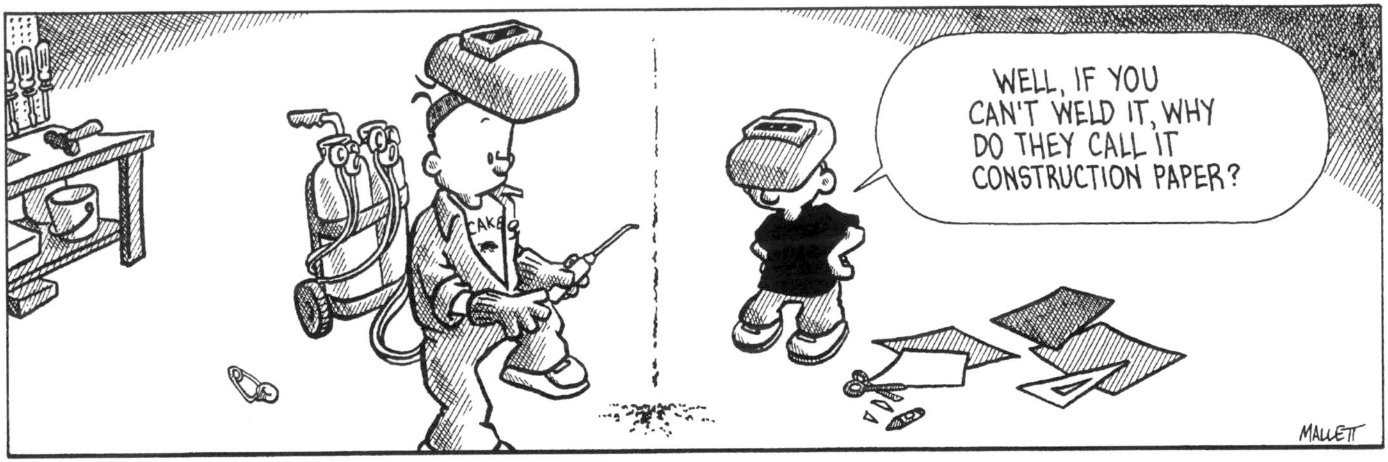

CAKE
WELL, IF YOU CAN'T WELD IT, WHY DO THEY CALL IT CONSTRUCTION PAPER?
MALLETT

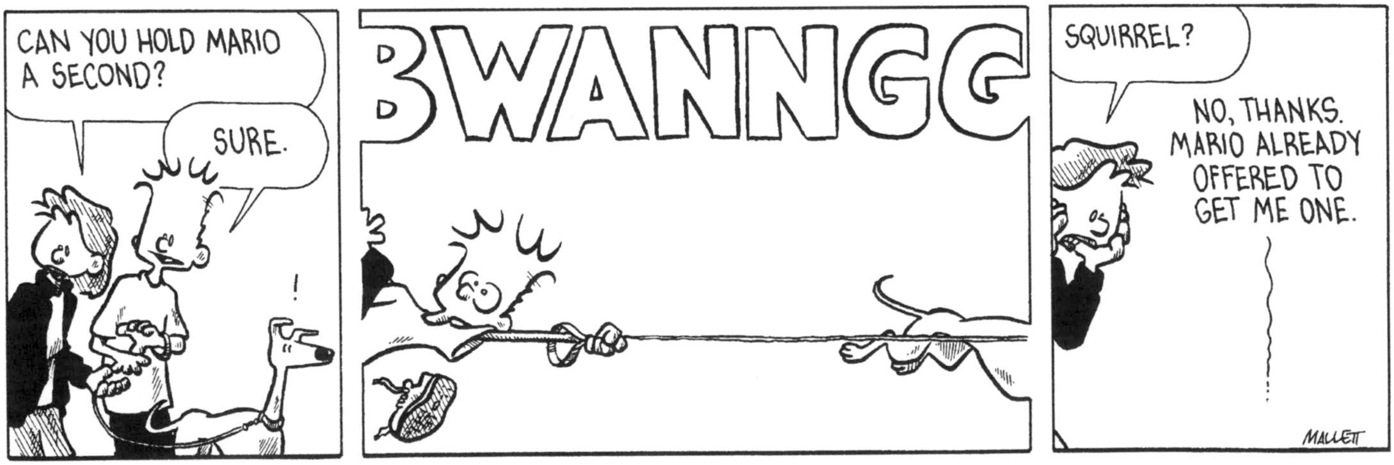

CAN YOU HOLD MARIO A SECOND?
SURE.
!
BWANNGG
SQUIRREL?
NO, THANKS. MARIO ALREADY OFFERED TO GET ME ONE.
MALLETT

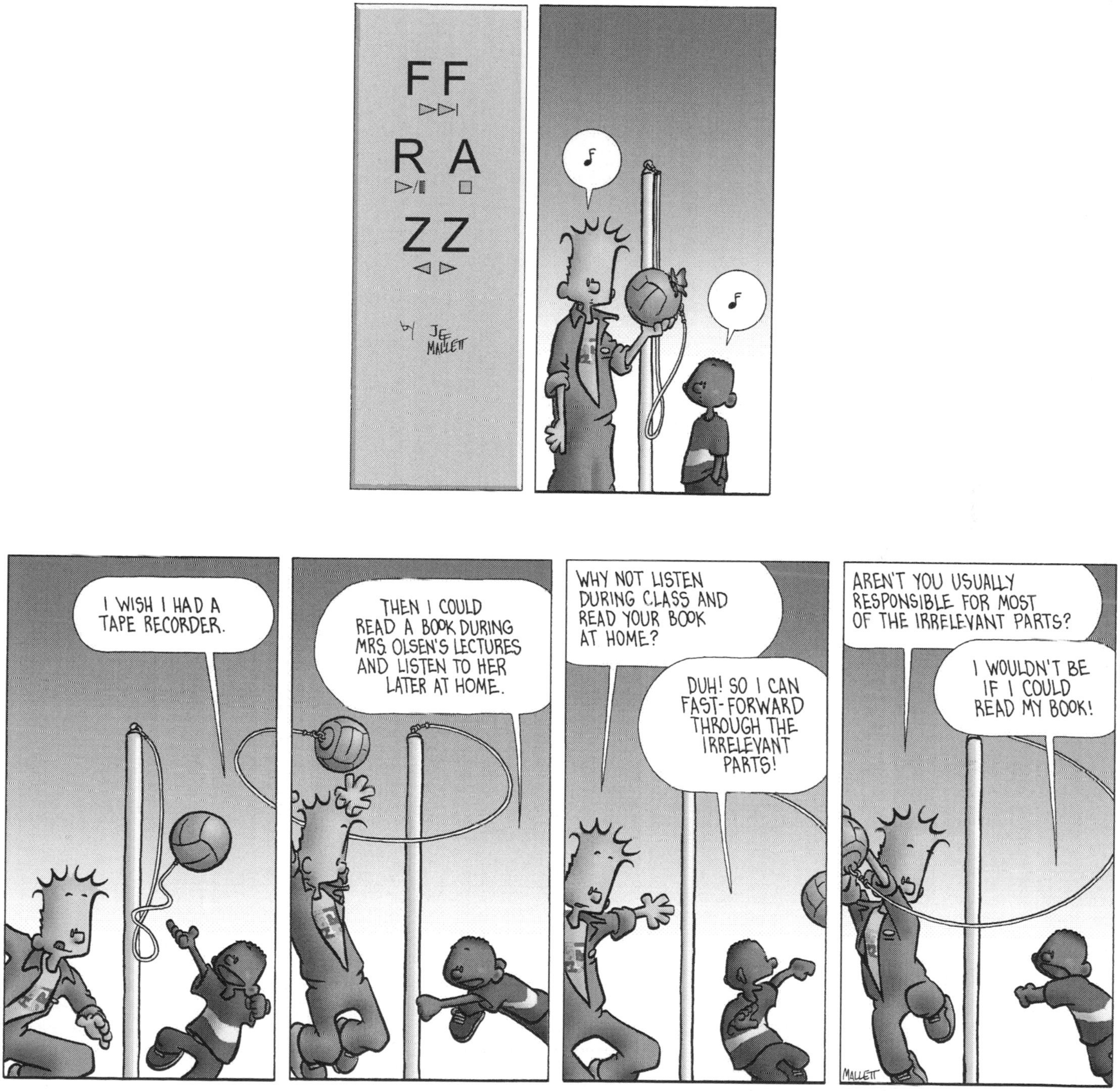
FRAZZ
by Jeff Mallett
I WISH I HAD A TAPE RECORDER.
THEN I COULD READ A BOOK DURING MRS. OLSEN'S LECTURES AND LISTEN TO HER LATER AT HOME.
WHY NOT LISTEN DURING CLASS AND READ YOUR BOOK AT HOME?
DUH! SO I CAN FAST-FORWARD THROUGH THE IRRELEVANT PARTS!
AREN'T YOU USUALLY RESPONSIBLE FOR MOST OF THE IRRELEVANT PARTS?
I WOULDN'T BE IF I COULD READ MY BOOK!
MALLETT

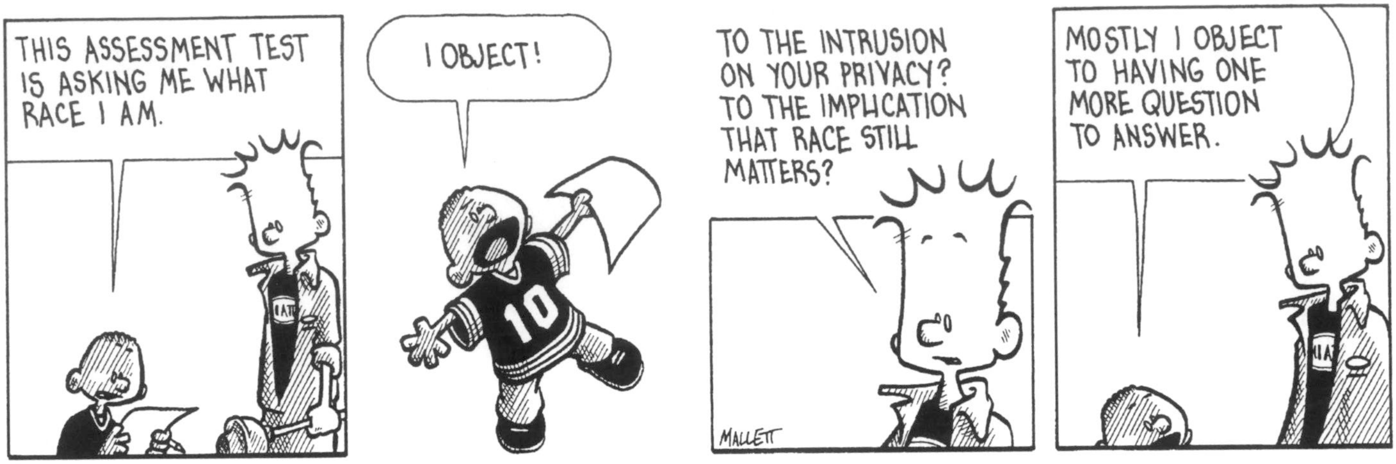
THIS ASSESSMENT TEST IS ASKING ME WHAT RACE I AM.
I OBJECT!
TO THE INTRUSION ON YOUR PRIVACY? TO THE IMPLICATION THAT RACE STILL MATTERS?
MALLETT
MOSTLY I OBJECT TO HAVING ONE MORE QUESTION TO ANSWER.

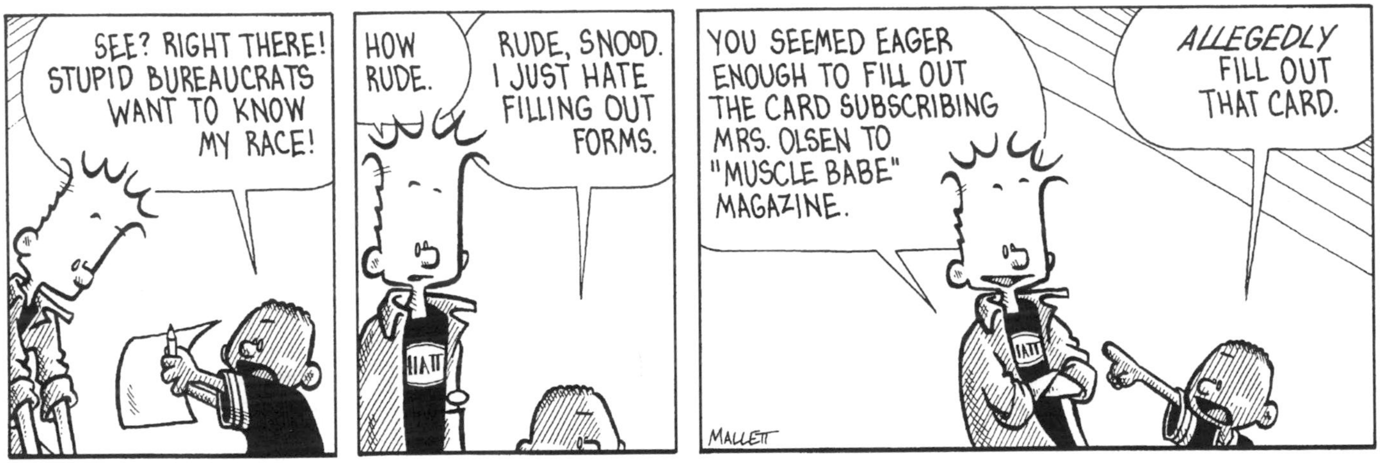
SEE? RIGHT THERE! STUPID BUREAUCRATS WANT TO KNOW MY RACE!
HOW RUDE.
RUDE, SNOOD. I JUST HATE FILLING OUT FORMS.
YOU SEEMED EAGER ENOUGH TO FILL OUT THE CARD SUBSCRIBING MRS. OLSEN TO "MUSCLE BABE" MAGAZINE.
ALLEGEDLY FILL OUT THAT CARD.
MALLETT

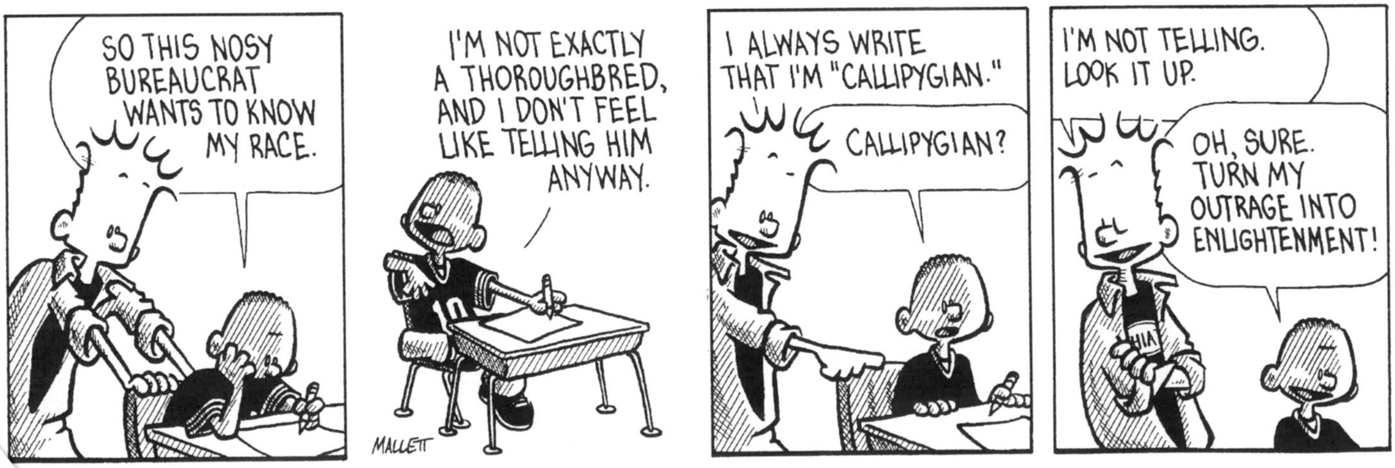
SO THIS NOSY BUREAUCRAT WANTS TO KNOW MY RACE.
I'M NOT EXACTLY A THOROUGHBRED, AND I DON'T FEEL LIKE TELLING HIM ANYWAY.
MALLETT
I ALWAYS WRITE THAT I'M "CALLIPYGIAN."
CALLIPYGIAN?
I'M NOT TELLING. LOOK IT UP.
OH, SURE. TURN MY OUTRAGE INTO ENLIGHTENMENT!

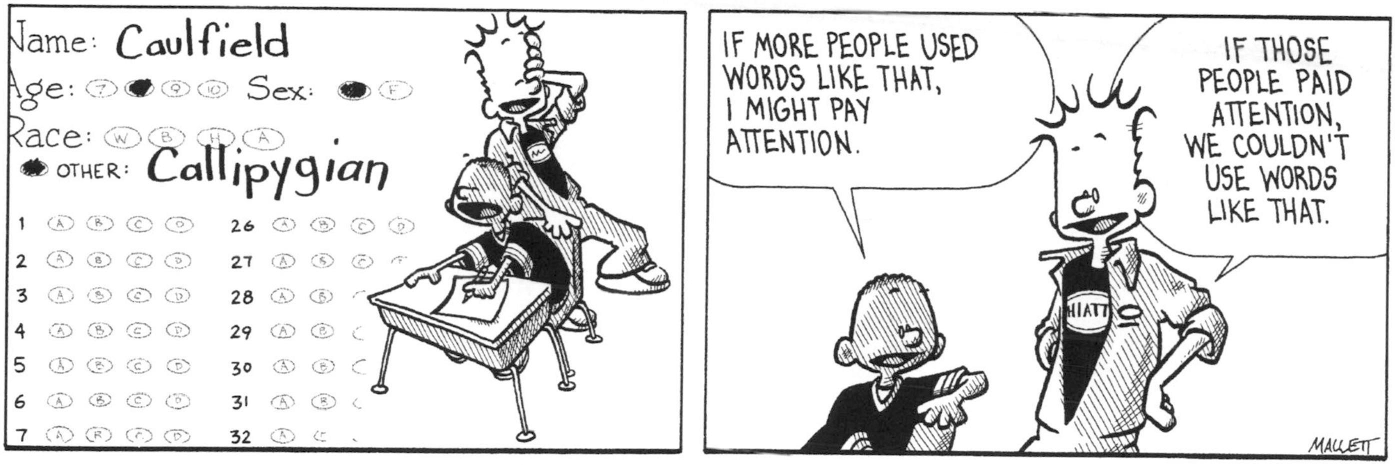
Name: Caulfield
Age: 7 9 10 Sex: F
Race: W B H A
OTHER: Callipygian
1 A B C D 26 A B C D
2 A B C D 27 A B C
3 A B C D 28 A B
4 A B C D 29 A B
5 A B C D 30 A B
6 A B C D 31 A B
7 A B C D 32 A
IF MORE PEOPLE USED WORDS LIKE THAT, I MIGHT PAY ATTENTION.
IF THOSE PEOPLE PAID ATTENTION, WE COULDN'T USE WORDS LIKE THAT.
HIATT
MALLETT

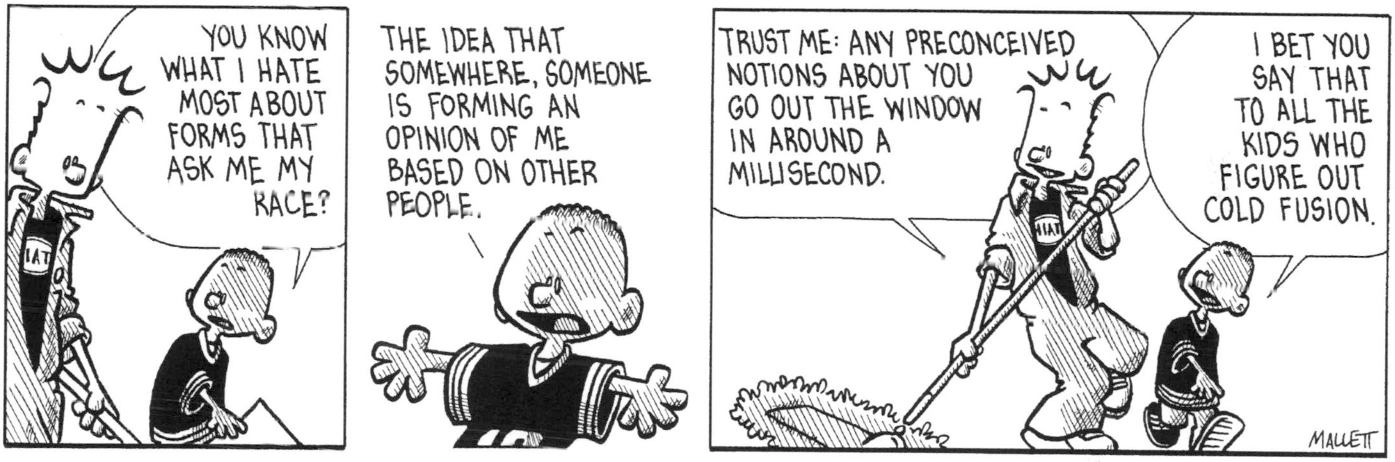
YOU KNOW WHAT I HATE MOST ABOUT FORMS THAT ASK ME MY RACE?
THE IDEA THAT SOMEWHERE, SOMEONE IS FORMING AN OPINION OF ME BASED ON OTHER PEOPLE.
TRUST ME: ANY PRECONCEIVED NOTIONS ABOUT YOU GO OUT THE WINDOW IN AROUND A MILLISECOND.
I BET YOU SAY THAT TO ALL THE KIDS WHO FIGURE OUT COLD FUSION.
HIATT
MALLETT

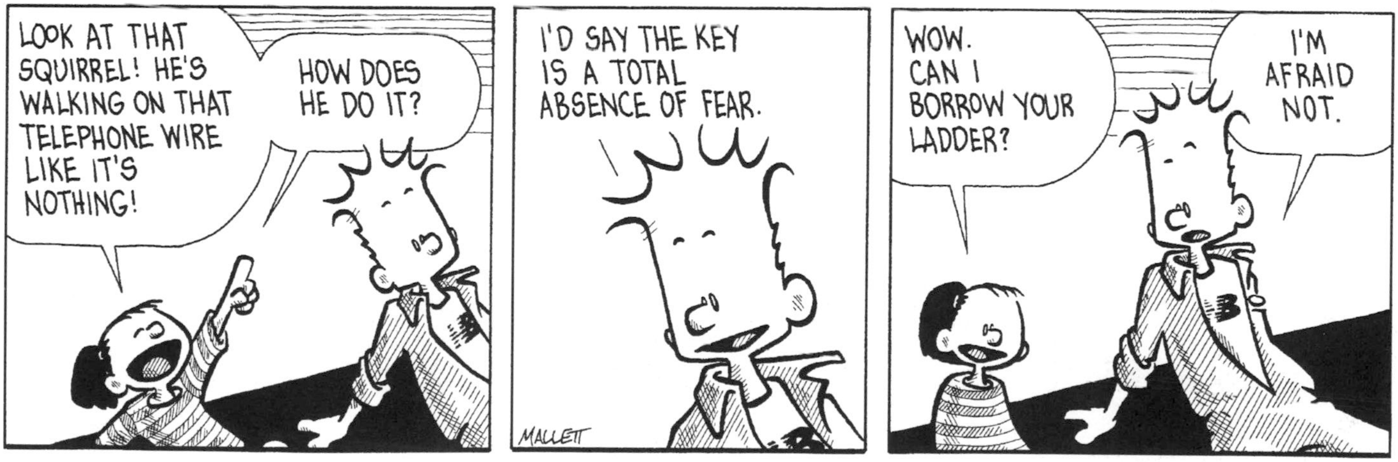
LOOK AT THAT SQUIRREL! HE'S WALKING ON THAT TELEPHONE WIRE LIKE IT'S NOTHING!
HOW DOES HE DO IT?
I'D SAY THE KEY IS A TOTAL ABSENCE OF FEAR.
MALLETT
WOW. CAN I BORROW YOUR LADDER?
I'M AFRAID NOT.

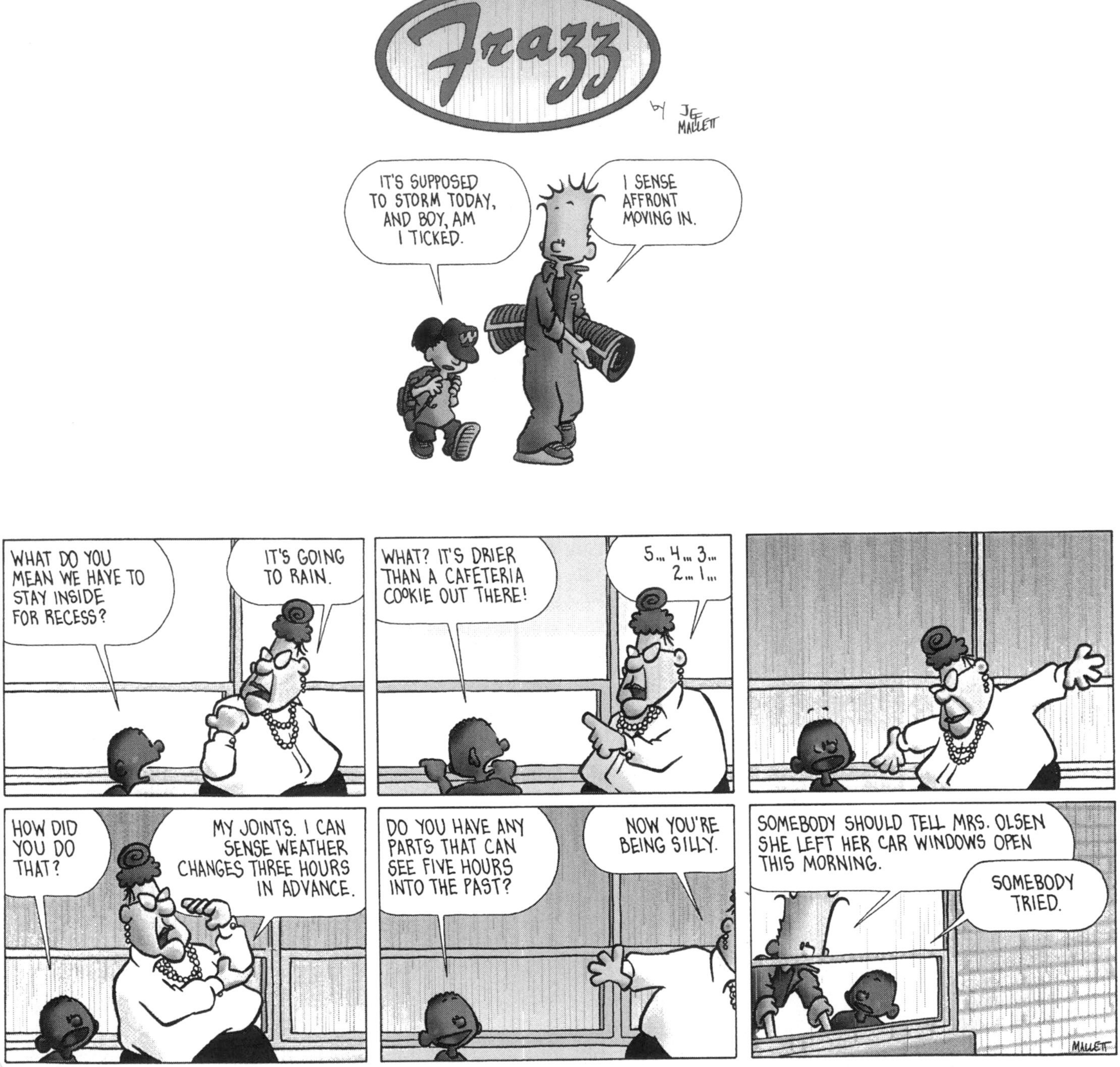
Frazz
by JEFF MALLETT
IT'S SUPPOSED TO STORM TODAY, AND BOY, AM I TICKED.
I SENSE AFFRONT MOVING IN.
WHAT DO YOU MEAN WE HAVE TO STAY INSIDE FOR RECESS?
IT'S GOING TO RAIN.
WHAT? IT'S DRIER THAN A CAFETERIA COOKIE OUT THERE!
5... 4... 3... 2... 1...
HOW DID YOU DO THAT?
MY JOINTS. I CAN SENSE WEATHER CHANGES THREE HOURS IN ADVANCE.
DO YOU HAVE ANY PARTS THAT CAN SEE FIVE HOURS INTO THE PAST?
NOW YOU'RE BEING SILLY.
SOMEBODY SHOULD TELL MRS. OLSEN SHE LEFT HER CAR WINDOWS OPEN THIS MORNING.
SOMEBODY TRIED.
MALLETT

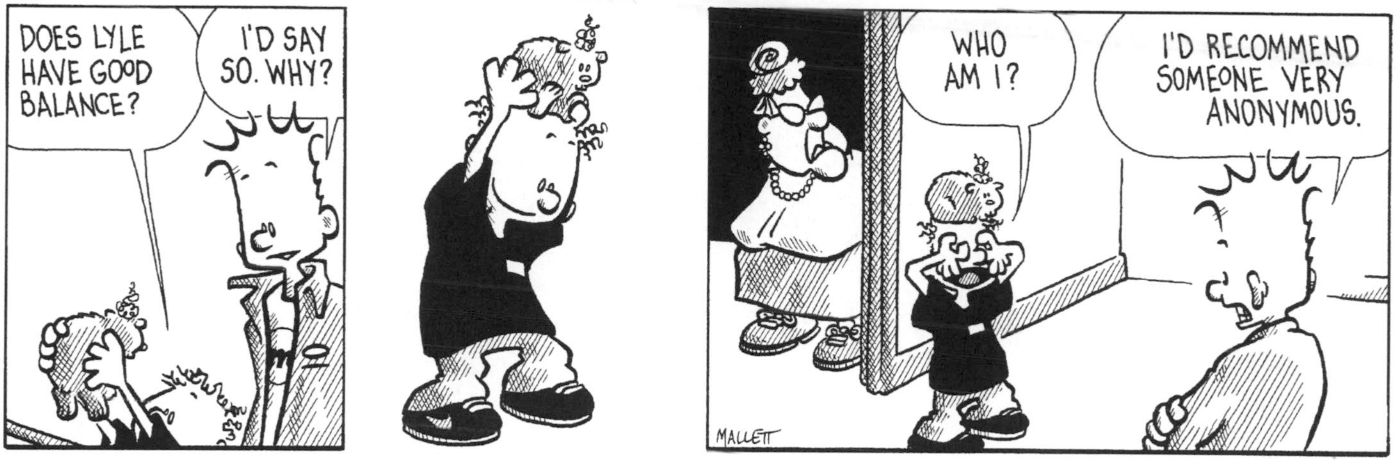
DOES LYLE HAVE GOOD BALANCE?
I'D SAY SO. WHY?
WHO AM I?
I'D RECOMMEND SOMEONE VERY ANONYMOUS.
MALLETT

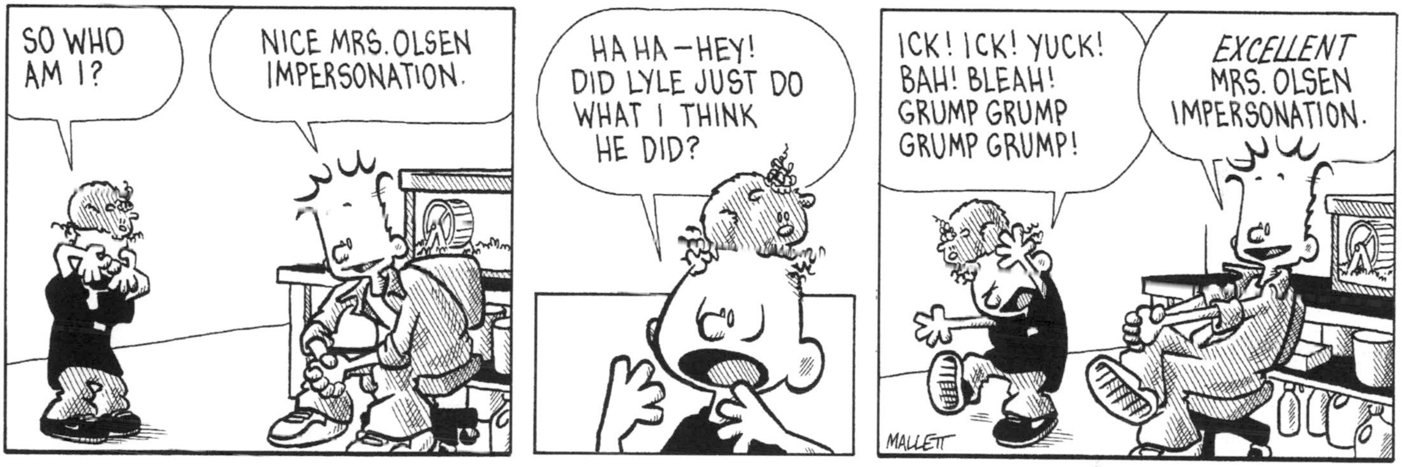
SO WHO AM I?
NICE MRS. OLSEN IMPERSONATION.
HA HA—HEY! DID LYLE JUST DO WHAT I THINK HE DID?
ICK! ICK! YUCK! BAH! BLEAH! GRUMP GRUMP GRUMP GRUMP!
EXCELLENT MRS. OLSEN IMPERSONATION.
MALLETT

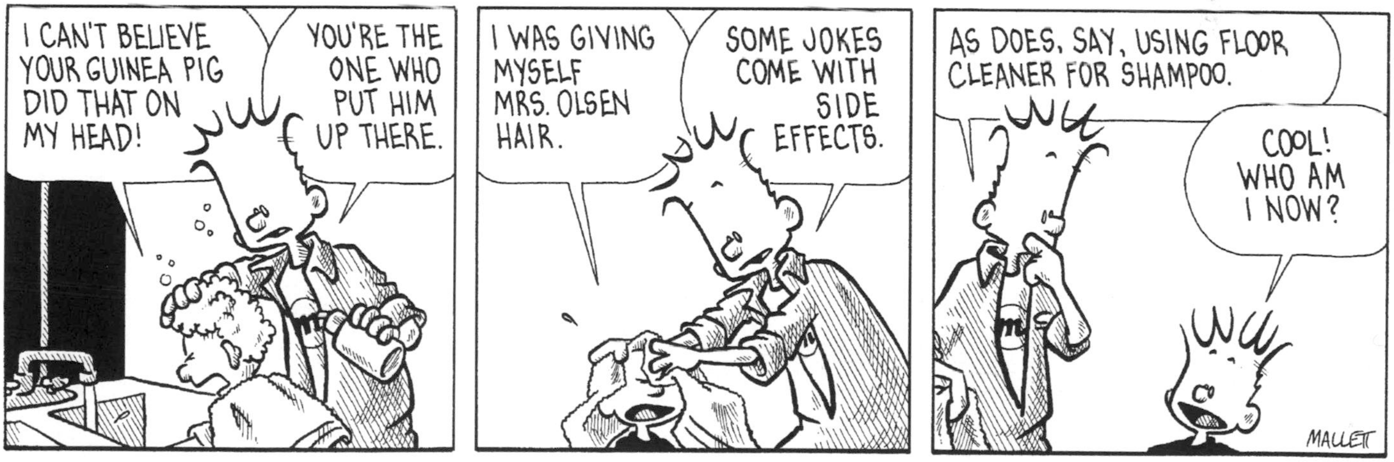
I CAN'T BELIEVE YOUR GUINEA PIG DID THAT ON MY HEAD!
YOU'RE THE ONE WHO PUT HIM UP THERE.
I WAS GIVING MYSELF MRS. OLSEN HAIR.
SOME JOKES COME WITH SIDE EFFECTS.
AS DOES, SAY, USING FLOOR CLEANER FOR SHAMPOO.
COOL! WHO AM I NOW?
MALLETT

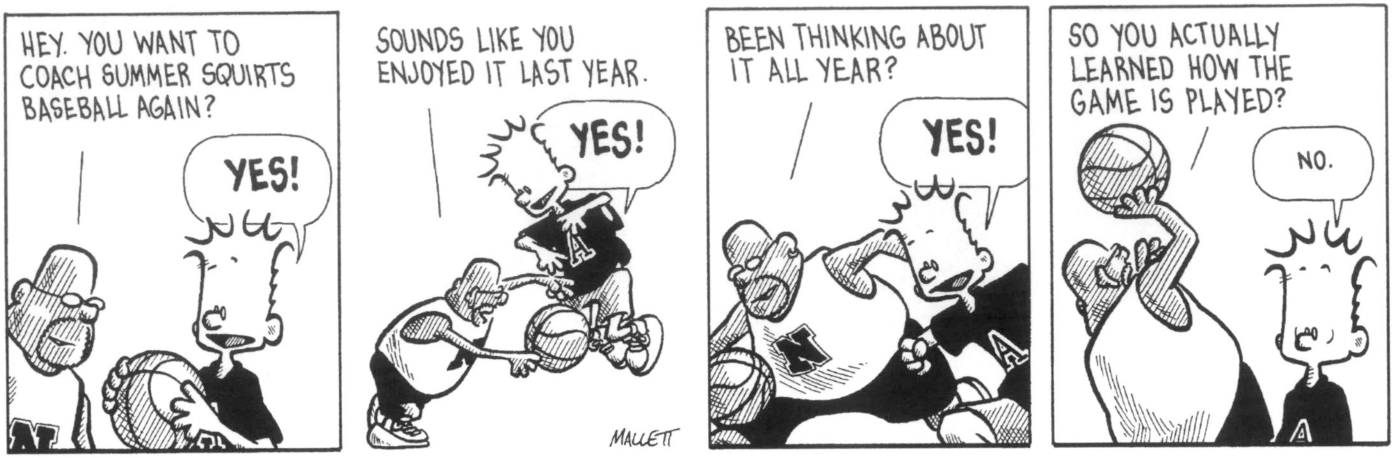
HEY. YOU WANT TO COACH SUMMER SQUIRTS BASEBALL AGAIN?
YES!
SOUNDS LIKE YOU ENJOYED IT LAST YEAR.
YES!
BEEN THINKING ABOUT IT ALL YEAR?
YES!
SO YOU ACTUALLY LEARNED HOW THE GAME IS PLAYED?
NO.
MALLETT

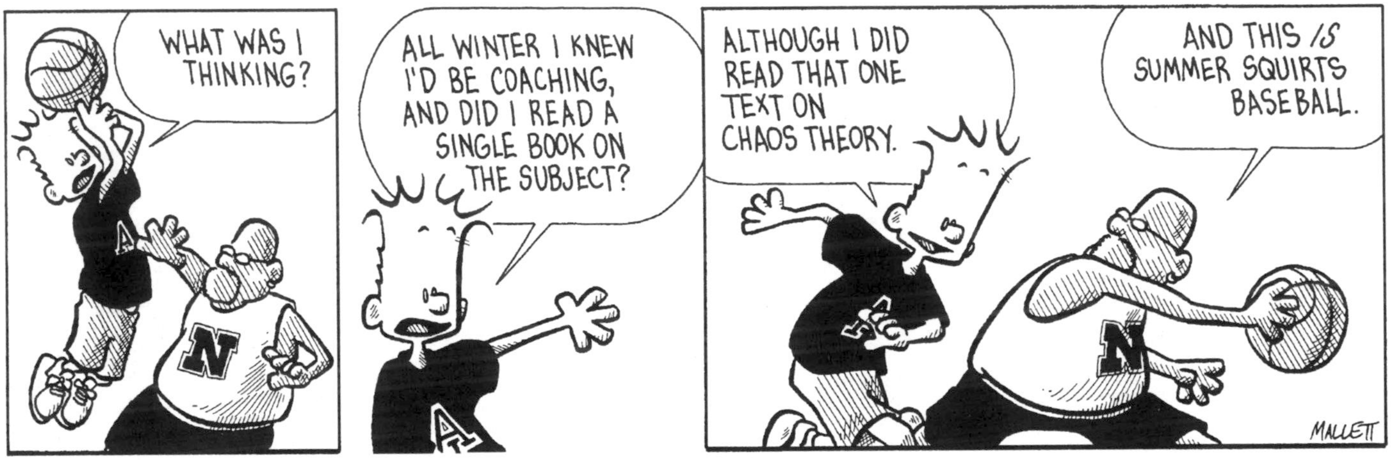
WHAT WAS I THINKING?
ALL WINTER I KNEW I'D BE COACHING, AND DID I READ A SINGLE BOOK ON THE SUBJECT?
ALTHOUGH I DID READ THAT ONE TEXT ON CHAOS THEORY.
AND THIS *IS* SUMMER SQUIRTS BASEBALL.
MALLETT

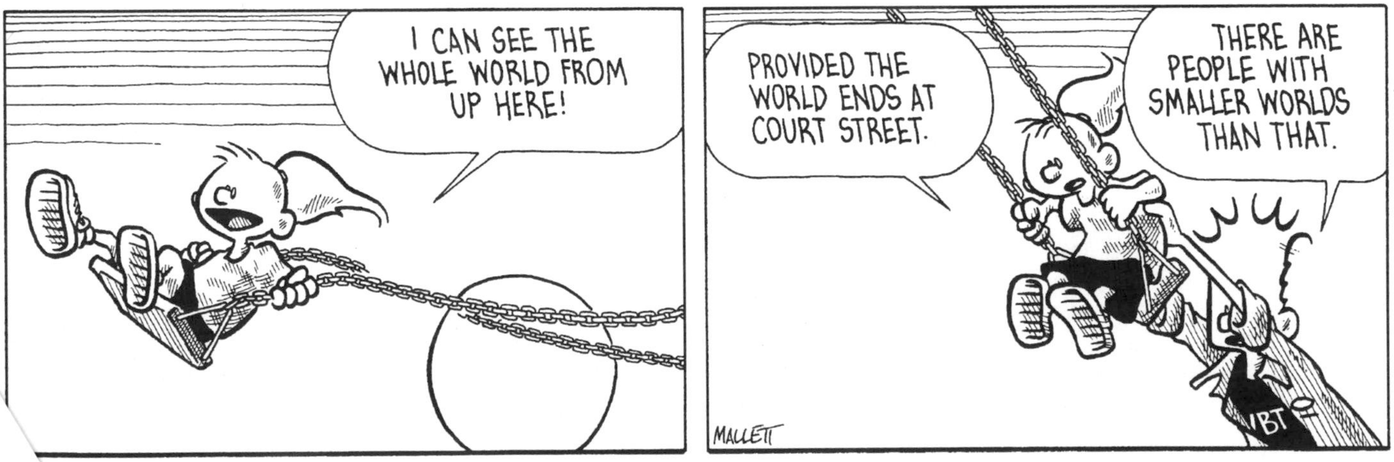
I CAN SEE THE WHOLE WORLD FROM UP HERE!
PROVIDED THE WORLD ENDS AT COURT STREET.
THERE ARE PEOPLE WITH SMALLER WORLDS THAN THAT.
MALLETT

Frazz

by Jef Mallett

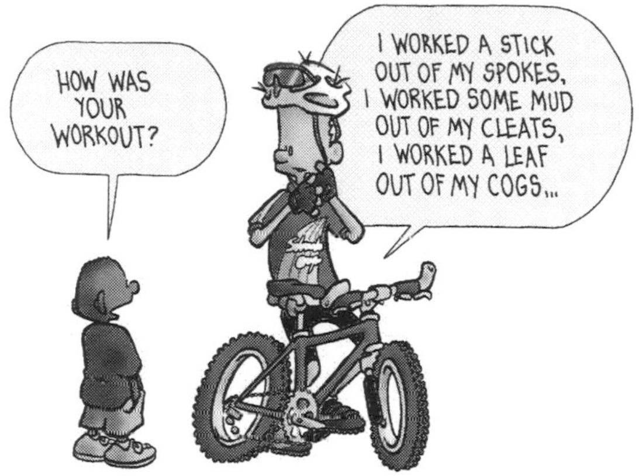
HOW WAS YOUR WORKOUT?
I WORKED A STICK OUT OF MY SPOKES, I WORKED SOME MUD OUT OF MY CLEATS, I WORKED A LEAF OUT OF MY COGS...

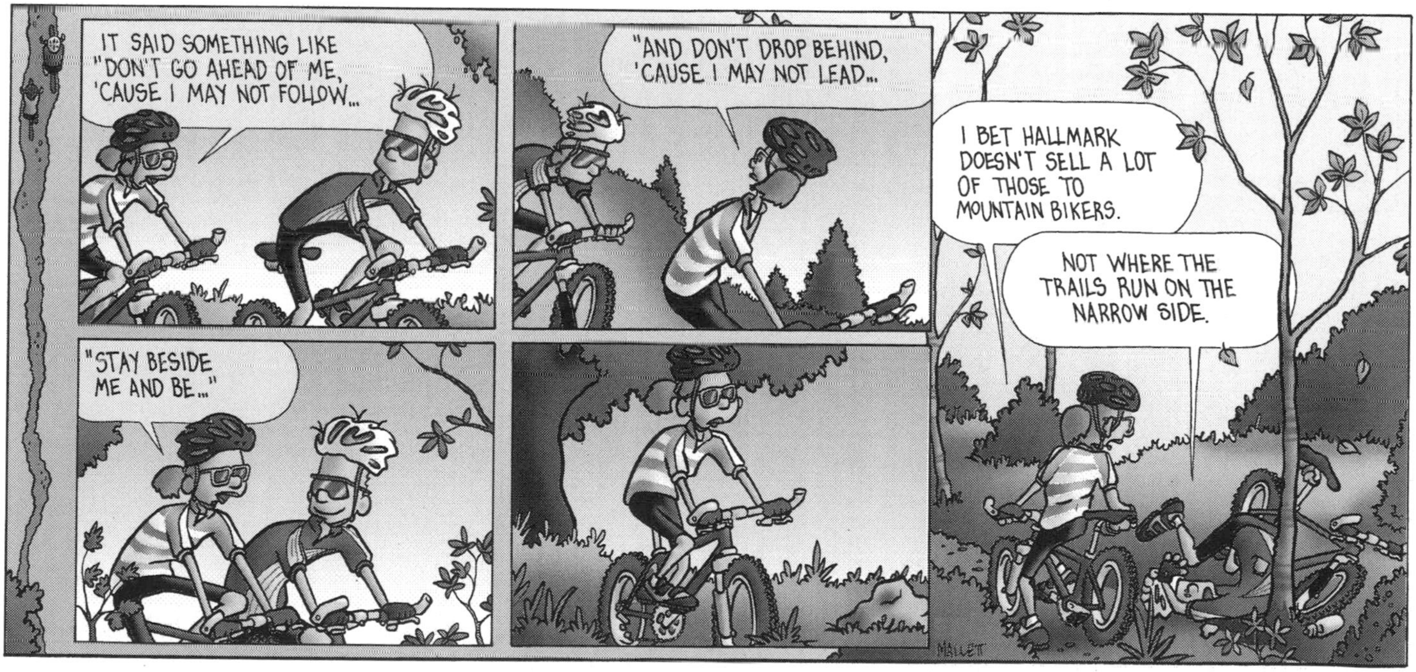
IT SAID SOMETHING LIKE "DON'T GO AHEAD OF ME, 'CAUSE I MAY NOT FOLLOW...
"AND DON'T DROP BEHIND, 'CAUSE I MAY NOT LEAD...
"STAY BESIDE ME AND BE..."
I BET HALLMARK DOESN'T SELL A LOT OF THOSE TO MOUNTAIN BIKERS.
NOT WHERE THE TRAILS RUN ON THE NARROW SIDE.
MALLETT

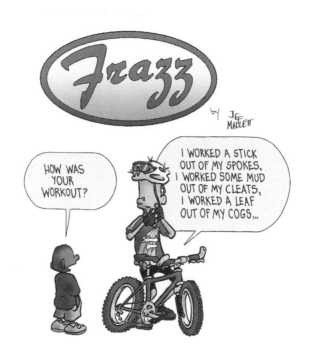

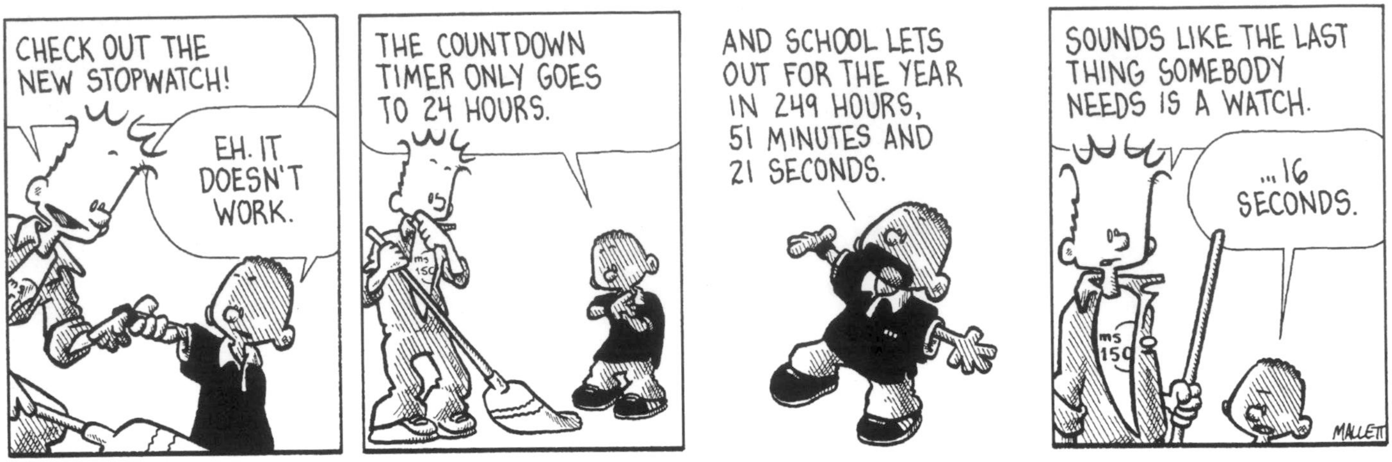
CHECK OUT THE NEW STOPWATCH!
EH. IT DOESN'T WORK.
THE COUNTDOWN TIMER ONLY GOES TO 24 HOURS.
AND SCHOOL LETS OUT FOR THE YEAR IN 249 HOURS, 51 MINUTES AND 21 SECONDS.
SOUNDS LIKE THE LAST THING SOMEBODY NEEDS IS A WATCH.
...16 SECONDS.
MALLETT

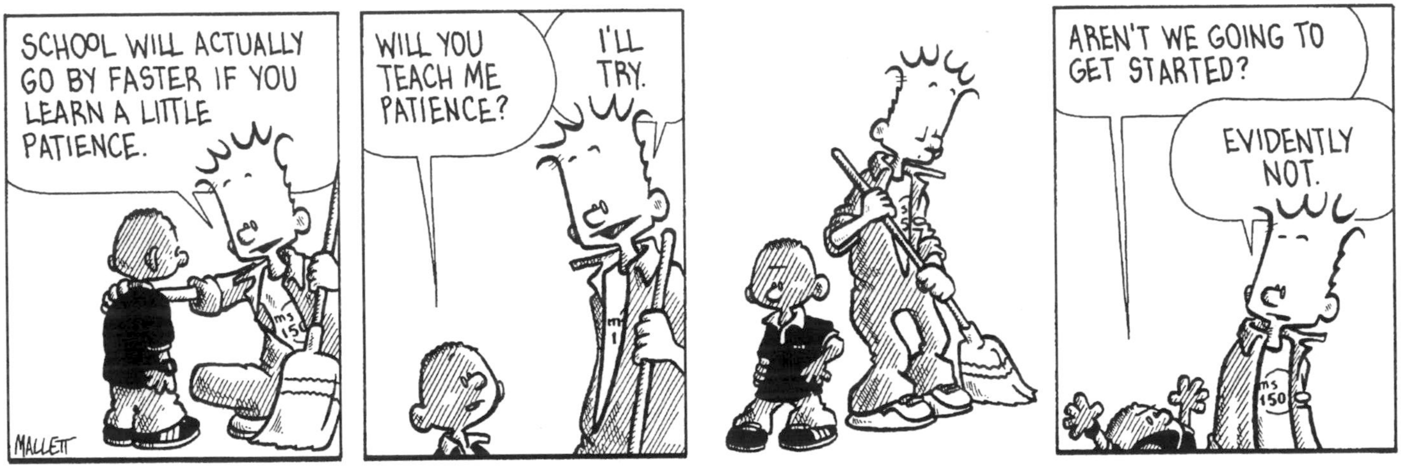
SCHOOL WILL ACTUALLY GO BY FASTER IF YOU LEARN A LITTLE PATIENCE.
WILL YOU TEACH ME PATIENCE?
I'LL TRY.
AREN'T WE GOING TO GET STARTED?
EVIDENTLY NOT.
MALLETT

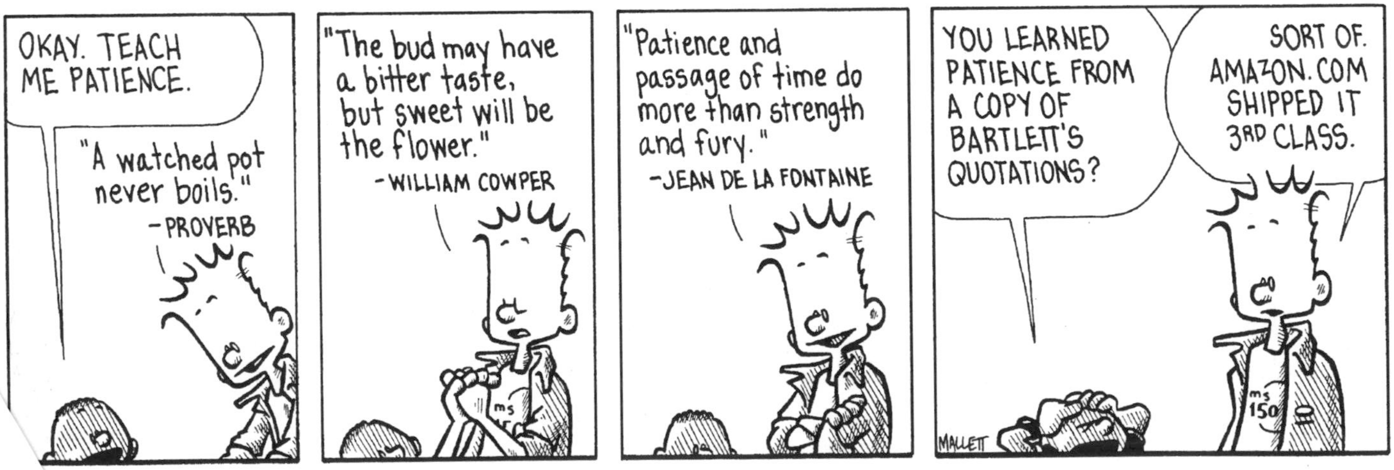
OKAY. TEACH ME PATIENCE.
"A watched pot never boils."
-PROVERB
"The bud may have a bitter taste, but sweet will be the flower."
-WILLIAM COWPER
"Patience and passage of time do more than strength and fury."
-JEAN DE LA FONTAINE
YOU LEARNED PATIENCE FROM A COPY OF BARTLETT'S QUOTATIONS?
SORT OF. AMAZON.COM SHIPPED IT 3RD CLASS.
MALLETT

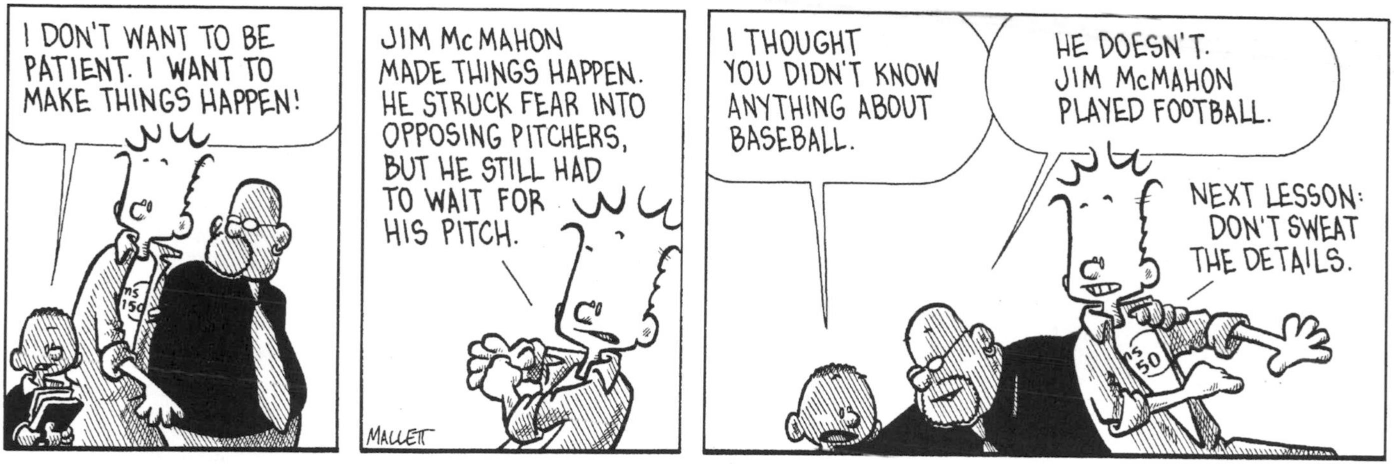
I DON'T WANT TO BE PATIENT. I WANT TO MAKE THINGS HAPPEN!
JIM McMAHON MADE THINGS HAPPEN. HE STRUCK FEAR INTO OPPOSING PITCHERS, BUT HE STILL HAD TO WAIT FOR HIS PITCH.
MALLETT
I THOUGHT YOU DIDN'T KNOW ANYTHING ABOUT BASEBALL.
HE DOESN'T. JIM McMAHON PLAYED FOOTBALL.
NEXT LESSON: DON'T SWEAT THE DETAILS.

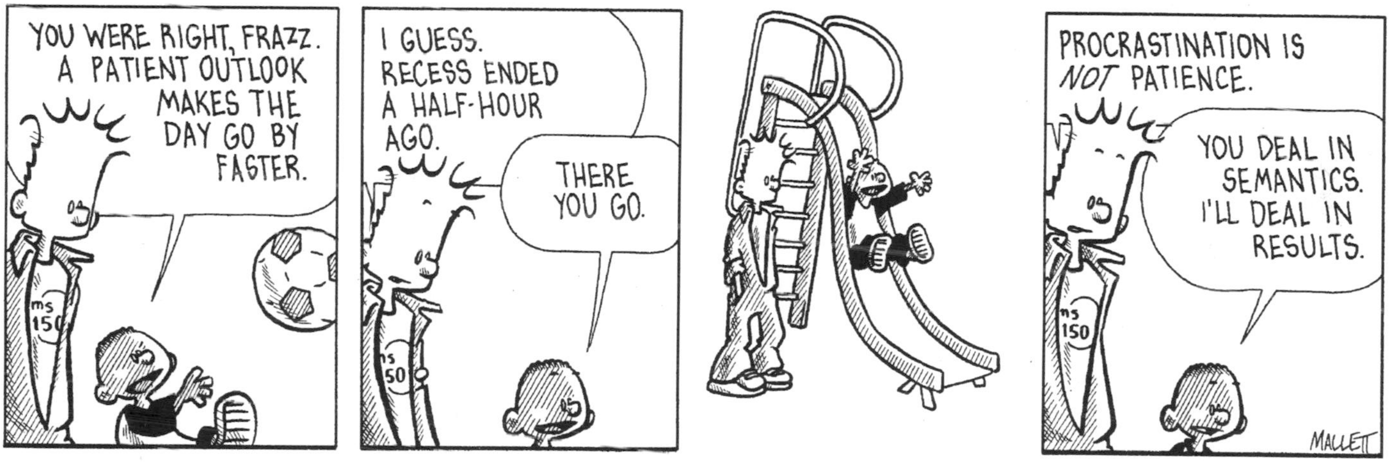
YOU WERE RIGHT, FRAZZ. A PATIENT OUTLOOK MAKES THE DAY GO BY FASTER.
I GUESS. RECESS ENDED A HALF-HOUR AGO.
THERE YOU GO.
PROCRASTINATION IS *NOT* PATIENCE.
YOU DEAL IN SEMANTICS. I'LL DEAL IN RESULTS.
MALLETT

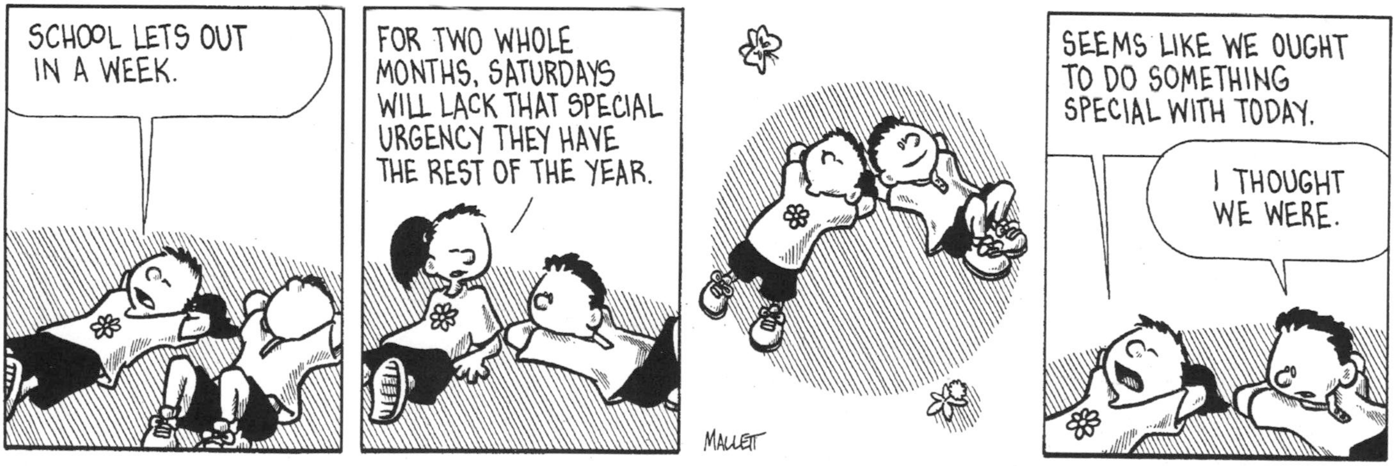
SCHOOL LETS OUT IN A WEEK.
FOR TWO WHOLE MONTHS, SATURDAYS WILL LACK THAT SPECIAL URGENCY THEY HAVE THE REST OF THE YEAR.
MALLETT
SEEMS LIKE WE OUGHT TO DO SOMETHING SPECIAL WITH TODAY.
I THOUGHT WE WERE.

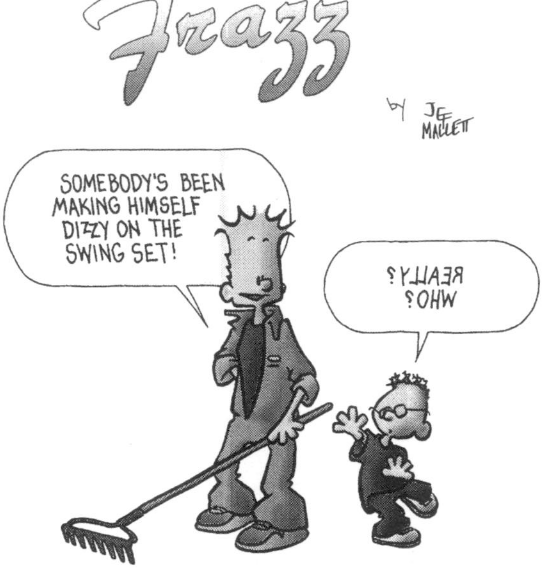
Frazz
by Jef Mallett
SOMEBODY'S BEEN MAKING HIMSELF DIZZY ON THE SWING SET!
REALLY? WHO?

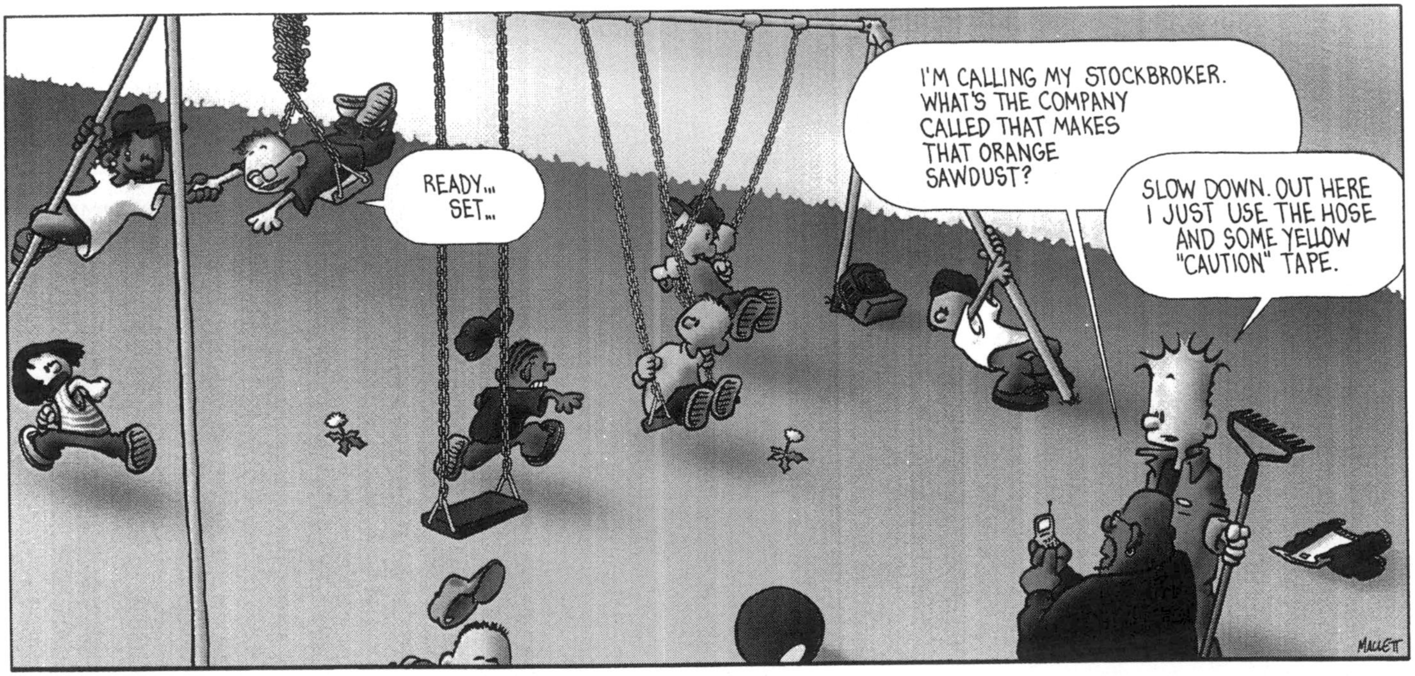
READY... SET...
I'M CALLING MY STOCKBROKER. WHAT'S THE COMPANY CALLED THAT MAKES THAT ORANGE SAWDUST?
SLOW DOWN. OUT HERE I JUST USE THE HOSE AND SOME YELLOW "CAUTION" TAPE.
MALLETT

MRS. OLSEN IS WRITING STUFF IN HER PLANNER!

'KAY.

IT'S THE LAST DAY OF SCHOOL!

SHE'S EITHER WRECKING HER OWN SUMMER OR PLOTTING TO RUIN MINE!

WHY CAN'T THAT LADY LEARN TO LIGHTEN UP?

LACK OF ROLE MODELS?

MALLETT

I'VE GOT TO PEEK IN MRS. OLSEN'S PLANNER.

PLEASE DON'T.

SHE'S PLOTTING ASSIGNMENTS TO RUIN MY SUMMER!

MALLETT

YOU CAN'T GO SNOOPING IN OTHER PEOPLE'S STUFF.

MR. SPAETZLE MADE YOU LOOK IN MY LOCKER.

WHEN MRS. OLSEN'S PLANNER STARTS SMELLING LIKE A 5-DAY-OLD CARP, WE'LL TALK.

IT WAS FOR SHOW AND TELL!

WOO! MRS. OLSEN'S PLANNER!

MALLETT

MY CHANCE TO SEE HOW SHE'S PLOTTING TO FILL UP MY SUMMER!

7	MONDAY
	Putter in garden
8	TUESDAY
	Putter in garden
9	WEDNESDAY
	Putter in garden
	(& Hammock)
10	THURSDAY
	Putter in garden
11	FRIDAY

JUL

I AM SHOCKED.

YES, YES YOU ARE.

115

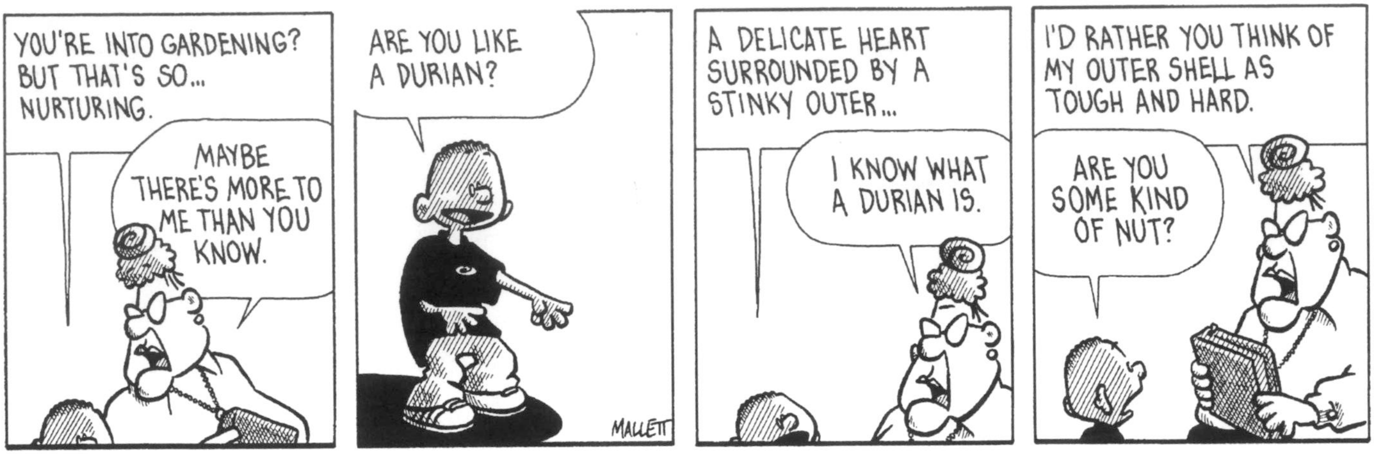
YOU'RE INTO GARDENING? BUT THAT'S SO... NURTURING.
MAYBE THERE'S MORE TO ME THAN YOU KNOW.
ARE YOU LIKE A DURIAN?
MALLETT
A DELICATE HEART SURROUNDED BY A STINKY OUTER...
I KNOW WHAT A DURIAN IS.
I'D RATHER YOU THINK OF MY OUTER SHELL AS TOUGH AND HARD.
ARE YOU SOME KIND OF NUT?

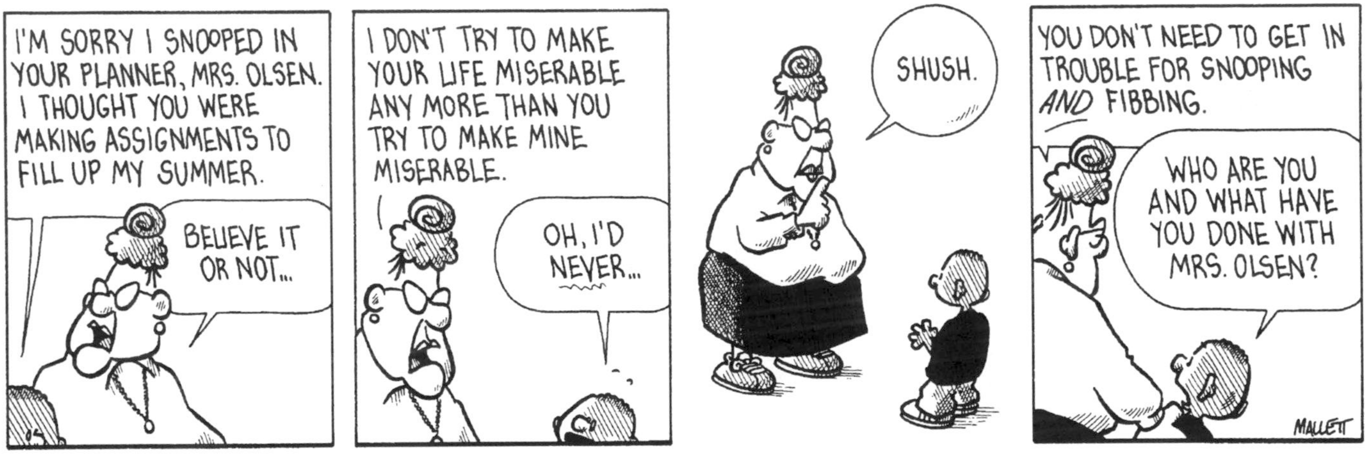
I'M SORRY I SNOOPED IN YOUR PLANNER, MRS. OLSEN. I THOUGHT YOU WERE MAKING ASSIGNMENTS TO FILL UP MY SUMMER.
BELIEVE IT OR NOT...
I DON'T TRY TO MAKE YOUR LIFE MISERABLE ANY MORE THAN YOU TRY TO MAKE MINE MISERABLE.
OH, I'D NEVER...
SHUSH.
YOU DON'T NEED TO GET IN TROUBLE FOR SNOOPING AND FIBBING.
WHO ARE YOU AND WHAT HAVE YOU DONE WITH MRS. OLSEN?
MALLETT

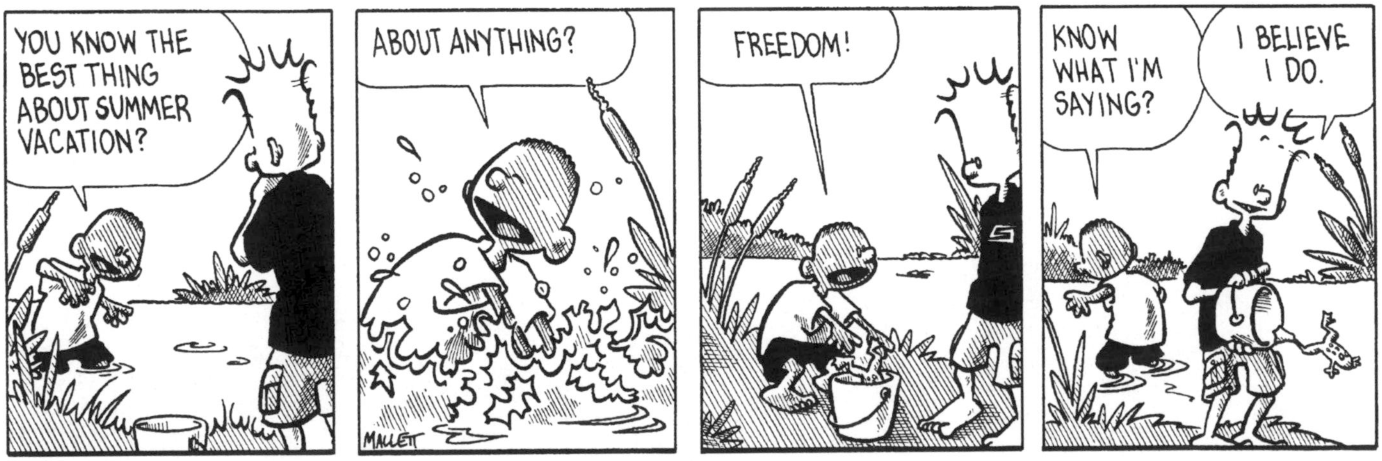
YOU KNOW THE BEST THING ABOUT SUMMER VACATION?
ABOUT ANYTHING?
MALLETT
FREEDOM!
KNOW WHAT I'M SAYING?
I BELIEVE I DO.

FRAZZ

by Jef Mallett

MALLETT
WHY EXACTLY IS THIS CALLED "WALKING" THE DOG?
SOMETHING TO DO WITH AVERAGE SPEED, I'M GUESSING.

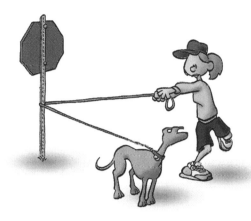

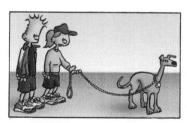

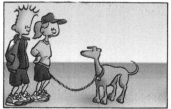

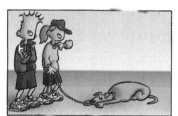

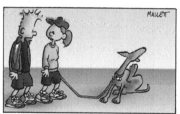

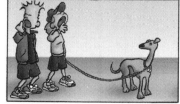

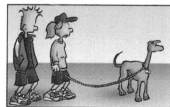

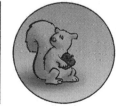

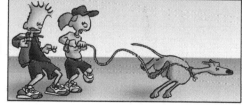

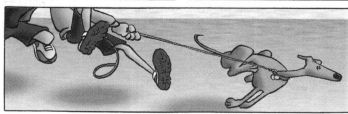

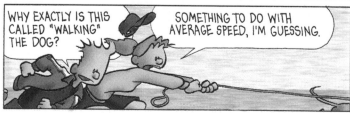

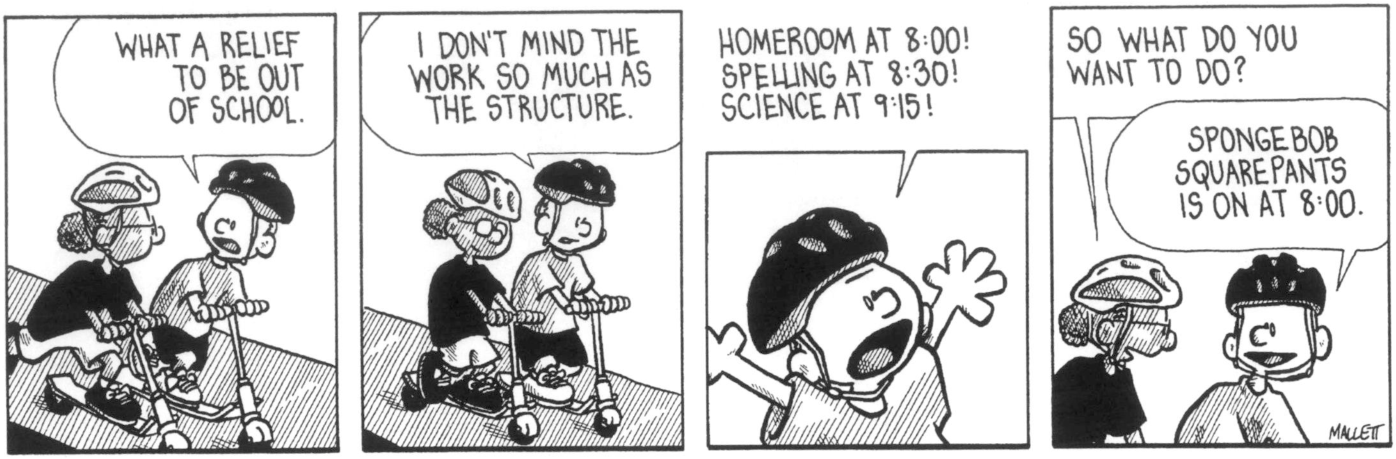
WHAT A RELIEF TO BE OUT OF SCHOOL.
I DON'T MIND THE WORK SO MUCH AS THE STRUCTURE.
HOMEROOM AT 8:00! SPELLING AT 8:30! SCIENCE AT 9:15!
SO WHAT DO YOU WANT TO DO?
SPONGEBOB SQUAREPANTS IS ON AT 8:00.
MALLETT

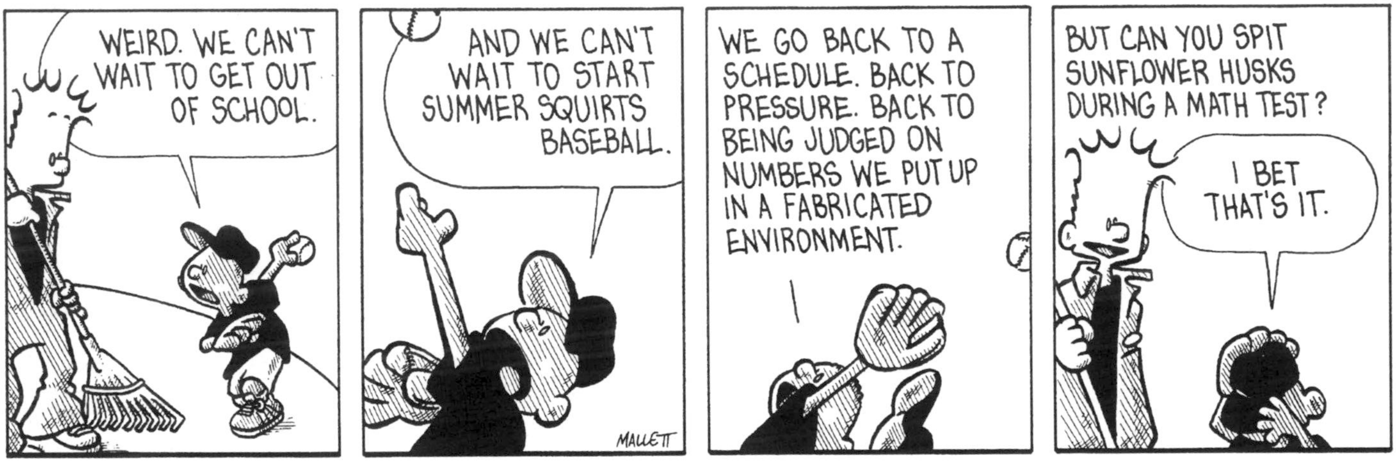
WEIRD. WE CAN'T WAIT TO GET OUT OF SCHOOL.
AND WE CAN'T WAIT TO START SUMMER SQUIRTS BASEBALL.
MALLETT
WE GO BACK TO A SCHEDULE. BACK TO PRESSURE. BACK TO BEING JUDGED ON NUMBERS WE PUT UP IN A FABRICATED ENVIRONMENT.
BUT CAN YOU SPIT SUNFLOWER HUSKS DURING A MATH TEST?
I BET THAT'S IT.

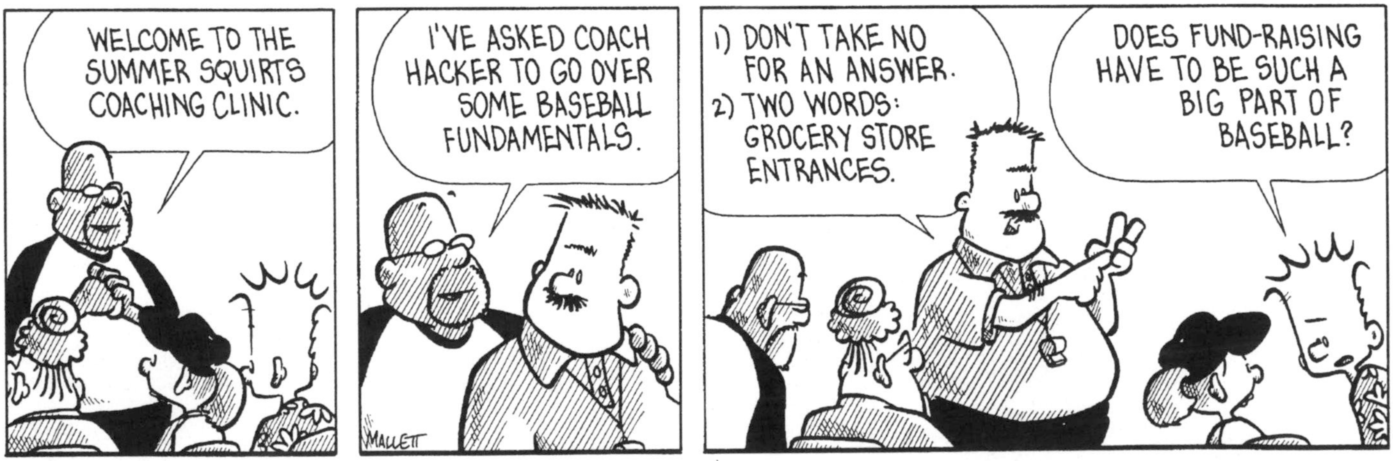
WELCOME TO THE SUMMER SQUIRTS COACHING CLINIC.
I'VE ASKED COACH HACKER TO GO OVER SOME BASEBALL FUNDAMENTALS.
MALLETT
1) DON'T TAKE NO FOR AN ANSWER. 2) TWO WORDS: GROCERY STORE ENTRANCES.
DOES FUND-RAISING HAVE TO BE SUCH A BIG PART OF BASEBALL?

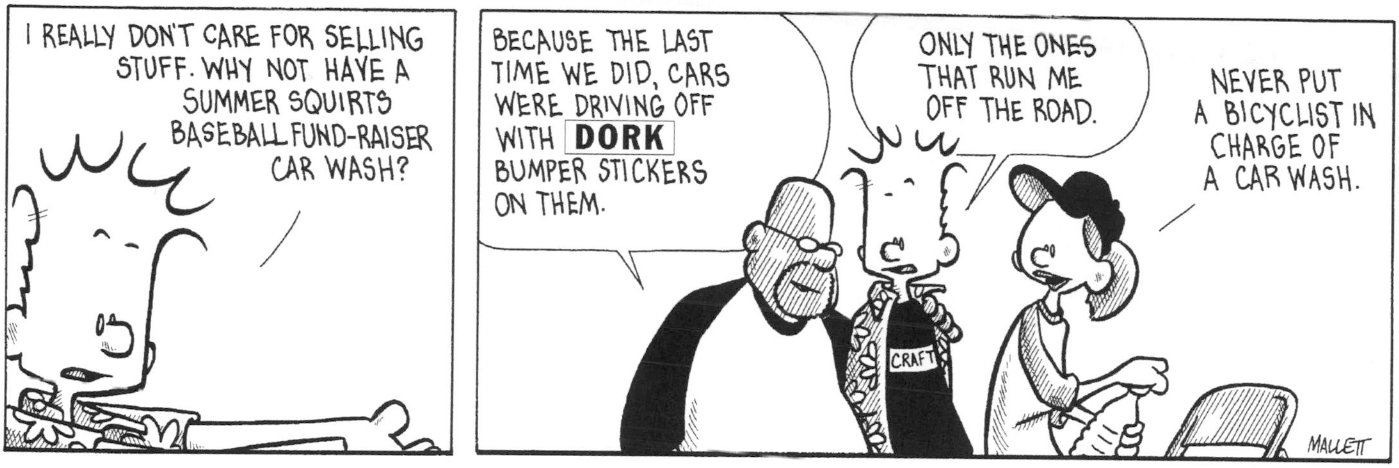
I REALLY DON'T CARE FOR SELLING STUFF. WHY NOT HAVE A SUMMER SQUIRTS BASEBALL FUND-RAISER CAR WASH?
BECAUSE THE LAST TIME WE DID, CARS WERE DRIVING OFF WITH DORK BUMPER STICKERS ON THEM.
ONLY THE ONES THAT RUN ME OFF THE ROAD.
NEVER PUT A BICYCLIST IN CHARGE OF A CAR WASH.
CRAFT
MALLETT

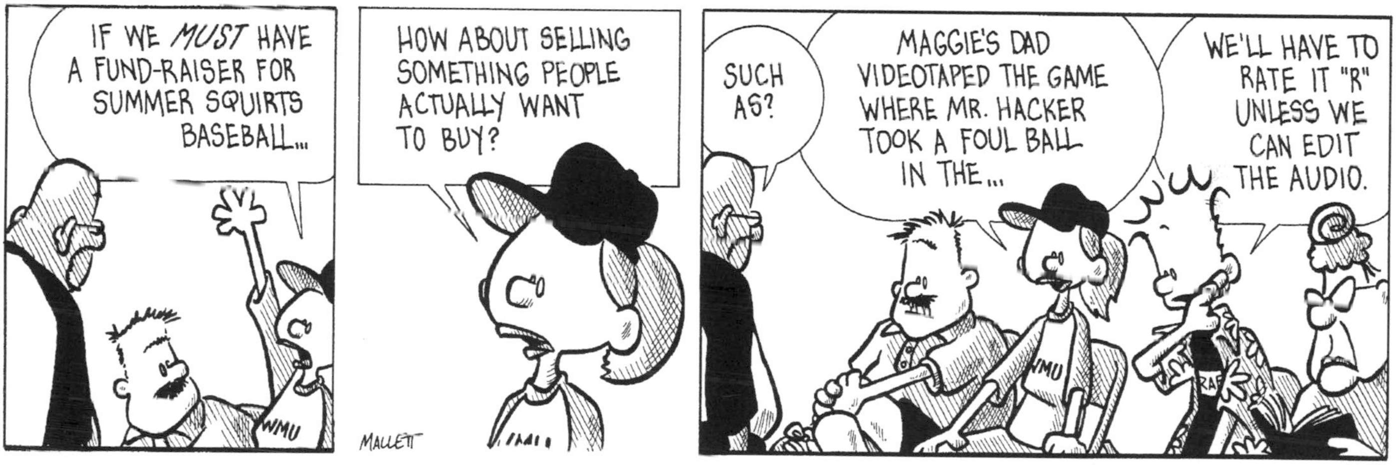
IF WE MUST HAVE A FUND-RAISER FOR SUMMER SQUIRTS BASEBALL...
WMU
HOW ABOUT SELLING SOMETHING PEOPLE ACTUALLY WANT TO BUY?
MALLETT
SUCH AS?
MAGGIE'S DAD VIDEOTAPED THE GAME WHERE MR. HACKER TOOK A FOUL BALL IN THE...
WE'LL HAVE TO RATE IT "R" UNLESS WE CAN EDIT THE AUDIO.

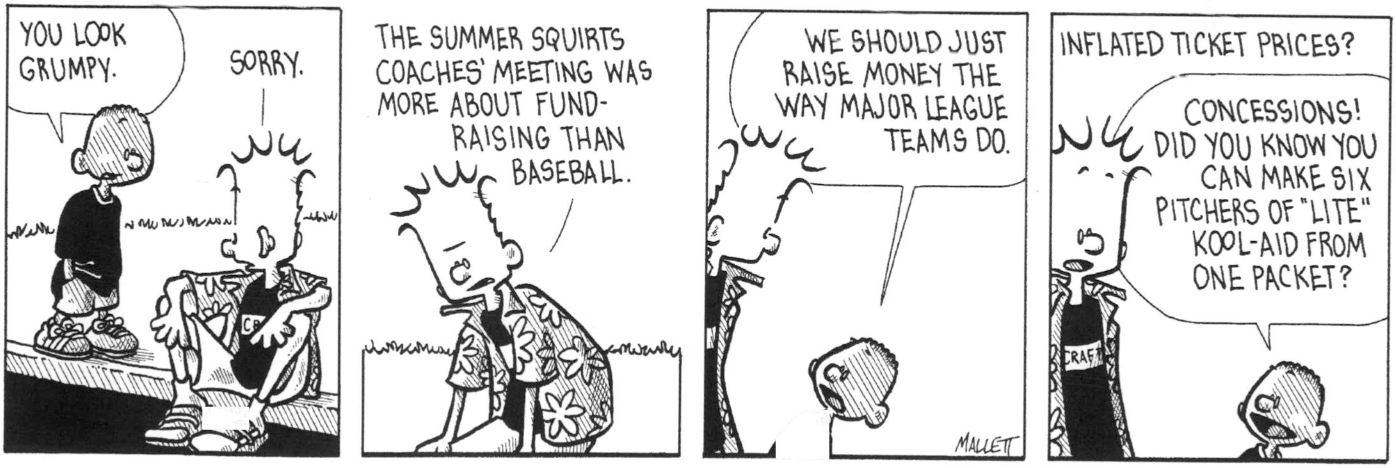
YOU LOOK GRUMPY.
SORRY.
THE SUMMER SQUIRTS COACHES' MEETING WAS MORE ABOUT FUND-RAISING THAN BASEBALL.
WE SHOULD JUST RAISE MONEY THE WAY MAJOR LEAGUE TEAMS DO.
MALLETT
INFLATED TICKET PRICES?
CONCESSIONS! DID YOU KNOW YOU CAN MAKE SIX PITCHERS OF "LITE" KOOL-AID FROM ONE PACKET?
CRAFT

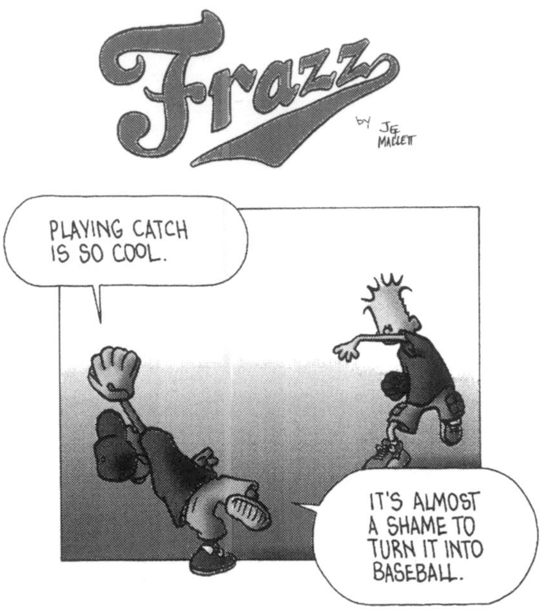
Frazz
by JEF MALLETT
PLAYING CATCH IS SO COOL.
IT'S ALMOST A SHAME TO TURN IT INTO BASEBALL.

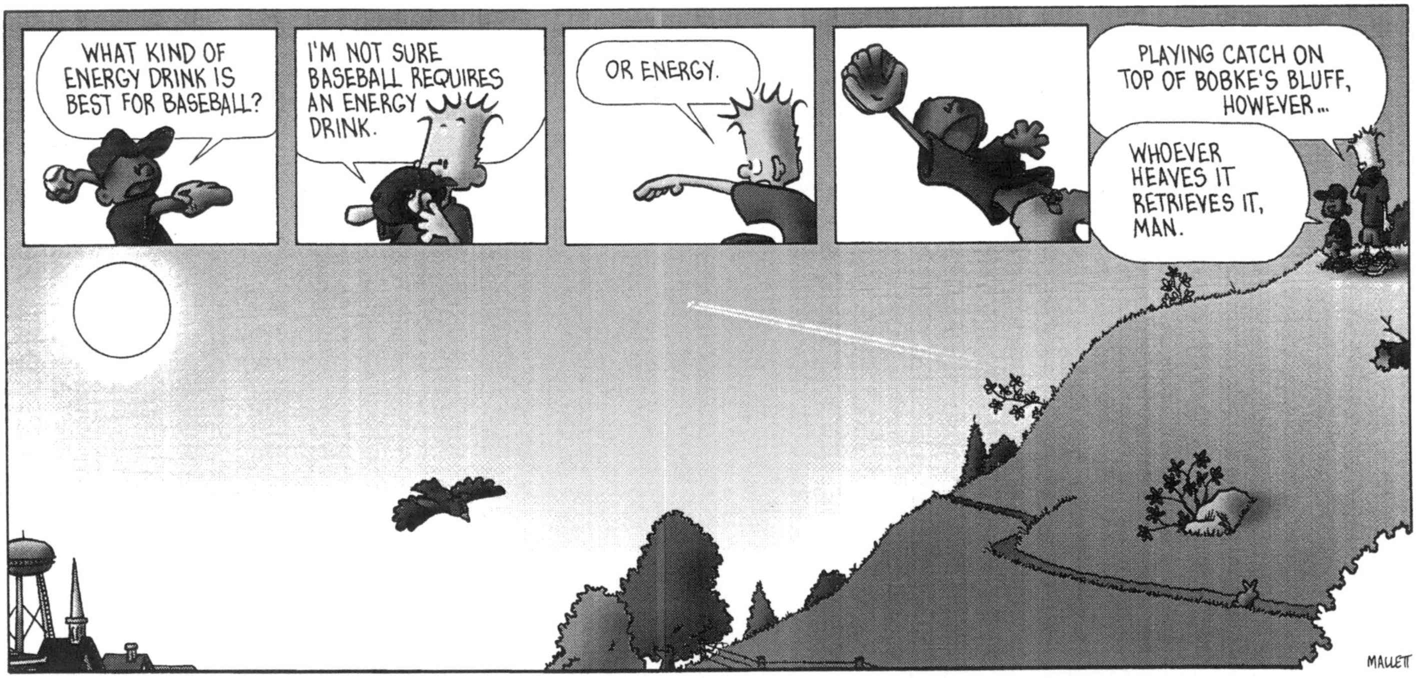
WHAT KIND OF ENERGY DRINK IS BEST FOR BASEBALL?
I'M NOT SURE BASEBALL REQUIRES AN ENERGY DRINK.
OR ENERGY.
PLAYING CATCH ON TOP OF BOBKE'S BLUFF, HOWEVER...
WHOEVER HEAVES IT RETRIEVES IT, MAN.
MALLETT

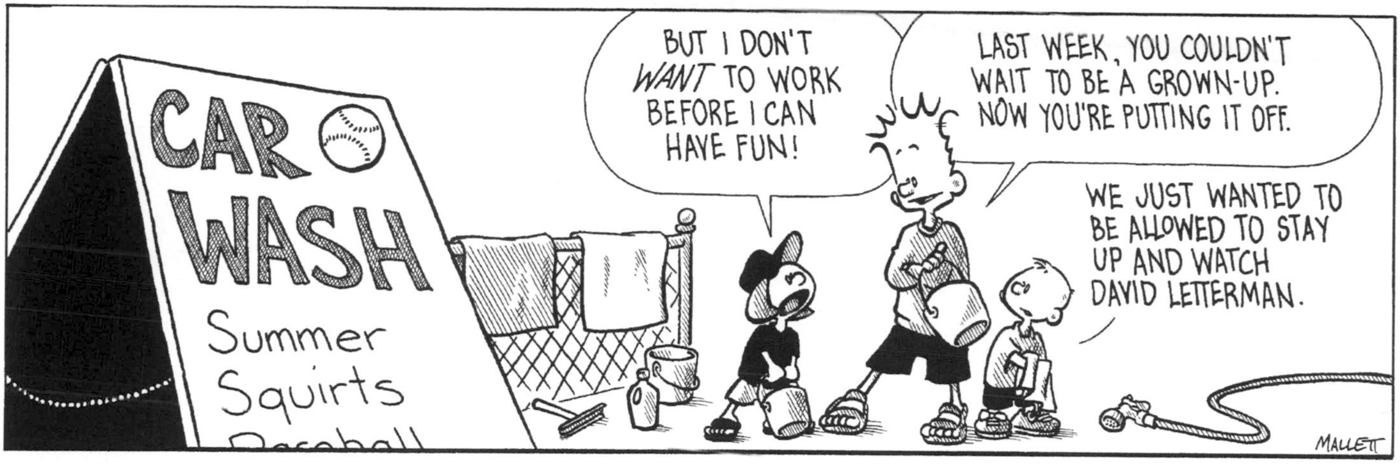
CAR WASH
Summer Squirts
BUT I DON'T *WANT* TO WORK BEFORE I CAN HAVE FUN!
LAST WEEK, YOU COULDN'T WAIT TO BE A GROWN-UP. NOW YOU'RE PUTTING IT OFF.
WE JUST WANTED TO BE ALLOWED TO STAY UP AND WATCH DAVID LETTERMAN.
MALLETT

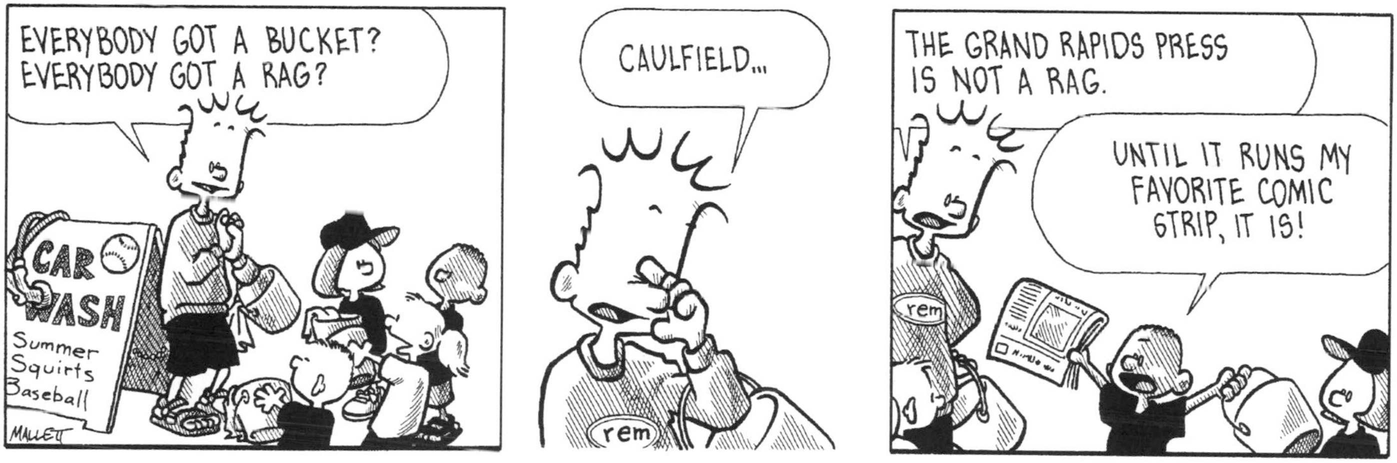
EVERYBODY GOT A BUCKET? EVERYBODY GOT A RAG?
CAR WASH
Summer Squirts Baseball
MALLETT
CAULFIELD...
rem
THE GRAND RAPIDS PRESS IS NOT A RAG.
UNTIL IT RUNS MY FAVORITE COMIC STRIP, IT IS!
rem

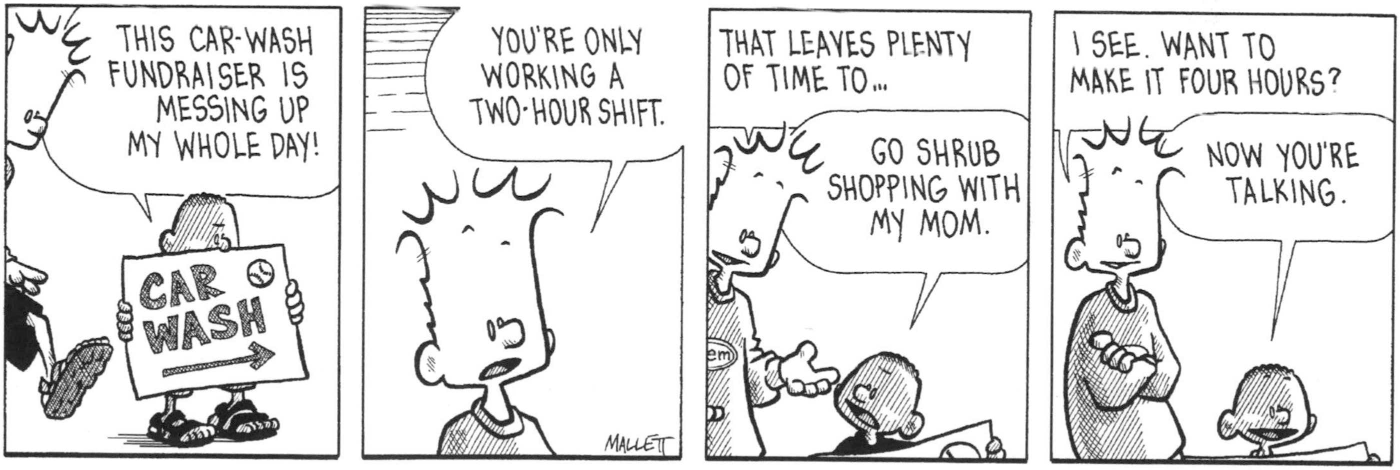
THIS CAR-WASH FUNDRAISER IS MESSING UP MY WHOLE DAY!
CAR WASH
YOU'RE ONLY WORKING A TWO-HOUR SHIFT.
MALLETT
THAT LEAVES PLENTY OF TIME TO...
GO SHRUB SHOPPING WITH MY MOM.
rem
I SEE. WANT TO MAKE IT FOUR HOURS?
NOW YOU'RE TALKING.

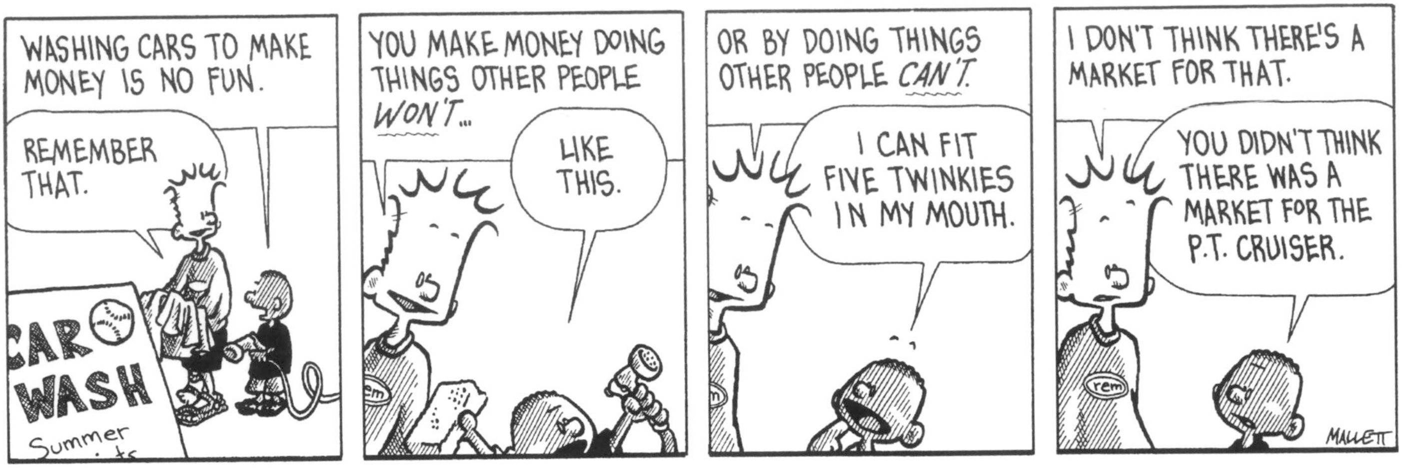
WASHING CARS TO MAKE MONEY IS NO FUN.
REMEMBER THAT.
CAR WASH
Summer
YOU MAKE MONEY DOING THINGS OTHER PEOPLE WON'T...
LIKE THIS.
OR BY DOING THINGS OTHER PEOPLE CAN'T.
I CAN FIT FIVE TWINKIES IN MY MOUTH.
I DON'T THINK THERE'S A MARKET FOR THAT.
YOU DIDN'T THINK THERE WAS A MARKET FOR THE P.T. CRUISER.
rem
MALLETT

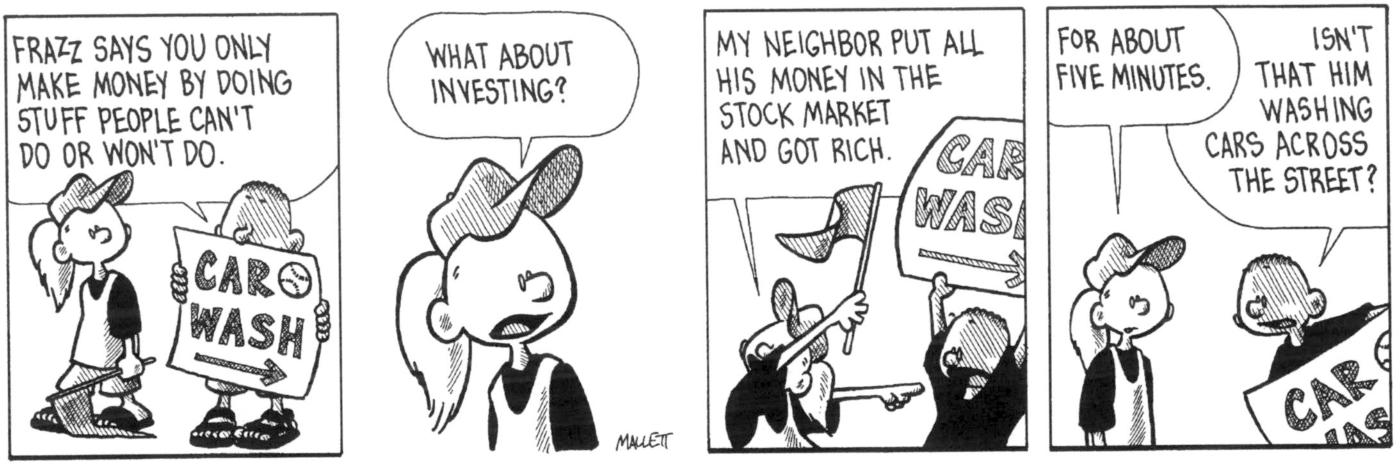
FRAZZ SAYS YOU ONLY MAKE MONEY BY DOING STUFF PEOPLE CAN'T DO OR WON'T DO.
CAR WASH
WHAT ABOUT INVESTING?
MALLETT
MY NEIGHBOR PUT ALL HIS MONEY IN THE STOCK MARKET AND GOT RICH.
FOR ABOUT FIVE MINUTES.
ISN'T THAT HIM WASHING CARS ACROSS THE STREET?

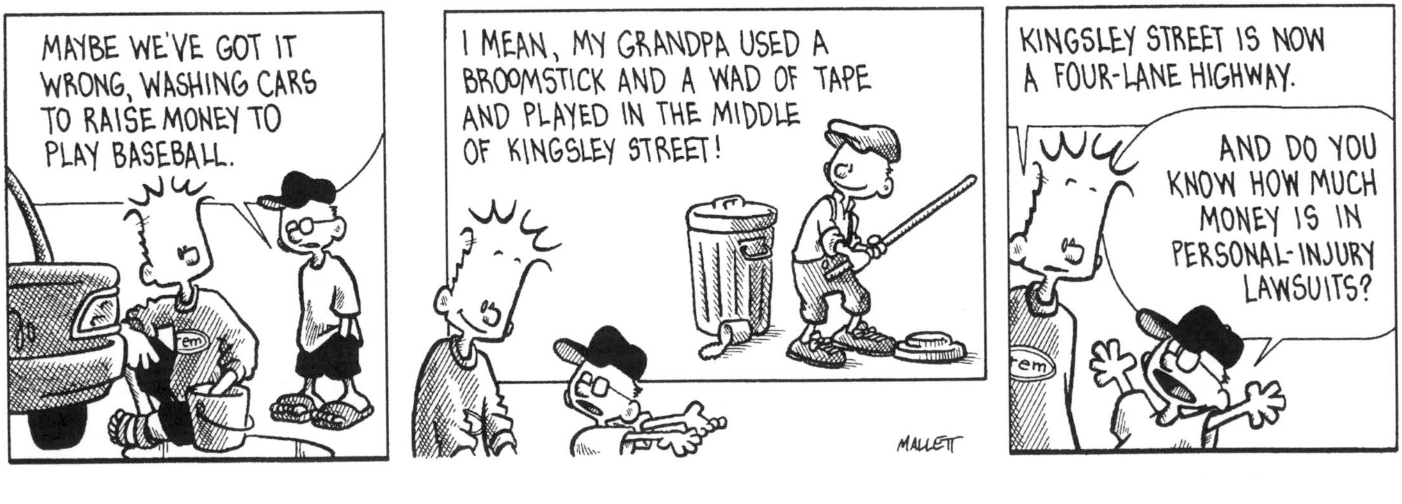
MAYBE WE'VE GOT IT WRONG, WASHING CARS TO RAISE MONEY TO PLAY BASEBALL.
I MEAN, MY GRANDPA USED A BROOMSTICK AND A WAD OF TAPE AND PLAYED IN THE MIDDLE OF KINGSLEY STREET!
MALLETT
KINGSLEY STREET IS NOW A FOUR-LANE HIGHWAY.
AND DO YOU KNOW HOW MUCH MONEY IS IN PERSONAL-INJURY LAWSUITS?
rem

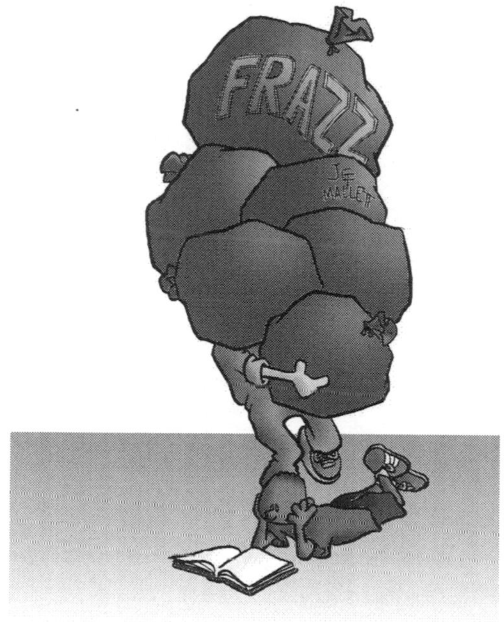
FRAZZ

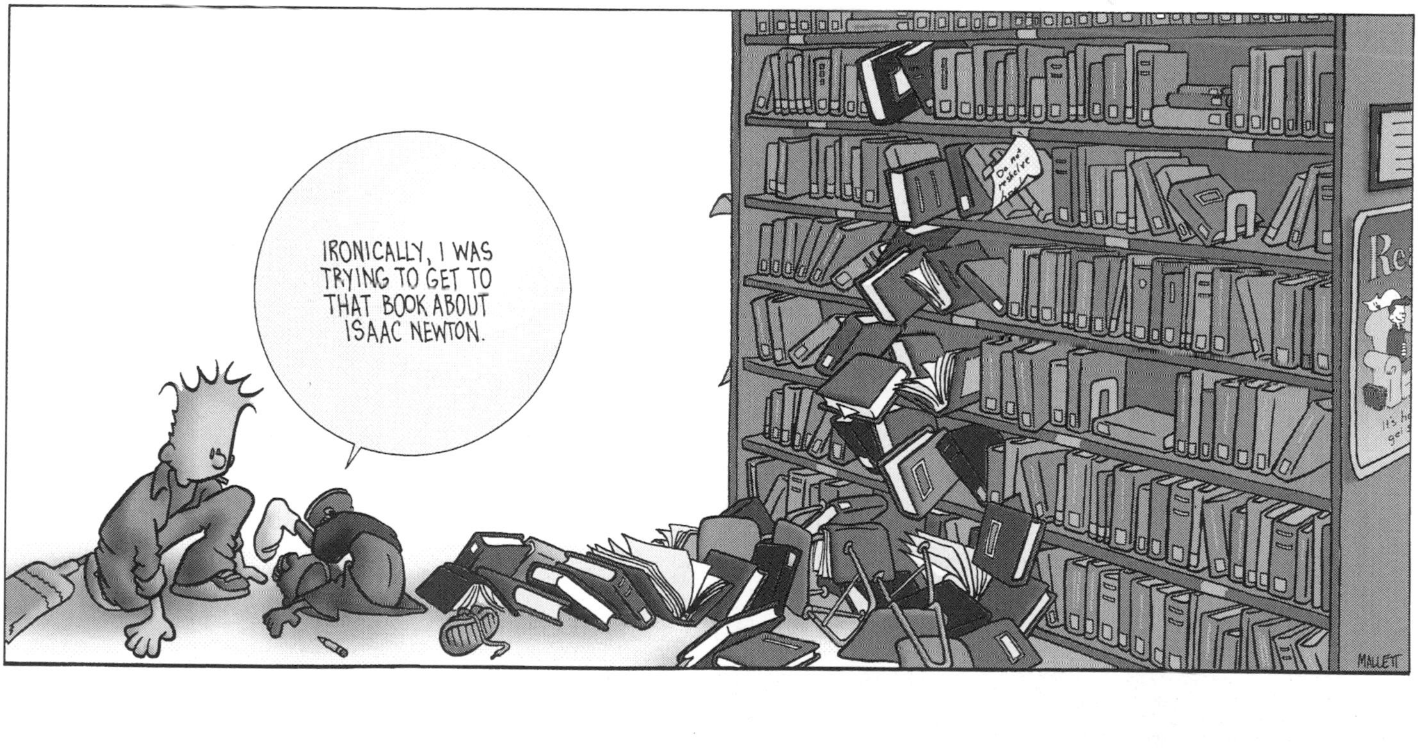
IRONICALLY, I WAS TRYING TO GET TO THAT BOOK ABOUT ISAAC NEWTON.
MALLETT

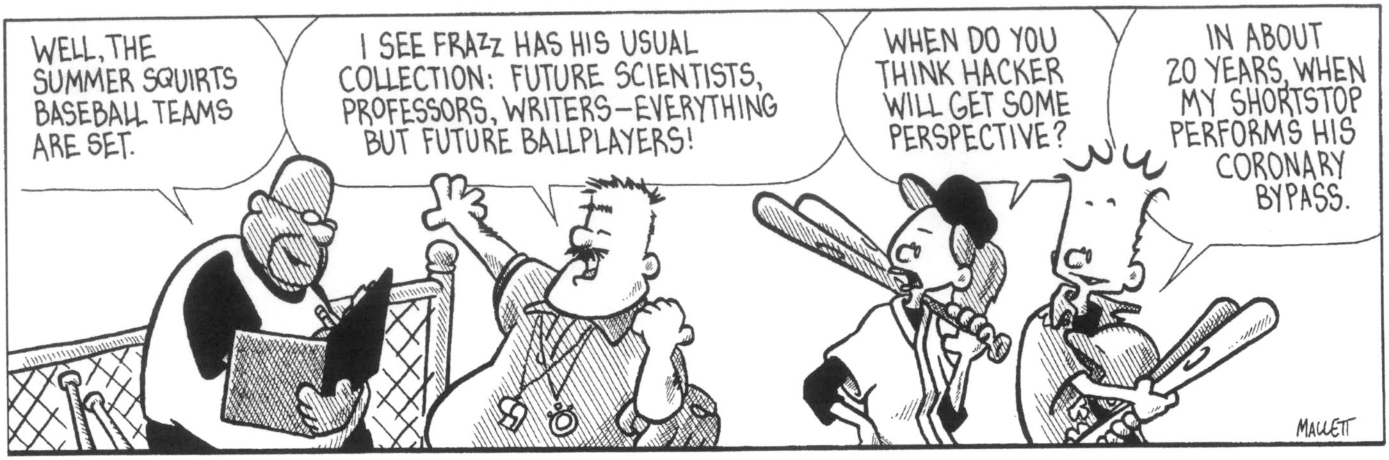

WELL, THE SUMMER SQUIRTS BASEBALL TEAMS ARE SET.
I SEE FRAZZ HAS HIS USUAL COLLECTION: FUTURE SCIENTISTS, PROFESSORS, WRITERS—EVERYTHING BUT FUTURE BALLPLAYERS!
WHEN DO YOU THINK HACKER WILL GET SOME PERSPECTIVE?
IN ABOUT 20 YEARS, WHEN MY SHORTSTOP PERFORMS HIS CORONARY BYPASS.
MALLETT

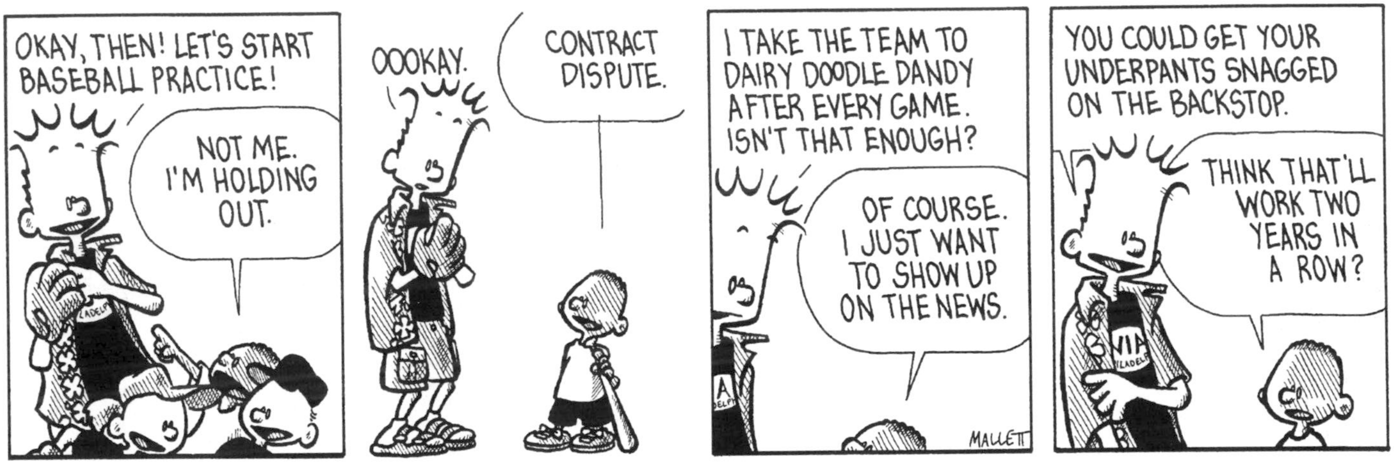

OKAY, THEN! LET'S START BASEBALL PRACTICE!
NOT ME. I'M HOLDING OUT.
OOOKAY.
CONTRACT DISPUTE.
I TAKE THE TEAM TO DAIRY DOODLE DANDY AFTER EVERY GAME. ISN'T THAT ENOUGH?
OF COURSE. I JUST WANT TO SHOW UP ON THE NEWS.
MALLETT
YOU COULD GET YOUR UNDERPANTS SNAGGED ON THE BACKSTOP.
THINK THAT'LL WORK TWO YEARS IN A ROW?

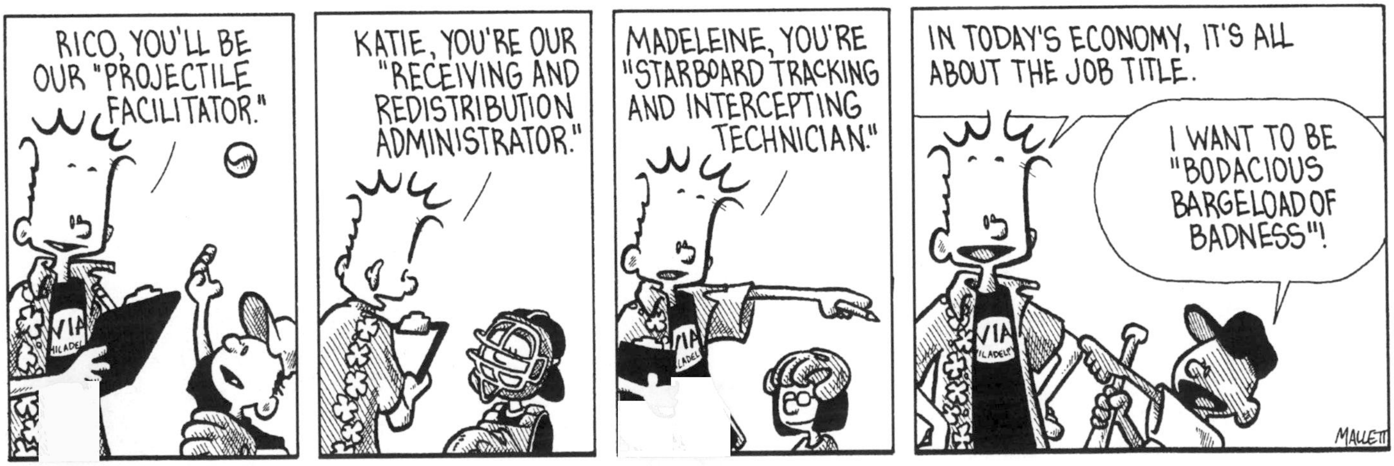

RICO, YOU'LL BE OUR "PROJECTILE FACILITATOR."
KATIE, YOU'RE OUR "RECEIVING AND REDISTRIBUTION ADMINISTRATOR."
MADELEINE, YOU'RE "STARBOARD TRACKING AND INTERCEPTING TECHNICIAN."
IN TODAY'S ECONOMY, IT'S ALL ABOUT THE JOB TITLE.
I WANT TO BE "BODACIOUS BARGELOAD OF BADNESS"!
MALLETT

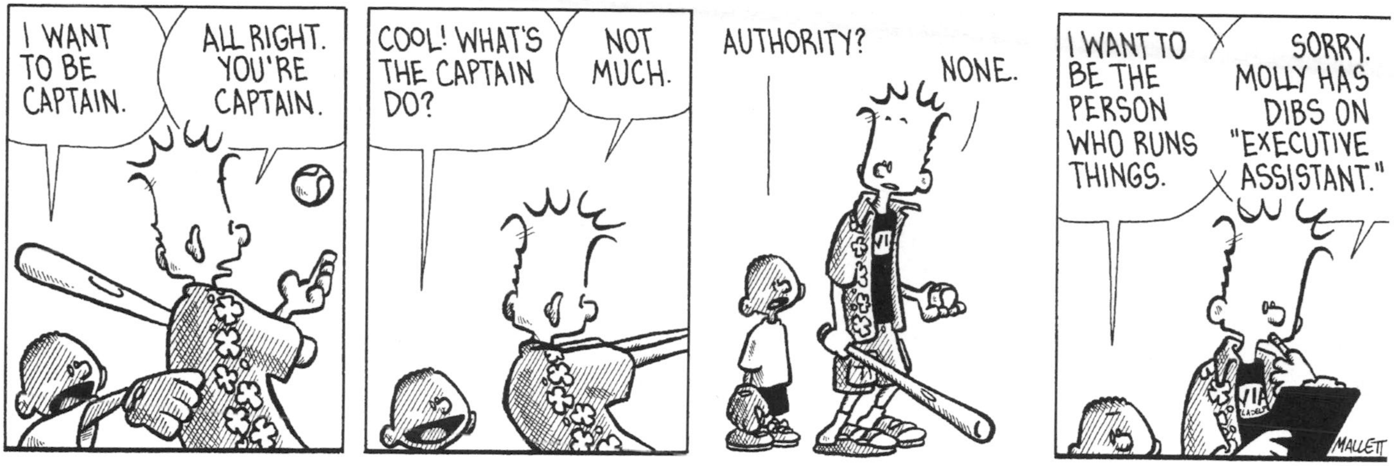
I WANT TO BE CAPTAIN.
ALL RIGHT. YOU'RE CAPTAIN.
COOL! WHAT'S THE CAPTAIN DO?
NOT MUCH.
AUTHORITY?
NONE.
I WANT TO BE THE PERSON WHO RUNS THINGS.
SORRY. MOLLY HAS DIBS ON "EXECUTIVE ASSISTANT."
MALLETT

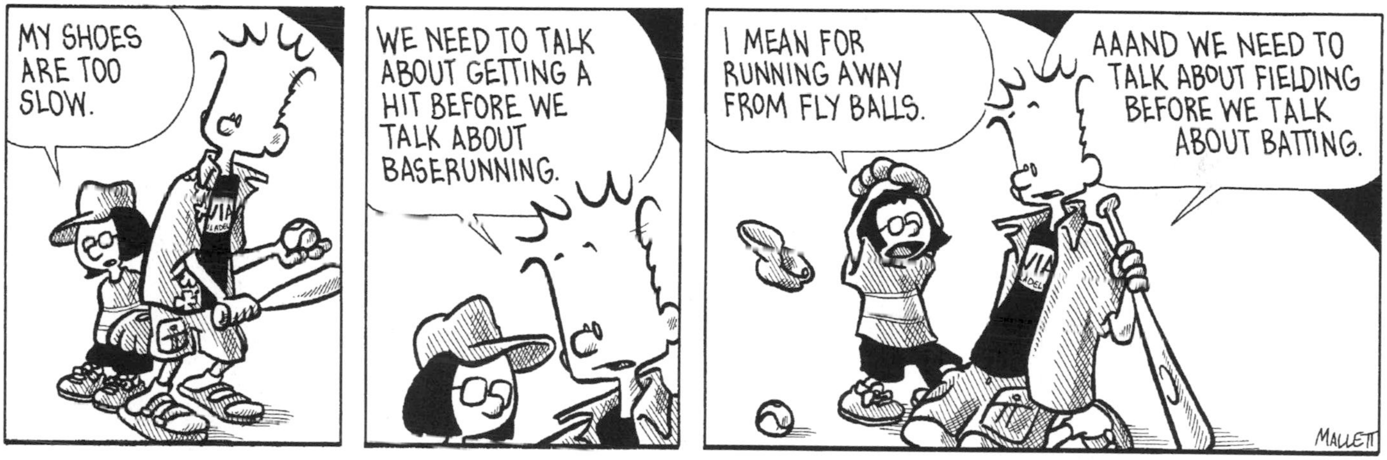
MY SHOES ARE TOO SLOW.
WE NEED TO TALK ABOUT GETTING A HIT BEFORE WE TALK ABOUT BASERUNNING.
I MEAN FOR RUNNING AWAY FROM FLY BALLS.
AAAND WE NEED TO TALK ABOUT FIELDING BEFORE WE TALK ABOUT BATTING.
MALLETT

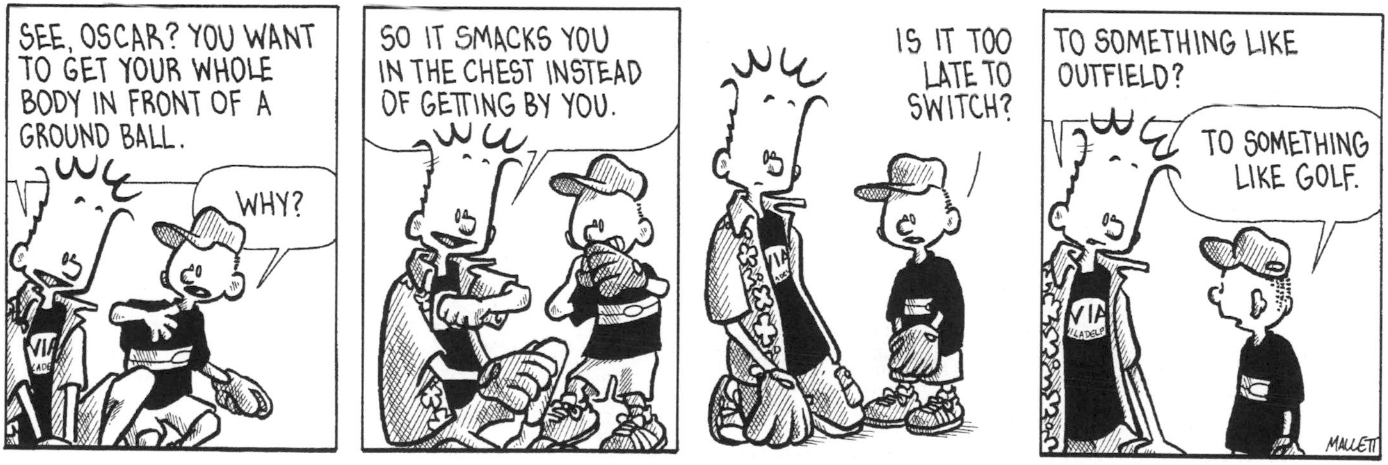
SEE, OSCAR? YOU WANT TO GET YOUR WHOLE BODY IN FRONT OF A GROUND BALL.
WHY?
SO IT SMACKS YOU IN THE CHEST INSTEAD OF GETTING BY YOU.
IS IT TOO LATE TO SWITCH?
TO SOMETHING LIKE OUTFIELD?
TO SOMETHING LIKE GOLF.
MALLETT

Frazz
by JEF MALLETT
HA HA HA.
FOR SALE BAT NEVER USED

STRIKE 94!
WHICH IS?
THE ATOMIC NUMBER OF PLUTONIUM!
WHICH IS RELEVANT HOW?
IT'S ABBREVIATED "Pu," SAME AS YOUR BATTING!
SIGH
HOW WAS BASEBALL PRACTICE?
EDUCATIONAL.
MALLETT

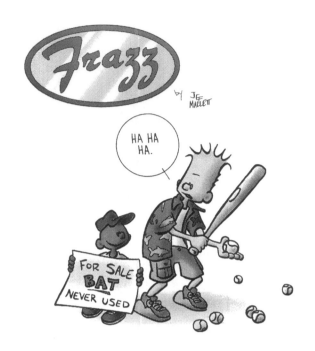

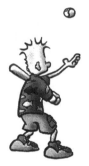

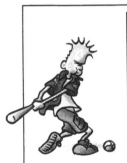

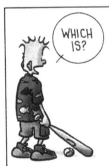

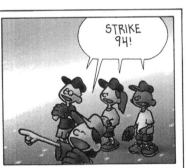

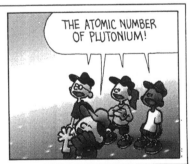

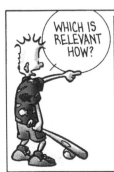

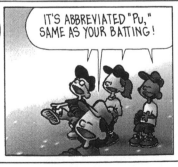

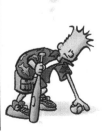

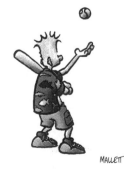

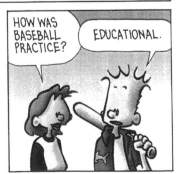

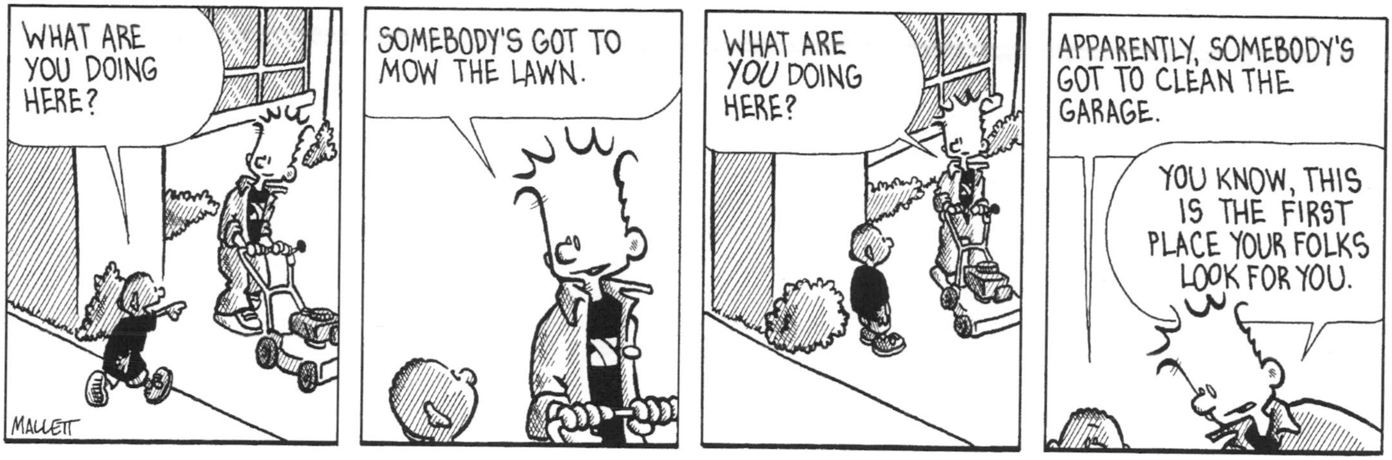
WHAT ARE YOU DOING HERE?
SOMEBODY'S GOT TO MOW THE LAWN.
WHAT ARE *YOU* DOING HERE?
APPARENTLY, SOMEBODY'S GOT TO CLEAN THE GARAGE.
YOU KNOW, THIS IS THE FIRST PLACE YOUR FOLKS LOOK FOR YOU.
MALLETT

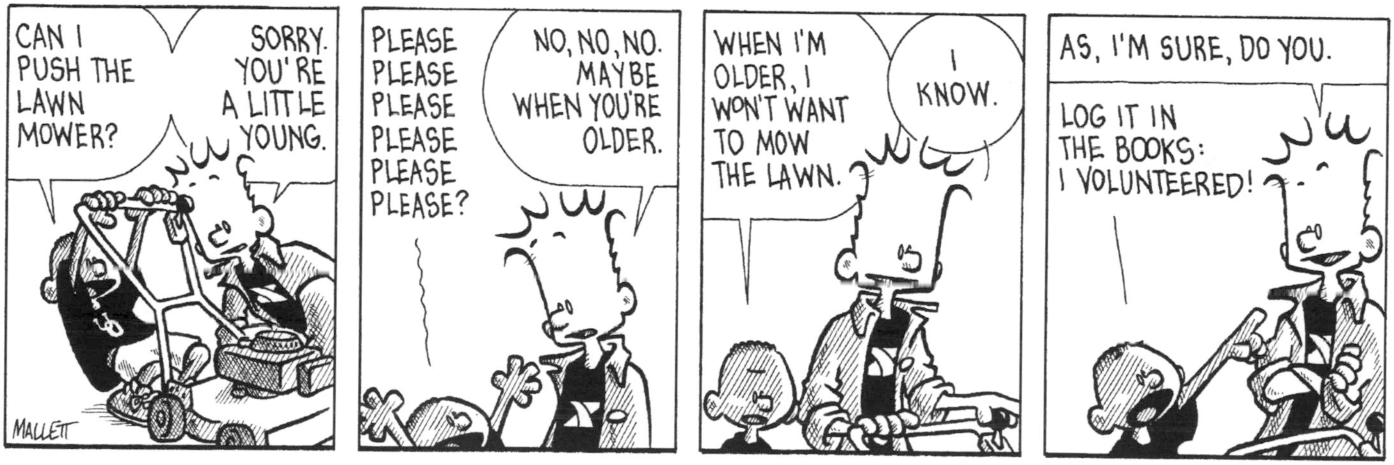
CAN I PUSH THE LAWN MOWER?
SORRY. YOU'RE A LITTLE YOUNG.
PLEASE PLEASE PLEASE PLEASE PLEASE PLEASE PLEASE?
NO, NO, NO. MAYBE WHEN YOU'RE OLDER.
WHEN I'M OLDER, I WON'T WANT TO MOW THE LAWN.
I KNOW.
AS, I'M SURE, DO YOU.
LOG IT IN THE BOOKS: I VOLUNTEERED!
MALLETT

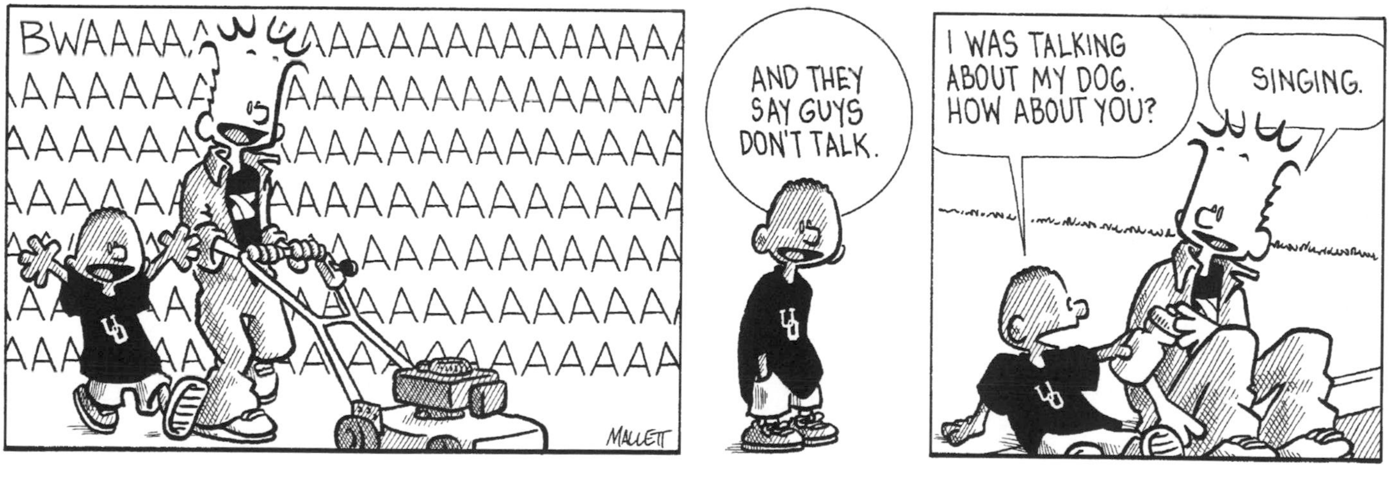
BWAAAAAAAAAAAAAAAAAAAAA AAAAAAAAAAAAAAAAAAAAAA AAAAAAAAAAAAAAAAAAAAAA AAAAAAAAAAAAAAAAAAAAAA AAAAAAAAAAAAAAAAA AAAAAAAAAAAAAAAA AAAAAAAAAAAAAAA
AND THEY SAY GUYS DON'T TALK.
I WAS TALKING ABOUT MY DOG. HOW ABOUT YOU?
SINGING.
MALLETT

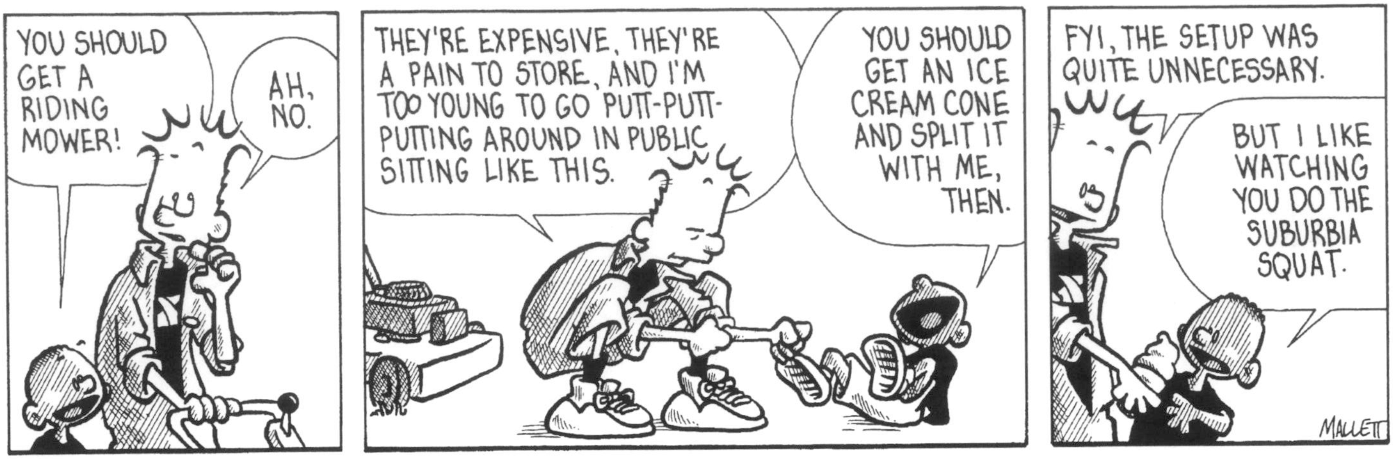
YOU SHOULD GET A RIDING MOWER!
AH, NO.
THEY'RE EXPENSIVE, THEY'RE A PAIN TO STORE, AND I'M TOO YOUNG TO GO PUTT-PUTT-PUTTING AROUND IN PUBLIC SITTING LIKE THIS.
YOU SHOULD GET AN ICE CREAM CONE AND SPLIT IT WITH ME, THEN.
FYI, THE SETUP WAS QUITE UNNECESSARY.
BUT I LIKE WATCHING YOU DO THE SUBURBIA SQUAT.
MALLETT

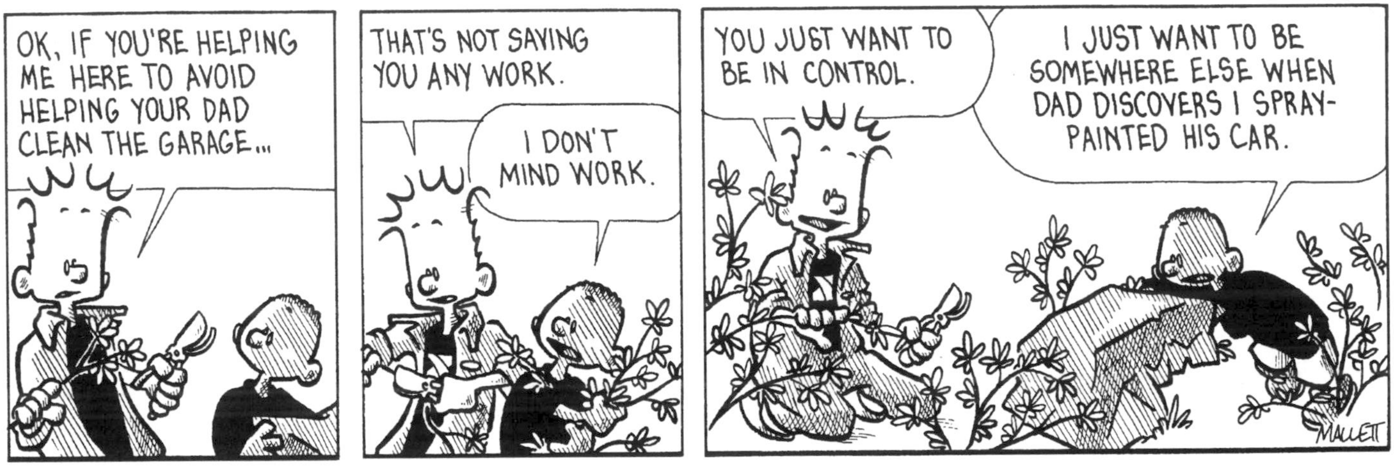
OK, IF YOU'RE HELPING ME HERE TO AVOID HELPING YOUR DAD CLEAN THE GARAGE...
THAT'S NOT SAVING YOU ANY WORK.
I DON'T MIND WORK.
YOU JUST WANT TO BE IN CONTROL.
I JUST WANT TO BE SOMEWHERE ELSE WHEN DAD DISCOVERS I SPRAY-PAINTED HIS CAR.
MALLETT

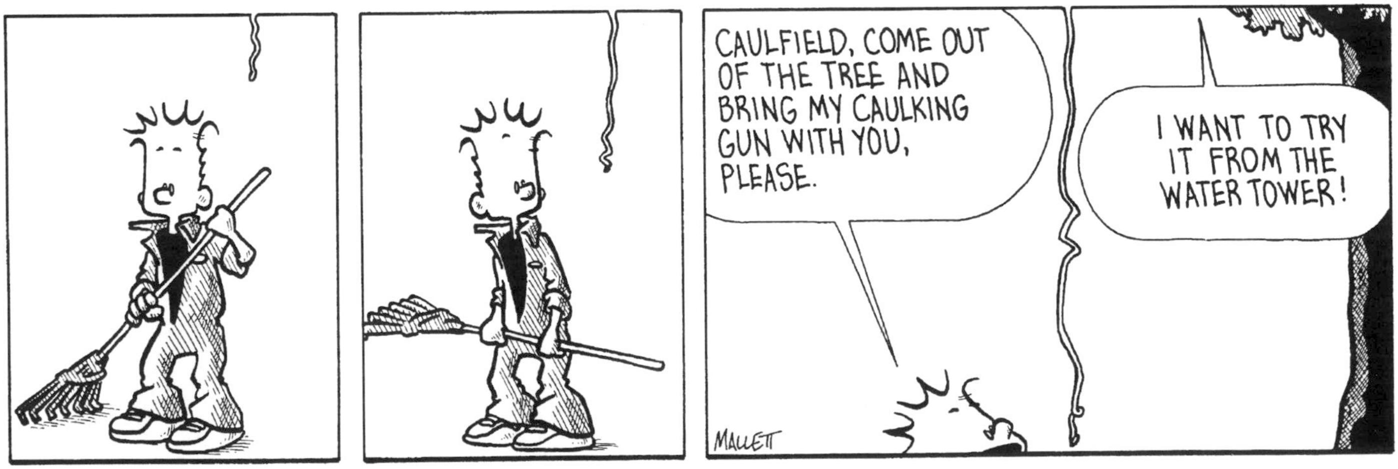
CAULFIELD, COME OUT OF THE TREE AND BRING MY CAULKING GUN WITH YOU, PLEASE.
I WANT TO TRY IT FROM THE WATER TOWER!
MALLETT